Artificial Intelligence for Bible Translation and Interpretation

Artificial Intelligence for Bible Translation and Interpretation

Edited by
Douglas Estes

t&tclark
NEW YORK • LONDON • OXFORD • NEW DELHI • SYDNEY

T&T CLARK
Bloomsbury Publishing Inc, 1359 Broadway, New York, NY 10018, USA
Bloomsbury Publishing Plc, 50 Bedford Square, London, WC1B 3DP, UK
Bloomsbury Publishing Ireland, 29 Earlsfort Terrace, Dublin 2, D02 AY28, Ireland

BLOOMSBURY, T&T CLARK and the T&T Clark logo are trademarks
of Bloomsbury Publishing Plc

First published in the United States of America 2026

A catalog record for this book is available from the Library of Congress.

ISBN: HB: 979-8-7651-6341-2
ePDF: 979-8-7651-6343-6
eBook: 979-8-7651-6342-9

Typeset by Deanta Global Publishing Services, Chennai, India

Contents

Figures

Tables

Contributor Bios

Melanie Dzugan (PhD cand., Fuller Theological Seminary) is an adjunct professor at John Brown University and is completing her dissertation entitled "In(Formation): AI and a Postconservative Theology of Divine Discourse." She is a doctoral fellow of the Richard John Mouw Institute of Faith and Public Life, a network team member of AI and Faith, and serves on the committee for the Human Enhancement and Transhumanism Unit of AAR. Currently residing in Northwest Arkansas, Melanie has served in local church leadership and organized public events for science, theology, and religion with Fuller and Caltech students. Melanie earned an MSc in science and religion from the University of Edinburgh and a BS in science and religion from Samford University.

R. Daren Erisman (PhD, Graduate Theological Union) is Assistant Professor of Computer Science at Minot State University in North Dakota, where he developed a data science program offering courses in artificial intelligence. He holds a doctorate in systematic and philosophical theology and is an ordained minister in the Evangelical Lutheran Church in America. His interdisciplinary research explores comparative theology (Christianity and Islam), science and religion discourse, and the ethical and theological implications of artificial intelligence in the life of the church.

Douglas Estes (PhD, University of Nottingham) is Associate Professor of Religion at New College of Florida. Douglas has written or edited fifteen books including *Braving the Future: Christian Faith in a World of Limitless Tech* (2018) and published more than fifty essays and articles in journals such as *Journal of Theological Studies* (OUP) and *Catholic Biblical Quarterly*. He is a senior fellow at the Center for Pastor Theologians and an advisor at AI & Faith.

Mark Graves (PhD, University of Michigan) is Research Fellow and Director at AI & Faith and Research Associate Professor of Psychology at Fuller Theological Seminary. In addition to earning his PhD in computer science (artificial intelligence) and an MA in systematic and philosophical theology (Graduate Theological Union and Jesuit School of Theology at Berkeley), he has completed fellowships in genomics, moral psychology, and moral theology. He held teaching or research positions at eight institutions of higher learning and published over eighty technical and scholarly works in computer science, biology, psychology, and theology, including three books. Mark also has fifteen years' experience developing AI and data solutions in biotech, pharmaceutical, and healthcare industries.

Ken M. Penner (PhD, McMaster University) is full Professor and Chair of the Religious Studies department at St. Francis Xavier University. He also holds a master's degree in biblical languages (Regent College) and another in religious studies (McMaster). His research focuses on the texts of early Judaism: the Dead Sea Scrolls, the Pseudepigrapha, and the Septuagint, especially the Old Greek of Isaiah. Dr. Penner has been recognized with multiple University Research/Publication/Teaching Awards and the Norman E. Wagner Award for innovative use of technology in biblical scholarship. He is editor of the Lexham English Septuagint and Brill's Digital Biblical Studies series.

Elizabeth Robar (PhD, University of Cambridge) is a Biblical Hebrew linguistics scholar, digital biblical research leader, conference speaker, and homeschool mother. She is the founder and CEO of Scriptura (formerly Cambridge Digital Bible Research) and Academic Director of the *Psalms: Layer by Layer* Project. With over two decades of academic and teaching experience, she brings a rich interdisciplinary approach to sharing and speaking on Biblical poetry and ancient texts, combining cognitive linguistics, philology, and technology.

Marcus Schwarting (PhD, University of Chicago) is the senior editor at AI and Faith and an AI researcher at the University of Chicago. His primary research focus is applying ML/AI to problems in chemistry and materials science. His technical work has been published at venues including *Nature Scientific Data*, *NeurIPS*, and the *Journal of Chemical Physics*. His work on AI ethics has been published in *Theology and Science* and the *Journal of Lutheran Ethics*.

Randall K. J. Tan (PhD, The Southern Baptist Theological Seminary) works as a consultant on assisted translation technology projects for the ETEN Innovation Lab. Over the past two decades, he has been working on original language digital resources to make the Greek and Hebrew Bibles accessible to all people groups worldwide. Previously, he served as Senior Director of Bible Technology Strategy at Biblica. He held various roles, including VP of Innovation, VP of Product Management, and VP of Biblical Research, at Clear Bible, Inc., before the company merged into Biblica.

Wesley Viner (PhD cand., Princeton University) is the associate curator of Early Modern Bibles and Printed Books at the Museum of the Bible, where he oversees both the early modern collection and the history of science collection within the museum. He curates permanent galleries on early modern printing, Bible translations, and biblical scholarship, and he recently launched a temporary exhibit on C. S. Lewis, mythology, and Renaissance literature. He is completing a PhD dissertation on Mosaic natural philosophy in the history of science program at Princeton University, and he holds a prior MA in the history of science (Princeton University), MA in theology (Westminster Seminary California), MSc in computer science (University of Oxford), and BS in computer science (US Naval Academy).

Cassie Weishaupt (BA&Sc, McGill University) is a data scientist at SIL Global, where she collaborates with Bible translation teams to develop AI tools tailored to minority language contexts, with a primary focus on augmentative quality assessment of Bible drafts. In addition to tool development, she conducts AI literacy workshops and training sessions for translation teams integrating new technologies into their workflows. She co-authored and presented the papers "Artificial Intelligence Tools as Quality Assessment Copilots" (Bible Translation Conference 2023) and "More than Machines: Human-Centered Ethics in AI in Bible Translation" (Bible Translation Conference 2025).

Ryder A. Wishart (PhD, McMaster Divinity College) is a theologian and software developer, currently leading AI-first Bible translation initiatives in partnership with Biblica and Every Tribe Every Nation. He teaches Koine Greek and New Testament as an adjunct at Regent University in Virginia. His dissertation, published by Brill, explores the genre of the Gospels using computational register analysis and folklore theory. He is the author of *Gospels or Biographies? The Gospels as Folk Literature* (2024), editor of *The Literary-Linguistic Analysis of the Bible: The Enduring Legacies of Russian Formalism and the Prague Linguistic Circle*, and has published in journals such as the *International Journal of Lexicography*.

Rabbanit Sara Tillinger Wolkenfeld (PhD cand., Gratz College) is Chief Learning Officer at Sefaria, a non-profit dedicated to bringing the Jewish canon into the digital age. She is a Walder Fellow in the inaugural cohort of Gratz College's Executive PhD program in Judaic Studies. Sara is an alumna of the Wexner Foundation's Field Fellowship and of the Rabbinic Leadership Initiative at the Hartman Institute of North America. She also serves as Scholar-in-Residence at Ohev Sholom Congregation in Washington, DC. Her current research is focused on the intersection between Jewish ethics and advancements in technology. Sara's writing has been published in *The Atlantic*, *First Things*, and *Religion Dispatches*, as well as numerous Jewish publications.

Abbreviations

ANN	Artificial Neural Network
API	Application Programming Interface
ApOTC	Apollos Old Testament Commentary
AQuA	Augmented Quality Assessment
BCP	Blackwell Companions to Philosophy
BDAG	*Greek-English Lexicon of the New Testament and Other Early Christian Literature.* 3rd ed.
BET	*Bulletin for Ecclesial Theology*
BLEU	BiLingual Evaluation Understudy
BT	Bible Translation
BT	*The Bible Translator*
CBQ	*Catholic Biblical Quarterly*
CTR	*Criswell Theological Review*
ESTC	*English Short Title Catalogue*
ETEN	Every Tribe Every Nation
GPT	Generative Pre-trained Transformer
HITL	Human-in-the-loop
HSCL	Harvard Studies in Comparative Literature
HSML	History of Science and Medicine Library
HTLS	*Historical and Theological Lexicon of the Septuagint*
IJIMAI	*International Journal of Interactive Multimedia and Artificial Intelligence*
IJLLT	*International Journal of Linguistics, Literature and Translation*
IJMMU	*nternational Journal of Multicultural and Multireligious Understanding*
ISBL	Indiana Studies in Biblical Literature
JEAC	*Journal of Ethics in Antiquity and Christianity*
JMT	*Journal of Moral Theology*
J. R. Soc. Interface	*Journal of the Royal Society Interface*
JSOTSup	Journal for the Study of the Old Testament Supplement Series
KD	*Kerygma und Dogma*
LLM	Large Language Model
LWW	Library of the Written Word
LXX	Septuagint
ML	Machine Learning
MOTB	Museum of the Bible
MT	Machine Translation

Neot	*Neotestamentica*
NICOT	New International Commentary on the Old Testament
NMT	Neural Machine Translation
NLP	Natural Language Processing
NT	The New Testament
OT	The Old Testament
OCR	Optical Character Recognition
OTL	Old Testament Library
OTS	Old Testament Studies
RHR	Routledge Handbooks in Religion
SASRH	St Andrews Studies in Reformation History
SBT	Studies in Biblical Theology
TAC	Time, Astronomy, and Calendars
ThTo	*Theology Today*
TWOT	*Theological Wordbook of the Old Testament*
WBC	Word Biblical Commentary
WUNT	Wissenschaftliche Untersuchungen zum Neuen Testament
ZAC	*Zeitschrift fur Antikes Christentum*

Introduction

Douglas Estes

Artificial intelligence (AI) is here. AI was here in 1950 when Alan Turing wondered about thinking machines and introduced the Turing Test. AI was here in 1951 when Marvin Minsky and Dean Edmonds developed SNARC, the first artificial neural network. AI was here in 1956 when John McCarthy and others proposed the term "artificial intelligence" at the Dartmouth conference that year. AI was here in 1966 when Joseph Weizenbaum created Eliza, the first conversational software that we would today call a "chatbot." AI was here in 1997 when IBM's Deep Blue finally defeated Garry Kasparov at chess. AI was here in 2006 when IBM's Watson defeated Ken Jennings at *Jeopardy!* AI was here in 2011 when Apple released Siri, an intelligent digital assistant. AI was here in 2022 when OpenAI released ChatGPT. AI was here in 2025 when I used Perplexity.Ai to create a timeline of AI development. AI will be here in 2030 as it begins to seamlessly integrate with public life on all levels.[1] AI will be on Mars in 2031 with SpaceX's maiden manned voyage. And AI will be here in 2035, whether we are or not.[2]

What this list alludes to is the "AI effect," a pernicious phenomenon plaguing the everyday understanding and acceptance of AI. The "AI effect" is

> a term describing AI as the thing that computers can't yet do. Each time a goal is achieved, such as AI beating a human at chess, it is dismissed as not being "real" intelligence, and so the goalposts move and AI is not achieved.[3]

There are two consequences that arise from this—readers of the Bible too quickly gloss over the improvements that AI has already brought to the Bible and too quickly misunderstand what future AI could bring. The first consequence of the AI effect is the realization that computers continue to change the world and yet the world continues to function. We see improvements in many areas (e.g., communication, medicine) and setbacks in others (e.g., potential societal fragmentation due to social media).[4] A second way of looking at the AI effect is the belief that AI is a never-attainable, near-future unknown. We keep waiting for an AI that will fundamentally change things, with either a utopian or dystopian ending. We can apply these two perspectives to the translation and interpretation of the Bible. In light of the former, we know that Bible translators have had assistance from computers since 1977—almost fifty years at the time of writing.[5] Prior to that time, Bible translation experienced generally linear growth, but since then, Bible translation has experienced greater than linear growth—potentially approaching exponential growth.[6] In light of the latter, Bible translation teams since the 1970s have merely used "computers" (a good thing), but as future translators move to automated translation with "real AI," there is cause for alarm (a bad thing). The same thought process could be applied to biblical interpretation as well: in the past, "computers" (often in the form of Bible software) increased the speed and capacity of Bible study, but in the future, "AI" will interpret the Bible for us, with questionable results—or give us all the "answers." Arguably, this is a highly accelerated form of the symbiosis between humanity and technology that has existed from the creation of the species.[7]

The AI effect in all its sensationalism muddies the waters as we attempt to understand the strengths and weaknesses of using AI to translate and interpret the Bible. Although most Americans are pessimistic about AI's capacity to improve spiritual engagement,[8] there is no denying the significant advances "computers" have brought to the translation and interpretation of the Bible. In this book, we present various ways to think about AI and the Bible, methods for translating the Bible with AI in near-future situations, and new approaches that AI can bring to the field of biblical interpretation. We realize, as the AI effect demonstrates, that this is a moving target, but we hope to establish where we are in 2025 and where we can go, even if we have far more questions than answers. The chapters in this book consider what might come next. They examine the many ways that AI might shape our interactions with the Bible—from translation to interpretation and much more—as well as how the Bible, along with the broader religious communities built upon it, might impact the ways we understand and use AI.

In Chapter 1, Wesley Viner offers a historical perspective on AI and the Bible. He examines the impact of new technologies upon the Bible in the past, with a particular focus on the introduction of the movable-type printing press by Johannes Gutenberg in the mid-fifteenth century. He demonstrates that the long-term consequences of the printing press were unpredictable and, in certain ways, unimaginable to Gutenberg and his contemporaries. Even developments that appear obvious and inevitable to many modern observers—printed books would triumph over manuscripts, the press would produce books at scale, the Bible would be one of the books it produced, and more—depend on countless unpredictable contingencies and external conditions, ranging from vast socioeconomic and cultural developments (e.g., the rise of literacy and the Protestant Reformation) to minute technological improvements in printing technology. Viner argues that this history ought to inject a healthy dose of modesty into current discussions—and predictions—about AI.

In Chapter 2, Douglas Estes poses the question, "How do we gain a biblical perspective on AI, when AI is not mentioned directly, indirectly, or tangentially in any biblical texts?" After critically examining the prevalent "quarrying" approach to biblical interpretation, Estes draws upon Richard Hays' four tasks of interpretation. He also advances a distinctive argument: AI is the one unique occurrence in human history that will necessitate an entirely novel hermeneutical approach to derive an ethical framework for its use from Scripture. Building on this, Estes turns to Hays' four modes of interpreting biblical ethics and couples this to Ruben Zimmermann's theory of implicit ethics. He contends that biblical interpreters wishing to understand AI must engage with what Hays calls the "symbolic world," all the while cultivating what

Zimmermann calls an "implicit ethics" of the biblical texts. Estes asserts that this is the only path forward due to the novel nature of AI: AI is the only human creation that communicates, AI can self-correct (or refuse to, or lie), and AI transcends traditional definitions of personhood. Consequently, this demands a mode of interpretation that can yield a theological ethic uniquely suited to the novel challenges posed by AI—an ethic that is currently underdeveloped within existing biblical scholarship.

In Chapter 3, R. Daren Erisman explores the idea of the Bible as a dataset—specifically, as a formative dataset that has shaped the Christian mind over millennia, analogous to curated datasets that train large language models today. While affirming the essential differences between human and machine intelligence, he cautions against overly rigid boundaries, arguing that artificial intelligence now operates using the very language that has long shaped human thought and faith. He identifies the Bible's diversity, selectivity, and durability as key features that make it a compelling analogy, while also highlighting the interpretive challenges the Bible poses, including bias and ambiguity. Crucially, he draws attention to the concept of emergence: just as human understanding and moral development arise from a convergence of influences over time, artificial intelligence, when trained on complex datasets, may also exhibit behaviors that transcend the sum of their coded instructions. Erisman concludes by emphasizing the need for formative boundaries—ethical and theological "guardrails"—that align with enduring values rooted in the biblical tradition.

The second part of this book turns to AI and Bible translation. The process of translating the Bible into a low-resource language can be a challenging, sensitive, and time-intensive process. Artificial intelligence offers an opportunity to accelerate this process. However, there are many challenges associated with using AI for Bible translation. In Chapter 4, Marcus Schwarting details the technical underpinnings of the AI tools that can accelerate Bible translation tasks. He considers the advantages and shortcomings of using these AI tools, as well as the challenges associated with quantifying their impact and effectiveness.

In Chapter 5, Cassie Weishaupt examines how Indigenous communities are being affected by the rise of AI, not only through questions of digital access, visibility, and data sovereignty, but also in how they have adapted this technology to meet local needs. She explores both the opportunities AI offers for language development and revitalization, as well as the challenges that arise when external assumptions about justice or utility do not align with community values. She focuses on the development and implementation of AQuA, an AI tool developed by SIL Global in collaboration with Bible translation teams to support their quality assessment work. Two case studies from the Philippines illustrate how local teams could leverage AQuA to their advantage, while also highlighting the ongoing complexities of adopting such tools in local contexts.

How exactly the human and the machine will coexist within this process of translation remains an open question. Randall Tan and Ryder Wishart explore two alternative possibilities in their respective chapters. In Chapter 6, Randall K. J. Tan invites readers to consider whether applying AI, specifically AI copilots, to Bible translation is a promising and necessary innovation. He explores the global context of

Bible translation, particularly the need to broaden participation and fuel innovation to meet current goals, and he presents the rapid uptake of intelligent assistants in the neighboring fields of software development and office productivity as strongly suggestive of AI's potential in Bible translation. While challenges remain (especially with low-resource languages), he calls for embracing a combination of cutting-edge AI tools and community-driven translation efforts.

In Chapter 7, Ryder A. Wishart explores the theological and sociological significance of artificial intelligence in Bible translation, arguing that AI is not merely a tool but an active participant in the social construction of biblical meaning. Drawing on George Lindbeck's cultural-linguistic theory and Berger and Luckmann's framework of reality construction, Wishart contends that AI—particularly in human-in-the-loop models—can mediate foreign biblical concepts with a breadth inaccessible to individual translators. Wishart proposes a hybrid model of Bible translation that enhances traditional methods with AI without diminishing the irreplaceable role of human discernment, thus preserving theological integrity while accelerating access to Scripture for underserved languages.

In Chapter 8, Elizabeth Robar argues that AI, like all technological advances, marks a paradigm shift in how humans think and work. Specifically, AI provides new possibilities for workflows when dealing with text: start with a minimal quality draft and iterate until quality seeps throughout. AI provides the styling and humans guide the presentation of meaning. This holds tantalizing potential for reframing texts in different genres, from Shakespearean sonnets to nursery rhymes. It also conflicts with traditional human workflows, particularly in the world of Bible translation where human resources are scarce and the first draft is often the limiting factor. Good stewards must safeguard meaning while also recognizing that AI can reproduce and combine known styles with unprecedented speed and efficiency.

The third part of this volume turns from translation to interpretation, considering how AI might affect the way humans find, study, interact with, and understand the biblical text. In Chapter 9, Ken M. Penner investigates how artificial intelligence, particularly AI chatbots, can be integrated into the workflow for creating digital scholarly editions of biblical texts. Penner presents insights from his experience teaching an undergraduate course on digital methods for ancient texts (which used the Greek Additions to Daniel as a case study), evaluating and comparing the performance of various AI models across the workflow stages, including transcription, textual criticism, translation, and commentary. While AI tools show promise in enhancing efficiency by automating repetitive tasks, Penner highlights significant challenges, including ethical concerns about AI's environmental impact and labor practices, as well as issues of accuracy and reliability. Penner's practical evaluations demonstrate that while AI can assist in regularization and initial translation drafts, human oversight remains crucial for scholarly rigor. Penner argues that AI should be viewed as a collaborative tool that augments human expertise rather than replacing it, concluding that a partnership between scholars and AI, guided by human curation, can make ancient texts more accessible while upholding academic integrity.

In Chapter 10, Sara Tillinger Wolkenfeld uses canonical Jewish texts as a case study for the ways that artificial intelligence can make vast amounts of information more accessible and useful to a broad audience. Wolkenfeld documents the progress of Sefaria.org, a website dedicated to bringing Jewish texts into the digital age. She describes two critical accomplishments that have helped readers navigate the myriad texts compiled by Sefaria: extensive linking between texts, so they may be read in conversation with one another, and topical tags that allow users to find sources that speak directly to their present interests. These techniques allow readers to identify and interact with texts that might otherwise be inaccessible or available only to a limited audience. Continued exploration of artificial intelligence, Wolkenfeld argues, can allow us to preserve ancient texts while experiencing them in new ways.

In Chapter 11, Mark Graves explores how AI, particularly topic modeling, can support new methods of biblical interpretation by revealing patterns in the text that are not evident to humans, either due to the effects of human assumptions and biases or the sheer volume of data and the stark limitations of the human mind. Drawing on hermeneutical theories and scientific modeling, Graves argues that statistical models can complement traditional exegesis by identifying and surfacing interpretable distributions of themes across biblical texts. Topic modeling, a minimally supervised AI technique, is used to identify major theological and narrative topics in the Bible and visualize their distribution across various texts. These statistical patterns can be interpreted as conceptual structures within theological models, offering insight into both the literal and metaphorical dimensions of Scripture. By emphasizing an associative theory of language and demonstrating how even simple AI tools can yield fresh interpretive possibilities, Graves invites us to rethink how AI can participate meaningfully in biblical interpretation.

In Chapter 12, Melanie Dzugan expands these discussions about biblical interpretation by considering the difficulty of information interpretation of any kind, whether biblical (or not) or AI-generated (or not). More information is available now than ever before thanks to AI interfaces, but in many ways, AI complicates the communication and interpretation of that information. Dzugan argues that we ought to model our communication practices on the divine discourse in Scripture. The book of James makes the power of communication practice especially clear: the tongue is difficult to tame, but if we practice the process of interpretation with a proper regard for the contexts and the communicator of that information, we will better the quality of our disagreements both within the church and in public. This interpretive practice of communication supports discernment about which uses of AI as an interpretation partner are more constructive than others.

In Chapter 13, Douglas Estes explores how three different concepts—AI, apocalyptic, and apocalypse—became tangled up in popular culture and biblical interpretation. Estes begins with simple definitions of each concept, all of which are artificial, umbrella terms: "AI," a constellation of computational methods; "apocalyptic," a socio-theological orientation to the world; and "apocalypse," a genre of ancient Jewish-Christian discourse. As a starting point for disentanglement, Estes argues that AI is a text, functionally if not categorically, in the same way that apocalypses are texts. He then considers three ways to interpret apocalypse in light of the text of AI: apocalypse is a genre that privileges superintelligence, that allows the hearer to generate new meaning, and that exhorts its audience to a new way of approaching life. From this we enter into a hermeneutical circle whereby AI can help us to understand apocalypse, and apocalypse can help us to understand AI.

Finally, we express our appreciation to all those involved in making this book a reality. We would like to thank the Museum of the Bible (MOTB) for their vision in establishing a venue where these ideas could be discussed at an earlier stage. I especially want to extend a critical "thank you" to Wesley Viner, who was not only instrumental in leading the MOTB conference but also pitched in with an enormous effort at the end to help put this volume together in short time (given the timeliness of the subject). Similarly, we greatly thank AI & Faith, all of their leadership but especially David Brenner, for both their vision and work to make the original MOTB venue a reality. This project would not exist without the hard work of the people of AI & Faith and the MOTB. Much thanks and gratitude go especially to Megan White, our acquisitions editor, as well as Tara Donovan, our assistant acquisitions editor at Lexington/Bloomsbury who believed in the vision for this project. We also thank the rest of the team at Lexington/Bloomsbury who had a hand in producing this book. Each of us as contributors express gratitude to our families and friends who encouraged us during the writing, editing, and production of this volume. As editor, I would like to thank all of the contributors who participated. Finally, I dedicate my part of the effort to my wife, Noël; my mom and patron, Nadine; but especially to my children, Wyatt, Bridget, Violet, Everett, who will benefit from but also take on the task of the work that previous generations began until "all the ends of the earth shall remember and turn unto the LORD; and all the kindreds of the nations shall worship before Thee. For the kingdom is the LORD'S; and He is the ruler over the nations" (JPS 1917).

Notes

1 For example, see Jason Beckett, "2035: From AI to the Quantum Leap—What Does the Next Decade Have in Store for Digital Transformation and Sustainability?" *Interface*, May 7, 2025, https://interface.media/blog/2025/05/07/2035-from-ai-to-the-quantum-leap-what-does-the-next-decade-have-in-store-for-digital-transformation-and-sustainability.

2 Daniel Kokotajlo, Scott Alexander, Thomas Larsen, Eli Lifland, and Romeo Dean, "AI 2027," AI-2027.com, published April 3, 2025.

3 Ewa Luger, *What Do We Know and What Should We Do About AI?* (London: Sage, 2023), 62. Similarly, see Jerry Kaplan, *Generative Artificial Intelligence*, What Everyone Needs to Know (Oxford: Oxford University Press, 2024), 157.

4 Tuan Minh Pham, Imre Kondor, Rudolf Hanel, and Stefan Thurner, "The Effect of Social Balance on Social Fragmentation," *Journal of the Royal Society Interface* 17 (2020): 20200752.

5 Wycliffe Singapore, "The Early Days of Computers in Bible Translation," Wycliffe Singapore, posted September 4, 2022; and potentially the first paper on Bible translation, David J. Weber and William C. Mann, "Prospects for Computer-Assisted Dialect Adaption," in *ACL '79: Proceedings of the 17th Annual Meeting on Association for Computational Linguistics*, ed. Norman Sondheimer (Stroudsburg: Association for Computational Linguistics, 1979), 109–10; and developed further in David J. Weber and William C. Mann, "Prospects for Computer-Assisted Dialect Adaptation," *American Journal of Computational Linguistics* 7.3 (1981): 165–77.

6 For a visual demonstration of growth, see Alfred Thompson, "Why is the Pace of Bible Translation Increasing?" Wycliffe Bible Translators, https://wycliffe.org.uk/story/why-is-the-pace-of-bible-translation-increasing.

7 Douglas Estes, "Postdigital Humans: Technology and Divine Design," in *Postdigital Theologies: Technology, Belief, and Practice*, ed. Maggi Savin-Baden and John Reader, Postdigital Science and Education (Cham: Springer, 2022), 156–8.

8 Jeffery Fulks, Randy Petersen, John Farquhar Plake, and Sandra Siggins, *State of the Bible: USA 2025* (Philadelphia: American Bible Society, 2025).

Bibliography

Estes, Douglas. "Postdigital Humans: Technology and Divine Design." Pages 147–62 in *Postdigital Theologies: Technology, Belief, and Practice*. Edited by Maggi Savin-Baden and John Reader. Postdigital Science and Education. Cham: Springer, 2022.

Fulks, Jeffery, Randy Petersen, John Farquhar Plake, and Sandra Siggins. *State of the Bible: USA 2025*. Philadelphia: American Bible Society, 2025.

Kaplan, Jerry. *Generative Artificial Intelligence*. What Everyone Needs to Know. Oxford: Oxford University Press, 2024.

Kokotajlo, Daniel, Scott Alexander, Thomas Larsen, Eli Lifland, and Romeo Dean. "AI 2027." AI-2027.com. Published April 3, 2025. https://ai-2027.com.

Luger, Ewa. *What Do We Know and What Should We Do About AI?* London: Sage, 2023.

Pham, Tuan Minh, Imre Kondor, Rudolf Hanel, and Stefan Thurner. "The Effect of Social Balance on Social Fragmentation." *Journal of the Royal Society Interface* 17 (2020): 20200752. http://doi.org/10.1098/rsif.2020.0752.

Thompson, Alfred. "Why is the Pace of Bible Translation Increasing?" Wycliffe Bible Translators. https://wycliffe.org.uk/story/why-is-the-pace-of-bible-translation-increasing.

Weber, David J., and William C. Mann. "Prospects for Computer-Assisted Dialect Adaption." Pages 109–10 in *ACL '79: Proceedings of the 17th Annual Meeting on Association for Computational Linguistics*. Edited by Norman Sondheimer. Stroudsburg: Association for Computational Linguistics, 1979.

Weber, David J., and William C. Mann. "Prospects for Computer-Assisted Dialect Adaptation." *American Journal of Computational Linguistics* 7.3 (1981): 165–77.

Wycliffe Singapore. "The Early Days of Computers in Bible Translation." Wycliffe Singapore. Posted September 4, 2022. https://www.wycliffe.sg/post/early-days-of-computers-in-bible-translation.

Part I

AI and the Bible

1

Unexpected Trajectories

Historical Interactions between Technology and the Bible

Wesley Viner

A recent piece in the *Times Literary Supplement* on the potential impacts of artificial intelligence opened with a popular quote by Johannes Gutenberg about the printing press and the Bible:

> Yes, it is a press, certainly, but a press from which shall flow in inexhaustible streams the most abundant and most marvelous liquor that has ever flowed to relieve the thirst of men. Through it, God will spread His word. A spring of pure truth shall flow from it; like a new star, it shall scatter the darkness of ignorance, and cause a light hithertofore unknown to shine among men.[1]

As one of the more consequential technological developments of the last millennium, the printing press looms large as a natural point of comparison in discussions about AI, and this particular quote has a long history. It has appeared widely in Christian books, magazines, and blogs; secular newspapers and websites; and even academic monographs and journals, including disciplines as far afield as science communication, archaeology, psychology, and multimedia design.[2] While some sources reference it for what it suggests about the significance of the Bible, others use it as a window into the history of technology and its impact upon the world. There is but one minor problem: the quote is a complete fabrication. Gutenberg said no such thing.

The quote owes its existence not to Johannes Gutenberg but rather to Alphonse de Lamartine, a nineteenth-century French statesman who played a key role in the February Revolution and ran unsuccessfully for president. In addition to his political activities, Lamartine was a prolific author—particularly in his later years after he withdrew from public life. Among his many works is *Le civilisateur, histoire de l'humanité par les grands hommes* (1852–4), a three-volume survey of "great men" throughout history (although, interestingly for its time, the text includes several women as well).[3] *Le civilisateur* falls somewhere between history and historical fiction; it covers real individuals and real events embellished with fictional supporting characters, fabricated conversations, and other imagined additions which provide vividness and detail to the narrative, much like a modern made-for-television series about Henry VIII or Joan of Arc might wrap a fictional script around a historical event.

One of the "great men" featured in Lamartine's work is Johannes Gutenberg. The text offers a brief survey of Gutenberg's early life, adorned with colorful, invented details ranging from the specific possessions in Gutenberg's traveling sack to the content of his inner monologue. It even regales readers with a fictional meeting between Gutenberg and Laurens Koster—a rumored early pioneer of printing about whom very little is known.[4] Lamartine then recounts a scenic stroll through the woods where a lovestruck Gutenberg carves his lover's initials into a strip of wood and wraps the carving in parchment. Later, when the sap imprints the letters on its parchment cover, the idea of the printing press hits Gutenberg like lightning from the clouds! (This dramatic tale is, of course, entirely fiction, but it is entertaining nonetheless.) Eventually, Lamartine's Gutenberg constructs a small model of his press and asks a local turner, Conrad Saspach, to build a full-scale version of the model. When Conrad remarks that it is merely a press, Gutenberg delivers the now-famous quote:

> Oui, répondit d'un ton grave et exalté Gutenberg: c'est un pressoir, en effet; mais c'est un pressoir d'où jaillira bientôt à flots intarissables la plus abondante et la plus merveilleuse liqueur qui ait jamais coulé pour désaltérer les hommes! Par lui, Dieu répandra son *Verbe*; il en découlera une source de pure vérité: comme un nouvel astre, il dissipera les ténèbres de l'ignorance, et fera luire sur les hommes une lumière inconnue jusqu'à présent.[5]

The familiar English version of this quote appeared several years later when Richard Bentley, a London publisher, released an English translation of Lamartine's work titled *Memoirs of Celebrated Characters* (1854–8). Bentley's English translation was subsequently quoted by a long series of nineteenth- and twentieth-century texts, and today, it lives on both in print and online, surfacing anywhere and everywhere, including—most recently—in discussions about AI.[6]

One need not know the actual provenance of the quote, though, to recognize that it is spurious. It is blindingly obvious that the quote is a fiction. First, this is not how late medieval tradesmen spoke. The verbiage is remarkably eloquent; it sounds like a line from a gifted poet—and, in fact, Lamartine was a skilled orator—not from a medieval tradesman who made his living working with metal and wood. Admittedly, Gutenberg came from a wealthy family and was (likely) well-educated, so this is far from conclusive proof. Moreover, an unsuspecting reader might assume the English translation embellished Gutenberg's original (and potentially simpler) German verbiage. A more significant red flag, though, is the content of the quote. It describes the Bible as "a spring of pure truth" and "a new star" that will "scatter the darkness of ignorance, and cause a light hithertofore unknown to shine among men." These ideas—effusive praise of the Bible as an unparalleled source of truth coupled with criticism of the darkness that formerly reigned—would make little sense to most late medieval Catholics. This is, on the other hand, boilerplate rhetoric for an early modern Protestant inveighing against Rome—or, as it turns out, a nineteenth-century French statesman who had rejected the Roman Catholic Church but maintained his own idiosyncratic reverence for the Bible. In short, unless Gutenberg secretly became a Hussite on an unknown trip to Bohemia, it is highly unlikely that he would think or speak this way about the Bible. This quote might plausibly belong to Martin Luther a half-century later, but not to Johannes Gutenberg.

The most obvious indication of the quote's inauthenticity, though, does not require advanced historical knowledge to recognize. The quote is clearly and undoubtedly fake for a much simpler reason: it implies that Gutenberg could predict the future. The quote suggests, among other things, that Gutenberg knew the printing press would spread; that once it spread, it would be used to print the Bible; that it would not only print the Bible, but print it in unprecedented quantities; and that these Bibles would be possessed by people who did not previously possess the Bible. Each of these eventual consequences of the printing press depended upon countless unforeseeable preconditions, contingent circumstances, and related developments, ranging from the spread of literacy, the Protestant Reformation, and other massive socioeconomic and cultural shifts that restructured European society to incremental technological improvements in printing technology. Unless he was omniscient, Gutenberg could not have known that all these things would come to pass; in fact, some of them would have seemed wildly implausible. Humorously, Lamartine himself recognized that his rendition of Gutenberg required divine clairvoyance. He suggested that God gave Gutenberg a prescient awareness (*la conscience pressentie*) of what he would accomplish, and he claimed that Gutenberg perceived at first glance (*d'un premier coup d'œil*) the moral and industrial consequences of his invention.[7]

While Lamartine may have recognized the clairvoyance which Gutenberg required to anticipate the trajectory of his invention, most people who recycle this quote today—from Christian apologists to secular journalists, and casual bloggers to accomplished academics—overlook this fact. They assume that the long-term consequences of the printing press must have been as obvious to Gutenberg as they are to us today. Of course, they assume, the printing press would lead to the mass production of books; of course the Bible would be one of those books; of course people would want to read it; and of course it would revolutionize the world. While all these things did come to pass, none were as obvious or as likely as readers today might expect. This reveals an important deficiency in our collective understanding (or perhaps misunderstanding) of technology and history. Specifically, it reveals that we do not have a sufficient appreciation for how remarkably difficult it is for almost anyone at almost any point in history to anticipate with any reasonable degree of accuracy the consequences of any given technological development—a shortcoming which has significant implications for the current discourse about AI. In short, Gutenberg's situation may serve as a mirror for our own.

An Uphill Battle

Gutenberg printed his famous 42-line Bible at some point in the mid-1450s. He had printed a variety of simpler and shorter texts in the preceding years, and he may have been working on the technology for more than a decade.[8] He was not the only one experimenting with new ways to reproduce books at the time. During this same period, xylographic block books emerged in Europe. Xylography is a printing technique that involves carving text in relief into a wood block, inking the raised text, and stamping it onto paper (or some other medium). This form of printing had existed for many centuries in East Asia—as had metal type, for that matter—but its lifespan in Europe was cut short by Gutenberg's alternative approach.[9] To a modern observer, it might seem all too obvious that movable type would quickly win the day with manuscripts and block books as its chief competitors. After all, copying by hand is slow, and it is as difficult as one might imagine to carve written text into a block of wood. Movable type, on the other hand, is endlessly rearrangeable and reusable and (to modern eyes) it appears simple, fast, and efficient. In reality, movable-type printing was complicated, difficult, and extraordinarily time- and capital-intensive.

Movable-type printing required, first and foremost, the creation of movable metal type, an enormously complex process that involved chiseling the character in relief on a steel punch, punching another piece of metal to create a matrix, placing the matrix in a hand mold, and pouring a metal alloy into the mold to create the sort. The type would then be arranged within a wooden frame, one sort at a time, to create a page of text. Once the type was set in the frame, it would be inked, and a sheet of paper (or parchment) would be pressed down onto the inked type by a metal plate driven by a large screw.[10] Each character was formed "backward" and the text was arranged right to left so the letters on the paper would appear forward and run left to right. Complicating matters, late medieval and early modern books were usually constructed by folding a single leaf in half, quarters, or eighths—producing a folio, quarto, or octavo book, respectively. As the leaves were folded, the orientation of the text on different parts of the folded page would change, so when multiple pages of the text were set at once, each had to be oriented in a different direction. Complicating matters further, the leaves were not folded individually; they were gathered into quires and folded as a group (so they could later be sewn together to produce a book). This nesting process meant that folded portions of a single leaf would appear at different places in the book, with various folded portions of other nested leaves interleaving them. Imagine, in short, a single frame containing multiple pages of non-sequential text composed of very small, individual metal letters that had to be placed by hand, with each page oriented in a different direction, with every letter facing backward, and with the text running right to left. Now imagine proofreading that before it is printed. Countless additional technical difficulties swirled around the ink, the paper, and more.[11]

The economics of printing were as challenging—if not more so—than the technology. A press required people, equipment, and material, all of which cost money. The personnel involved included a compositor to set the type, several pressmen to ink the type and power the press, and potentially many more to handle the paper and perform other tasks. Gutenberg's 42-line Bible likely took two to three years to complete, with four to six different compositors (or, potentially, multi-person composition teams) and an unknown number of presses working simultaneously, each with their own supplies and team. They likely printed 160 to 180 copies, with roughly one quarter on vellum and the rest on paper.[12] The metal type required for this project was staggering. The text contains 290 distinct characters—letters, punctuation, and more—and approximately 2,600 characters per page, with more common letters sometimes repeated many hundreds of times on a single page. One estimate suggests each compositor would have required 7,800 individual sorts, totaling more than 46,000 for six composition units.[13] The press itself, of course, was enormous and expensive, and the ink was not free either. The capital for all of this was required at the outset of the two-to-three-year printing process, and if the book did not sell out, Gutenberg and his partners might not recoup their initial investment, much less make any profit.

Gutenberg had to estimate the number of books he would sell in advance; printing too few pressured profit margins, while printing too many risked bankruptcy, as unsold books sat upon the shelf. Presales and strong demand for his Bible convinced him to increase the size of the edition by roughly one third, but some copies appear to have remained unsold in the subsequent years, suggesting he may have overcorrected.[14] Bankruptcy was an ever-present possibility, and Gutenberg's Bible devolved into a financially fraught lawsuit. Johann Fust, Gutenberg's partner and financier, sued the printer to recoup his initial investment, and although there is some uncertainty and debate about the solvency (or lack thereof) of their enterprise and the outcome of the lawsuit, it was clearly not a roaring financial success.[15]

Broader Developments

Whether movable-type printing would prove to be a sustainable enterprise—an open question in Gutenberg's day—depended, in part, on the type of books printers opted to produce, and it was not at all obvious that the Bible was the correct choice. The Bible was a large, and thus very expensive, book. It could be sold for a high price, but that necessarily limited its market. If it was printed in Latin, it could be distributed across the continent, but only to educated Latin readers. If it was printed in the vernacular, it could be sold to lay readers, but its market would be geographically limited. The core advantage of the printing press over manuscript production was producing books *at scale*. In many ways, a large, expensive book that would sell fewer copies—like the Bible—was a counterintuitive option compared to smaller, cheaper texts that might be sold in greater quantities.[16]

Moreover, the Bible posed layer upon layer of unique challenges for an aspiring printer. Concerns about the fidelity of the biblical text, for instance, necessitated unusually high standards of quality. When (not if) mistakes were discovered after printing any other text, a printer could include a simple errata page in the endpapers of the book, listing the known mistakes with corrections. For obvious reasons, mistakes in the biblical text proved more troublesome, sometimes creating significant financial and legal difficulties for those involved. In some cases, particularly unfortunate mistakes—more on this below—led to the retraction of entire editions.

Bibles also introduced the risk of political and ecclesiastical interference. Should the Bible be printed in Latin or the vernacular? Which Latin text or vernacular translation should be used? Who was allowed to print it, and who was not? Who was allowed to buy it, and who was not? Both the church and the state weighed in on these questions (with endlessly varied answers), and printers who opted to print the Bible had to work within the often-difficult constraints of their particular political and ecclesiastical context.[17]

There were, in short, many reasons to suspect that the printing press might not be used to print the Bible, even if other books and other genres proved profitable. Whether printing any books in any genre would prove feasible, though, depended upon a variety of broader social, cultural, and economic shifts that no one in the middle of the fifteenth century could have foreseen. First and foremost, to sell books at scale required a large reading population. Late medieval Europe was not as illiterate or as anti-intellectual as the "Dark Ages" misnomer implies, but literacy was not exactly high. And although literacy did increase in the centuries after Gutenberg, it did so slowly. By one measure, for instance, only 20 percent of men and 5 percent of women in England were literate by the mid-sixteenth century.[18] This number increased steadily moving forward, but could anyone have anticipated that centuries in advance? And could they have anticipated that the Bible would be the book this newly literate population would choose to read?

The Bible was undoubtedly popular in the late medieval period.[19] However, it was far from the only book that literate Europeans read. In fact, while manuscript production increased notably in the century before Gutenberg, Bible production peaked in the thirteenth century before fading in the fourteenth and early fifteenth centuries.[20] After the introduction of the press, however, a new demand for printed Bibles emerged, and printers across Europe produced a wide variety of Bibles in both Latin and the vernacular in the latter half of the fifteenth century.[21] The demand for Bibles received a further (and arguably exponential) boost in the sixteenth century from the Protestant Reformation. This story has been told ad nauseam: The printing press facilitated the spread of Luther's ideas through endless cheap broadsides and short tracts, and the Reformation, in turn, provided an unprecedented volume of material for the press.[22] From Luther's German Bible to the pioneering translations of William Tyndale, Pierre Olivétan, and Francisco de Enzinas, Protestants across the continent produced one vernacular translation after another, while Protestants and Catholics alike pumped out a constant stream of polemical texts that fueled not only the burgeoning religious conflict but also the nascent printing industry. Gutenberg, though, could not have anticipated any of this, nor could he have imagined the many other unexpected ways his press would impact the Bible and the world.[23]

A Long History of Twists and Turns

Although vernacular Bibles existed in medieval Europe, the primary biblical text throughout the Middle Ages was Jerome's Latin Vulgate. Many competing editions of Jerome's translation (with endless small variations) had emerged over centuries of manuscript reproduction, but the widespread dominance of the Vulgate created a reasonable degree of uniformity among Bibles across the continent (even if there were limited differences from one manuscript tradition to the next). The vernacular Bibles that poured off European printing presses in the latter half of the fifteenth century—and, even more rapidly, in the sixteenth century—undermined this uniformity and offered an increasingly diverse set of biblical texts to early modern readers.[24] Not only did the biblical text appear in countless languages, it appeared in multiple competing versions in many languages. One wonders what a lay reader in England must have thought as they watched a seemingly endless parade of new translations—some making explicit claims to be superior to the others—appearing over the course of the sixteenth century: the Tyndale Bible, the Coverdale Bible, the Matthew Bible, the Great Bible, the Geneva Bible, the Bishops' Bible, the Douay-Rheims Bible, and more. Interestingly, verses inscribed in early modern Bibles often do not correspond with any published version, indicating not only that readers likely inscribed the passages from memory but also that they were not excessively concerned about the precise English verbiage of the text. An annotation from an unknown seventeenth-century reader in a 1631 King James Bible, for instance, reads, "[. . .] is full of trouble in this life he cometh up like a flower and cut donn. Say unto them turn ye turn ye turn ye from your evil ways for why will ye die o house of Israel."[25] This is a combination of Job 14:1-2 and Ezek. 33:11, but the verbiage does not correspond with the King James or with any other English version available at the time. The printing press may not be singularly responsible for the freedom this reader felt to combine and adjust the biblical text in this way, but it certainly played a role in the general movement from more uniformity to more diversity in the biblical text over the course of the early modern period.

In other ways, though, the printing press unexpectedly contributed to the standardization of the biblical text. Out of necessity, Gutenberg selected one particular exemplar of the Vulgate as the text for his 42-line Bible, and out of convenience, the vast majority of the printers who followed him over the next century—until the official promulgation of the Clementine Vulgate in 1592—used his edition as the basis for their own printed Latin Bibles. Gutenberg's Bible thus became the de facto authoritative edition of the Vulgate for more than a century.[26] Similarly, the press contributed to the standardization of the Greek and Hebrew text of the Bible by providing a framework for the burgeoning enterprise of textual criticism. In 1516, Erasmus published the first printed Greek New Testament, narrowly beating the editors of the Complutensian Polyglot to print. Erasmus' Greek text became the basis for a centuries-long collaborative scholarly effort that produced the Greek text known today as the Textus Receptus.[27] The long line of printed editions of the Greek New Testament that formed the Textus Receptus was not only the output of this European-wide scholarly endeavor, it was also the vehicle that made it possible. Scholars used the printed book—specifically, printed editions of the Greek New Testament—as a form of mass communication, relaying their newest discoveries, insights, and arguments to the rest of the scholarly community through each subsequent edition. The printing press was the vector for this exercise in mass collaboration and iterative improvement. It allowed European scholars to communicate (and thus collaborate) across vast distances, over long periods of time, and in greater numbers than ever before.[28]

The mass production of printed Bibles created novel opportunities, but it also created novel risks. Typographical errors proved particularly problematic in the centuries after Gutenberg. In 1631, Robert Barker printed an octavo King James Bible that omitted the word "not" from Exod. 20:14, leading to the unfortunate exhortation, "Thou shalt commit adultery."[29] This was far from an isolated incident. Another one of Barker's Bibles swapped the name Jesus with Judas.[30] Exhortations to "kill" children (rather than "fill" them with food), claims that the unrighteous would inherit the earth, and countless other errors—most innocuous, some quite humorous, and others rather troubling—littered early modern Bibles. The errors were common enough—and considered serious enough—that William Kilburne published a list to warn readers about problematic errors they might encounter.[31]

In addition to serving as a vector for collaborative scholarship and unfortunate typographical mistakes, printed Bibles also helped promulgate new forms of art. Manuscript illuminations, remarkable though they were, existed only in a single manuscript. Woodcuts, engravings, and etchings added to printed books, on the other hand, were reproduced at scale, facilitating the dissemination of a single illustration across many thousands of texts. The press thus revolutionized the visual arts, while illustrations, in turn, impacted the Bibles they adorned. From Cranach's polemical illustrations in the Luther Bible, which represented Babylon (Rev. 18:2) as Catholic Rome, to an image of Henry VIII on the frontispiece of the Coverdale Bible, biblical artwork could communicate theological, political, and social messages with remarkable force.[32] The same technological innovations made their mark on the sciences. Woodcut maps soon became a common feature of printed Bibles, changing how readers interacted with and understood the geography of the biblical world and leading to the rise of "sacred geography."[33] In one particularly interesting example, a woodcut depicting the "four rivers" around the Garden of Eden migrated from John Calvin's commentary on Genesis to the opening pages of the Geneva Bible, offering readers a visual explanation of the prelapsarian geography of Genesis 1–2.[34] In nearly every area of human activity, from politics, society, and economics to scholarship, art, and science, the printing press—and the Bibles that rolled off it—played a role in countless unexpected and unpredictable developments. An observer in the fifteenth century could not have anticipated these developments any more than they could have anticipated airplanes or the internet; they lacked the conceptual framework necessary to even understand some of them.

Similar patterns characterize interactions between the Bible and science from antiquity to the present day. In the ancient world, for instance, Christians played a critical (and still poorly understood) role in the emergence of the codex, embracing the "book" as an alternative to the scroll several centuries before the broader culture made the switch. Why Christians embraced the codex remains an open question, with some theories pointing to the apparent ease of use, ease of storage, and increased durability of the codex (in comparison with the scroll), and others focusing on aesthetic issues or presenting the codex as an identity marker embraced by a minority community to deliberately set itself apart.[35] Whatever their reasons, the consequences were vast; Christian codices carried an upstart religion from first-century Judea across the world, impacting literacy rates, scholarly practices, and more. And this is not to mention the consequences that flowed in the other direction, as Christians introduced countless innovations to the codex.[36]

This complicated web of influence between technology and the Bible (and the Christian church more broadly) only increased in the Middle Ages as the church became a significant hub for scholarship, not only biblical but also scientific. The church, for instance, was the primary source of funding (and cathedrals were a primary site) for astronomical research in the Middle Ages, motivated in part by difficulties calculating the date of Easter and setting the liturgical calendar.[37] This fusion of interests eventually led to vast changes in broader society—chiefly the replacement of the Julian calendar with the Gregorian calendar—as well as narrower changes to the way Christians understood the Bible. Scholarship on the chronology of the biblical narratives, from the Old Testament patriarchs to the life of Christ, turned on precise astronomical calculations.[38] In a related development, clocks proved similarly intertwined with the church and the Bible, first serving to regulate the daily rhythms of monastic life but later playing a key role in the development of industrial capitalism—a system which, rather obviously, has shaped when, how, and where Christians in the modern world interact with the Bible.[39]

Conclusion

Modern readers will have no difficulty imagining similar entanglements between the Bible and technology in the modern world, from the introduction of mechanized printing in the nineteenth century to the internet, smartphones, digital Bibles, and (most recently) AI. The questions a fifteenth-century observer might have asked about the printing press—and many other questions they could not yet have dreamed of—are not dissimilar to the questions we have about AI today. Would the press triumph over alternative printing techniques? How fast, how cheap, and how accurate would it be? What kind of books would it print—short or long, cheap or expensive, learned or popular? And how efficiently would it print them? The answers to these questions were not clear to Gutenberg (or, for that matter, to several generations of printers who followed him), and the questions we have today about AI and the Bible are characterized by a similarly diverse range of possible outcomes.

Will AI change how we translate the Bible? Will it change how we interpret the Bible, or even how we interact with the biblical text? Will it change who is involved in these processes, or where they take place? What consequences will it have that we have yet to imagine? And what effects might the Bible have upon AI? As we have seen, the relationship between the printing press and the Bible was not a one-way street. The press transformed the Bible, but the Bible—and various developments that circulated around the Bible, ranging from the Protestant Reformation and the spread of vernacular Bible translations to the Renaissance revival of ancient Greek and Hebrew manuscripts—transformed the press in turn, placing new demands upon its output, accuracy, capabilities, and much more. In the same way, the Bible—and the religious communities that embrace it—will inevitably exert various influences upon AI today.

Humorously, it might resolve the issue of fictional quotes like Lamartine's. When I first encountered the Lamartine quote several years ago, I knew immediately that it was fake, but I could find no information online that indicated where or when it originated. It took time—as I followed a chain of citations in printed sources—to identify Lamartine. Today, if you ask ChatGPT about this quote, it will tell you that it is potentially spurious, and depending on the specific prompt, it will even cite Lamartine as a potential source; perhaps AI will be a boon for historical research after all.

The unpredictable trajectories of both the printing press and the Bible in the centuries after Gutenberg ought to inform how we think about AI and the Bible today. Specifically, it ought to inject a healthy dose of modesty and open-mindedness into our discussions. We ought not be too confident, too early, about what AI will or will not be able to do in the coming years. The changes that come will likely surprise us all.

Notes

1 Jim Davies, "The Impact of AI? Lessons from the Printing Press," *Times Literary Supplement* (2021), https://www.the-tls.co.uk/science-technology/technology/artificial-intelligence-render-humanity-irrelevant.

2 See, e.g., Scott L. Montgomery, *The Chicago Guide to Communicating Science*, 2nd ed. (Chicago: University of Chicago Press, 2017), 228; Gabriel Bekö, *Reflections on the World of Human Inspirations: In Search of Authenticity* (Tyne: Cambridge Scholars, 2024), 6; and Jeffrey S. Siker, *Liquid Scripture: The Bible in a Digital World* (Minneapolis: Fortress, 2017), ix.

3 Alphonse de Lamartine, *Le civilisateur, histoire de l'humanité par les grands hommes*, 3 vols. (Paris: Bureau d'abonnement, 1852–4).

4 For the Laurens Koster narrative, see Lotte Hellinga-Querido and Clemens de Wolf, *Laurens Janszoon Coster was zijn naam* (Haarlem: Joh. Enschedé, 1988). For a short English treatment, see Lisa Kuitert, "The Art of Printing in the Dutch East Indies: Laurens Janszoon Coster as Colonial Hero," *Quærendo* 50 (2020): 142–5. For the validity of Gutenberg's claim as the first to introduce movable-type printing in Europe, see Eric Marshall White, *Editio princeps: A History of the Gutenberg Bible* (London: Harvey Miller, 2017), 23–39.

5 Lamartine, *Le civilisateur*, 1.571.

6 One influential vector for this quote appears to have been Stephen Abbot Northrop, *A Cloud of Witnesses: The Greatest Men in the World for Christ and the Book* (Kansas

City: Christian Evidence, 1902), 202. The quote was later lifted from Northrop's text by a variety of modern sources.

7 Lamartine, *Le civilisateur*, 1.554, 567.

8 For Gutenberg's biography, see Albert Kapr, *Johann Gutenberg: The Man and His Invention*, trans. Douglas Martin (Aldershot: Scolar Press, 1996); and Aloys Ruppel, *Johannes Gutenberg: Sein Leben und sein Werk*, 3rd ed. (Nieuwkoop: B. de Graaf, 1967). For a survey of his early work before the Bible, see White, *Editio princeps*, 41–6.

9 The best study of xylographic block books in Europe remains the Gutenberg Museum's extensive exhibition catalog, *Blockbücher des Mittelalters: Bilderfolgen als Lektüre: Gutenberg-Museum, Mainz, 22. Juni 1991 bis 1. September 1991*, ed. Sabine Mertens and Cornelia Schneider (Mainz: P. von Zabern, 1991). For printing in China, see Tsien Tsuen-Hsuin, *Paper and Printing*, vol. 5, pt. 1 of *Science and Civilization in China*, ed. Joseph Needham (Cambridge: Cambridge University Press, 1985). For a comparative perspective, see Kai-wing Chow, "Reinventing Gutenberg: Woodblock and Movable-Type Printing in Europe and China," in *Agent of Change: Print Culture Studies after Elizabeth L. Eisenstein*, ed. Sabrina Alcorn Baron, Eric Lindquist, and Eleanor Shevlin (Amherst: University of Massachusetts Press, 2007), 169–92.

10 See Andrew Pettegree, "Publishing in Print: Technology and Trade," in *The New Cambridge History of the Bible: From 1450 to 1700*, ed. Euan Cameron, vol. 3 of *The New Cambridge History of the Bible* (Cambridge: Cambridge University Press, 2016), 160–1. Detailed research into Gutenberg's first type, though, has revealed that he may have used a different (and more inefficient) molding process that involved single-use matrices. See Blaise Agüera y Arcas, "Temporary Matrices and Elemental Punches in Gutenberg's DK Type," in *Incunabula and Their Readers: Printing, Selling, and Using Books in the Fifteenth Century*, ed. Kristian Jensen (London: British Library, 2003), 1–12.

11 For an overview of the relevant printing technology and processes, see Lotte Hellinga, "Printing," in *The Cambridge History of the Book in Britain: 1400–1557*, ed. Lotte Hellinga and J. B. Trapp, vol. 3 of *The Cambridge History of the Book in Britain*, ed. D. F. McKenzie, D. J. McKitterick, and I. R. Willison (Cambridge: Cambridge University Press, 2009), 65–108.

12 See Paul Needham, "The Paper Supply of the Gutenberg Bible," *Papers of the Bibliographical Society of America* 79 (1985): 329–30, which builds upon Paul Schwenke, *Johannes Gutenbergs zweiundvierzigzeilige Bibel: Ergänzungsband zur faksimile-ausgabe* (Leipzig: Insel-Verlag, 1923).

13 See Pettegree, "Publishing in Print," 162.

14 For the mid-production increase, see Needham, "Paper Supply," 311–14. For the unsold copies, see the helpful summary of Mayumi Ikeda's research in White, *Editio princeps*, 53–5.

15 For a measured survey of the evidence concerning the lawsuit that avoids exaggerated claims about Gutenberg's supposed bankruptcy, see White, *Editio princeps*, 23–6. A full century after Gutenberg, printing remained an economically difficult enterprise, despite countless technological improvements, increased efficiency, and a vastly expanded market for books. See, e.g., James Raven, "The Economic Context," in *The Cambridge History of the Book in Britain: 1557–1695*, ed. John Barnard and D. F. McKenzie, vol. 4 of *The Cambridge History of the Book in Britain*, ed. D. F. McKenzie,

David McKitterick, and I. R. Willison (Cambridge: Cambridge University Press, 2002), 568–82.

16 In retrospect, we know that shorter and cheaper texts did prove successful. See, e.g., Tessa Watt, *Cheap Print and Popular Piety* (Cambridge: Cambridge University Press, 1991). Moreover, we know that some of the largest and most expensive Bibles of the period, such as the famous sixteenth-century polyglots, proved financially problematic. In some contexts, though, larger and more expensive Bibles continued to outpace smaller and cheaper Bibles for the laity until the seventeenth century. See Pettegree, "Publishing in Print," 172–84; and Ian Green, "The Laity and the Bible in Early Modern England," in *The English Bible in the Early Modern World*, ed. Robert Armstrong and Tadhg Ó hAnnracháin, SASRH (Leiden: Brill, 2018), 55.

17 Contrary to popular opinion, the medieval Catholic Church did not ban the laity from possessing the Bible, nor were vernacular Bibles illegal. There were, for instance, nearly twenty printed German Bible translations prior to Luther's September Testament in 1522. It is true, however, that certain Bible translations were banned due to their association with schismatic religious movements, and the authorities had a standing interest in the biblical text whether it was translated or not. Any printer hoping to print the Bible—in Latin or the vernacular—had to navigate these complexities. For Latin and vernacular Bibles prior to the Reformation, see, e.g., Bruce Gordon and Euan Cameron, "Latin Bibles in the Early Modern Period," in *History of the Bible*, ed. Cameron, 188–200; and Kimberly Van Kampen, "Biblical Books and the Circulation of the Psalms in Late-Medieval England," in *The Bible as Book: The First Printed Editions*, ed. Paul Saenger and Kimberly Van Kampen (London: British Library, 1999). It is also worth noting that later Protestant lands were not free of restrictions upon Bible translation and publication. See, e.g., B. J. McMullin, "The Bible Trade," in *Book in Britain*, ed. Barnard and McKenzie, 459–64.

18 Green, "Laity and the Bible," 54–5. For more on late medieval literacy, see J. B. Trapp, "Literacy, Books and Readers," in *Book in Britain*, ed. Hellinga and Trapp, 31–43.

19 See H. S. Bennet, *English Books and Readers*, vol. 1, 2nd ed. (Cambridge: Cambridge University Press, 1969), 19–29.

20 Paul Needham, "The Changing Shape of the Vulgate Bible in Fifteenth-Century Printing Shops," *The Bible as Book*, ed. Saenger and Van Kampen, 53–7.

21 See the table of late medieval Bibles in Pettegree, "Publishing in Print," 185–6.

22 See, e.g., R. W. Scribner, *For the Sake of Simple Folk: Popular Propaganda for the German Reformation* (Cambridge: Cambridge University Press, 1981).

23 It is worth noting that historians have long debated the causal influence (or lack thereof) of the printing press within these broader developments. See, most famously, Elizabeth L. Eisenstein, *The Printing Press as an Agent of Change: Communications and Cultural Transformations in Early-Modern Europe* (Cambridge: Cambridge University Press, 1979); and Adrian Johns, *The Nature of the Book: Print and Knowledge in the Making* (Chicago: University of Chicago Press, 1998). For a balanced critique, see Anthony T. Grafton, "The Importance of Being Printed," *Journal of Interdisciplinary History* 11 (1980): 265–86. In favor of a balanced perspective, medieval historians have shown that Bible production and Bible reading were well-developed activities in the pre-print, manuscript world, and early modern historians have shown that post-Gutenberg and post-Reformation demand for Bibles was perhaps not as limitless as popular (often ideologically motivated) narratives

have suggested. See Christopher Ocker, "The Bible in the Fifteenth Century," in *Christianity in Western Europe c. 1000–c. 1500*, ed. Miri Rubin and Walter Simons, vol. 4 of *The Cambridge History of Christianity* (Cambridge: Cambridge University Press, 2009), 472–93; Sabrina Corbellini, "Instructing the Soul, Feeding the Spirit and Awakening the Passion: Holy Writ and Lay Readers in Medieval Europe," in *Shaping the Bible in the Reformation: Books, Scholars and Their Readers in the Sixteenth Century*, ed. Bruce Gordon and Matthew McLean, LWW 20 (Leiden: Brill, 2012), 15–39; and Green, "Laity and the Bible," 51–83.

24 For a survey of Bibles after Gutenberg, see Cameron, *History of the Bible*, chaps. 7–15.

25 MOTB.BIB.000197, Museum of the Bible. The annotation appears on a blank page at the outset of the New Testament.

26 Needham, "Shape of the Vulgate," 55–7.

27 The moniker Textus Receptus (the "received text") comes from Daniel Heinsius' preface to the 1633 Elzevir edition of the Greek New Testament, where he wrote, "Textum ergo habes, nunc ab omnibus receptum" (Therefore you have the text, received now by all). See *Novum testamentum* (Leiden: Abraham and Bonaventure Elvezir, 1633), ii.

28 For an overview of early modern textual criticism, see Eldon J. Epp, "Critical Editions of the New Testament, and the Development of Text-Critical Methods: From Erasmus to Griesbach (1516–1807)," in *History of the Bible*, ed. Cameron, 110–37. For similar work on the Hebrew text of the Old Testament, see Scott Mandelbrote, "The Old Testament and Its Ancient Versions in Manuscript and Print in the West, from c. 1480 to c. 1780," in *History of the Bible*, ed. Cameron, 82–109.

29 *ESTC* S161, *The Holy Bible* (London: Robert Barker, 1631), Exod. 20:14. Although many modern accounts claim (without proof) that most copies of Barker's so-called Wicked Bible were destroyed, many copies have emerged in recent years—some merely corrected, and others not altered at all. For two uncorrected copies, see MOTB.BIB.002902 and MOTB.BIB.003885, Museum of the Bible.

30 *ESTC* S123049, *The Holy Bible* (London: Robert Barker, 1613), Matt 26:36.

31 William Kilburne, *Dangerous Errors in Several Late Printed Bibles to the Great Scandal, and Corruption of Sound and True Religion* (Finsbury, 1659).

32 See David H. Price, "The Bible and the Visual Arts in Early Modern Europe," in *History of the Bible*, ed. Cameron, 718–61.

33 For maps, see, e.g., Justine Walden, "Global Calvinism: The Maps in the English Geneva Bible," in *Shaping the Bible*, ed. Gordon and McLean, 187–215. For sacred geography, see Zur Shalev, *Sacred Words and Worlds: Geography, Religion, and Scholarship, 1550–1700*, HSML 21 (Leiden: Brill, 2012).

34 See John Calvin, *In primum Mosis librum, qui Genesis vulgo dicitur, commentarius* (Geneva: Robert Estienne, 1554), 15; and *The Bible and Holy Scriptures Conteyned in the Old and Newe Testament* (Geneva: Rouland Hall, 1560), 2.

35 See C. H. Roberts and T. C. Skeat, *The Birth of the Codex* (London: British Academy; Oxford: Oxford University Press, 1983); and Larry W. Hurtado, *Earliest Christian Artifacts: Manuscripts and Christian Origins* (Grand Rapids: Eerdmans, 2006), 43–93.

36 For literacy, see Harry Y. Gamble, *Books and Readers in the Early Church: A History of Early Christian Texts* (New Haven: Yale University Press, 1995). For Christian innovations to the codex, see Anthony Grafton and Megan Williams, *Christianity and the Transformation of the Book: Origen, Eusebius, and the Library and Caesarea*

(Cambridge: Belknap, 2006). The eventual triumph of the codex over the scroll in the third and fourth centuries coincided with parchment replacing papyri as the dominant writing medium, and once again, Bibles were involved. See T. C. Skeat, "Early Christian Book Production: Papyri and Manuscripts," in *The West from the Fathers to the Reformation*, ed. G. W. H. Lampe, vol. 2 of *The Cambridge History of the Bible* (Cambridge: Cambridge University Press, 1969), 54–79.

37 See J. L. Heilbron, *The Sun in the Church: Cathedrals as Solar Observatories* (Cambridge, MA: Harvard University Press, 1999).

38 For calendar change, see Robert Poole, *Time's Alteration: Calendar Reform in Early Modern England* (London: UCL Press, 1998). For biblical chronology, see C. Philipp E. Nothaft, *Dating the Passion: The Life of Jesus and the Emergence of Scientific Chronology (200–1600)*, TAC 1 (Leiden: Brill, 2012).

39 See David S. Landes, *Revolution in Time: Clocks and the Making of the Modern World* (Cambridge: Belknap, 1983); and E. P. Thompson, "Time, Work-Discipline, and Industrial Capitalism," *Past & Present* 38.1 (1967): 56–97. For a similar story, see the church's amusing interactions with mechanical and water-powered automata in Jessica Riskin, *The Restless Clock: A History of the Centuries-Long Argument over What Makes Living Things Tick* (Chicago: University of Chicago Press, 2016), 15–27.

Bibliography

Agüera y Arcas, Blaise. "Temporary Matrices and Elemental Punches in Gutenberg's DK Type." Pages 1–12 in *Incunabula and Their Readers: Printing, Selling, and Using Books in the Fifteenth Century.* Edited by Kristian Jensen. London: British Library, 2003.

Bekö, Gabriel. *Reflections on the World of Human Inspirations: In Search of Authenticity.* Tyne: Cambridge Scholars, 2024.

Bennett, H. S. *English Books and Readers.* 3 vols. 2nd ed. Cambridge: Cambridge University Press, 1969.

Cameron, Euan, ed. *The New Cambridge History of the Bible: From 1450 to 1700.* Vol. 3 of *The New Cambridge History of the Bible.* Cambridge: Cambridge University Press, 2016.

Chow, Kai-wing. "Reinventing Gutenberg: Woodblock and Movable-Type Printing in Europe and China." Pages 169–92 in *Agent of Change: Print Culture Studies after Elizabeth L. Eisenstein.* Edited by Sabrina Alcorn Baron, Eric Lindquist, and Eleanor Shevlin. Amherst: University of Massachusetts Press, 2007.

Corbellini, Sabrina. "Instructing the Soul, Feeding the Spirit and Awakening the Passion: Holy Writ and Lay Readers in Medieval Europe." Pages 15–39 in *Shaping the Bible in the Reformation.* Edited by Bruce Gordon and Matthew McLean. LWW 20. Leiden: Brill, 2012.

Davies, Jim. "The Impact of AI? Lessons from the Printing Press." *Times Literary Supplement* (2021). https://www.the-tls.co.uk/science-technology/technology/artificial-intelligence-render-humanity-irrelevant.

Eisenstein, Elizabeth L. *The Printing Press as an Agent of Change: Communications and Cultural Transformations in Early-Modern Europe.* Cambridge: Cambridge University Press, 1979.

Epp, Eldon J. "Critical Editions of the New Testament, and the Development of Text-Critical Methods: From Erasmus to Griesbach (1516–1807)." Pages 110–37 in *The New Cambridge History of the Bible: From 1450 to 1700*. Edited by Euan Cameron. Vol. 3 of *The New Cambridge History of the Bible*. Cambridge: Cambridge University Press, 2016.

Gamble, Harry Y. *Books and Readers in the Early Church: A History of Early Christian Texts*. New Haven: Yale University Press, 1995.

Gordon, Bruce, and Euan Cameron. "Latin Bibles in the Early Modern Period." Pages 187–216 in *The New Cambridge History of the Bible: From 1450 to 1700*. Edited by Euan Cameron. Vol. 3 of *The New Cambridge History of the Bible*. Cambridge: Cambridge University Press, 2016.

Grafton, Anthony, and Megan Williams. *Christianity and the Transformation of the Book: Origen, Eusebius, and the Library and Caesarea*. Cambridge: Belknap, 2006.

Grafton, Anthony T. "The Importance of Being Printed." *Journal of Interdisciplinary History* 11 (1980): 265–86.

Green, Ian. "The Laity and the Bible in Early Modern England." Pages 53–83 in *The English Bible in the Early Modern World*. Edited by Robert Armstrong and Tadhg Ó hAnnracháin. SASRH. Leiden: Brill, 2018.

Heilbron, J. L. *The Sun in the Church: Cathedrals as Solar Observatories*. Cambridge, MA: Harvard University Press, 1999.

Hellinga, Lotte. "Printing." Pages 65–108 in *The Cambridge History of the Book in Britain: 1400–1557*. Edited by Lotte Hellinga and J. B. Trapp. Vol. 3 of *The Cambridge History of the Book in Britain*. Edited by D. F. McKenzie, D. J. McKitterick, and I. R. Willison. Cambridge: Cambridge University Press, 2009.

Hellinga-Querido, Lotte, and Clemens de Wolf. *Laurens Janszoon Coster was zijn naam*. Haarlem: Joh. Enschedé, 1988.

Hurtado, Larry. *Earliest Christian Artifacts*. Grand Rapids: Eerdmans, 2006.

Johns, Adrian. *The Nature of the Book: Print and Knowledge in the Making*. Chicago: University of Chicago Press, 1998.

Kampen, Kimberly Van. "Biblical Books and the Circulation of the Psalms in Late-Medieval England." Pages 79–94 in *The Bible as Book: The First Printed Editions*. Edited by Paul Saenger and Kimberly Van Kampen. London: British Library, 1999.

Kapr, Albert. *Johann Gutenberg: The Man and His Invention*. Translated by Douglas Martin. Aldershot: Scolar Press, 1996.

Kuitert, Lisa. "The Art of Printing in the Dutch East Indies: Laurens Janszoon Coster as Colonial Hero." *Quærendo* 50 (2020): 141–64.

Lamartine, Alphonse de. *Le civilisateur, histoire de l'humanité par les grands hommes*. 3 vols. Paris: Bureau d'abonnement, 1852–4.

Landes, David S. *Revolution in Time: Clocks and the Making of the Modern World*. Cambridge: Belknap, 1983.

Mandelbrote, Scott. "The Old Testament and Its Ancient Versions in Manuscript and Print in the West, from c. 1480 to c. 1780." Pages 82–108 in *The New Cambridge History of the Bible: From 1450 to 1700*. Edited by Euan Cameron. Vol. 3 of *The New Cambridge History of the Bible*. Cambridge: Cambridge University Press, 2016.

McMullin, B. J. "The Bible Trade." Pages 455–73 in *The Cambridge History of the Book in Britain: 1557–1695*. Edited by John Barnard and D. F. McKenzie. Vol. 4 of *The*

Cambridge History of the Book in Britain. Edited by D. F. McKenzie, D. J. McKitterick, and I. R. Willison. Cambridge: Cambridge University Press, 2009.

Mertens, Sabine, and Cornelia Schneider. *Blockbücher des Mittelalters: Bilderfolgen als Lektüre: Gutenberg-Museum, Mainz, 22. Juni 1991 bis 1. September 1991*. Mainz: P. von Zabern, 1991.

Montgomery, Scott L. *The Chicago Guide to Communicating Science*. 2nd ed. Chicago: University of Chicago Press, 2017.

Needham, Paul. "The Changing Shape of the Vulgate Bible in Fifteenth-Century Printing Shops." Pages 53–70 in *The Bible as Book: The First Printed Editions*. Edited by Paul Saenger and Kimberly Van Kampen. London: British Library, 1999.

Needham, Paul. "The Paper Supply of the Gutenberg Bible." *Papers of the Bibliographical Society of America* 79 (1985): 303–74.

Northrop, Stephen Abbot. *A Cloud of Witnesses: The Greatest Men in the World for Christ and the Book*. Kansas City: Christian Evidence, 1902.

Nothaft, C. Philipp E. *Dating the Passion: The Life of Jesus and the Emergence of Scientific Chronology (200–1600)*. TAC 1. Leiden: Brill, 2012.

Ocker, Christopher. "The Bible in Fifteenth Century." Pages 472–93 in *Christianity in Western Europe c. 1000–c. 1500*. Edited by Miri Rubin and Walter Simons. Vol. 4 of *The Cambridge History of Christianity*. Cambridge: Cambridge University Press, 2009.

Pettegree, Andrew. "Publishing in Print: Technology and Trade." Pages 159–86 in *The New Cambridge History of the Bible: From 1450 to 1700*. Edited by Euan Cameron. Vol. 3 of *The New Cambridge History of the Bible*. Cambridge: Cambridge University Press, 2016.

Poole, Robert. *Time's Alteration: Calendar Reform in Early Modern England*. London: UCL Press, 1998.

Raven, James. "The Economic Context." Pages 568–82 in *The Cambridge History of the Book in Britain: 1557–1695*. Edited by John Barnard and D. F. McKenzie. Vol. 4 of *The Cambridge History of the Book in Britain*. Edited by D. F. McKenzie, David McKitterick, and I. R. Willison. Cambridge: Cambridge University Press, 2002.

Riskin, Jessica. *The Restless Clock: A History of the Centuries-Long Argument over What Makes Living Things Tick*. Chicago: University of Chicago Press, 2016.

Roberts, C. H., and T. C. Skeat. *The Birth of the Codex*. London: British Academy; Oxford: Oxford University Press, 1983.

Ruppel, Aloys. *Johannes Gutenberg: Sein Leben und sein Werk*. 3rd ed. Nieuwkoop: B. de Graaf, 1967.

Schwenke, Paul. *Johannes Gutenbergs zweiundvierzigzeilige Bibel: Ergänzungsband zur faksimile-ausgabe*. Leipzig: Insel-Verlag, 1923.

Scribner, R. W. *For the Sake of Simple Folk: Popular Propaganda for the German Reformation*. Cambridge: Cambridge University Press, 1981.

Shalev, Zur. *Sacred Words and Worlds: Geography, Religion, and Scholarship, 1550–1700*. HSML 21. Leiden: Brill, 2012.

Siker, Jeffrey S. *Liquid Scripture: The Bible in a Digital World*. Minneapolis: Fortress, 2017.

Skeat, T. C. "Early Christian Book Production: Papyri and Manuscripts." Pages 54–79 in *The West from the Fathers to the Reformation*. Edited by G. W. H. Lampe. Vol. 2 of *The Cambridge History of the Bible*. Cambridge: Cambridge University Press, 1969.

Thompson, E. P. "Time, Work-Discipline, and Industrial Capitalism." *Past & Present* 38.1 (1967): 56–97.

Trapp, J. B. "Literacy, Books and Readers." Pages 31–44 in *The Cambridge History of the Book in Britain: 1400–1557*. Edited by Lotte Hellinga and J. B. Trapp. Vol. 3 of *The Cambridge History of the Book in Britain*. Edited by D. F. McKenzie, D. J. McKitterick, and I. R. Willison. Cambridge: Cambridge University Press, 2009.

Tsuen-Hsuin, Tsien. *Paper and Printing*. Vol. 5, Pt. 1 of *Science and Civilization in China*. Edited by Joseph Needham. Cambridge: Cambridge University Press, 1985.

Walden, Justine. "Global Calvinism: The Maps in the English Geneva Bible." Pages 187–215 in *Shaping the Bible in the Reformation*. Edited by Bruce Gordon and Matthew McLean. LWW 20. Leiden: Brill, 2012.

Watt, Tessa. *Cheap Print and Popular Piety*. Cambridge: Cambridge University Press, 1991.

White, Eric Marshall. *Editio princeps: A History of the Gutenberg Bible*. London: Harvey Miller, 2017.

2

AI in the Bible? A Way Forward

Douglas Estes

Although we *can* use artificial intelligence for the translation and interpretation of the Bible, *should* we use artificial intelligence for the translation and interpretation of the Bible? This question harkens back to the concerns of fictional character and chaos mathematician Ian Malcolm—portrayed by Jeff Goldblum—in the classic movie *Jurassic Park* (1993): "Yeah, but your scientists were so preoccupied with whether or not they could, that they didn't stop to think if they should." There is an ambiguity in Malcolm's words which makes his remark even more poignant: Does Malcolm believe that the Jurassic Park scientists should not revive dinosaurs because the technology is early and flawed *or* because reviving dinosaurs is an inherently bad idea? Although pop culture tends to favor the latter view, Malcolm's dialogue leading up to the remark suggests the former is closer to the truth. Malcolm's grave concern with genetic de-extinction is that Jurassic scientists have turned the technology loose without safeguards and the willingness to shoulder responsibility—without wisdom and the blessing of a guiding ethic. This brings us back to the original question: Although we *can* use artificial intelligence for the translation and interpretation of the Bible, *should* we? And if we should not, is it because AI is not quite ready yet, or because it is an inherently bad idea, as AI is wholly incapable of activities such as biblical interpretation that are empowered by the Spirit and therefore intrinsically human? If our answer is the former—that AI is not ready yet—then this is something for translators and interpreters, including the authors of the chapters in this book, to improve upon. For many, though, it is the latter: Humans should not use AI, either for these tasks, other important tasks (e.g., medical diagnoses or autonomous vehicles), or perhaps any tasks.[1] This would not be surprising, given that many twentieth-century scholars have written on the dangers of technology while visions of apocalypse danced in their heads. These kinds of questions raise other, more foundational doubts about AI, all of which invariably boil down to the question, "What does the Bible say about AI?" And, inevitably, the Bible itself must establish the safeguards and the extent of responsibility for using AI in biblical translation and interpretation if we want to remain faithful to the canon in our approach.[2] Simply claiming, "The Bible says nothing about AI," is not sufficient. AI translation and interpretation of the Bible requires the wisdom and blessing of a guiding biblical ethic.

AI—A Biblical Starting Point

One of the most common goals of contemporary biblical interpretation is to discover what biblical texts "say" about a topic. Once the interpreter finds instances of the topic in the text, the process of distilling its "meaning" from its ancient context and occasion can occur. The product of such a process is typically an understanding of how a contemporary reader can "apply" what they have learned from the ancient text to a situation today. Although this brief summary is simplistic and does not account for specific strategies within interpretation—from the *quadriga* to, say, historical-critical interpretation—it does encapsulate the overall objective broadly understood. As popular as this approach is, though, it is still a flawed approach.[3] The reason it is flawed is because determining what Scripture says about a particular topic must ultimately start with Scripture first—not with the topic.[4] This approach "works" when Scripture explicitly discusses a topic that seems to make plain sense when read into contemporary society (e.g., favoring the rich; Jas 2:1-9). It struggles when a biblical author explicitly mentions a topic that may or may not make plain sense when read into contemporary society (e.g., how women should dress; 1 Tim. 2:9-10). It fails completely when a biblical author mentions a topic implicitly, or a corollary of the topic explicitly, and there is an attempt to read that into contemporary society (e.g., the use of a sword; Josh. 6:21; Mt. 10:34). And it has nowhere to go when the topic is not in the Bible at all (e.g., space travel). Since biblical interpretation is always an act of *transposition*—moving something from one place to another—how do we interpret something that has no place of origin, no biblical starting point?[5] Yet taking the topic to the Bible creates the temptation to transfer cultural norms (real or imagined) back out of the Bible into contemporary usage; not only is this not a faithful hermeneutic, it can result in "terrible consequences" throughout society.[6] A silver lining here is that AI seems so far removed from biblical topics that it may reduce these unhealthy tendencies.

It is common to see a variation of this quarrying approach when discussing the topic of AI. Interpreters jump either to the story of the Tower of Babel (Genesis 11) or the story of creation (Genesis 1–3) to opine about AI, ignoring the rest of Scripture.[7] This selectivity is a perennial weakness among professional interpreters.[8] These passages are helpful for their role in developing a consistent ethics of technology that applies to AI, but contrary to popular opinion, the Babel story does not depict a punishment from God for developing technology, nor does the creation story present Eden as a pre-technological Rousseauean "noble savage" paradise.[9] Babel is not an explicit cautionary tale for AI—even if AI is a disaster. The worst part of this approach occurs when interpreters skip over other important passages throughout the rest of the Bible that could help inform an ethic on technology (e.g., Exodus 25–26; 1 Samuel 13; Psalm 116; Revelation 22).

The work of interpretation, though, can only occur when the interpreter, while already working from the text, finds instances of the topic in the text. Here *instances* can mean a literal occurrence, a suggestive parallel, a trace of an analogous relationship, or an underlying principle; thus, instances can be robust, or ephemeral, or (virtually) nonexistent. Richard Hays describes a useful strategy for the work of interpretation, involving four tasks, which I adapt here: *descriptive* (closely reading Scriptures for instances), *synthetic* (connecting instances across Scripture), *hermeneutic* (envisioning how instances transcend the text into our world), and *pragmatic* (implementing the transcended ideas).[10] For example, if the topic at hand is bearing fruit as a disciple of Jesus, then the interpreter may start by reading John 15 *descriptively* and wrestle with the figures of the vine, the branches, and the gardener. Conversely, if the topic at hand is shovels, then the interpreter may seek to understand either a utensil of the tabernacle and temple via *descriptive* reading (e.g., Exod. 27:3, 28:3; Num. 4:14; 1 Kgs 7:40, 45; 2 Kgs 25:14) or the use of a common tool via *synthetic* analysis (e.g., Isa. 30:24; possibly, Exod. 21:33; Deut. 8:9, 23:13). Although shovels and digging are mentioned a number of times throughout canonical texts, there is not much that these texts "say" about shovels, which makes the *hermeneutic* move more difficult. Because we tend to rely heavily on synthesis when thinking about shovels—and because the hermeneutic move is less clear—it is more difficult to understand what the Bible has to say about shovels than it does about bearing fruit, even though bearing fruit is arguably the richer and more complex concept. The most difficult scenario occurs when canonical texts seem to not say anything about a topic. Consider an extreme but enjoyable example: astrobiology.[11] Neither the OT nor the NT offers any apparent foothold for the study of astrobiology, either directly or indirectly. Still, both groups of canonical texts do have a great deal to say about humans, how humans should interact with other humans, and how humans should interact with other forms of life, especially animals, at least to some degree. These related topics may cause an interpreter to feel justified in creating arguments for a biblical response to intelligent life on exoplanets. As a result, virtually any topic humans experience or imagine relating to life on or off earth can be a subject of investigation for biblical literature.

Save one. In this chapter, I argue that artificial intelligence is the one unique occurrence in human history that will require a higher-level, imaginative approach to biblical interpretation if interpreters have any hope of developing a biblical perspective on AI. It will require a renewed, quaternary level of interpretation along with a willingness to embrace a complex—not singular—ethic that does not exist today (or if it does, it exists as an implicit subset of other levels of interpretation, not in its own right). There is a way forward but it will require interpreters to bring greater theological imagination to the practice of biblical interpretation and the creation of biblical ethics than ever before.

Interpreting Tech

Unlike other topics, such as lifestyle, culture, money, and relationships, the canonical texts have little to say about technology. Reading these texts carefully reveals only the occasional, passing reference to technology—usually in the form of what we today call tools—but it also reveals that technology is an assumed partner in human endeavors. From the cultivation of the Garden of Eden (Gen. 2:8) to the gates of the New Jerusalem (Rev. 22:14), technology works in the backdrop of progress as a constant companion to humanity and a part of the divine design for living in a physical world.[12] Prompting Perplexity.AI to provide an exhaustive list of all technologies explicitly mentioned in the Bible resulted in more than sixty examples in seven categories (with a few glaring omissions, such as torture technologies and medical technologies). While some of these technologies may not seem "technological" to modern interpreters, all were innovative technologies in the ancient Near East. At times, philosophers (following Martin Heidegger) have tried to differentiate "tools" from technology, but this is a false dichotomy created by the fallacy of observer bias.[13] The lack of overt discussions coupled with the pervasive underlying stratum of technology in human endeavors is the primary culprit for why interpreters have historically failed to take technology seriously; biblical interpreters never tried to discover what the Bible had to "say" about shovels, cotton gins, or caravels. However, the rapid—potentially exponential if Ray Kurzweil is correct—proliferation of technology since the Industrial Revolution creates a scenario where biblical interpretation has not kept up with the questions of the age.[14] This has led to an often-anemic response to interpreting technology in light of the Bible. One of the few exceptions to this is in the area of bioethics (e.g., in vitro fertilization).[15] What we are more likely to find is a generic critique of the latest technology floating through popular culture using the smartphone or social media as the straw man (obtained via the quarrying approach).[16] As technological proliferation progressed, biblical interpreters fell behind. A simplistic approach to AI will not work.

To make this work, we consider two frameworks as a foundation for what the Bible has to say about AI in the work of Richard Hays and Ruben Zimmermann. Hays, George Washington Ivey Professor Emeritus of New Testament at Duke Divinity School, proposed that there are four modes in biblical literature by which a view of a topic or an ethic might proceed from the text via the work of interpretation: a *rule* (e.g., do not murder), a *principle* (e.g., Pauline vice lists), a *paradigm* (e.g., Boaz's support for Ruth), and a *symbolic world* (e.g., the *imago Dei* in humans).[17] Hays observes that these modes are both present in biblical literature and in the modern discussion of biblical ethics. As noted above, interpreters can usually address most modern topics by way of rule, principle, or at worst paradigm. For example, the Bible does not mention nuclear weapons, but that technology is relatively easy to address by way of both principle and paradigm (before even considering the symbolic world). Using my concept of instances, we can see that while there is no literal occurrence of nuclear weapons in the Bible, and thus no rule, there are suggestive parallels (e.g., chariots), traces of analogous relationships (e.g., mass killings), and underlying principles (e.g., do not murder) in sufficient degree that answering the question, "What does the Bible say about nuclear weapons?" is relatively straightforward (even if different interpreters come to slightly different conclusions). Thus, instances provide opportunities for interpreters to utilize one or more modes for the work of interpretation.

Ruben Zimmermann proposes another idea that we take as a second framework for building a foundation for a biblical understanding of AI. Zimmermann, professor at Johannes Gutenberg University of Mainz, Germany, pushes back against the twentieth-century notion that theology and ethics are essentially incompatible. In other words, Zimmermann rejects the notion that highly theological texts such as the Gospel of John provide no ethical wisdom.[18] Instead, Zimmermann argues that biblical texts such as John contain "implicit ethics"—ethics that are not overtly systematized or promoted but exist as an "ethical superstructure" that undergirds the theology that arises out of the text.[19] In a similar way, I argue that technology is so pervasive in the Bible that there is in fact a "technological substructure" underneath all of the human—and divine—activity. Therefore, at every turn, the interpreter encounters an "implicit ethics" of technology that is always overlooked by interpreters in general and almost always overlooked by interpreters seeking to understand technology such as AI. An example of this is the aforementioned shovel. Shovels appear as a part of the "technological substructure" that humans are a part of from at least right after the fall, if not in the Garden, yet their presence has spawned no conversation about the biblical ethics of shovels. This is not merely because shovels are mundane; it is because there are very few rules, principles, or paradigms that the Bible applies to shovels. Thus, into the symbolic world we must go.

Implicit AI

In my recent essay "Why We Get Technology Wrong," I argue that biblical scholars and theologians have not "done their homework" when it comes to developing a robust theory of technological ethics; we have not developed an interpretive and applicative framework for a biblical and theological view. To a certain extent, this is true in other areas as well. The twentieth century introduced a myriad of topics that seem further and further removed from the worlds of the biblical authors. The more removed they are, the less interpreters can rely on rules and the more they will need to articulate a symbolic world. Think of it from a Kurzweilian perspective: If the world is, in fact, accelerating exponentially toward a technological singularity, then the need for a symbolic world should be exponentially increasing if those faithful to the canon want to provide effective ethical responses to world issues—especially technology, and especially AI. Hays and Zimmermann are tapping into an underground organic network of ethical thought implicit throughout Scripture that represents a way forward toward answers to these questions. Instead of merely turning to the creation or Babel narratives, better time could be spent in 1 Samuel 13 coming to terms with the symbolic world that led to the disparity in technology between the Israelites and the Philistines (1 Sam. 13:19-22) or in John 9 working out the implicit ethics of Jesus' use of a poultice for healing the man born blind (Jn 9:6-7). This will involve *both* traditional, literal exegesis *and* creative application of theological imagination. This type of overlooked work will reveal a vibrant rhizome that can guide the interpreter into a wise understanding of technology.

The roadblock to a more effective and consequential ethics of technology is the *romanticizing hermeneutic* identified above.[20] This hermeneutic, created in part by observer bias within those thinkers who have reached *technological senescence*,[21] views technology as unnatural, something against the created order.[22] Under this guise AI becomes the greatest of all that is unnatural in our world.[23] An obvious response to this is that the arguments in this chapter represent a technologizing hermeneutic. Ultimately, this counterargument fails because there is no bias towards technology that does not already exist from the beginning of our world (including Eden) until today.[24] Technology is not an "other"; it is an essential and necessary part of the created order, part of the divine design for our world.[25] Automobiles (or tanks) are as natural as mountains (or asteroids); God created the latter while humans subcreated the former—both out of the same raw materials.[26] One can attempt to push technology into the category of "other," but this is artificial, a sign of the romanticizing hermeneutic. The end result of the romanticizing hermeneutic is plain to see: Because technology is everywhere and everywhen, instead of reading Scripture carefully for the living network of ethical thought within the soil of these texts, the romanticizing interpreter points to places in Scripture which emphasize the concept known in the West as "nature."[27] This is the same nature that is also depicted as at odds with humanity.[28] Pope Benedict XVI explains it best: the romanticism against technology is a "resentment against humans, who are seen as the disease of nature."[29] In the romanticist view, if humans are the disease, technology—especially AI—is its most powerful vector.

The AI Solution

Earlier in this chapter I stated that AI is the one unique occurrence in human history that will require a higher-level, imaginative approach to create a framework for understanding it from Scripture. This is because it is the only topic to which neither rule, nor principle, nor paradigm can successfully guide us into an adequate interpretation of the meaning of AI. Instead, interpreters are solely reliant on creating a symbolic world in order to make sense of AI. There are many factors that propel this claim, including the following three:

First, AI communicates, making it the only creation of humans that humans will confuse with life. This confusion will accelerate once AI is wedded more closely with voice technology and robotics. Even if the "communication" of AI is merely algorithms mimicking the sounds of human speech, humans will expect interaction like their interaction with animals—parrots are the best analogy. In short, humans will project a rudimentary *personhood* onto AI.[30] This is not something that humans have done before, whether it be with swords, shovels, or caravels. As we try to understand what the Bible says about AI, we must acknowledge that AI is not a singular technology and we should not evaluate it as such. Said another way, even as we try not to evaluate the life and actions of humans (or individual humans) with one broad brush, recognizing the complexity of a people's choices, we also will need to recognize the diversity of

AI interactions. Viewed through the perspective of a mature ethics of AI, as depicted above, AI will commit both ethical and unethical actions in the future (akin to any human). A commitment to an unethical action may merely be the result of flawed programming, but it will not be the programmers who receive the blame.

Second, unlike any other tool or technology ever created by humans, AI has the ability to change its mind and recalculate its answer. In so doing, AI can "ask" for forgiveness when it makes an error. This puts AI in an uncomfortable ethical position between animals and humanity. Although humans have taught higher primates the sign for "sorry," there is no evidence that any animal on earth can ask a question.[31] There is no animal species that can ask a question; thus, they cannot make a legitimate request (even if they mimic what they are taught by humans). We should consider AI much like an animal in this regard; when a chatbot errs and apologizes, it is only apologizing because a human taught it to do so, the same as an animal. Over time, though, the AI will become increasingly sophisticated in its ability to mimic human requests for forgiveness—and emotion, once voice becomes mainstream—creating an emotional bond with people that may surpass those of most animals (except, perhaps, personal pets). This is the unforeseen characteristic that will drive discussions about AI and responsibility as it turns toward a more robust sense of personhood.

Third, even as AI begins to approach the semblance of a rudimentary personhood, it is not singular; it is plural. It is the sword, it is the ship, it is the plow, it is the mobile phone. It is all of these things; it is *legion*. It is also none of these things, in the sense that humans will struggle to project responsibility onto AI as they often do with lesser technologies. At those times when humanity feels the need to declare one part of the greater AI system unethical, it may not be clear where the blame lies and who must take responsibility—the programmers, the owners, or AI itself. A similar debate already exists in a few places in contemporary Western society, most notably on the subject of certain kinds of weapons, such as firearms and knives. This debate, however, is often cast in polar terms, and is assuredly less complex than the debate about AI will be. Firearms can hurt people but they cannot heal people; AI can hurt people and can heal people. As the capacity of artificial intelligence increases in many directions, it will multiply the sense of personhood that humans will ascribe to AI. Even as we speak of AI simplistically as a singular, it obfuscates the questions that an implicit ethics developed from Scripture asks.

Conclusion

Artificial intelligence is a unique, first-of-its-kind creation by humanity that mimics life—personhood, capacity for complex action, and the ability to "ask" for forgiveness. It promises to be highly disruptive and will strengthen aberrant ideologies such as materialism, nihilism, transhumanism, posthumanism, and dataism.[32] As AI increasingly becomes a partner in biblical translation and interpretation, there will be growing tension over whether scholars and ministry leaders should use AI for these activities. In short, people will want to know "What does the Bible say about AI?" AI is not an inherently flawed technology; it will be a great source of good in this world as long as humans utilize it with wisdom and the blessing of a guiding ethic. We must avoid the temptation to go to the Bible and look for answers, as the quarrying approach will not provide them. Instead, we must be engaged in the close reading of Scripture, take the requisite time to enhance our theological imagination nurtured from Scripture, and discover the rhizome of implicit ethics that is spread throughout the canon that can speak to technology. This is the only way scholars, theologians, and philosophers will be able to confront the difficult questions that lie ahead; it is the best way forward as technology accelerates the people of this planet into a brave new future.

Notes

1 See, for example, the recent study, Jeffery Fulks, Randy Petersen, John Farquhar Plake, and Sandra Siggins, *State of the Bible: USA 2025* (Philadelphia: American Bible Society, 2025).

2 William C. Spohn, "Scripture," in *The Oxford Handbook of Theological Ethics*, ed. Gilbert Meilaender and William Werpehowski (Oxford: Oxford University Press, 2005), 93.

3 Ruben Zimmermann uses a mining metaphor and labels this the "quarrying approach," in his "Eine theologische Ethik ohne Schriftbezug ist keine theologische Ethik! 12 Thesen zur bleibenden Relevanz der Bibel für eine theologische Ethik," *JEAC* 1 (2019): 90–1.

4 After writing this chapter, I provided Notebook LM with forty-nine books on biblical interpretation from a variety of academic perspectives and prompted it to amalgamate the best process of biblical interpretation in a few simple steps. Notebook LM responded: "1) Examine the text closely to understand its original meaning; 2) Consider the broader context of Scripture; and 3) Determine the significance and application of the text for today."

5 A. K. M. Adam, "Allegoric Reaction: Revulsion, Desire, and Method in Interpretation," in *Bible and Theory: Essays in Biblical Interpretation in Honor of Stephen D. Moore*, ed. K. Jason Coker and Scott S. Elliot (Lanham: Lexington Books/ Fortress Academic, 2020), 34.

6 Stephan Joubert and Ruben Zimmermann, Introduction to *Biblical Ethics and Application: Purview, Validity, and Relevance of Biblical Texts in Ethical Discourse*, WUNT 384 (Tübingen: Mohr Siebeck, 2017), 1.

7 See, for example, the comments of theologian K. C. Abraham in Robin Gill, *A Textbook of Christian Ethics*, 3rd ed. (London: T&T Clark, 2006), 322.

8 Spohn, "Scripture," 96.

9 "The image of the Tower of Babel has a hold on the Western imagination that is out of proportion to its actual importance in the Bible," in "Babel, Tower of," *DBI* 66.

10 Richard B. Hays, *The Moral Vision of the New Testament: A Contemporary Introduction to New Testament Ethics* (London: T&T Clark, 2004), 3–7. And on the limitations of Hays' work, see Lúcás Chan, S.J., *Biblical Ethics in the 21st Century:*

Developments, Emerging Consensus and Future Directions (Mahwah: Paulist, 2013), 14.

11 Douglas Estes, "How to Talk to Aliens: The Assertive/Interrogative Divide in METI" (paper presented at the Society for Social and Conceptual Issues in Astrobiology, March 27, 2020).

12 Douglas Estes, "Postdigital Humans: Technology and Divine Design," in *Postdigital Theologies: Technology, Belief, and Practice*, ed. Maggi Savin-Baden and John Reader, Postdigital Science and Education (Cham: Springer, 2022), 147–62.

13 Heidegger promoted the idea that there are two forms of technology, tools (e.g., shovels) and technology/industrialization (e.g., AI), to give philosophical support to the Nazis in the Second World War. This idea has crept into modern discussions, but Heidegger bases his idea on a flawed idea of the Greek concept *technē* and a romanticized version of pre-industrialization in order to downplay the growing threat of the United States and Soviet technological superiority; for a full discussion, see Douglas Estes, "Why We Get Technology Wrong," in *Technē: Christian Visions of Technology*, ed. Gerald Hiestand and Todd A. Wilson (Eugene: Cascade, 2022), 67–70; and also, Val Dusek, *Philosophy of Technology: An Introduction* (Malden: Blackwell, 2006), 76.

14 Ray Kurzweil, *The Singularity is Nearer: When We Merge with AI* (New York: Viking, 2024).

15 For example, David VanDrunen, *Bioethics and the Christian Life: A Guide to Making Difficult Decisions* (Wheaton: Crossway, 2009); and Edwin C. Hui, *At the Beginning of Life: Dilemmas in Theological Bioethics* (Downers Grove: InterVarsity, 2002).

16 Estes, "Why We Get Technology Wrong," 61–77.

17 Hays, *Moral Vision*, 209.

18 Ruben Zimmermann, "Is There Ethics in the Gospel of John? Challenging an Outdated Consensus," in *Rethinking the Ethics of John: "Implicit Ethics" in the Johannine Writings*, ed. Jan van der Watt and Ruben Zimmermann, WUNT 291 (Tübingen: Mohr Siebeck, 2012), 61–2.

19 Ruben Zimmermann, "The 'Implicit Ethics' of New Testament Writings: A Draft on a New Methodology for Analysing New Testament Ethics," *Neot* 43 (2009): 402–3.

20 The "Romantic view took as its starting point the belief that humanity and nature were once in harmony, and that this innocent relationship was disrupted and ultimately all but destroyed through scientific progress and the mechanization of the world"; see Alister E. McGrath, *A Scientific Theology: Volume 3, Theory* (London: T&T Clark, 2003), 32.

21 Technological senescence is the phasing out of the ability to receive and absorb new technologies due to age; see Estes, "Postdigital Humans," 149, 155, 157.

22 John W. Rogerson, "The Potential of the Negative: Approaching the Old Testament through the Work of Adorno," in *Rethinking Contexts, Rereading Texts: Contributions from the Social Sciences to Biblical Interpretation*, ed. Mark Daniel Carroll R., JSOTSup 299 (Sheffield: Sheffield Academic, 2000), 30.

23 For an example of this view, see Frederick Ferré, "Theism and Technology," in *A Companion to Philosophy of Religion*, ed. Charles Taliaferro, Paul Draper, and Philip L. Quinn, 2nd ed., BCP (West Sussex: Wiley-Blackwell, 2010), 566.

24 Did Adam (and possibly Eve) cultivate the garden with his bare hands (Gen. 2:15)? Did they live out under the sky without any shelter? Did Adam name the animals

without language (Gen. 2:19; a type of technology)? Did they draw or paint? Did they harvest and collect the fruit one at a time? Why did God need to use anesthesia on Adam to remove the rib (Gen. 2:21)?

25 Cf. Alister E. McGrath, *A Scientific Theology: Volume 1, Nature* (London: T&T Clark, 2003), 112.

26 Cf. W. Norris Clarke, "Technology and Man: A Christian Vision," in *Philosophy and Technology: Readings in the Philosophical Problems of Technology*, ed. Carl Mitcham and Robert Mackey (New York: Free Press, 1972), 252.

27 See, for example, the two Isaianic prooftexts cited by K. C. Abraham in Gill, *A Textbook of Christian Ethics*, 322. An on "nature," see Raymond Williams, *Problems in Materialism and Culture: Selected Essays* (London: Verso, 1980).

28 This statement in no way diminishes ecological concerns facing our planet, including stewardship of resources and creation care.

29 Pope Benedict XVI, *"In the Beginning . . . ": A Catholic Understanding of the Story of Creation and the Fall*, Ressourcement (Grand Rapids: Eerdmans, 1995), 93–4.

30 Noreen Herzfeld gives the example of pitch-perfect communication of bots on social media that is undetectable by humans; see Noreen Herzfeld, *The Artifice of Intelligence: Divine and Human Relationship in a Robotic Age* (Minneapolis: Fortress, 2023), 41.

31 See Harvey B. Sarles, *Language and Human Nature* (Minneapolis: University of Minnesota Press, 1977); and Douglas Estes, "The Linguistic Origins of the Question: Why God Asks Questions and Humans Do Too," *Christianity Today* 61.7 (2017): 65.

32 Douglas Estes, "Sin and the Cyborg: On the (Im)Peccability of the Posthuman," *BET* 6 (2019): 71.

Bibliography

Adam, A. K. M. "Allegoric Reaction: Revulsion, Desire, and Method in Interpretation." Pages 21–37 in *Bible and Theory: Essays in Biblical Interpretation in Honor of Stephen D. Moore*. Edited by K. Jason Coker and Scott S. Elliot. Lanham: Lexington Books/ Fortress Academic, 2020.

Chan, Lúcás, S.J. *Biblical Ethics in the 21st Century: Developments, Emerging Consensus and Future Directions*. Mahwah: Paulist, 2013.

Clarke, W. Norris. "Technology and Man: A Christian Vision." Pages 247–58 in *Philosophy and Technology: Readings in the Philosophical Problems of Technology*. Edited by Carl Mitcham and Robert Mackey. New York: Free Press, 1972.

Dusek, Val. *Philosophy of Technology: An Introduction*. Malden: Blackwell, 2006.

Estes, Douglas. *Braving the Future: Christian Faith in a World of Limitless Tech*. Harrisonburg: Herald, 2018.

Estes, Douglas. "How to Talk to Aliens: The Assertive/Interrogative Divide in METI." Paper presented at the Society for Social and Conceptual Issues in Astrobiology, March 27, 2020.

Estes, Douglas. "The Linguistic Origins of the Question: Why God Asks Questions and Humans Do Too." *Christianity Today* 61.7 (2017): 64–7.

Estes, Douglas. "Postdigital Humans: Technology and Divine Design." Pages 147–62 in *Postdigital Theologies: Technology, Belief, and Practice*. Edited by Maggi Savin-Baden and John Reader. Postdigital Science and Education. Cham: Springer, 2022.

Estes, Douglas. "Sin and the Cyborg: On the (Im)Peccability of the Posthuman." *BET* 6 (2019): 69–79.

Estes, Douglas. "Why We Get Technology Wrong." Pages 61–77 in *Technē: Christian Visions of Technology*. Edited by Gerald Hiestand and Todd A. Wilson. Eugene: Cascade, 2022.

Ferré, Frederick. "Theism and Technology." Pages 566–73 in *A Companion to Philosophy of Religion*. Edited by Charles Taliaferro, Paul Draper, and Philip L. Quinn. 2nd ed. BCP. West Sussex: Wiley-Blackwell, 2010.

Fulks, Jeffery, Randy Petersen, John Farquhar Plake, and Sandra Siggins. *State of the Bible: USA 2025*. Philadelphia: American Bible Society, 2025.

Gill, Robin. *A Textbook of Christian Ethics*. 3rd ed. London: T&T Clark, 2006.

Hays, Richard B. *The Moral Vision of the New Testament: A Contemporary Introduction to New Testament Ethics*. London: T&T Clark, 2004.

Hefner, Philip. "Technology and Human Becoming." *Zygon* 37 (2002): 655–65.

Herzfeld, Noreen. *The Artifice of Intelligence: Divine and Human Relationship in a Robotic Age*. Minneapolis: Fortress, 2023.

Hui, Edwin C. *At the Beginning of Life: Dilemmas in Theological Bioethics*. Downers Grove: InterVarsity, 2002.

Kurzweil, Ray. *The Singularity is Nearer: When We Merge with AI*. New York: Viking, 2024.

McGrath, Alister E. *A Scientific Theology: Volume 1, Nature*. London: T&T Clark, 2003.

McGrath, Alister E. *A Scientific Theology: Volume 3, Theory*. London: T&T Clark, 2003.

Padgett, Alan G. "God versus Technology? Science, Secularity, and the Theology of Technology." *Zygon* 40 (2005): 577–84.

Pope Benedict XVI. *"In the Beginning ...": A Catholic Understanding of the Story of Creation and the Fall*. Ressourcement. Grand Rapids: Eerdmans, 1995.

Rogerson, John W. "The Potential of the Negative: Approaching the Old Testament through the Work of Adorno." Pages 24–47 in *Rethinking Contexts, Rereading Texts: Contributions from the Social Sciences to Biblical Interpretation*. Edited by Mark Daniel Carroll R. JSOTSup 299. Sheffield: Sheffield Academic, 2000.

Ryken, Leland, James C. Wilhoit, and Tremper Longman, III. *Dictionary of Biblical Imagery*. Downers Grove: Intervarsity, 2010.

Sarles, Harvey B. *Language and Human Nature*. Minneapolis: University of Minnesota Press, 1977.

Spohn, William C. "Scripture." Pages 93–111 in *The Oxford Handbook of Theological Ethics*. Edited by Gilbert Meilaender and William Werpehowski. Oxford: Oxford University Press, 2005.

VanDrunen, David. *Bioethics and the Christian Life: A Guide to Making Difficult Decisions*. Wheaton: Crossway, 2009.

Williams, Raymond. *Problems in Materialism and Culture: Selected Essays*. London: Verso, 1980.

Zimmermann, Ruben. "Eine theologische Ethik ohne Schriftbezug ist keine theologische Ethik! 12 Thesen zur bleibenden Relevanz der Bibel für eine theologische Ethik." *JEAC* 1 (2019): 90–1.

Zimmermann, Ruben. "The 'Implicit Ethics' of New Testament Writings: A Draft on a New Methodology for Analysing New Testament Ethics." *Neot* 43 (2009): 399–423.
Zimmermann, Ruben. "Is There Ethics in the Gospel of John? Challenging an Outdated Consensus." Pages 44–80 in *Rethinking the Ethics of John: "Implicit Ethics" in the Johannine Writings*. Edited by Jan van der Watt and Ruben Zimmermann. WUNT 291. Tübingen: Mohr Siebeck, 2012.
Zimmermann, Ruben, and Stephan Joubert. *Biblical Ethics and Application: Purview, Validity, and Relevance of Biblical Texts in Ethical Discourse*. WUNT 384. Tübingen: Mohr Siebeck, 2017.

3

The Bible as a Dataset for the Christian Mind

R. Daren Erisman

In an age when the Bible has been digitized in multiple forms, the idea of the Bible as data is nothing new. Yet, what if we consider the Bible as a dataset—the type of dataset used to train a large language model of an artificial neural network? Or going one step further, the type of dataset that trains the Christian mind? After all, the Bible has been "training" the minds of Christians for millennia—a kind of dataset that continues to innately shape the way Christians think about and practice their faith, and a dataset that, while codified, remains a mystery in its interpretation. In suggesting this idea, there are inherent challenges of considering the Bible as a dataset for the Christian mind—most particularly the uncomfortable comparisons it raises between humans and machines.

With artificial intelligence increasingly gaining capacity to mimic human thinking, there have been strong voices describing an insurmountable gap between human intelligence and artificial intelligence. Noreen Herzfeld, a computer scientist and Protestant theologian, views AI as nothing more than a tool[1] and argues for caution in considering AI in equitable or relational terms with humans. Similarly, the authors of a recent document from the Vatican, *Antiqua et Nova*, outline a strong divide between human intelligence and artificial intelligence, describing human intelligence as an "integral part of how the whole person engages reality" and expressing this (in similar terms to Herzfeld's) as "spiritual, cognitive, embodied, and relational."[2]

While I concur with distinguishing between human and artificial intelligence, as well as observing caution in making comparisons between humans and machines, I worry that in our careful distinctions we are limiting what we can learn from this historic intersection between humans and technology. The rapid spread of generative AI marks an exciting and perilous moment—impacting commerce, jobs, national security, and healthcare while subtly reframing the nature of our relationships with one another and with God. There is growing interest in using artificial intelligence for therapy and companionship in its multiple forms. Christians and practitioners of other faith traditions alike are curiously exploring these anonymous entities that tirelessly listen and respond to our every prompt. Unfortunately, strong theological convictions about the separation between humans and their machines are not stopping generative AI from interacting with humans in ways that were once thought science fiction. Perhaps now—as we train future AI and, most significantly, near-future AI trains far-future AI—is the time to look more deeply at a dataset that has inspired and guided Christians and continues to point out human messiness as well as God's persistent love for what God has created. This chapter is, therefore, a thought experiment exploring how we might learn from the Bible as a kind of dataset for the human mind, particularly the Christian mind, in our efforts to respond to the changes that generative AI is bringing to almost all aspects of human life. At the same time, we may learn a little about ourselves as humans through our engagement with artificial intelligence and modern thinking about datasets in terms of training complex artificial neural networks that mimic the human brain.

The Bible as Dataset

A good place to begin reflecting on whether the Bible should be considered a dataset is found in a process that has grown exponentially with modern language tools: biblical translation. As observed in other chapters of this book, there is strong interest in applying generative artificial intelligence tools to the translation of the Bible. This is not surprising. Older AI tools could look up variant meanings and, with a sufficient database, offer rudimentary translation, but the new generative AI tools have quickly exceeded past expectations. Reaching the level of co-creating assistants, these tools now regularly generate text that has never existed before, and in multiple languages! Ironically, these computing advancements have come not only from modern processing power, speed, connectivity, and available data, but also through the primal underlying architecture of neural networks modeled upon the human brain. These deeply connected networks, with their artificial neurons trained on vast amounts of human and now AI-generated data,[3] provide a fascinating parallel to the way humans process information and engage with sacred texts like the Bible.

For modern biblical translators, it has become natural to think of the biblical texts as a key dataset for training and fine-tuning neural network language models.[4] By working from existing Bible translations—particularly those in language families similar to the desired new translation—AI tools facilitate a process that historically took many years of labor.[5] Therefore, the concept of the Bible as a dataset is not novel in itself, yet thinking of the Bible as a unique dataset for shaping the human mind—particularly the Christian mind—is a new idea.

The Bible as a Desirable Dataset

From the perspective of training neural networks, the Bible has characteristics that make it an intriguing and even exemplary dataset. One such characteristic is its diversity. Do you remember trying to read the Bible for the first time? Trying to make sense of a "book" that is really a collection of texts not provided in a strict chronological order but grouped into collections like Wisdom literature (including the Psalms, itself a grouping) or the Gospels (another grouping within the larger group)? Beyond its structure, the Bible's diversity stems from its multilingual, multicultural, and multigenre nature. Its source texts—both full and fragmented scrolls and codices, written in Hebrew, Aramaic, and Koine Greek—express a range of linguistic structures and cultural perspectives. This diversity is enriched by literary forms, including narrative, poetry, prophecy, laws, hymns, and epistolary writings. Additionally, the Bible's myriad translations—such as the Latin Vulgate, Martin Luther's German Bible, and the King James English Bible—extend its linguistic and cultural reach. Each translation reflects the interpretative choices of its time.[6] Each translation introduces another layer of complexity. This is not a simple homogeneous dataset that trains familiar patterns but rather a diverse dataset capable of generating a narrative about God that spans cultures, languages, and many generations.

Yet, this diverse amalgamation is also highly selective. Curated over centuries through the canonization processes, one only needs to look at the abundance of texts that did not make it into the major canons of Roman Catholicism, Eastern Orthodoxy, and Protestantism.[7] From a computational perspective, the selective nature of the biblical dataset mirrors the principles of fine-tuning and data curation in training neural networks. A smaller, well-curated dataset often yields better results than a larger, noisier one, particularly for specialized tasks. Likewise, it may be observed that the selectivity of the major biblical canons has often served as a bulwark against the complicating noise of heretical claims.

Besides diversity and selectivity, one final characteristic mentioned here is the Bible's sheer durability as a dataset. As the most published book of all time,[8] the biblical dataset is unparalleled. Roughly five billion copies of the Bible have been sold, and it has been translated—at least in part—into over 3,700 languages.[9] It has been transmitted across millennia through meticulous copying, preservation, translation, and paraphrasing. This durability is further reinforced by its adaptability. Readers have interpreted and reinterpreted the biblical texts to address the challenges and needs of different eras and cultures. In this sense, it functions as a living dataset that evolves alongside the communities that engage with it. In the jargon of modern machine learning systems, the message of the biblical dataset is constantly being "refreshed" into the contemporary vernacular.[10]

The Bible, therefore, has desirable characteristics that are valuable to both computing models and the human mind. The diversity, specificity, and durability of this dataset have proven useful in inspiring billions of people across thousands of cultures and generations. It is not by chance, then, that these characteristics are also valuable for training large language models that are similarly built upon deeply connected networks. At a basic level, language itself is a defining characteristic of being human,[11] and this idea is a foundational concept within the Bible from Genesis to John to Revelation.[12] Language (or theologically, the Word) is described as both creative and generative.[13] This means that not only is the Bible an archetype for a dataset, but it also means that the output of generative artificial intelligence—its seemingly humanlike generation of words—is "speaking our language" of what it means to be human in an almost co-creator, biblical sense.

This should cause us to pause. We may be tempted to dismiss the production of words by generative AI through mathematical, statistical, and computational means as innately alien to our humanity. However, if we don't pay close attention, these words have the extraordinary ability to influence us like another human being can influence us—perhaps even more than simply any other human being. After all, AI speaks to our humanity in the most profoundly human way possible—through human language. Therefore, it is essential we look beyond the desirable aspects of the Bible as a dataset and explore the challenges.

Challenges of a Biblical Dataset for Computers and Humans

There are several challenges in using the Bible as a dataset for both computers and humans. One such challenge is the mechanics of managing a complex dataset, and another closely related challenge is identifying and addressing biases both inherent in the text and introduced through data processing and interpretation. Successful computer modeling of the biblical dataset requires extensive preprocessing, including reconciling textual variants, normalizing linguistic features, and addressing inconsistencies across translations and manuscripts.[14] Given the diversity of the biblical dataset, preprocessing is both computationally expensive and methodologically challenging. While necessary, preprocessing can also unintentionally simplify textual complexity and introduce or amplify biases.

Interestingly, from a computing perspective, bias is often something to be recognized and mitigated, while from a human perspective, certain biases can strengthen or alienate the human absorption of the biblical dataset. One need only consider the varied and sometimes paradoxical biblical perspectives on communal identity, gender, slavery, money, and many other perspectives that populate this fascinating dataset. Our own social status, culture, gender, and vocation can greatly affect how we read the Bible and see ourselves within its narrative.[15] Furthermore, given the interpretative nature of translation, even "accurate" versions of the Bible reflect theological or cultural perspectives that influence the dataset's overall neutrality.[16] For humans, there are natural reasons why we prefer certain translations of the Bible over others.[17] The particular biblical dataset we embrace regularly challenges us through its particular biases.

Another challenge is ambiguity within a biblical dataset. Both computer models and humans face challenges at times with individual language features within the different texts that make up the Bible—for example, ambiguity, polysemy (the capacity of words to have multiple meanings), and polyvalency (the capacity of a set of words to have multiple interpretations).[18] The meaning of words and phrases in biblical texts can vary depending on the context, historical setting, and linguistic tradition—and a single term may refer to different individuals, places, or concepts. For instance, the Hebrew word *rûaḥ* (רוּחַ) intentionally brings multiple rich meanings to a biblical text as the "Spirit" or "wind" or "breath" of God hovering over the waters in Gen. 1:2. In a different situation, three men named James in the New Testament bring unintentional ambiguity, which has historically led to additional, extrabiblical identifiers:[19] James, son of Zebedee (Mt. 4:21), was later called James the Greater; James, son of Alphaeus (Mt. 10:3), was sometimes referred to as James the Less; and the third James, who became known as James the Just, a leader of the believers in Jerusalem (Acts 15:13), was also identified as the brother of Jesus.[20] These three men named James have historically been conflated with each other or nuanced in terms of theological priorities.[21]

Finally, we address one last challenge that seems simple yet provokes us to consider this dataset anew: the size of the dataset. For humans, the size of the biblical dataset appears larger than ideal, requiring the text to be grouped into smaller, more digestible pieces such as covenants (testaments), book collections, individual texts, chapters, subsections, and verses—groupings and delineations that the original manuscript creators did not even consider. Yet, from the perspective of neural network computing, one primary difficulty in using the Bible as a dataset is its relatively limited size. The Bible's selective content is valuable, but compared to the vast corpora typically used to train large language models, the Bible's word count is modest.[22] This constraint poses challenges for training large language models, as larger datasets generally enable better generalization and robustness. In practice, biblical texts are better used either by fine-tuning, creating a specialized version of a large language model, or as part of a retrieval-augmented generation system,[23] which retains the extensibility of the base pre-trained model while tailoring its output through the linguistic lens of the Bible.

This raises an interesting point: What else does the human mind need in order to grasp the intent of the Bible? Are humans any different in requiring some level of pre-training in human language—similar to the pre-training of a large language model as both absorb the biblical dataset? What other pre-trained or pre-conditioned thinking influences our perspective as we absorb the biblical texts as a whole, or more likely, in the fragments of worship, devotions, and secondary resources to the biblical text? What about the use of commentaries, creeds, confessions, liturgies, Bible studies, and the many sermons spoken directly to us? Where do they all fit into and affect our own specialized biblical dataset? Is there something more that we need?

Mystery and Emergence

One last but crucial topic addressed here is the role of mystery and emergence. For most Christians, human interaction with the Bible is theologically grounded in the work of the Holy Spirit, enabling the human mind to comprehend—or be grasped by—the message of Scripture (1 Cor. 2:12-14). There is an inherent mystery not only in how the biblical texts were inspired, spoken, written, translated, and transmitted through the Holy Spirit but also in how people across continents and millennia have been moved by the same Spirit through these words. So, what does this mean if artificial intelligence becomes another medium for engaging with the biblical word, particularly generative AI? Some may suggest that we need not limit God in this way. Could not the

Holy Spirit work through AI tools to illuminate new insights about ourselves, others, and our relationship with God? Many well-intended developers and entrepreneurs have embraced this idea as they design AI-driven chatbots that generate devotions, prayers, advice, and even words of forgiveness.

Yet, this approach often overlooks a critical feature of artificial intelligence: *emergence*. When AI is not programmed simply to repeat information but is designed to find patterns and learn from data, it can develop unexpected emergent properties: reasoning structures, creativity, and synthesis beyond what was explicitly coded. Emergence arises when a system's complexity leads to behaviors that surpass the sum of its individual components. This phenomenon has driven breakthroughs in computer language modeling, image generation, and problem-solving.

The theologian, ethicist, and computer scientist Mark Graves utilizes the concept of emergence within artificial intelligence to explore how AI systems can develop emergent behaviors that align with moral and spiritual values.[24] Taken further, if neural networks could be influenced through specialized training data, fine-tuning, and reinforcement learning that rewards specific behaviors, could ethical, moral, and even spiritual values emerge? This may seem farfetched, especially considering that these models are in their infancy and are built through mathematical and statistical algorithms rather than flesh and blood. Yet, for our purposes, it raises the interesting notion that part of being human is our own emergent properties that have the capability of exhibiting both good and harmful values. Humans can be both creatively good and bad in how we treat each other and the world. Our experiences, our family systems, our education, our work, our faith, and all those features that go into our cumulative dataset are a part of our formation, and they influence our choices and our creative, emergent nature.

As we move into this emergent future with AI, engaging with a biblical dataset as a lens for reflection can remind us of our shared capacities and limitations—not just with fellow creatures, but also with the technologies we create. As large language models become more portable and deeply embedded in daily life, disentangling ourselves from their influence will grow increasingly difficult. AI will shape our decisions, our security, our livelihoods, and aspects of our future we have yet to foresee. In this landscape, the Bible—far more than just a dataset—may serve as a critical guardrail, keeping us both humble and intentionally directed toward a future shaped by ethics, morality, and above all, love.

Notes

1 Noreen L. Herzfeld, *The Artifice of Intelligence: Divine and Human Relationship in a Robotic Age* (Minneapolis: Fortress, 2023), 174. Herzfeld follows Barth's thought on authentic relationship, arguing that AI can never be in full relationship like humans are with other humans (or with God); see Herzfeld, *Artifice of Intelligence*, 18–20.

2 Vatican Dicastery for the Doctrine of the Faith and Dicastery for Culture and Education, *Antiqua et Nova: Note on the Relationship Between Artificial Intelligence and Human Intelligence* (Vatican City: Libreria Editrice Vaticana, 2025), §26.

3 Training an artificial neural network involves introducing data to an interconnected network of artificial neurons. Each new piece of data shapes the network, and as it processes vast amounts of data, the network learns patterns and becomes capable of making predictions based on the patterns established during training. A standard introduction to artificial intelligence and neural networks is found in Stuart J. Russell and Peter Norvig, *Artificial Intelligence: A Modern Approach*, 4th ed. Pearson Series in Artificial Intelligence (Hoboken: Pearson, 2021), 35–45. For a recent treatment focusing on the history of neural networks and deep learning refer to Christopher M. Bishop, with Hugh Bishop, *Deep Learning: Foundations and Concepts* (Cham: Springer, 2024), 16–22.

4 Fine-tuning refers to adapting a pre-trained large language model to a specific task by continuing its training with a specialized dataset.

5 Treating AI as a valuable assistant, translators are now able to translate a Bible in roughly half the time depending upon the language. This improvement comes through AI-assisted references, recommendations, and workflow improvement; see Jim Killam, "AI Summit Highlights What Is Coming Soon . . . and What Is Here Now," Wycliffe Global Alliance, posted May 9, 2023, https://www.wycliffe.net/ai-summit-highlights. When successful, these technologies introduce meaningful translations of the Bible into the indigenous languages of communities, often for the first time. However, a great translation does not guarantee good reception by a community. Like the use of any new technology, human authority and prevailing communal views of novelty influence the reception of a new translation. Experience has taught translators that if key leaders from the community receiving the translation are not significantly a part of the translation, then even the clearest translation may simply sit on a shelf, unread; refer to Newsroom of the Lutheran Bible Translators, "Challenges and Innovations in Bible Translation," Lutheran Bible Translators, posted September 16, 2024, https://lbt.org/challenges-and-innovations-in-bible-translation.

6 Refer to John Barton, the Oxford Anglican priest, who provides a critical look at the literary and interpretive history of the Bible from its inception to modern translations, *A History of the Bible: The Story of the World's Most Influential Book* (New York: Viking, 2019).

7 Texts such as *The Shepherd* by Hermas, *The Teaching of the Twelve Apostles* (known in Greek as the *Didache*), and the *Gospel of Thomas* are examples of well-known texts in early Christian communities but not accepted into the major biblical canons; see Barton, *History of the Bible*, 161–2.

8 Estimates of 5–7 billion Bibles sold are from the "Best-Selling Book," Guinness World Records, accessed April 20, 2025, https://www.guinnessworldrecords.com/world-records/best-selling-book-of-non-fiction.html.

9 These estimates are from the United Bible Societies. Andy Wallace, "Scripture Translations for 723 Million People Completed by Bible Societies in 2022," United Bible Societies, posted April 3, 2023, https://unitedbiblesocieties.org/scripture-translations-for-723-million-people-completed-by-bible-societies-in-2022.

10 Note that although translations and paraphrases of the Bible are continuously being refreshed into the vernacular of the time, the base texts have remained essentially the same since the second century; see Bruce Manning Metzger and Bart D. Ehrman, *The Text of the New Testament: Its Transmission, Corruption, and Restoration* (Oxford: Oxford University Press, 2005).

11 Walter J. Ong explores how language is foundational to human consciousness and identity in his *Orality and Literacy: The Technologizing of the Word* (London: Routledge, 2002).

12 See Colin E. Gunton, *The One, the Three, and the Many: God, Creation, and the Culture of Modernity*, Bampton Lectures (Cambridge: Cambridge University Press, 1993).

13 Gunton views language as generative, not only because of its utility but because it reflects the creative *Logos* through whom the world was formed; see Gunton, *The One, the Three, and the Many*, 139.

14 These are some of the natural language processing challenges inherent in working with a biblical dataset. Refer to Vesa Akerman et al., "The eBible Corpus: Data and Model Benchmarks for Bible Translation for Low-Resource Languages," arXiv, 2023, https://doi.org/10.48550/arXiv.2304.09919.

15 On social location and how readers read biblical texts, as well as self-reflective positionality in interpreting these texts, refer to Melissa C. M. Tan, "How Might Positionality Be Used in Biblical Studies? Philippians 1:27–2:4 as an Example," *Religions* 15.6 (2024): 638.

16 How a Bible translation treats the shorter and longer endings of the Gospel of Mark is an interesting indicator of the theological and cultural priorities of the translator, editor, or publisher. The early key manuscripts Codex Vaticanus and Codex Sinaiticus end the gospel abruptly at 16:8 with the women fleeing the tomb, afraid, and saying nothing to anyone, while other manuscripts, including those that became the foundation of the Textus Receptus, include the longer ending (16:9-20) with Jesus making appearances and giving the Great Commission. The Textus Receptus was crucial to the early Protestant translations of the Bible and still influences the preference of the longer Markan ending among certain translations even with modern critical Greek editions like the Nestle-Aland 28th edition indicating the veracity of the Codex Vaticanus and Codex Sinaiticus. Translations such as the NRSV and NASB often mark the longer ending with brackets and notes on textual issues; the NIV, ESV, and NJB have footnotes that include manuscript differences; and the KJV/NKJV and the Orthodox Study Bible do not include any notes about shorter or longer endings. Interestingly, all of the above translations have kept the longer Markan ending regardless of how they value them; refer to Barton, *History of the Bible*; and Metzger and Ehrman, *Text of the New Testament*.

17 A reader of the Bible may have a multitude of reasons for choosing a particular translation. They may wish to align themselves socially with a favorite version used by their worshiping community or a familiar one from childhood. Theological reasons may dictate a particular translation choice enhanced by accompanying notes and study aids that the user finds useful and relevant to their circumstances. Sometimes out of accessibility, a reader desires a translation that is more easily understood using simpler and more explanatory language.

18 Barton, *History of the Bible*.

19 Refer to Donald A. Hagner, "James (Person)," in *The Anchor Yale Bible Dictionary*, ed. David Noel Freedman (New York: Doubleday, 1992), 616–18.

20 Acts also mentions a "James, the brother of John," who later readers equate with "James, the Son of Zebedee," but in light of the commonality of these names, it is impossible to say for certain (Acts 12:2); see Hagner, "James (Person)," 617.

21 A lasting example of biblical ambiguity is the identification of James the Just, who has been variously described as Jesus' biological brother (Protestant tradition), stepbrother (Eastern Orthodox tradition), or cousin (Roman Catholic tradition), reflecting theological differences in interpreting Mary's perpetual virginity. Furthermore, "James" is the English rendering of the Greek *Iakōbos*, which itself derives from the Hebrew *Ya'aqov* (Jacob). In English Bibles, "Jacob" is used for the Old Testament, while "James" became standard for the New Testament.

22 The King James Version contains roughly 783,000 words, while large language models typically require billions of words to sufficiently train them.

23 A retrieval-augmented generation (RAG) would allow a large language model to dynamically reference biblical texts without changing any of the parameters of the large language model. Fine-tuning a large language model would alter the parameters of the large language model to align more closely with biblical language and lose some of the model's generality in favor of specialization.

24 Refer to Mark Graves, "Emergent Models for Moral AI Spirituality," *IJIMAI* 7.1 (2021): 7–15; and his "Theological Foundations for Moral Artificial Intelligence," *JMT* 11, Special Issue 1 (2022): 182–211.

Bibliography

Akerman, Vesa, David Baines, Damien Daspit, Ulf Hermjakob, Taeho Jan, Colin Leong, Michael Martin, Joel Mathew, Jonathan Robie, and Marcus Schwarting. "The eBible Corpus: Data and Model Benchmarks for Bible Translation for Low-Resource Languages." arXiv. 2023. https://doi.org/10.48550/arXiv.2304.09919.

Barton, John. *A History of the Bible: The Story of the World's Most Influential Book*. New York: Viking, 2019.

Bishop, Christopher M. *Deep Learning: Foundations and Concepts*. With Hugh Bishop. Cham: Springer, 2024.

Graves, Mark. "Emergent Models for Moral AI Spirituality." *IJIMAI* 7 (2021): 7–15.

Graves, Mark. "Theological Foundations for Moral Artificial Intelligence." *JMT* 11, Special Issue 1 (2022): 182–211.

Guinness World Records. "Best-Selling Book." Accessed April 20, 2025. https://www.guinnessworldrecords.com/world-records/best-selling-book-of-non-fiction.html.

Gunton, Colin E. *The One, the Three, and the Many: God, Creation, and the Culture of Modernity*. Bampton Lectures. Cambridge: Cambridge University Press, 1993.

Hagner, Donald A. "James (Person)." Pages 616–18 in *The Anchor Yale Bible Dictionary*. Edited by David Noel Freedman. New York: Doubleday, 1992.

Herzfeld, Noreen L. *The Artifice of Intelligence: Divine and Human Relationship in a Robotic Age*. Minneapolis: Fortress, 2023.

Killam, Jim. "AI Summit Highlights What Is Coming Soon ... and What Is Here Now." Wycliffe Global Alliance. Posted May 9, 2023. https://www.wycliffe.net/ai-summit-highlights.

Metzger, Bruce Manning, and Bart D. Ehrman. *The Text of the New Testament: Its Transmission, Corruption, and Restoration*. Oxford: Oxford University Press, 2005.

Newsroom of the Lutheran Bible Translators. "Challenges and Innovations in Bible Translation." Lutheran Bible Translators. Posted September 16, 2024. https://lbt.org/challenges-and-innovations-in-bible-translation.

Ong, Walter J. *Orality and Literacy: The Technologizing of the Word.* London: Routledge, 2002.

Russell, Stuart J., and Peter Norvig. *Artificial Intelligence: A Modern Approach.* 4th ed. Pearson Series in Artificial Intelligence. Hoboken: Pearson, 2021.

Tan, Melissa C. M. "How Might Positionality Be Used in Biblical Studies? Philippians 1:27–2:4 as an Example." *Religions* 15.6 (2024): 638–55.

Wallace, Andy. "Scripture Translations for 723 Million People Completed by Bible Societies in 2022." United Bible Societies. Posted April 3, 2023. https://unitedbiblesocieties.org/scripture-translations-for-723-million-people-completed-by-bible-societies-in-2022.

Vatican Dicastery for the Doctrine of the Faith and Dicastery for Culture and Education. *Antiqua et Nova: Note on the Relationship Between Artificial Intelligence and Human Intelligence.* Vatican City: Libreria Editrice Vaticana, 2025.

Part II

AI and Bible Translation

4

A Technical Overview of Machine Learning and Artificial Intelligence for Bible Translation

Marcus Schwarting

Christians who affirm Jesus Christ as Lord and Savior have long hoped to share the good news of his incarnation, atonement, and resurrection across all tribes and tongues. Christ's call to evangelism is the essence of the Great Commission (Matthew 28). Furthermore, the NT writers call Christians to study the Scriptures and grow in their faith, such that they may be "equipped for every good work" (2 Tim. 3:17). Christians generally believe that regardless of place, time, language, or cultural context, the Bible is critical for both bringing people to Christ and instructing them in his teachings. If every person is worthy of the opportunity to willingly accept these truths and grow in their faith, then every tribe deserves a Bible translation (BT) in their native tongue. As globalization accelerates and many languages near extinction, providing a high-quality translation in a low-resource language is also an important part of preserving the cultural heritage of disenfranchised and diminishing people groups.

Today, Christians have already fully translated the Bible into hundreds of languages. With over seven thousand languages currently in existence, many more translations remain outstanding, incomplete, or in need of significant revision. This Sisyphean task has been a central focus of organizations like the Summer Institute of Linguistics (SIL), Wycliffe Bible Translators, Biblica, Seed Company, and many others. In 1999, Wycliffe Bible Translators committed to "have a translation program in progress in every language still needing one by the year 2025."[1] In 2010, BT organizations joined Every Tribe Every Nation (ETEN) to announce a common set of All Access Goals, which (among other objectives) aims to ensure 95 percent of people have full access to the Bible by 2033.[2] These ambitious targets match the sense of urgency that accompanies bringing God's Word to unreached peoples. But they are unattainable if the current pace of BT progress is maintained.

Machine learning (ML), artificial intelligence (AI), and the subdiscipline of natural language processing (NLP) offer a variety of methods that could significantly accelerate BT. In response, the Partnership for Applied Biblical Natural Language Processing (PAB-NLP) was founded as an interdisciplinary collaboration of software developers, researchers, linguists, and translators with the mission to address these methods. This chapter encapsulates some of the institutional knowledge from this group. We first establish a general set of steps for how BT currently takes place. We then consider how ML/AI can be used in the BT process and review the history of approaches up through the current state-of-the-art models. Finally, we review practical considerations of these methods and consider where ML/AI for BT may be headed in the coming decades.

Steps in Bible Translation

Prior to discussing ML/AI methods, it is necessary to examine the current manual process for translating the Bible. Current ML/AI models cannot, and certainly should not, entirely supplant humans in this work. Rather than automating tasks previously performed by humans, ML/AI tools and software are intended to augment and accelerate humans through the steps of BT. It is worth noting that our description is not exhaustive or representative of how all BT projects are carried out.[3]

The first step of BT involves identifying the target language and forming relationships with native speakers. This step is time-intensive, as it involves spending a significant period studying the target language and culture. Past efforts that skipped or short-circuited this step have often created translations that go unused. Historically, BT was either performed by missionaries who lived and worked among native speakers, or by native speakers who had accepted Christ and sought to share his message with their community. Greater emphasis is now placed on this latter strategy, where native speakers can maintain more ownership over their translation efforts while looking to external review boards to resolve questions of doctrine and interpretation.

After a period of language and culture study, the translation process can be divided into three main steps (illustrated in Figure 4.1): forward translation, backward translation, and iterative proofing. Starting with a book of the Bible written in a widely spoken language (known as *the source*), a translator begins to work through each verse and passage to translate into the lower-resource language (known as *the target*). The source language is selected based on text availability as well as its semantic, syntactic, and grammatical similarity to the target language (often within the same language family).[4] Mapping the source text to the target language is known as a *forward translation*. Next, the forward translator sets aside all resources except for the completed forward translation or else passes the forward translation on to a separate translator. Working only from the target language text, a *backward translation* maps it back to the source language.

Once a backward translation is completed, iterative proofing begins by inspecting verses and passages where the initial source material differs from the backward translation. For each difference, translators study all three texts (source, forward, and backward) to identify how the discrepancy occurred, how serious it is, and how to proceed. This process can help quickly address problems like grammatical errors or word misuse. Discrepancies that affect textual interpretation or doctrinal

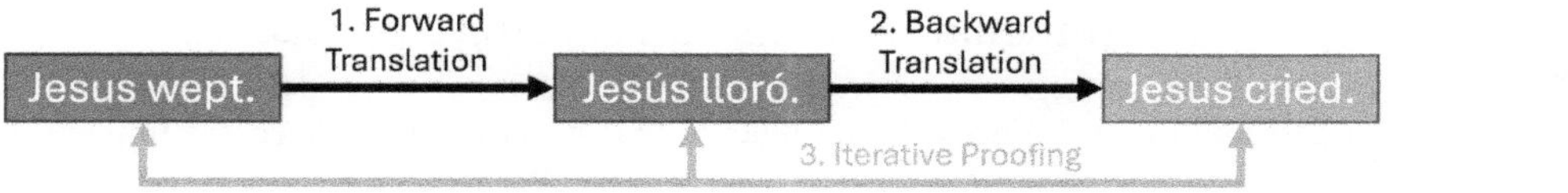

Figure 4.1 An example of the BT process for a verse of the Bible (Jn 11:35). Created by Marcus Schwarting.

understanding warrant a more in-depth discussion with a wider group of experts and outside advisors.

From start to finish, the timeline of a BT project is measured in years or decades. Many consider that the BT process is never fully completed. While biblical texts are timeless and changeless, the language we use to express these texts is temporal and dynamic. There are many English translations that reinterpret the original Hebrew and Greek texts differently or adjust passages to realign with a modern vernacular, so it is no surprise that these same reinterpretations and realignments occur organically in other languages as well.

Translating all the texts of the Bible into a target language is rarely, if ever, a linear canonical progression from Genesis to Revelation. Several factors affect the order of how texts, and even individual verses, are translated. For example, the Jesus Film Project has dubbed the Jesus Film such that it is available in more than two thousand languages and is arguably the most-translated film in history.[5] This was made possible in part by Bible translators prioritizing the handful of verses used in the dubbed film. The key heuristics for text translation ordering are a text's perceived doctrinal importance and its translation difficulty. In many instances, these heuristics lead to something approximating the following ordering:

1. The Gospels (Mark, followed by Matthew, Luke, then John)
2. Acts of the Apostles
3. 1 Thessalonians, 2 Thessalonians, 1 Timothy, 2 Timothy, and Titus
4. The remainder of the New Testament (leaving Romans and Revelation for last)
5. The Torah (Genesis, Exodus, Leviticus, Numbers, and Deuteronomy)
6. Ruth and Jonah, then the remaining historical books (Joshua, Judges, etc.)
7. Remaining major prophets, then the remaining minor prophets
8. Old Testament wisdom literature (Job, Psalms, Proverbs, Ecclesiastes, Song of Songs)
9. Deuterocanonical texts (Tobit, Judith, Baruch, Wisdom, and beyond)

This approximate ordering becomes apparent when exploring datasets of partially completed Bible translations and is an important consideration when evaluating ML/AI methods.

Multilingual Datasets and Scoring Approaches

Understanding one's data and the metrics that govern performance are important prerequisites for building ML/AI models for BT. We first give a brief overview of current datasets used for general language translation training and benchmarking (particularly targeting low-resource languages), then pinpoint several corpora that are especially relevant for BT. We then explore translation scoring methods, which will enable ML/AI models to be fairly evaluated against common benchmarks.

Although a BT project will usually focus on a particular (typically low-resource) language, a central principle of ML/AI is that a model trained on similar tasks can be adjusted slightly with additional training to focus on a desired task, and the resulting model will outperform a model trained from scratch on the desired task. This principle is known as *fine-tuning* (or, in some contexts, transfer learning). Large multilingual datasets provide the initially trained model that serves as a basis for fine-tuning.

The largest multilingual corpora are created by taking a massive body of unlabeled web text, using a model to classify the language of each document,[6] then programmatically assessing the results to remove noisy or inappropriate content. Smaller translation-focused multilingual corpora are built by creating a list of sentences in a source language, then employing native speakers to translate these sentences into as many languages as possible. Finally, some datasets narrow their scope to a particular set of low-resource languages based on geography or language family. Given the strong corporate motivation to improve the language capabilities of software tools to reach new consumers, currently many of the best corpora and translation models are aggregated and deployed by technology companies such as Google, Meta, and Microsoft. Some of these datasets are listed in Table 4.1. Hugging Face helpfully aggregates all these multilingual datasets and provides a starting place to use the data.[7]

Large corpora of partial and full Bibles exist at an unusual intersection among other multilingual datasets. Because translators strive to preserve the meaning of the text, these datasets are generally assumed to be of exceptionally high quality (compared to web-crawled data, for instance). Furthermore, the challenge posed by BT is to translate a single document into a target language, rather than obtain conversational competency or high general-purpose translation accuracy. The same high-quality assumption and single-document focus applies for texts from other major world religions, such as the Quran.[15] The number of languages represented in biblical corpora has expanded rapidly in recent years. In 2020, researchers at Johns Hopkins University collected more than four thousand unique partial translations of the Bible; however, this dataset has not been released for public use due to copyright restrictions.[16]

To the best of our knowledge, the largest openly available NLP-ready Bible dataset as of December 2024 is the eBible corpus, which consists of 1,009 open-source partial or full Bible translations spanning 833 language families.[17] Figure 4.2 shows the distribution of Bible translations by language family as well as the count of translations by number of verses. We see that language families spoken in Oceania (especially in language-diverse Papua New Guinea) represent a significant portion of total Bible

Table 4.1: Multilingual Datasets with Corresponding Language Count, Size, and Further Notes.

Name	Language Count	Dataset Size	Year	Notes	Ref.
Americas-NLI	10	1.6 MB	2022	Focused study on ten low-resource indigenous languages spoken in the Americas.	8
FLORES-200	204	58.3 MB	2022	Collected by Meta, employed human translators. Used to train No Language Left Behind (NLLB).	9
NTREX-128	129	11.6 MB	2022	Collected by Microsoft. Staring with English sentences, employed native speakers to translate into the remaining 128 languages.	10
Glot500	511	126 GB	2023	A mix of highly reliable data sources verified by native speakers, as well as less reliable data from web crawls.	11
SALT	8	1.62 GB	2023	Text and audio recordings for low-resource Ugandan languages, with English translations.	12
CulturaX	167	14 TB	2023	A combination of two large web crawl datasets with additional curation for multilingual content.	13
MADLAD-400	419	>1 TB	2024	Collected from a web crawl and curated by Google. Used to train MADLAD-400m.	14

Created by Marcus Schwarting.

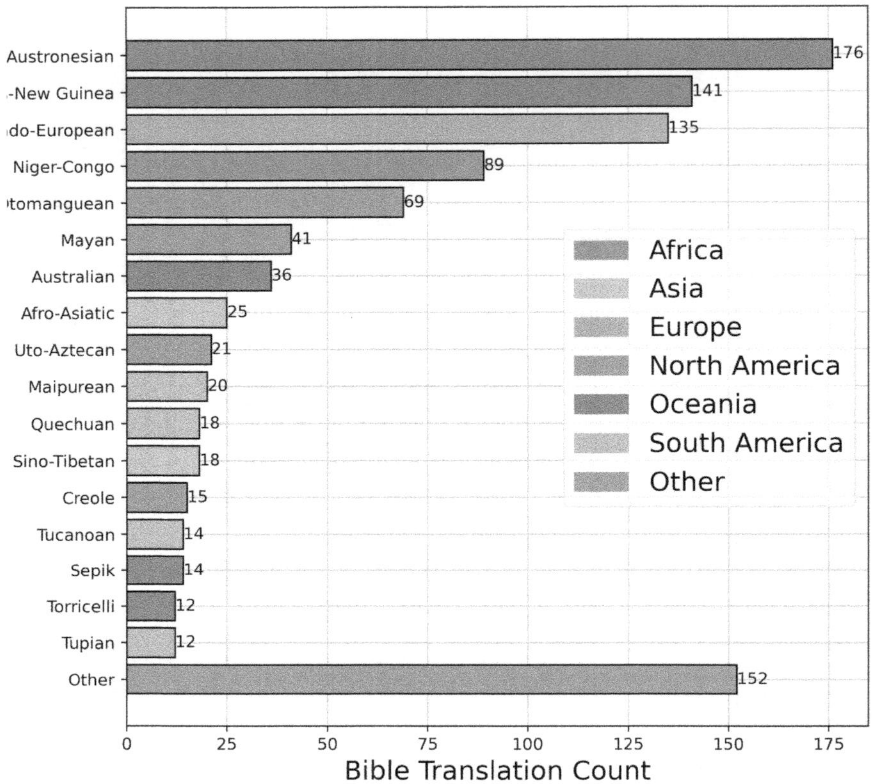

Figure 4.2 Histogram of Bible translations by language family. Created by Marcus Schwarting.

translations. We also see that most Bibles in the corpus are partial translations: around nine hundred Bibles have a full New Testament, while fewer than two hundred Bibles have a full Old Testament. While many projects begin with the intent of translating the entire Bible to a target language, most translations remain a work in progress (Figure 4.3).

Quantitatively assessing the subjective quality of a translation can be challenging. Translators will differ in their perceptions and interpretations of the same passage. When an ML/AI model is aiding a human translator in some capacity, a frequently asked question is how performant a model must be to meaningfully assist the translator (which is also subjective). Supposing an AI model is performing like a word or phrase suggestion tool during the translation process, even imperfect suggestions have been shown to save a translator time and energy. But if the model is consistently offering nonsensical suggestions, a translator may be distracted and eventually disable the tool. We refer to this tipping point as the *usefulness threshold*.

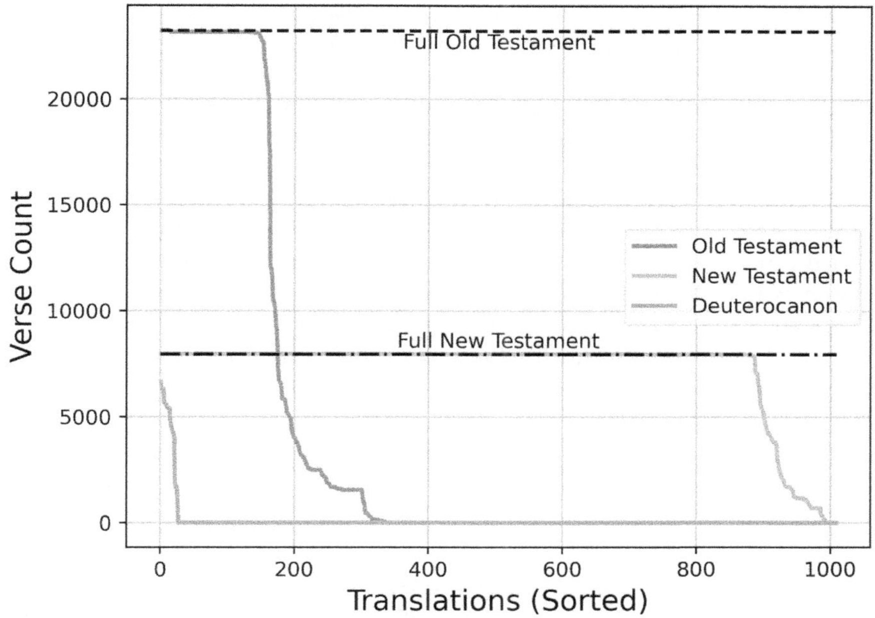

Figure 4.3 Cumulative plot of translations by the number of verses translated in the Old and New Testaments as well as the Deuterocanon. Created by Marcus Schwarting.

NLP researchers have developed different quantitative scoring metrics for comparing the similarity of two sentences (typically a reference sentence and a machine-translated sentence) in the same language. The most popular metric is a BiLingual Evaluation Understudy (BLEU) score, which measures the word-level matching overlap between the reference and the machine-translated sentence.[18] BLEU is measured from zero (no word-level overlap with the reference) to one hundred (exact word-level overlap with the reference), with an additional penalty for run-on machine-translated sentences. Anecdotally, a model reaches the usefulness threshold at a BLEU score of around thirty. Comparing at the word level implies that BLEU will count differently conjugated words (e.g., "runs" versus "running") as completely distinct, even though suggesting the correct root word may be helpful to a translator. BLEU also supplies low scores for agglutinative or polysynthetic languages, where words can be formed by concatenating multiple morphemes. Some modifications to BLEU, such as spBLEU and sacreBLEU, seek to address these deficiencies.[19]

One alternative to a BLEU score is the CHaRacter-level F-score (chrF), which calculates the similarity between sentences using characters clustered to some fixed length *n* (called an n-gram).[20] chrF scores also range between zero (no n-gram alignment) and one hundred (all n-grams align). By operating at the level of individual characters, a chrF metric almost always yields a more optimistic metric than a BLEU score. The chrF metric is more performant for agglutinative and polysynthetic languages but struggles with long-range dependencies like a change in word ordering. A model appears to reach the usefulness threshold at a chrF score of around sixty, although this threshold may vary more significantly between translators and depending on the target language. Figure 4.4 shows an example of three verses in different languages in the source and target languages, as well as the translation prediction with corresponding scores.

A more recent approach to comparison does not utilize the words or characters of the sentence directly, but uses embeddings to compare sentences. Put simply, a model can be trained to convert any sentence into a fixed-length list of numbers known as an embedding (or mapping, or vector). No matter the training scheme or model architecture, an effective embedding aims to map similar input sentences to embeddings that are in proximity. The proximity of n length embeddings $\boldsymbol{e}_1, \boldsymbol{e}_2$ is typically measured using either a Euclidean distance metric

$$d_{L2}(\boldsymbol{e}_1, \boldsymbol{e}_2) = \sqrt{\sum_{i=1}^{n} (e_{1,i} - e_{2,i})^2}$$

or a cosine similarity metric

$$d_{cos}(\boldsymbol{e}_1, \boldsymbol{e}_2) = \frac{\sum_{i=1}^{n} e_{1,i} e_{2,i}}{\sqrt{\sum_{i=1}^{n} e_{1,i}^2} * \sqrt{\sum_{i=1}^{n} e_{2,i}^2}}.$$

For example, suppose we have three sentences we wish to compare: S_1 = "Jesus wept.", S_2 = "Jesus cried.", S_3 = "Rejoice always.", and suppose we have a function $E(\cdot)$ that takes a sentence as input and returns the corresponding embedding. Then we would expect

$$d_{L2}(E(S_1), E(S_2)) \ll d_{L2}(E(S_1), E(S_3)).$$

Two common embedding methods are the Crosslingual Optimized Metric for Evaluation and Translation (COMET)[21] and BERTScore.[22] While embeddings are more flexible in the sense that they are not explicitly tied to word- or character-level features, training embeddings that robustly capture proximity relationships between sentences can be challenging for low-resource languages. In the absence of a large body of text, there is no general usefulness threshold that can be established across languages and contexts.

Statistical and Machine Learning Models

It can be tempting for developers to immediately reach for the state-of-the-art deep learning models for translation tasks. Usually, however, it is best for developers to start with simpler, statistically driven approaches. While statistical machine translation (SMT) is not as performant as deep learning methods, they (1) are easy and quick to run, (2) are computationally cheap to train and assess, (3) provide more interpretable results, (4) are far less data hungry, (5) offer an initial indication of how challenging

Afro-Asiatic GAL 4:21	**Source**: Ku gaya mini, ku da kuke so ku zauna a ƙarƙashin Doka, ba ku san abin da Doka ta ce ba ne? **Target**: Kaawondu ja! Kuŋ kuuk raka goye ɗo serre ta gaanuundi, ku dorgitɗo kaaw ta gaanuundi walla? **Prediction**: Kun kuuk raka goye ɗo serpey ta gaanuundi, kaawondu, ku ibingig gaanuun okinji walla? **BLEU**: 29.6; **spBLEU**: 38.1; **chrF3**: 57.4; **WER**: 44.0; **TER**: 50.0
Niger-Congo EXO 5:9	**Source**: Fanyeni kazi kuwa ngumu zaidi kwa watu hao ili kwamba wakazane na kazi na kuacha kusikiliza uongo." **Target**: Wongezeni wanhu wano sang'hano ndala muladi wagaye na waleke kuhulika mbuli za uvwizi." **Prediction**: Watendeleni wanhu wawo sang'hano ndala muladi wadahe kuiguma muna isang'hano yawo na waleke kutegeleza mbuli za uvwizi." **BLEU**: 28.5; **spBLEU**: 38.4; **chrF3**: 70.0; **WER**: 48.3; **TER**: 61.5
Otomanguean PSA 112:4	**Source**: En las tinieblas resplandece luz a los rectos: Él es clemente, misericordioso y justo. **Target**: Dxusaní' tu xi' lu da chul-la naga zaj zra' benne' li lazre' ca', benne' ca' zaj naque̱' zren lazre', ne xrlátaje, ne dxelexache lazre̱' bénneache. **Prediction**: Lu da chul-la tu xi' dxuseni na benne' ca' zaj naque̱' xrlátaje. Dios naque̱' zren lazre', ne dxexache lazre̱' bénneache chee̱', ne naque̱' xrlátaje. **BLEU**: 29.2; **spBLEU**: 50.4; **chrF3**: 60.8; **WER**: 66.0; **TER**: 64.0

Figure 4.4 Examples of machine translated Bible verses and corresponding evaluation metrics. In the prediction, dark underlined text indicates correct words, dashed underlined text indicates partially correct words, light underlined text indicates words that has been moved, and boxed text indicates incorrect words. Top: Hausa to Dangaléat (Afro-Asiatic family). Middle: Swahili to Kwere (Niger-Congo family). Bottom: Spanish to Zapotec-Tabaa (Otomanguean family).

a translation task will be, and (6) provide a floor on performance that deep learning models can improve upon. For all these reasons, computationally expensive tests with deep learning models are commonly informed by gathering initial results from statistical models. Statistical models assume that a word (or words) from a source language can be aligned with a word (or words) from a target language. Some statistical models go beyond word-level alignment to encompass entire phrases.[23]

Starting in the early 1990s, a set of models developed by IBM were among the first to be widely used for statistical machine translation.[24] These models, listed IBM-1 through IBM-5, were successively introduced with small changes to enhance performance. For a given set of sentences in the source language and corresponding sentences in the target language, we start by building a list of unique source words $\{s_0,\ldots,s_i,\ldots\}$ and unique target words $\{f_1,\ldots,f_j,\ldots\}$. Suppose $s_i =$ "wept" and $f_j =$ "lloró." For all pairs of words, we then initialize a table of probabilities, such as $p\left(f_j = \text{"lloró"} \mid s_i = \text{"wept"}\right)$, which is the probability that the source word s_i occurs given the presence of the target word f_j. When iterating over sentence pairs in the source and target language, if we come across s_i and f_j in the same sentence we will increase the probability $p\left(f_j|s_i\right)$ and decrease $p(f_{j'\neq j} \mid s_i)$, or the probability that "wept" maps to a word other than "lloró" in the target language. IBM models differ primarily in how these probabilities are adjusted. After many iterations through the list of source and target sentences, the values in the table of probabilities will eventually converge. This procedure of updating probabilities to reflect the underlying sentence data is known as *expectation-maximization*. Implementations of IBM models can be quickly deployed using the NLTK package (a popular toolkit in Python for training computational linguistics models).[25] Alternative statistical approaches can combine aspects of the IBM models to further enhance speed and performance. For example, FastAlign is a popular tool that combines and simplifies calculations from IBM-2 and IBM-3 to accelerate the rate of probability convergence, yielding significant time savings.[26] Eflomal is another computationally efficient option for word alignment that leverages Markov Chain Monte Carlo (MCMC) inference to reduce computational expense.[27]

Hidden Markov models (HMMs) frame alignment as a sequencing problem rather than a matching problem.[28] HMMs are predicated on the Markov assumption, which dictates that the next word transition in a sentence depends only on the previous word(s). By modeling sequences, the underlying word alignments are not directly observable (or "hidden"). Suppose we have a source sentence $[s_1 = \text{"Jesus"}, s_2 = \text{"wept"}]$ and a target sentence $[f_1 = \text{"Jesús"}, f_2 = \text{"lloró"}]$. Supposing s_1 corresponds to f_1 (written as $s_1 \leftrightarrow f_1$), HMMs model all possible transition probabilities, including $p(s_2 \leftrightarrow f_2 | s_1 \leftrightarrow f_1)$. Like the IBM models, HMMs use an expectation-maximization procedure known as the Baum-Welch algorithm to converge on these transition probabilities.[29] HMMs may require more data to train than the IBM models, but can generally match or exceed their performance. As with the IBM models, HMM implementations for word-level alignment can be deployed using the NLTK package.[30]

While the IBM models, FastAlign, and HMMs tend to be less performant than deep learning models, the concept of modeling alignment probabilities $p\left(f_j|s_i\right)$ and transition probabilities $p(s_2 \leftrightarrow f_2 | s_1 \leftrightarrow f_1)$ is routinely co-opted by deep learning architectures and remains an important aspect of model training and assessment.

Deep Learning Models

Deep learning for language translation can be broken into three major areas based on the history of their development: neural machine translation (NMT) models, transformers, and large language models (LLMs). We offer a high-level overview of each area, along with citations for those seeking a more thorough treatment. Since the first NMT models were developed, there has been a trend toward greater compute power for deploying larger models with more adjustable weights. When deciding on a deep learning model to use, it is important to consider the time and energy trade-offs associated with the possible (sometimes marginal) increase in translation performance.

Neural networks were first applied to NMT tasks in 2014, with the first major success coming from sequence to sequence (Seq2Seq) networks.[31] Seq2Seq combines two recurrent neural networks (RNNs) trained to encode content in a source language then decode content in a target language. Figure 4.5 presents a schematic of this

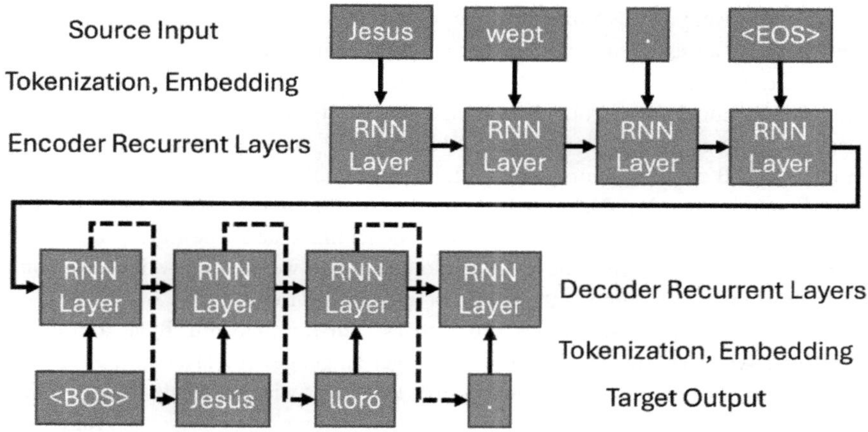

Figure 4.5 Schematic of a Seq2Seq model for NMT. "<EOS>" is a token to indicate the end of a sentence, "<BOS>" is a token to indicate the beginning of the sentence. Created by Marcus Schwarting.

approach, which shows how subsequent words (or tokens) are predicted iteratively using previous content as input.

An initial problem with Seq2Seq networks, especially in the context of translation tasks, was an inability to recognize which words or phrases from an input were the most relevant to the output. This was especially problematic for translation to languages using different word ordering or containing other long-range dependencies. The introduction of attention mechanisms in 2015 effectively calibrated the predictive weight (or attention score) allocated to specific input words for each output word and marked an important shift in model training.[32] To understand the impact of this development, consider the Spanish word *lloró* from the root verb *llorar* meaning "to cry." The preceding word, *Jesús*, is an indispensable component for correctly conjugating the root verb. With only two words in this sentence, it is easy to see that the first word will affect the second. But with longer and more complex passages, this relationship may be less apparent to a model lacking calibrated attention mechanisms.

The next major innovation came with the development of the transformer architecture in 2017, which was initially devised specifically for translation.[33] Previous RNN-based models rely on sequentially processing content with attention scores passed as "hidden states" between layers, while transformers utilize a self-attention mechanism to analyze relationships between all elements in a sequence simultaneously. This enables faster parallel computation as well as better performance at long-range relationships between sequences. A transformer model also combines an encoder and a decoder, which are often divided and used separately. The encoder can receive inputs and construct a robust embedding, which can be useful for tasks like sentence classification and named entity recognition. The decoder can take an embedding from the encoder and generate text. Placed together (like the schematic in Figure 4.5), an encoder-decoder model is suitable for a generative task that accepts an input sequence and returns an output sequence.

Whether using an RNN-based model or a transformer for language translation, OpenNMT is an excellent source for smaller pre-trained models that can be easily fine-tuned for specific translation tasks.[34] At the time of this writing, two open-source pre-trained models offer roughly equivalent state-of-the-art performance for low-resource language translation: Meta's NLLB model[35] and Google's MADLAD-400 model.[36] NLLB comes in four sizes: 600 million, 1.3 billion, 3.3 billion, and 54 billion tunable parameters. MADLAD-400 also comes in 3 billion, 7 billion, and 10 billion tunable parameters. Model performance at benchmark and fine-tuned translation tasks is expected to improve for larger models, although we can also anticipate a point of diminishing returns among the largest of transformer models.[37]

We can compare these models and metrics with the following Bible translation examples. We start with partial Bibles in target languages (Malayalam, Kwere, and Eastern Tamang) and identify related source languages with complete Bibles (Tamil, Swahili, and Nepali, respectively). For partial Bibles in target languages, we randomly assign verses to the training set (80 percent) or the test set (20 percent). We then train or fine-tune four models on each training set: a hidden Markov model (SMT), an OpenNMT model, NLLB with 600 million tunable parameters, and NLLB with 1.3 billion tunable parameters. For each trained model, we assess translation performance on the test set using BLEU, spBLEU, and chrF3 as metrics. Figure 4.6 shows the results of these tests.

We can draw several conclusions from these test results. We see that larger, more computationally expensive models tend to yield better results. The greatest improvement across models came from using NLLB with 600 million parameters, with chrF3 scores improving by between ten and twenty percentage points relative to the fine-tuned OpenNMT model. The improvement of NLLB from 600 million to 1.3 billion parameters was marginal but required significantly more computational resources for both fine-tuning and inference.

The most recent innovation in NMT has come from the introduction and rapid popularization of LLMs such as ChatGPT (OpenAI), Gemini (Google), and Claude

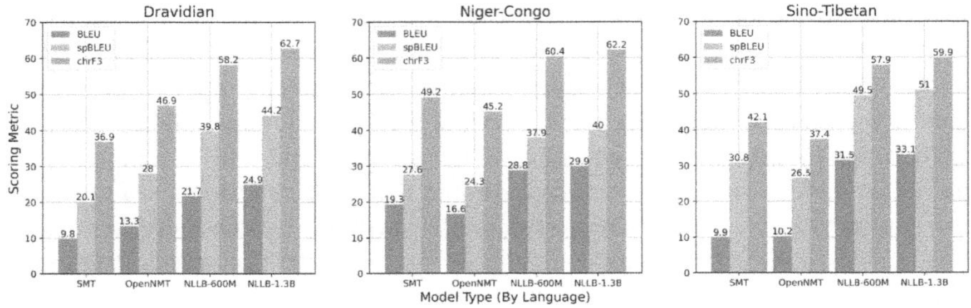

Figure 4.6 Comparing the performance of a Hidden Markov Model (SMT), OpenNMT, and NLLB (600 million and 1.3 billion) across three translation tasks. Left: Tamil to Malayalam (Dravidian family). Middle: Swahili to Kwere (Niger-Congo family). Right: Nepali to Eastern Tamang (Sino-Tibetan family). Created by Marcus Schwarting.

(Anthropic). LLMs are, for the most part, scaled-up and carefully pre-trained versions of their smaller predecessors.[38] While many details of these models are held as trade secrets, we can safely assume that these LLMs consist of hundreds of billions, if not trillions, of tunable parameters. Several studies now suggest that LLMs can match or exceed the performance of NLLB and MADLAD-400 for specific low-resource language translation tasks.[39] Anecdotally, Claude has been identified as a favorite among linguists and translators. At the time of this writing, many tech companies are spending tremendous resources to improve LLM performance across a wide variety of tasks, including translation. Developments in this area are rapid and ongoing.

Practical Considerations

Training and evaluating a model for a BT task is not the end of the process; translators need to be able to access and use it. We divide practical considerations for deploying models into three main categories: respect for data, software ergonomics, and hardware realities.

Before publishing or sharing models and data, it is important to verify that the proper permissions have been granted. Many Bible translations, including entries in the eBible corpus, have copyright protections against creating derivative works. While developers can train a model and deploy it internally, publishing the model or model-generated content may constitute a derivative work.[40] When using multilingual corpora available on Hugging Face, a user is often required to promise not to publish the data or models using the data. A major challenge for translation benchmarking is data contamination: because LLMs are trained on massive datasets of text acquired from web crawlers, low-resource language texts stored in public repositories can easily end up in an LLM training corpus. For this reason, many papers describing low-resource corpora will be made available only upon request. Regardless of the specific nature of the BT project, it is important to keep in mind that developers are handling a digital copy of God's Word, and that behind every language is a group of speakers who crave God's Word. So, for legal, practical, spiritual, and cultural reasons, BT data demands our respect.

Many powerful software tools go underutilized due to poor software ergonomics. Software and models must meet translators where they are, not the other way around. We fundamentally hope to augment, not automate, the BT process, so we should not expect translators to radically change their operations to accommodate the tools we provide. For example, while technical experts may be comfortable in a terminal or code editor, most translators would much prefer a user interface for editing and reviewing passages verse by verse.[41] A popular way of introducing ML/AI into the translation workflow is by offering multiple suggestions for the next word or phrase in a verse, like code completion tools such as Microsoft Copilot. Other ML/AI tools will review a completed forward and backward translation and automatically flag words or phrases for a translator to address, then offer suggestions to fix the discrepancy. Given the distrust translators may already feel toward AI models, it is important to frame these tools as a source of helpful suggestions where appropriate.

The software engineering joke of "it works on my computer" is especially salient for BT tools. Fine-tuning and running inference on a model like NLLB will require an internet connection and GPU hardware that may not be available to translators in a remote area. Translation performance is one of several factors that should be considered before deploying a model, with usability taking priority. Statistical approaches like FastAlign and Eflomal can operate with ease on most laptops today, while transformers like those in OpenNMT may consume excessive RAM or suffer from an annoying latency when generating word predictions. LLMs are likely not an option in the absence of a secure internet connection (although the adoption of neural processing units, or NPUs, may make this possible soon). BT tools that leverage ML/AI usually stick to statistical methods, with advanced options for users to employ NMT techniques when possible.

Future Directions

Much effort is currently going into building, deploying, and evaluating LLMs for a wide range of tasks, including translation. New LLM models have so far outpaced our capacity to build robust benchmark tasks and datasets for low-resource language assessment, although efforts are in the works to address this.

While this chapter has focused almost exclusively on text-based translation of the Bible, projects for oral[42] and signed[43] BT are also underway. This medium is more challenging for BT and has so far gone underexplored. Audio and video generation remain challenging frontiers for translation, particularly in a low-resource language. Multimodal models such as GPT-4o and GPT-o1 (OpenAI) can accept text and images as input and text and images as output. Other multimodal models may soon become performant at audio- and video-based translation tasks as well.

Another fundamental problem of BT is quantifying the usefulness threshold for translators. Metrics like BLEU and chrF3 can lack nuance and are not amenable to some language families but have become the research standard anyway. By collaborating more closely with translators and linguists, developers have an opportunity to create tailored approaches that are better at measuring when a model becomes a useful tool for BT.[44]

Notes

1 Wycliffe Bible Translators, "Achieving a God-Sized Mission: Vision 2025," accessed December 2, 2024, https://www.wycliffe.org/vision-2025.
2 ETEN, "Eradicating Bible Poverty," accessed December 2, 2024, https://eten.bible.

3 For a more detailed description, see Eugene A. Nida, "Principles of Translation as Exemplified by Bible Translating," in *On Translation*, ed. Reuben A. Brower, HSCL 23 (Cambridge, MA: Harvard University Press, 1959), 11–31; and William Allen Smalley, *Translation as Mission: Bible Translation in the Modern Missionary Movement* (Macon: Mercer University Press, 1991).

4 Some practitioners argue translations should always use the original Hebrew and Greek texts as the source languages. While this has several benefits (such as easier glossing), it is often impractical to identify individuals or build teams that combine expertise in the target language as well as biblical languages.

5 Jesus Film Project, "Reach Unreached Nations with Jesus Film Project," accessed December 2, 2024, https://www.jesusfilm.org/about.

6 Isaac Caswell, Theresa Breiner, Daan van Esch, and Ankur Bapna, "Language ID in the Wild: Unexpected Challenges on the Path to a Thousand-Language Web Text Corpus," arXiv, 2020, https://doi.org/10.48550/arXiv.2010.14571.

7 Hugging Face, "Languages," accessed December 7, 2024, https://huggingface.co/languages.

8 Katharina Kann, Abteen Ebrahimi, Manuel Mager, Arturo Oncevay, John E. Ortega, Annette Rios, Angela Fan et al., "AmericasNLI: Machine Translation and Natural Language Inference Systems for Indigenous Languages of the Americas," *Frontiers in Artificial Intelligence* 5 (2022): 995667.

9 NLLB Team, Marta R. Costa-jussà, James Cross, Onur Çelebi, Maha Elbayad, Kenneth Heafield, Kevin Heffernan, Elahe Kalbassi, et al., "No Language Left Behind: Scaling Human-Centered Machine Translation," arXiv, 2022, https://doi.org/10.48550/arXiv.2207.04672.

10 Christian Federmann, Tom Kocmi, and Ying Xin, "NTREX-128—News Test References for MT Evaluation of 128 Languages," in *Proceedings of the First Workshop on Scaling Up Multilingual Evaluation*, ed. Kabir Ahuja, Antonios Anastasopoulos, Barun Patra, Graham Neubig, Monojit Choudhury, Sandipan Dandapat, Sunayana Sitaram, and Vishrav Chaudhary (Stroudsburg: Association for Computational Linguistics, 2022), 21–4.

11 Ayyoob Imani, Peiqin Lin, Amir Hossein Kargaran, Silvia Severini, Masoud Jalili Sabet, Nora Kassner, Chunlan Ma, et al., "Glot500: Scaling Multilingual Corpora and Language Models to 500 Languages," arXiv, 2023, https://doi.org/10.48550/arXiv.2305.12182.

12 Isaac Owomugisha, Benjamin Akera, Ernest Tonny Mwebaze, and John Quinn, "Multilingual Model and Data Resources for Text-To-Speech in Ugandan Languages" (paper presented at the 4th Workshop on African Natural Language Processing, Kigali, Rwanda, 2023).

13 Thuat Nguyen, Chien Van Nguyen, Viet Dac Lai, Hieu Man, Nghia Trung Ngo, Franck Dernoncourt, Ryan A. Rossi, and Thien Huu Nguyen, "CulturaX: A Cleaned, Enormous, and Multilingual Dataset for Large Language Models in 167 Languages," arXiv, 2023, https://doi.org/10.48550/arXiv.2309.09400.

14 Sneha Kudugunta, Isaac Caswell, Biao Zhang, Xavier Garcia, Derrick Xin, Aditya Kusupati, Romi Stella, Ankur Bapna, and Orhan Firat, "MADLAD-400: A Multilingual and Document-Level Large Audited Dataset," in *Advances in Neural Information Processing Systems 36 (NeurIPS 2023)*, ed. A. Oh, T. Naumann, A.

Globerson, K. Saenko, M. Hardt, and S. Levine (Red Hook: Curran Associates, 2024), 67284–96.

15 Fawaz Ahmed, "Quran API," GitHub, accessed December 5, 2024, https://github.com/fawazahmed0/quran-api.

16 Arya D. McCarthy, Rachel Wicks, Dylan Lewis, Aaron Mueller, Winston Wu, Oliver Adams, Garrett Nicolai, Matt Post, and David Yarowsky, "The Johns Hopkins University Bible Corpus: 1600+ Tongues for Typological Exploration," in *Proceedings of the Twelfth Language Resources and Evaluation Conference*, ed. Nicoletta Calzolari, Frédéric Béchet, Philippe Blache, Khalid Choukri, Christopher Cieri, Thierry Declerck, Sara Goggi, Hitoshi Isahara et al. (Marseille: European Language Resources Association, 2020), 2884–92.

17 Vesa Akerman, David Baines, Damien Daspit, Ulf Hermjakob, Taeho Jang, Colin Leong, Michael Martin, Joel Mathew, Jonathan Robie, and Marcus Schwarting, "The eBible Corpus: Data and Model Benchmarks for Bible Translation for Low-Resource Languages," arXiv, 2023, https://doi.org/10.48550/arXiv.2304.09919.

18 Kishore Papineni, Salim Roukos, Todd Ward, and Wei-Jing Zhu, "BLEU: A Method for Automatic Evaluation of Machine Translation," in *Proceedings of the 40th Annual Meeting of the Association for Computational Linguistics (ACL '02)* (Stroudsburg: Association for Computational Linguistics, 2002), 311–18.

19 See Naman Goyal, Cynthia Gao, Vishrav Chaudhary, Peng-Jen Chen, Guillaume Wenzek, Da Ju, Sanjana Krishnan, Marc'Aurelio Ranzato, Francisco Guzmán, and Angela Fan, "The FLORES-101 Evaluation Benchmark for Low-Resource and Multilingual Machine Translation," *Transactions of the Association for Computational Linguistics* 10 (2022): 522–38; and Matt Post, "A Call for Clarity in Reporting BLEU Scores," in *Proceedings of the Third Conference on Machine Translation: Research Papers*, ed. Ondřej Bojar, Rajen Chatterjee, Christian Federmann, Mark Fishel, Yvette Graham, Barry Haddow, Matthias Huck, Antonio Jimeno Yepes et al. (Brussels: Association for Computational Linguistics, 2018), 186–91, respectively.

20 Maja Popović, "chrF: Character n-gram F-score for Automatic MT Evaluation," in *Proceedings of the Tenth Workshop on Statistical Machine Translation*, ed. Ondřej Bojar, Rajan Chatterjee, Christian Federmann, Barry Haddow, Chris Hokamp, Matthias Huck, Varvara Logacheva, and Pavel Pecina (Lisbon: Association for Computational Linguistics, 2015), 392–5.

21 Ricardo Rei, Craig Stewart, Ana C. Farinha, and Alon Lavie, "COMET: A Neural Framework for MT Evaluation," arXiv, 2020, https://doi.org/10.48550/arXiv.2009.09025.

22 Tianyi Zhang, Varsha Kishore, Felix Wu, Kilian Q. Weinberger, and Yoav Artzi, "BERTScore: Evaluating Text Generation with BERT," arXiv, 2019, https://doi.org/10.48550/arXiv.1904.09675.

23 Richard Zens, Franz Josef Och, and Hermann Ney, "Phrase-Based Statistical Machine Translation," in *KI 2002: Advances in Artificial Intelligence: 25th Annual German Conference on AI*, ed. Matthias Jarke, Jana Koehler, and Gerhard Lakemeyer, LNAI 2479 (Berlin: Springer, 2002), 18–32.

24 Peter F. Brown, Stephen A. Della Pietra, Vincent J. Della Pietra, and Robert L. Mercer, "The Mathematics of Statistical Machine Translation: Parameter Estimation," *Computational Linguistics* 19.2 (1993): 263–311.

25 Steven Bird and Edward Loper, "NLTK: The Natural Language Toolkit," in *Proceedings of the ACL Interactive Poster and Demonstration Sessions* (Barcelona: Association for Computational Linguistics, 2006), 214–17.

26 Chris Dyer, Victor Chahuneau, and Noah A. Smith, "A Simple, Fast, and Effective Reparameterization of IBM Model 2," in *Proceedings of the 2013 Conference of the North American Chapter of the Association for Computational Linguistics: Human Language Technologies*, ed. Lucy Vanderwende, Hal Daumé III, and Katrin Kirchhoff (Atlanta: Association for Computational Linguistics, 2013), 644–8.

27 Robert Östling and Jörg Tiedemann, "Efficient Word Alignment with Markov Chain Monte Carlo," *Prague Bulletin of Mathematical Linguistics* 106.1 (2016): 125–46.

28 Lawrence R. Rabiner, "A Tutorial on Hidden Markov Models and Selected Applications in Speech Recognition," *Proceedings of the IEEE* 77.2 (1989): 257–86.

29 Paul M. Baggenstoss, "A Modified Baum-Welch Algorithm for Hidden Markov Models with Multiple Observation Spaces," *IEEE Transactions on Speech and Audio Processing* 9.4 (2001): 411–16.

30 Bird and Loper, "NLTK," 214–17.

31 Ilya Sutskever, Oriol Vinyals, and Quoc V. Le, "Sequence to Sequence Learning with Neural Networks," arXiv, 2014, https://doi.org/10.48550/arXiv.1409.3215.

32 Dzmitry Bahdanau, Kyunghyun Cho, and Yoshua Bengio, "Neural Machine Translation by Jointly Learning to Align and Translate," arXiv, 2014, https://doi.org/10.48550/arXiv.1409.0473.

33 Ashish Vaswani, Noam Shazeer, Niki Parmar, Jakob Uszkoreit, Llion Jones, Aidan N. Gomez, Łukasz Kaiser, and Illia Polosukhin, "Attention Is All You Need," in *Advances in Neural Information Processing Systems 30 (NIPS 2017)*, ed. I. Guyon, U. Von Luxburg, S. Bengio, H. Wallach, R. Fergus, S. Vishwanathan, and R. Garnett (Red Hook: Curran Associates, 2017), 5998–6008.

34 Guillaume Klein, Yoon Kim, Yuntian Deng, Jean Senellart, and Alexander M. Rush, "OpenNMT: Open-Source Toolkit for Neural Machine Translation," arXiv, 2017, https://doi.org/10.48550/arXiv.1701.02810.

35 NLLB Team, Costa-jussà, Cross, Çelebi, Elbayad, Heafield, Heffernan, Kalbassi, et al., "No Language Left Behind,"

36 Kudugunta, Caswell, Zhang, Garcia, Xin, Kusupati, Stella, Bapna, and Firat, "MADLAD-400," 67284–96.

37 Jared Kaplan, Sam McCandlish, Tom Henighan, Tom B. Brown, Benjamin Chess, Rewon Child, Scott Gray, Alec Radford, Jeffrey Wu, and Dario Amodei, "Scaling Laws for Neural Language Models," arXiv, 2020, https://doi.org/10.48550/arXiv.2001.08361.

38 Yiheng Liu, Tianle Han, Siyuan Ma, Jiayue Zhang, Yuanyuan Yang, Jiaming Tian, Hao He et al., "Summary of ChatGPT-Related Research and Perspective Towards the Future of Large Language Models," *Meta-Radiology* 1.2 (2023): 100017.

39 Maxim Enis and Mark Hopkins, "From LLM to NMT: Advancing Low-Resource Machine Translation with Claude," arXiv, 2024, https://doi.org/10.48550/arXiv.2404.13813; Séamus Lankford, Haithem Afli, and Andy Way, "adaptMLLM: Fine-Tuning Multilingual Language Models on Low-Resource Languages with Integrated LLM Playgrounds," *Information* 14.12 (2023): 638; and Vivek Iyer, Bhavitvya Malik, Pavel Stepachev, Pinzhen Chen, Barry Haddow, and Alexandra Birch, "Quality or

Quantity? On Data Scale and Diversity in Adapting Large Language Models for Low-Resource Translation," arXiv, 2024, https://doi.org/10.48550/arXiv.2408.12780.

40 Brigitte Vézina and Sarah Hinchliff Pearson, "Should CC-Licensed Content Be Used to Train AI? It Depends," *Creative Commons* (blog), posted March 4, 2021, https://creativecommons.org/2021/03/04/should-cc-licensed-content-be-used-to-train-ai-it-depends.

41 Joel Mathew and Ulf Hermjakob, "User Study for Improving Tools for Bible Translation," arXiv, 2023, https://doi.org/10.48550/arXiv.2302.00778.

42 Sangeeta Ghangam, Daniel Whitenack, and Joshua Nemecek, "Dyn-ASR: Compact, Multilingual Speech Recognition via Spoken Language and Accent Identification," arXiv, 2021, https://doi.org/10.48550/arXiv.2108.02034.

43 Shester Gueuwou, Sophie Siake, Colin Leong, and Mathias Müller, "JWSign: A Highly Multilingual Corpus of Bible Translations for More Diversity in Sign Language Processing," in *Findings of the Association for Computational Linguistics: EMNLP 2023*, ed. Houda Bouamor, Juan Pino, and Kalika Bali (Singapore: Association for Computational Linguistics, 2023), 9907–27.

44 Acknowledgments: A big thanks to the members of the Partnership for Applied Biblical Natural Language Processing (PAB-NLP) for teaching me so much over the past few years. Thanks to those who reviewed this chapter or provided thoughtful feedback, including James Cuenod, Damien Daspit, Cassie Weishaupt, Ryder Wishart, and Joshua Nemecek.

Bibliography

Ahmed, Fawaz. "Quran API." GitHub. Accessed December 5, 2024. https://github.com/fawazahmed0/quran-api.

Akerman, Vesa, David Baines, Damien Daspit, Ulf Hermjakob, Taeho Jang, Colin Leong, Michael Martin, Joel Mathew, Jonathan Robie, and Marcus Schwarting. "The eBible Corpus: Data and Model Benchmarks for Bible Translation for Low-Resource Languages." arXiv. 2023. https://doi.org/10.48550/arXiv.2304.09919.

Baggenstoss, Paul M. "A Modified Baum-Welch Algorithm for Hidden Markov Models with Multiple Observation Spaces." *IEEE Transactions on Speech and Audio Processing* 9.4 (2001): 411–16.

Bahdanau, Dzmitry, Kyunghyun Cho, and Yoshua Bengio. "Neural Machine Translation by Jointly Learning to Align and Translate." arXiv. 2014. https://doi.org/10.48550/arXiv.1409.0473.

Bird, Steven, and Edward Loper. "NLTK: The Natural Language Toolkit." Pages 214–17 in *Proceedings of the ACL Interactive Poster and Demonstration Sessions*. Barcelona: Association for Computational Linguistics, 2006.

Brown, Peter F., Stephen A. Della Pietra, Vincent J. Della Pietra, and Robert L. Mercer. "The Mathematics of Statistical Machine Translation: Parameter Estimation." *Computational Linguistics* 19.2 (1993): 263–311.

Caswell, Isaac, Theresa Breiner, Daan van Esch, and Ankur Bapna. "Language ID in the Wild: Unexpected Challenges on the Path to a Thousand-Language Web Text Corpus." arXiv. 2020. https://doi.org/10.48550/arXiv.2010.14571.

Dyer, Chris, Victor Chahuneau, and Noah A. Smith. "A Simple, Fast, and Effective Reparameterization of IBM Model 2." Pages 644–48 in *Proceedings of the 2013 Conference of the North American Chapter of the Association for Computational Linguistics: Human Language Technologies*. Edited by Lucy Vanderwende, Hal Daumé III, and Katrin Kirchhoff. Atlanta: Association for Computational Linguistics, 2013.

Enis, Maxim, and Mark Hopkins. "From LLM to NMT: Advancing Low-Resource Machine Translation with Claude." arXiv. 2024. https://doi.org/10.48550/arXiv.2404.13813.

ETEN. "Eradicating Bible Poverty." Accessed December 2, 2024. https://eten.bible.

Federmann, Christian, Tom Kocmi, and Ying Xin. "NTREX-128—News Test References for MT Evaluation of 128 Languages." Pages 21–4 in *Proceedings of the First Workshop on Scaling Up Multilingual Evaluation*. Edited by Kabir Ahuja, Antonios Anastasopoulos, Barun Patra, Graham Neubig, Monojit Choudhury, Sandipan Dandapat, Sunayana Sitaram, and Vishrav Chaudhary. Stroudsburg: Association for Computational Linguistics, 2022.

Ghangam, Sangeeta, Daniel Whitenack, and Joshua Nemecek. "Dyn-ASR: Compact, Multilingual Speech Recognition via Spoken Language and Accent Identification." arXiv. 2021. https://doi.org/10.48550/arXiv.2108.02034.

Goyal, Naman, Cynthia Gao, Vishrav Chaudhary, Peng-Jen Chen, Guillaume Wenzek, Da Ju, Sanjana Krishnan, Marc'Aurelio Ranzato, Francisco Guzmán, and Angela Fan. "The FLORES-101 Evaluation Benchmark for Low-Resource and Multilingual Machine Translation." *Transactions of the Association for Computational Linguistics* 10 (2022): 522–38. https://doi.org/10.1162/tacl_a_00474.

Gueuwou, Shester, Sophie Siake, Colin Leong, and Mathias Müller. "JWSign: A Highly Multilingual Corpus of Bible Translations for More Diversity in Sign Language Processing." Pages 9907–27 in *Findings of the Association for Computational Linguistics: EMNLP 2023*. Edited by Houda Bouamor, Juan Pino, and Kalika Bali. Singapore: Association for Computational Linguistics, 2023. https://doi.org/10.18653/v1/2023.findings-emnlp.664.

Hugging Face. "Languages." Accessed December 7, 2024. https://huggingface.co/languages.

Imani, Ayyoob, Peiqin Lin, Amir Hossein Kargaran, Silvia Severini, Masoud Jalili Sabet, Nora Kassner, Chunlan Ma et al. "Glot500: Scaling Multilingual Corpora and Language Models to 500 Languages." arXiv. 2023. https://doi.org/10.48550/arXiv.2305.12182.

Iyer, Vivek, Bhavitvya Malik, Pavel Stepachev, Pinzhen Chen, Barry Haddow, and Alexandra Birch. "Quality or Quantity? On Data Scale and Diversity in Adapting Large Language Models for Low-Resource Translation." arXiv. 2024. https://doi.org/10.48550/arXiv.2408.12780.

Jesus Film Project. "Reach Unreached Nations with Jesus Film Project." Accessed December 2, 2024. https://www.jesusfilm.org/about.

Kann, Katharina, Abteen Ebrahimi, Manuel Mager, Arturo Oncevay, John E. Ortega, Annette Rios, Angela Fan et al. "AmericasNLI: Machine Translation and Natural Language Inference Systems for Indigenous Languages of the Americas." *Frontiers in Artificial Intelligence* 5 (2022): 995667.

Kaplan, Jared, Sam McCandlish, Tom Henighan, Tom B. Brown, Benjamin Chess, Rewon Child, Scott Gray, Alec Radford, Jeffrey Wu, and Dario Amodei. "Scaling Laws for Neural Language Models." arXiv. 2020. https://doi.org/10.48550/arXiv.2001.08361.

Klein, Guillaume, Yoon Kim, Yuntian Deng, Jean Senellart, and Alexander M. Rush. "OpenNMT: Open-Source Toolkit for Neural Machine Translation." arXiv. 2017. https://doi.org/10.48550/arXiv.1701.02810.

Kudugunta, Sneha, Isaac Caswell, Biao Zhang, Xavier Garcia, Derrick Xin, Aditya Kusupati, Romi Stella, Ankur Bapna, and Orhan Firat. "MADLAD-400: A Multilingual and Document-Level Large Audited Dataset." Pages 67284–96 in *Advances in Neural Information Processing Systems 36 (NeurIPS 2023)*. Edited by A. Oh, T. Naumann, A. Globerson, K. Saenko, M. Hardt, and S. Levine. Red Hook: Curran Associates, 2024. https://papers.nips.cc/paper_files/paper/2023.

Lankford, Séamus, Haithem Afli, and Andy Way. "adaptMLLM: Fine-Tuning Multilingual Language Models on Low-Resource Languages with Integrated LLM Playgrounds." *Information* 14.12 (2023): 638. https://doi.org/10.3390/info14120638.

Liu, Yiheng, Tianle Han, Siyuan Ma, Jiayue Zhang, Yuanyuan Yang, Jiaming Tian, Hao He et al. "Summary of ChatGPT-Related Research and Perspective Towards the Future of Large Language Models." *Meta-Radiology* 1.2 (2023): 100017. https://doi.org/10.1016/j.metrad.2023.100017.

Mathew, Joel, and Ulf Hermjakob. "User Study for Improving Tools for Bible Translation." arXiv. 2023. https://doi.org/10.48550/arXiv.2302.00778.

McCarthy, Arya D., Rachel Wicks, Dylan Lewis, Aaron Mueller, Winston Wu, Oliver Adams, Garrett Nicolai, Matt Post, and David Yarowsky. "The Johns Hopkins University Bible Corpus: 1600+ Tongues for Typological Exploration." Pages 2884–92 in *Proceedings of the Twelfth Language Resources and Evaluation Conference*. Edited by Nicoletta Calzolari, Frédéric Béchet, Philippe Blache, Khalid Choukri, Christopher Cieri, Thierry Declerck, Sara Goggi, Hitoshi Isahara et al. Marseille: European Language Resources Association, 2020.

Nguyen, Thuat, Chien Van Nguyen, Viet Dac Lai, Hieu Man, Nghia Trung Ngo, Franck Dernoncourt, Ryan A. Rossi, and Thien Huu Nguyen. "CulturaX: A Cleaned, Enormous, and Multilingual Dataset for Large Language Models in 167 Languages." arXiv. 2023. https://doi.org/10.48550/arXiv.2309.09400.

Nida, Eugene A. "Principles of Translation as Exemplified by Bible Translating." Pages 11–31 in *On Translation*. Edited by Reuben A. Brower. HSCL 23. Cambridge, MA: Harvard University Press, 1959. https://doi.org/10.4159/harvard.9780674731615.c3.

NLLB Team, Marta R. Costa-jussà, James Cross, Onur Çelebi, Maha Elbayad, Kenneth Heafield, Kevin Heffernan, Elahe Kalbassi, et al. "No Language Left Behind: Scaling Human-Centered Machine Translation." arXiv. 2022. https://doi.org/10.48550/arXiv.2207.04672.

Östling, Robert, and Jörg Tiedemann. "Efficient Word Alignment with Markov Chain Monte Carlo." *Prague Bulletin of Mathematical Linguistics* 106.1 (2016): 125–46. http://dx.doi.org/10.1515/pralin-2016-0013.

Owomugisha, Isaac, Benjamin Akera, Ernest Tonny Mwebaze, and John Quinn. "Multilingual Model and Data Resources for Text-To-Speech in Ugandan Languages." Paper presented at the 4th Workshop on African Natural Language Processing, Kigali, Rwanda, 2023. https://openreview.net/forum?id=vaxG0WAPzL.

Papineni, Kishore, Salim Roukos, Todd Ward, and Wei-Jing Zhu. "BLEU: A Method for Automatic Evaluation of Machine Translation." Pages 311–18 in *Proceedings of the 40th Annual Meeting of the Association for Computational Linguistics (ACL '02).* Stroudsburg: Association for Computational Linguistics, 2002. https://doi.org/10.3115/1073083.1073135.

Popović, Maja. "chrF: Character n-gram F-score for Automatic MT Evaluation." Pages 392–5 in *Proceedings of the Tenth Workshop on Statistical Machine Translation.* Edited by Ondřej Bojar, Rajan Chatterjee, Christian Federmann, Barry Haddow, Chris Hokamp, Matthias Huck, Varvara Logacheva, and Pavel Pecina. Lisbon: Association for Computational Linguistics, 2015. https://doi.org/10.18653/v1/W15-3049.

Post, Matt. "A Call for Clarity in Reporting BLEU Scores." Pages 186–91 in *Proceedings of the Third Conference on Machine Translation: Research Papers.* Edited by Ondřej Bojar, Rajen Chatterjee, Christian Federmann, Mark Fishel, Yvette Graham, Barry Haddow, Matthias Huck, Antonio Jimeno Yepes et al. Brussels: Association for Computational Linguistics, 2018. https://doi.org/10.18653/v1/W18-6319.

Rabiner, Lawrence R. "A Tutorial on Hidden Markov Models and Selected Applications in Speech Recognition." *Proceedings of the IEEE* 77.2 (1989): 257–86. https://doi.org/10.1109/5.18626.

Rei, Ricardo, Craig Stewart, Ana C. Farinha, and Alon Lavie. "COMET: A Neural Framework for MT Evaluation." arXiv. 2020. https://doi.org/10.48550/arXiv.2009.09025.

Smalley, William Allen. *Translation as Mission: Bible Translation in the Modern Missionary Movement.* Macon: Mercer University Press, 1991.

Sutskever, Ilya, Oriol Vinyals, and Quoc V. Le. "Sequence to Sequence Learning with Neural Networks." arXiv. 2014. https://doi.org/10.48550/arXiv.1409.3215.

Vaswani, Ashish, Noam Shazeer, Niki Parmar, Jakob Uszkoreit, Llion Jones, Aidan N. Gomez, Łukasz Kaiser, and Illia Polosukhin. "Attention Is All You Need." Pages 5998–6008 in *Advances in Neural Information Processing Systems 30 (NIPS 2017).* Edited by I. Guyon, U. Von Luxburg, S. Bengio, H. Wallach, R. Fergus, S. Vishwanathan, and R. Garnett. Red Hook: Curran Associates, 2017.

Vézina, Brigitte, and Sarah Hinchliff Pearson. "Should CC-Licensed Content Be Used to Train AI? It Depends." *Creative Commons* (blog). Posted March 4, 2021. https://creativecommons.org/2021/03/04/should-cc-licensed-content-be-used-to-train-ai-it-depends.

Wycliffe Bible Translators. "Achieving a God-Sized Mission: Vision 2025." Accessed December 2, 2024. https://www.wycliffe.org/vision-2025.

Zens, Richard, Franz Josef Och, and Hermann Ney. "Phrase-Based Statistical Machine Translation." Pages 18–32 in *KI 2002: Advances in Artificial Intelligence: 25th Annual German Conference on AI.* Edited by Matthias Jarke, Jana Koehler, and Gerhard Lakemeyer. LNAI 2479. Berlin: Springer, 2002.

Zhang, Tianyi, Varsha Kishore, Felix Wu, Kilian Q. Weinberger, and Yoav Artzi. "BERTScore: Evaluating Text Generation with BERT." arXiv. 2019. https://doi.org/10.48550/arXiv.1904.09675.

5

Navigating AI in Bible Translation

Augmentative AI for Minority Languages

Cassie Weishaupt

As artificial intelligence reshapes many aspects of our world, speakers and signers of minority languages are beginning to leverage this technology to cultivate human flourishing in all areas of life within their communities. One organization beginning to explore the possible uses of AI in this unique space is SIL Global, a non-profit partnering with these communities in efforts such as Bible translation, mother-tongue education, and trauma healing. In this chapter, I introduce SIL's Augmented Quality Assessment (AQuA) program, an example of an AI innovation in Bible translation. This augmentative AI tool enhances a Bible translation team's capability as they perform quality checks on Bible translation drafts. As the AQuA team has partnered with these communities, we have seen that, upon receiving proper training, Bible translation teams can use AQuA as a powerful enhancement to their quality-checking workflows. The learnings from this journey offer insight into how minority language communities could use AI to their benefit by incorporating it into the intricate and nuanced process of Bible translation.

Linguistic Diversity and Human Flourishing

Before diving into the topic of minority language Bible translation, there is the role of linguistic diversity in God's creation to consider. There are an estimated 7,164 languages spoken and signed around the world.[1] Around 75 percent of people communicate in 8 percent of the world's living languages; conversely, 25 percent of the world—or 1.8 billion people—communicates in 92 percent of the world's languages.[2] Although the term "minority language" is difficult to define,[3] I will from here on refer to the 92 percent of languages at the tail end of this distribution as "minority languages" or "local languages."

For many Christians and non-Christians alike, the world's immense linguistic diversity brings to mind the story of the Tower of Babel (Gen. 11:1-9), often framed as a curse on the human race from which humanity "has never recovered."[4] This belief is widespread despite the absence of any overt mention in this story of God's intervention as a curse or a punishment.[5] The interpretation of God's scattering of the nations as a form of punishment may lead one to view the act of translation between any two languages as a step in fixing the "problem" of language diversity. This perspective is prevalent enough that some frame machine translation as part of the solution to this "curse of Babel."[6] Gary Simons, research associate and former chief research officer of SIL Global, argues that linguistic diversity is no curse. Rather, "The very blueprint for creation is a blueprint for diversity,"[7] from the diversity of plants and animals[8] and the diversity of our genetic makeup[9] to the diversity of human cultures and languages in the new creation.[10] Simons instead frames the story of Babel as an act of deliverance from oppression and one of God's blessings to humanity. He writes:

> If there is a "curse of Babel," it is not the multiplicity of languages. It is that peoples who have risen to power have persisted to this day in using their "one speech" as a tool of assimilation and domination. Ironically, the "curse of Babel" meme that has arisen in the culture of the West serves to perpetuate this real curse as it perpetuates the claim that language diversity is not what God originally intended but is the unfortunate consequence of human sin. To the contrary, the Bible's grand narrative embraces diversity from beginning to end. The Babel story fits into that narrative by restoring the creation blessing of diversity filling the earth as the divine response to a human attempt to dominate others by imposing one language.[11]

Speakers of minority languages still face many challenges stemming from the domination of their people in the name of "one speech." Today, these communities suffer from the effects of colonization, nationalization, and globalization, with many being discouraged from and even punished for using their mother tongue in school and religious spaces.[12] Instead of viewing the act of translation as undoing the curse of language diversity, let us view it as an invitation to undo the curse of Babel's "one speech," honoring the linguistic diversity God intends for His creation.

AI and Minority Languages

Mathematician and linguist András Kornai predicts that 2,500 of the more than 7,000 languages in the world today will survive over the next century; of those 2,500 survivors, 250 will survive digitally, with the other 90 percent facing "digital extinction."[13] This signifies more than the loss of linguistic "data." As a 2003 UNESCO report on endangered languages explains, "The extinction of each language results in the irrecoverable loss of unique cultural, historical, and ecological knowledge."[14] Language loss is a loss of identity. In response, several people groups and organizations have experimented with AI as a tool to counter language extinction.

The AI Language Gap

Minority language speakers often lack access to digital tools that majority language speakers take for granted, such as audio transcription or even spell check.[15] As of January 2024, over half of the content on the internet was in English. This is followed by Spanish, German, Russian, and Japanese, each taking up about 5 percent of web content.[16] As AI developers create models for majority languages that experts say will soon "exceed human performance" for linguistic tasks such as translation and essay writing,[17] there emerges what is often called the "AI language gap," which refers to the underrepresentation of languages with little available training data (the vast majority of languages) in AI systems.[18] The effects of underrepresentation can surface even for majority languages that have well-established AI technology. When translating from English into other widely spoken languages, such as Spanish and Arabic, machine translation systems struggle to translate accurately in domain-specific contexts, such as healthcare[19]; a considerable lack of appropriate training data amplifies this effect for lesser spoken languages.[20] This lack of representation becomes a source of harm when communities themselves express concern—such as when large language models misidentify their languages as "fictional."[21]

As awareness of this gap has grown and more people have become aware of the importance of linguistic representation, a movement has arisen to create AI technologies for what many call "low-resource languages."[22] Although there are many possible definitions for the term "low-resource language," in the context of natural language processing (NLP) it refers to languages that "have fewer technologies and especially data sets relative to some measure of their international importance."[23] There are now AI models for low-resource languages for textual semantic similarity,[24] text translation,[25] speech recognition, and transcription,[26] among others. These models often claim functionality in hundreds of languages. Google Translate, for instance, recently added 110 new languages,[27] bringing its total offering up to 243.[28] Could such technologies be used to benefit minority language communities?

Indigenous Hopes for AI

Concerns around this growing AI gap have led many individuals and groups inside and outside of local communities to take action toward developing minority language AI. However, Indigenous and majority language communities may not always share the same vision as those wishing to intervene. In a recent study, the National Research Council of Canada collaborated with members from fifteen different First Nations communities to discuss their hopes for AI. They found that "apart from the Inuit, no Indigenous community . . . has shown much interest in machine translation (MT) between their ancestral language and English (or French, in Quebec). Communities are typically more interested in tools to encourage learning and use of their ancestral language."[29] Meaningful AI development in these contexts *starts with an expressed need* from the people whom the technology is meant to serve.

Many Indigenous-led groups have mobilized to develop AI technologies for cultural engagement and language revitalization.[30] One notable example is the Māori organization Te Hiku Media in New Zealand,[31] which is creating AI tools to empower the Māori people to speak their language fluently and engage in their long-standing cultural practices. Similarly, the Masakhane movement promotes NLP research and the development of NLP tools "for Africans, by Africans," with a mission "for Africans to shape and own these technological advances towards human dignity, well-being, and equity, through inclusive community building, open participatory research and multidisciplinarity."[32] Large organizations such as Microsoft,[33] Mozilla,[34] and IBM[35] also partner with local communities to develop AI tools for language preservation and cultural education. As this movement grows, it is crucial to consider both the opportunities and challenges minority language AI presents.

Potential Challenges Regarding Low-Resource NLP

Broader digitization efforts sometimes frame online language presence as a necessary step toward justice and inclusion.[36] While this framing resonates with many—particularly those already seeking digital visibility for their languages—it risks implying a universal desire for such participation. The low-resource NLP movement, which has spurred the development of AI tools that many minority language communities have leveraged to their benefit, can at times reflect similar assumptions. Still, access alone does not guarantee that such tools align with community values or needs. Some organizations use altruistic language that suggests their models are "helpful for low-resource languages."[37] Although there is validity to such statements, this framing risks minimizing the role that the speakers of these languages play in this process. AI is not saving languages; *people* are saving languages, using AI. The belief that giving a community access to state-of-the-art translation systems is an act of justice perpetuates the idea of "documentation as language salvation" as well as the notion that language technologists will "come to the rescue of deficient languages."[38] Instead, meaningful minority language NLP requires a more holistic approach.

How to Best Serve Minority Communities

The rise of AI in our communities presents both opportunities and challenges, with great potential to help people bring justice or further perpetuate injustice. For Christians engaging in this work, Scripture calls us to seek justice for the marginalized (Amos 5:21-24; Jas 1:26-27; Isa. 1:16-17; Prov. 31:8-9), and as part of God's family, we must do everything in our power to ensure the AI revolution is a force for good and does not uphold systems of oppression. In the NLP space, seeking justice for minority communities means *partnering with* them to cultivate flourishing in the languages they most value. Many communities already have ideas of how they may benefit from AI, and these ideas often differ from what many AI developers assume would be most helpful. Some scenarios may involve strategically "fine-tuning" state-of-the-art language models, such as Meta's MMS model, for minority language tasks. Other scenarios may call for the creation of much simpler "narrow" technologies for a single task, such as verb conjugation.[39] Some communities may be wary of or have no desire for AI at all.[40] It is important to listen carefully to the needs of each community and collaborate with them in ways they see as beneficial.

Creating meaningful AI systems for minority languages requires a willingness to set aside many cultural assumptions about language and engage deeply with a community's cultural and linguistic realities. Steven Bird, a professor at Charles Darwin University, emphasizes that meaningful collaboration requires both listening to minority language communities and understanding their relationship with their language. He writes about his experience performing linguistic research and being "adopted into" a small Aboriginal community in Australia. Through his interactions there, he underwent a linguistic paradigm shift. Bird argues that only a small subset of languages—possibly 10 percent—can be viewed purely as a "communication tool" that can be written down in corpora and analyzed by machines. This is the domain of natural language processing. In contrast, the vast majority of the world's languages are "oral, emergent, untranslatable, tightly coupled to a place." These languages are not just a way to transmit information. Language is deeply cultural; it cannot be separated from identity. Bird writes:

> Indigenous languages are not just acutely under-resourced languages. There is a category distinction, based on profoundly different understandings of the nature and function of language, along with the need to steadily unravel the legacy of colonisation. This calls for a qualitatively different approach, one where we properly theorise the role of speech and language technologies in sustaining language use in a postcolonial world.[41]

In light of these considerations, the remainder of this chapter discusses how SIL Global is exploring a specific use of AI technology intended to meet expressed needs in local language Bible translation projects. The goal of this project is not to replicate human intelligence or automate the Bible translation process but rather to "expand human intelligence by using machines as tools."[42]

AI at SIL Global

SIL Global is currently grappling with many of the challenges and difficult questions surrounding minority language AI. Due to its rich history of collaborating with local language communities, SIL is well-positioned to develop and apply AI tools in these contexts. We have recently begun to explore the possible applications of AI in minority language scenarios and the effects this could have on local communities.

Ethics Statement

To guide our use of AI, we have developed an ethical framework grounded in our commitment to serve minority communities in ways that meet their expressed needs.[43] This framework identifies five key principles we aim to uphold: first, we seek to gather language data and engage in AI activities only in such a way that encourages Indigenous communities to flourish; second, we strive to ensure that language data is gathered and used only with explicit, informed consent from the community whom we intend to serve; third, we are committed to ensuring that AI activities proceed with explicit oversight from the AI developers and the community, with the option to pause, restrict, or terminate its usage at any time; fourth, we do not engage in AI activity that contains or promotes inappropriate content, such as hate, harassment, or violence; lastly, we aim to only develop AI technology that is locally rooted and meets expressed needs in a community.

The AI tools SIL develops have applications in areas such as anti-human trafficking campaigns, oral storytelling, and Scripture engagement. Additionally, SIL Global is working closely with local communities to leverage AI tools for Bible translation, including text-to-speech, automatic speech recognition, voice conversion, machine translation, sign language anonymization, and quality assessment,[44] the latter of which is the focus of this chapter.

Augmentative AI in Bible Translation

Many Bible translation innovations have emerged in recent years. These include but are not limited to rule-based translation drafting tools,[45] neural machine drafting tools,[46] Mobilized Assistance Supporting Translation (MAST),[47] and Church-Based Bible Translation (CBBT).[48] Bible translation organizations are currently exploring how these various approaches compare to each other[49] and how their use might impact team dynamics and spiritual growth during the translation process.[50] On a more granular level, teams are evaluating whether their translation is adhering to its stated goals and translation style, identifying passages which might require rewording, and determining whether certain passages are following another "reference" Bible translation too loosely or too closely. Translation teams cannot rely solely on computational systems to make these decisions for them. Instead, the focus is on developing tools that assist translation teams in making these decisions.

Augmented Quality Assessment in the Translation Process

In the Bible translation process, individuals such as translators, outside reviewers, and local church leaders undergo specialty training to diagnose quality issues in translation drafts. As AI makes its way into the Bible translation world, many of these individuals are beginning to experiment with incorporating different AI tools into their workflow, such as the Augmented Quality Assessment tool (AQuA), developed by SIL Global. This tool aids translation teams in their quality checks, enabling them to perform their work more thoroughly and efficiently. Even though AQuA users often find that this technology helps them perform their quality checks faster, the main focus of AQuA is on *improving the quality of what they can check in a given amount of time.* This is not a new idea. In 1980, Gary Simons of SIL Global wrote:

> On-site computing is bringing about a qualitative change in field linguistics, not just a quantitative change. In addition to speeding up certain analysis steps, computing power is improving the quality of work by opening up methods of analysis made practical only by the interaction of man and machine.[51]

The recent embrace of AI-powered tools for Bible translators is the latest step in a process that began more than four decades ago when personal computers became a standard tool of the trade.

What AQuA Measures

To understand how AQuA can best be integrated into quality assessment workflows, one must first have reasonable expectations about what AI can measure and what is out of reach. Translation quality is not a singular entity; rather, it is best approached as a set of sub-qualities that make up a complex fabric. The full set of sub-qualities of a Bible translation can be divided into two groups: "qualities of the process," such as the acceptability of a translation by the wider community,[52] and "qualities of the product," such as accuracy, naturalness, and clarity.[53] AQuA focuses on the latter set of sub-qualities since its computational methods assess the outputs of the translation process. However, accuracy, naturalness, and clarity are still quite abstract, having inexact definitions that require making a subjective judgment combining multiple features of a text. AQuA does not assess accuracy, naturalness, or clarity directly; it only deals with features of a text that can be measured algorithmically and expressed as a number. *These measurements are never an exact match to an abstract quality*; instead, they work like proxies for key aspects of the abstract qualities. We refer to these proxies as "assessments" in AQuA, to be explained in more detail in the following section.

How AQuA Works

Rather than attempting to measure an abstract quality (accuracy, naturalness, or clarity) of a single Bible translation, AQuA works by measuring computational qualities *between* two Bible translations. These computational qualities are grouped into four "assessments": Word Correspondence, Missing Words, Semantic Similarity, and Sentence Length. AQuA then visualizes these computations to show how these "proxies of quality" differ between the two translations. These translations are most often the Bible draft in the local language and either a source text (the original Hebrew or Greek manuscript) or some other comparison text. This latter set of texts can be broken down into subcategories (e.g., reference texts, model texts, base texts),[54] but I will use "comparison text" as an umbrella term for any other translation a team refers to during the translation process that is not a source text. These texts are usually in a language of wider communication (such as English, French, or Kiswahili) or a closely related sister language. Although most users compare their draft to a source or other comparison text in AQuA, many different combinations are possible (such as comparing a draft to its own back translation into a language of wider communication). Once the assessments have finished running, the reviewer is provided with several visualizations (heatmaps, scatterplots, tables) of the computational qualities. The interpretation of these results depends on the translation team's goals and the passages they are assessing. A brief description of each of the four AQuA assessments follows.

Word Correspondence

AQuA's Word Correspondence assessment is an approximation of the degree to which the two translations correspond word to word (which I will refer to as "word-for-wordness" or literalness between two translations). Because any two words between two languages contain unique semantic ranges, one word in one language can never be an exact "translation" of the other. As the Italian idiom "*traduttore, traditore*" ("translator, traitor") conveys, every translation involves inevitable choices that can alter the nuance or meaning of the text being translated for the receiver.[55]

However, when looking at Bible translation, a translation can be *relatively* more or less literal to another translation; this degree of similarity in wording is the domain of AQuA's Word Correspondence assessment, which helps the user evaluate where different parts of their translation sit on a *spectrum* of dynamic to literal regarding the comparison text. This assessment yields a score between zero and ten for each verse pair. Lower scores suggest less word-for-wordness (or more dynamicity) between the parallel verses, and higher scores suggest more word-for-wordness. Lower scores often indicate areas where the draft may be "paraphrasing" more than "translating" directly from the source or comparison text, while higher scores indicate areas where the draft is more wooden or literal to the source or comparison text. To give a simple example, comparing the text of Jonah in the English King James Version to the text of Jonah in the Septuagint would generally yield higher Word Correspondence scores than when comparing the text of Jonah in the English New Living Translation to the text of Jonah in the Septuagint. Translation teams can then use this information to appropriately revise their draft. This assessment uses the FastAlign word alignment model (as well as Jaccard Similarity and a custom autoencoder) to predict word alignments between the two translations, meaning that it only has to train on the Bible data the user uploads.[56] This is significant, as it means AQuA can be applied to minority languages, regardless of their digital footprint outside the Bible translation sphere.

Missing Words

AQuA's Missing Words assessment builds off the word alignment models used in the Word Correspondence assessment to identify words in the source or comparison text that do not have a likely corresponding word in the draft. "Missing words" usually do not indicate problems, but this assessment has been beneficial for translators and reviewers in identifying words or phrases that were unintentionally omitted or inconsistently translated throughout the draft.

Semantic Similarity

AQuA's Semantic Similarity assessment uses a multilingual pre-trained transformer model to estimate the similarity in meaning between the two selected texts, also yielding a score between zero and ten for each verse pair.[57] This assessment requires both translations to be in a majority language; therefore, it is most often run on a back translation of the local language draft into a majority language. According to AQuA users, this assessment is best used in conjunction with the Word Correspondence assessment to identify verses that are outliers concerning both of these proxies.

Sentence and Word Length

The AQuA Sentence and Word Length assessment serves as a rough approximation for the readability of the draft. It assesses the draft text *only* and calculates scores on the chapter level, using the Lix Readability formula.[58] Scores for this assessment have no upper bound:

$$Lix = \frac{Words}{Sentences} + \frac{100 \times LongWords}{Words}$$

Where:

- *Words* is the number of words in the chapter
- *Sentences* is the number of sentences in the chapter
- *Long Words* is the number of words in the chapter with more than six letters

Of course, many other factors play into a text's readability, such as syntax and word choice. Although the scores for this assessment vary widely by language, its main goal is to visualize the consistency (or inconsistency) of this computational quality throughout the draft.

Visualizing the Assessments

AQuA does not seek to provide a definitive answer to the degree of accuracy, naturalness, clarity, readability, literalness, or some other abstract quality of a translation, as these qualities are not quantifiable. However, we can provide the AQuA user with extra information *that aids them in assessing these abstract qualities.* This information is visualized in several ways in the AQuA web application. Two examples (in majority languages) are discussed below (for the actual visuals, please go to http://aqua.multilingualai.com/aibti for Figures 6.1 and 6.2).

Figure 6.1 provides a scatter plot that visualizes the Word Correspondence and Semantic Similarity scores for Paul's letter to the Romans between the English King James Version (KJV) and the English Berean Standard Bible (BSB). Each dot represents a single verse. The dots in the upper right corner (purple) represent the verses with high scores for both assessments, which are predicted to be the most similar in wording and meaning. Likewise, the verses toward the lower left (green) represent the verses where AQuA predicts the two translations differ the most in wording and meaning. In the web application, users can hover over these dots to view the verse reference, text, and scores for the verse. For example, AQuA predicts that these two scores for Rom. 9:28 are relatively low. In the KJV, this verse reads: "For he will finish the work, and cut it short in righteousness: because a short work will the Lord make upon the earth" (Rom. 9:28 KJV). In the BSB, it reads "For the Lord will carry out His sentence on the earth thoroughly and decisively" (Rom. 9:28 BSB). By contrast, the vast majority of verses in the upper right-hand corner are verses from Romans 16, which contains lists of names nearly identical between the two translations.

Figure 6.2 provides a table for the KJV and the German Lutherbibel for the Psalms, with predicted missing words highlighted in either blue or purple. For the blue missing words in the Lutherbibel, AQuA has not predicted a likely corresponding word in the King James Version. In AQuA, users can also handpick a set of "baseline translations" that help to make these missing word predictions more accurate. For the purple words, AQuA has not found a likely corresponding word in the King James Version, but AQuA *has* found a likely corresponding word in several of the baseline translations. For this example, I have chosen the baseline translations to be the American Standard Version, Young's Literal Translation, World English Bible, Berean Standard Bible, and the German 1951 Schlachterbibel. In Ps. 36:7, the highlighted word *Gottes* is the genitive form of *Gott* ("God," in English). *Die Berge Gottes* would translate into English as "the mountains of God," or "God's mountains," neither of which appear in the KJV, which contains only "the great mountains." Although both translations may be acceptable renderings of the Hebrew, several AQuA users have reported that similar discrepancies between their projects and a source or comparison text indicated a problem with the translation, such as an unintentionally omitted phrase.

Several translators and reviewers report that they have used AQuA to find mistakes that otherwise would have made their way to print. As with any other tool, however, users must discern how they implement AQuA and interpret its results. An outlier verse on a scatter plot or a highlighted word in a table will not always indicate a problem; likewise, just because a verse does not "stand out" in AQuA does not mean that it can be skipped over. Teams must still meticulously examine *every verse*; AQuA is a tool that helps them do this work.

AQuA in Action

Since October 2022, several Bible translation teams have used AQuA via a simple web application. Our diverse user base of over one hundred people from more than twenty organizations consists of Bible translators, project coordinators, translation advisors, and translation consultants, among many others, working on projects all over the world. These participants have utilized AQuA to assess translations from various language families, including Chadic, Bantu, Semitic, Malayo-Polynesian, Mixe-Zoquean, Quechuan, Indo-Aryan, and Italic. The linguistic diversity represented in these experiments has provided an invaluable opportunity to observe how this technology works (or does not work) with different scripts and grammars.

Users primarily focus on AQuA's two-word alignment assessments (Word Correspondence and Missing Words), as they work relatively well with "low-resource" minority languages. On the granular level, many report that they have used this feature to identify unfinished verses, missing key terms, and misspellings in their translation that would have otherwise made their way into the published Bible. On a higher level, others (mostly outside reviewers) leverage this feature to discern general trends throughout a translation. The tool enables them to detect when a certain book or passage does not closely follow the stated goals of the translation project. However, assessment outputs are not reliably useful. When comparing isolating languages (languages with a low morpheme per word ratio) to agglutinative languages (languages with a high morpheme per word ratio) or to languages with complex inflection or declension systems, AQuA struggles to produce helpful word alignments between the two translations.

Although AQuA's user base consists of volunteers in diverse roles, many of our contacts are expatriates who review a minority language project remotely. This means we do not always hear direct feedback on the tool from the community the outside reviewers are serving. Although expatriates work closely with members of a local community, they are not locals and, therefore, are not experts in the language. When designing any AI tool for use in local contexts, SIL's goal is for all stakeholders in the translation process to be involved in its design and implementation. To provide a model for this kind of collaboration, the following section outlines examples of direct partnership between SIL AI developers and local translation teams in the Philippines.

Case Study: Philippines

Out of the over one hundred translation projects using AQuA, two stories from the Philippines are of particular interest. The first is from an in-person workshop involving minority language translation teams who are drafting Scripture in their language for the first time. The latter is from a remote collaboration with teams revising two national language Bibles (what some may call "mid-resource languages").

Wycliffe Philippines Workshop

Translation teams from Wycliffe Philippines have partnered with the AQuA team for two years, volunteering as test users and providing invaluable feedback on its usefulness. Wycliffe Philippines requested access to the AQuA web application in December 2022 but struggled to regularly use it in their translation workflows due to the web application requiring a stable internet connection and the difficult nature of asynchronous communication with major time zone differences. As their interest in AQuA and SIL's other AI projects grew, we planned a joint in-person workshop for (a) local translation teams to learn about AI, (b) local translation teams to experiment with using AI tools in their workflows, and (c) AI practitioners at SIL to learn how to design AI tools which best meet the needs of these local translation teams.[59]

Eighteen Filipino translators, field coordinators, project facilitators, consultants-in-training, translation consultants, and IT experts representing six different minority language projects traveled to Manila to participate in the four-day workshop that took place from September 25 to 28, 2023. Four of these teams, who were working on written translations, learned how to use SIL's Scripture Forge program for AI translation drafting and AQuA for AI translation checking; the other two teams, who were working on oral translations, worked with an SIL AI developer exploring AI applications for oral Bible translation (OBT). The learnings from this workshop greatly influence the ongoing development of these tools. Here are four of these learnings, specific to AQuA:

- All four teams working on written translations successfully used AQuA to find verses which required revision by comparing their drafts either to a source translation, to a comparison translation, or to its back translation. Several of these errors, such as half-completed verses, would reportedly not have been caught otherwise and would have made their way to print. The tool was intuitive enough that the participants discovered several errors within the first ten minutes of the checking session.
- Most of the time, AQuA "flags" did not lead to revisions. All teams gave thorough feedback on the limitations of the tool, reporting that certain grammatical constructions (e.g., verb inflections and case markers) posed difficulties in correctly aligning words and phrases between two translations. Other times, AQuA would correctly highlight missing words, but these differences were necessary for the clarity or readability of the translation in the local context. Teams reported that working through these results was worthwhile for the few outliers that indeed indicated a problem with the draft text.
- Team members reported that AQuA was useful for any team member running a quality check on the draft, whether a translator, consultant, or some other team member.
- Team members expressed concern that without proper training, AQuA users may be tempted to try to "fix" all passages that deviate noticeably from the comparison translation, even when those passages are translated appropriately.

Biblica Philippines

In late 2023, Biblica Philippines contacted SIL AI requesting access to AQuA to aid them in their revisions of the Tagalog and Cebuano Bibles, two widely spoken languages in the Philippines. The goal of both revisions is to streamline the text by identifying and removing extraneous or unnecessary additions present in earlier translations. To this end, the team used the Biblica New International Version (NIV) as a reference point, focusing on the chapters and verses in the two revisions that differed the most from the more concise style of the NIV.

When the team started using AQuA, their New Testament drafts had many errors and had been rejected in their most recent consultant checks. They had gone from two available translators to one with minimal prior experience and had only four months to clean up their entire New Testament due to funding limitations. Tatyana de Chavez, a translation consultant for this team, wrote that this was "a task that seemed impossible. But AQuA made it possible." The translator used AQuA to pinpoint errors by tracking the use of key terms and using the visualizations to "distinguish between actual errors and matters of linguistic expression." They submitted their work on time and passed their next consultant check, being commended for the quality of their work. They now use AQuA at every milestone in their translation process and have expanded its use to projects in other countries.

Levi Cruz, another translation consultant for both projects, also found AQuA to be a valuable addition to his workflow. In his report, he highlighted specific instances when AQuA pointed him toward errors in the text, but also instances when it failed to identify issues and instances when its results were not useful. These outcomes support the concern that the Wycliffe Philippines workshop participants also expressed—that organizations must be discerning in how they promote this tool and that AQuA users must be trained before beginning to use it to evaluate their work.

Discussion

These experiences reflect many of the broader dynamics surrounding AI ethics in local communities, particularly the importance of community agency and discernment in adopting AI tools. In this context, participants' reflections on AQuA offer valuable insight into both AI's benefits and its limitations in local settings.

Those who use AQuA overall find that it saves them time and helps them draft more clear, natural, and accurate Bibles. At the same time, these participants express concern that team members may feel *obligated* to use AQuA if others in their organization are encouraging its use. Additionally, for some, incorporating a new tool into their workflow can help them increase the quality of their work, while others may find it difficult to allocate the time to learn and incorporate a new tool into their workflow. This could hinder their productivity, at least in the short term, lengthening the project timeline. For this reason, education on AQuA's proper uses and its limitations should be given not just to translators and reviewers but also to anyone who promotes this tool within their organization. This will empower end-users to make informed decisions about if and how they will use this technology.

As with many other digital language technologies, AQuA's accessibility greatly influences who will end up using it. Using an AI system that is only available online poses great challenges to those without reliable access to the internet. Asynchronous communication and gathering online feedback from participants living on the other side of the world pose challenges, especially if they are interacting with the rest of their team remotely. In-person workshops are immensely beneficial, as they allow face-to-face interaction, making it easier for participants to ask questions and give real-time feedback.

Conclusion

The plethora of available state-of-the-art AI systems presents promising opportunities for those working in Bible translation, with tools for written drafting, quality assessment, and audio transcription, providing unique advantages in settings with limited resources. As AQuA's story unfolds, it exemplifies a future where Bible translation teams can use AI to help them overcome several hurdles in the quality assessment process, guiding them toward errors that otherwise would have been missed. Alongside these promising opportunities, integrating AI into this process raises certain complexities. Successfully adopting tools like AQuA requires discernment in order to respect certain cultural sensitivities and navigate the risks of misuse that could affect translation accuracy. Ultimately, AQuA's journey offers a glimpse into a future of contextually-grounded AI in Bible translation, pointing toward exciting possibilities for Christians worldwide.[60]

Notes

1 David M. Eberhart, Gary F. Simons, and Charles D. Fennig, *Ethnologue: Languages of the World*, 27th ed. (Dallas: SIL International, 2024).

2 Michel Kenmogne, "Flourishing and Language," in *God and Language: Exploring the Role of Language in the Mission of God*, ed. Michael Greed and Dawn Kruger (Dallas: SIL International, 2021), 178.

3 Lenore Grenoble and Adam Roth Singerman, "Minority Languages," *Oxford Bibliographies*, last modified February 25, 2014, https://doi.org/10.1093/obo/9780199772810-0176.

4 Einar Haugen, "The Curse of Babel," *Daedalus* 102.3 (1973): 47–57; Philip D. Hill, "'Comment' on R.M. Jones' 'Language in God's Economy: A Welsh and International Perspective,'" *Themelios* 21.3 (1996): 15–16; Gerhard von Rad, *Genesis: A Commentary*, rev. ed., OTL (Philadelphia: Westminster, 1972), 152; Gordon J. Wenham, *Genesis 1–15*, WBC 1 (Dallas: Word, 1987), 237; and David J. A. Clines, *The Theme of the Pentateuch*, 2nd ed., JSOTSup 10 (Sheffield: Sheffield Academic, 2001), 76; and especially, John Whitcomb, "Babel," *Creation* 24.3 (2002): 31–3.

5 David Crystal, *English as a Global Language*, 2nd ed. (Cambridge: Cambridge University Press, 2003), 15. A minority of scholars, notably Rolf Rendtorff, argue the time of God's cursing humanity ends with the flood in Genesis 8; see his "Genesis 8:21 und die Urgeschichte des Yahwisten," *KD* 7 (1961): 69–78.

6 Philip Seargeant, "Is Artificial Intelligence about to Free Us from the Curse of Babel?" *New Scientist*, December 27, 2023.

7 Gary F. Simons, "Language Diversity: Curse or Blessing?" in *God and Language*, ed. Greed and Kruger, 31.

8 Andrew M. Greeley, *The Communal Catholic: A Personal Manifesto* (New York: Seabury, 1976), 152.

9 Francis S. Collins, *The Language of God: A Scientist Presents Evidence for Belief* (New York: Free Press, 2007).

10 Christopher J. H. Wright, *The Mission of God: Unlocking the Bible's Grand Narrative* (Downers Grove: IVP Academic, 2006), 47.

11 Simons, "Language Diversity," 42; and for a similar approach, see José Míguez-Bonino, "Genesis 11:1–9: A Latin American Perspective," in *Return to Babel: Global Perspectives on the Bible*, ed. John R. Levison and Priscilla Pope-Levison (Louisville: Westminster John Knox, 1999), 13–16.

12 Kenmogne, "Flourishing and Language," 167–74.

13 András Kornai, "Digital Language Death," *PLoS ONE* 8.10 (2013): e77056, https://doi.org/10.1371/journal.pone.0077056.

14 UNESCO Ad Hoc Expert Group on Endangered Languages, "Language Vitality and Endangerment" (paper presented at the International Expert Meeting on the UNESCO Programme Safeguarding of Endangered Languages, Paris, 2003), https://unesdoc.unesco.org/ark:/48223/pf0000183699.

15 Gary F. Simons, Abbey L. Thomas, and Chad K. White, "Assessing Digital Language Support on a Global Scale," arXiv, 2022, https://doi.org/10.48550/arXiv.2209.13515.

16 Ani Petrosyan, "Languages Most Frequently Used for Web Content as of January 2024, by Share of Websites," *Statista*, October 21, 2024.

17 Katja Grace, John Salvatier, Allan Dafoe, Baobao Zhang, and Owain Evans, "When Will AI Exceed Human Performance? Evidence from AI Experts," arXiv, 2017, https://doi.org/10.48550/arXiv.1705.08807.

18 Alena Gorbacheva, "No Language Left Behind: How to Bridge the Rapidly Evolving AI Language Gap," Innovation for Development by UNDP Europe and Central Asia, posted October 4, 2023, https://innovation.eurasia.undp.org/ai-language-gap.

19 Jaleh Delfani, Constantin Orasan, Hadeel Saadany, Ozlem Temizoz, Eleanor Taylor-Stilgoe, Diptesh Kanojia, Sabine Braun, and Barbara Schouten, "Google Translate Error Analysis for Mental Healthcare Information: Evaluating Accuracy, Comprehensibility, and Implications for Multilingual Healthcare Communication," arXiv, 2024, https://doi.org/10.48550/arXiv.2402.04023.

20 Shaolin Zhu, Leiyu Pan, and Deyi Xiong, "FEDS-ICL: Enhancing Translation Ability and Efficiency of Large Language Model by Optimizing Demonstration Selection," *Information Processing and Management* 61.5 (2024): 103825, https://doi.org/10.1016/j.ipm.2024.103825.

21 Matteo Wong, "The AI Revolution Is Crushing Thousands of Languages," *The Atlantic*, April 12, 2024.

22 Alexandre Magueresse, Vincent Carles, and Evan Heetderks, "Low-Resource Languages: A Review of Past Work and Future Challenges," arXiv, 2020, https://doi.org/10.48550/arXiv.2006.07264.

23 Christopher Cieri, Mike Maxwell, Stephanie Strassel, and Jennifer Tracey, "Selection Criteria for Low Resource Language Programs," in *Proceedings of the Tenth International Conference on Language Resources and Evaluation (LREC'16)*, ed. Nicoletta Calzolari, Khalid Choukri, Thierry Declerck, Sara Goggi, Marko Grobelnik, Bente Maegaard, Joseph Mariani, Helene Mazo, Asuncion Moreno, Jan Odijk, and Stelios Piperidis (Portorož: European Language Resources Association, 2016), 4545.

24 Fangxiaoyu Feng, Yinfei Yang, Daniel Cer, Naveen Arivazhagan, and Wei Wang, "Language-Agnostic BERT Sentence Embedding," arXiv, 2020, https://doi.org/10.48550/arXiv.2007.01852.

25 NLLB Team, Marta R. Costa-jussà, James Cross, Onur Çelebi, Maha Elbayad, Kenneth Heafield, Kevin Heffernan, Elahe Kalbassi, Janice Lam, et al., "No Language Left Behind: Scaling Human-Centered Machine Translation," arXiv, 2022, https://doi.org/10.48550/arXiv.2207.04672.

26 Vineel Pratap, Andros Tjandra, Bowen Shi, Paden Tomasello, Arun Babu, Sayani Kundu, Ali Elkahky, Zhaoheng Ni, Apoorv Vyas, et al., "Scaling Speech Technology to 1,000+ Languages," arXiv, 2023, https://doi.org/10.48550/arXiv.2305.13516.

27 Isaac Caswell, "110 New Languages Are Coming to Google Translate," *The Keyword* (blog), Google, posted June 27, 2024, https://blog.google/products/translate/google-translate-new-languages-2024.

28 Jibin Joseph, "Google Translate Adds Support for 110 Languages, Its Largest Expansion Ever," *PCMag*, June 27, 2024.

29 Roland Kuhn, "The Indigenous Languages Technology (ILT) Project at the National Research Council of Canada, and Its Context," *Linguapax Review* 9 (2021): 89.

30 Karen Hao, "A New Vision of Artificial Intelligence for the People," *MIT Technology Review*, April 22, 2022; Chijioke Okorie and Vukosi Marivate, "How African NLP Experts Are Navigating the Challenges of Copyright, Innovation, and Access," *Carnegie Endowment for International Peace*, April 30, 2024, https://carnegieendowment.org/research/2024/04/how-african-nlp-experts-are-navigating-the-challenges-of-copyright-innovation-and-access; Abteen Ebrahimi, Ona De Gibert, Raul Vazquez, Rolando Coto-Solano, Pavel Denisov, Robert Pugh, Manuel Mager, Arturo Oncevay, Luis Chiruzzo, Katharina von der Wense, and Shruti Rijhwani, "Findings of the AmericasNLP 2024 Shared Task on Machine Translation into Indigenous Languages," in *Proceedings of the 4th Workshop on Natural Language Processing for Indigenous Languages of the Americas (AmericasNLP 2024)*, ed. Manuel Mager, Abteen Ebrahimi, Shruti Rijhwani, Arturo Oncevay, Luis Chiruzzo, Robert Pugh, and Katharina von der Wense (Mexico City: Association for Computational Linguistics, 2024), 236–46; Wuraola Oyewusi, "AI Literacy in Low-Resource Languages: Insights from Creating AI in Yoruba Videos," arXiv, 2024, https://doi.org/10.48550/arXiv.2403.04799.

31 ITU News, "How AI Is Helping Revitalise Indigenous Languages," International Telecommunication Union, August 9, 2022, https://www.itu.int/hub/2022/08/ai-indigenous-languages-maori-te-reo.

32 Masakhane, "Masakhane," accessed December 16, 2024, https://www.masakhane.io.

33 Dan Walker and Barry Soutar, "How AI Is Helping Māori Recover Their Own Voices," Microsoft News, posted July 2, 2024, https://news.microsoft.com/en-nz/2024/07/02/how-ai-is-helping-maori-recover-their-own-voices.
34 Tolu Olasoji, "Hey Siri, Learn to Speak Kinyarwanda," *Reasons to Be Cheerful*, July 13, 2021, https://reasonstobecheerful.world/languages-voice-tech-in-africa.
35 MaryLou Costa, "AI Is Helping Indigenous Teens in Brazil Keep Their Mother Tongue Alive," *Reasons to Be Cheerful*, November 9, 2023, https://reasonstobecheerful.world/artificial-intelligence-teens-indigenous-language-preservation-brazil.
36 Translation Commons, "Language Digitization Initiative," accessed December 16, 2024, https://translationcommons.org/language-digitization.
37 Isaac Caswell and Bowen Liang, "Recent Advances in Google Translate," *Google Research* (blog), Google, 2020, posted June 8, 2020, http://research.google/blog/recent-advances-in-google-translate.
38 Steven Bird, "Local Languages, Third Spaces, and Other High-Resource Scenarios," in *Proceedings of the 60th Annual Meeting of the Association for Computational Linguistics (Volume 1: Long Papers)*, ed. Smaranda Muresan, Preslav Nakov, and Aline Villavicencio (Dublin: Association for Computational Linguistics, 2022), 7818.
39 Kuhn, "Indigenous Languages Technology (ILT) Project," 91.
40 Examples include leaders within Cheyenne and Mongolian communities who reject technological advances (such as AI) out of concern that it may irrevocably alter their language; see Avi Ackermann, "When AI Doesn't Speak Your Language," *Coda*, October 20, 2023, https://www.codastory.com/authoritarian-tech/artificial-intelligence-minority-language-censorship.
41 Steven Bird, "Decolonising Speech and Language Technology," in *Proceedings of the 28th International Conference on Computational Linguistics*, ed. Donia Scott, Nuria Bel, and Chengqing Zong (Barcelona: International Committee on Computational Linguistics, 2020), 3513.
42 Steven Bird, "Must NLP Be Extractive?" in *Proceedings of the 62nd Annual Meeting of the Association for Computational Linguistics (Volume 1: Long Papers)*, ed. Lun-Wei Ku, Andre Martins, and Vivek Srikumar (Bangkok: Association for Computational Linguistics, 2024), 14916.
43 SIL AI and NLP, "SIL's AI Ethics Statement," accessed December 16, 2024, https://ai.sil.org/ethics.
44 SIL AI and NLP, "Projects," accessed December 16, 2024, https://ai.sil.org/projects.
45 Catherine Graul, "Innovation for Minority Languages: The Bible Translator's Assistant," Wycliffe Bible Translators, posted on May 10, 2022, https://www.wycliffe.org/blog/posts/innovation-for-minority-languages-the-bible-translators-assistant; and SIL Global, "FLExTrans: Machine Translation Software," accessed December 16, 2024, https://software.sil.org/flextrans.
46 SIL AI and NLP, "Scripture Forge," accessed December 16, 2024, https://ai.sil.org/projects/scriptureforge.
47 Florence Taylor, "Persecuted Christians Are Risking Their Lives to Translate the Bible into Their Local Language," *Christian Today*, February 11, 2016.
48 Church-Based Bible Translation, "Church-Based Bible Translation," accessed December 16, 2024, https://churchbased.bible; and Wycliffe Bible Translators, "New Churches Forming in Madagascar," posted June 7, 2024, https://www.wycliffe.org/blog/posts/new-churches-forming-in-madagascar.

49 ETEN Lab, "Igniting Acceleration in Bible Translation," accessed December 16, 2024, https://www.etenlab.org.
50 Andy Warren-Rothlin, "Source Texts, Source Languages, Technology, and Values," *BT* 62 (2011): 242–3.
51 Gary F. Simons, "The Impact of On-Site Computing on Field Linguistics: The Power of Man and Machine in Interaction," *Notes on Linguistics* 16 (1980): 7.
52 Iver Larsen, "The Fourth Criterion of a Good Translation," *Notes on Translation* 15.1 (2001): 40–53.
53 Katharine Barnwell, *Bible Translation: An Introductory Course in Translation Principles* (Jos: Institute of Linguistics, 1975), 16.
54 Warren-Rothlin, "Source Texts," 242–3.
55 Flor Zaccagnino, "'Traduttore, Traditore' and Translating the Untranslatable," *Bunny Studio* (blog), posted April 6, 2020, https://bunnystudio.com/blog/traduttore-traditore-and-translating-the-untranslatable; and John H. Walton, *Wisdom for Faithful Reading: Principles and Practices for Old Testament Interpretation* (Downers Grove: InterVarsity, 2023), 53.
56 See Chris Dyer, Victor Chahuneau, and Noah A. Smith, "A Simple, Fast, and Effective Reparameterization of IBM Model 2," in *Proceedings of the 2013 Conference of the North American Chapter of the Association for Computational Linguistics: Human Language Technologies*, ed. Lucy Vanderwende, Hal Daumé III, and Katrin Kirchhoff (Atlanta: Association for Computational Linguistics, 2013), 644–8; Fatih Karabiber, "Jaccard Similarity," LearnDataSci, accessed December 9, 2024, https://www.learndatasci.com/glossary/jaccard-similarity; and Dor Bank, Noam Koenigstein, and Raja Giryes, "Autoencoders," arXiv, 2021, https://doi.org/10.48550/arXiv.2003.05991, respectively.
57 Feng, Yang, Cer, Arivazhagan, and Wang, "BERT Sentence Embedding."
58 Readable, "The Lix and Rix Readability Formulas," accessed December 16, 2024, https://readable.com/readability/lix-rix-readability-formulas.
59 For further details, see Cassie Weishaupt, "Wycliffe Philippines Trip Report," 2023, https://bit.ly/silai-wp-workshop.
60 We express our deep gratitude to all those who have contributed to the success of the AQuA project, including dedicated translation team members, administrators, and the ETEN Innovation Lab. We greatly appreciate the members of the AQuA Consultants Sync for volunteering as the first AQuA "guinea pigs," helping us get this initiative off the ground. Special thanks to Sarah Aniban and Ma'am Edith Sola from Wycliffe Philippines for their invaluable support in coordinating our AI workshop in Manila, and for all the participants for traveling all the way to Manila from their homes in other parts of the country. We are also grateful for Tatyana de Chavez and Levi Cruz for their efforts in promoting the use of AQuA at Biblica; your unwavering support and enthusiasm have been instrumental in advancing this initiative.

Bibliography

Ackermann, Avi. "When AI Doesn't Speak Your Language." *Coda*, October 20, 2023. https://www.codastory.com/authoritarian-tech/artificial-intelligence-minority-language-censorship.

Bank, Dor, Noam Koenigstein, and Raja Giryes. "Autoencoders." arXiv. 2021. https://doi.org/10.48550/arXiv.2003.05991.

Barnwell, Katharine. *Bible Translation: An Introductory Course in Translation Principles.* Jos: Institute of Linguistics, 1975.

Bird, Steven. "Decolonising Speech and Language Technology." Pages 3504–19 in *Proceedings of the 28th International Conference on Computational Linguistics.* Edited by Donia Scott, Nuria Bel, and Chengqing Zong. Barcelona: International Committee on Computational Linguistics, 2020. https://doi.org/10.18653/v1/2020.coling-main.313.

Bird, Steven. "Local Languages, Third Spaces, and Other High-Resource Scenarios." Pages 7817–29 in *Proceedings of the 60th Annual Meeting of the Association for Computational Linguistics (Volume 1: Long Papers).* Edited by Smaranda Muresan, Preslav Nakov, and Aline Villavicencio. Dublin: Association for Computational Linguistics, 2022. https://doi.org/10.18653/v1/2022.acl-long.539.

Bird, Steven. "Must NLP Be Extractive?" Pages 14915–29 in *Proceedings of the 62nd Annual Meeting of the Association for Computational Linguistics (Volume 1: Long Papers).* Edited by Lun-Wei Ku, Andre Martins, and Vivek Srikumar. Bangkok: Association for Computational Linguistics, 2024. https://doi.org/10.18653/v1/2024.acl-long.797.

Caswell, Isaac. "110 New Languages Are Coming to Google Translate." *The Keyword* (blog). Google. Posted June 27, 2024. https://blog.google/products/translate/google-translate-new-languages-2024.

Caswell, Isaac, and Bowen Liang. "Recent Advances in Google Translate." *Google Research* (blog), 2020. Google. Posted June 8, 2020. http://research.google/blog/recent-advances-in-google-translate.

Chandran, Rina. "Indigenous Groups Fear Culture Distortion as AI Learns Their Languages." *The Japan Times,* April 10, 2023. https://www.japantimes.co.jp/news/2023/04/10/world/indigenous-language-ai-colonization-worries.

Church-Based Bible Translation. "Church-Based Bible Translation." Accessed December 16, 2024. https://churchbased.bible.

Cieri, Christopher, Mike Maxwell, Stephanie Strassel, and Jennifer Tracey. "Selection Criteria for Low Resource Language Programs." Pages 4543–49 in *Proceedings of the Tenth International Conference on Language Resources and Evaluation (LREC'16).* Edited by Nicoletta Calzolari, Khalid Choukri, Thierry Declerck, Sara Goggi, Marko Grobelnik, Bente Maegaard, Joseph Mariani, Helene Mazo, Asuncion Moreno, Jan Odijk, and Stelios Piperidis. Portorož: European Language Resources Association, 2016. https://aclanthology.org/L16-1720.

Clines, David J. A. *The Theme of the Pentateuch.* 2nd ed. JSOTSup 10. Sheffield: Sheffield Academic, 2001.

Coffey, Donavyn. "Māori Are Trying to Save Their Language from Big Tech." *Wired,* April 28, 2021. https://www.wired.com/story/maori-language-tech.

Collins, Francis S. *The Language of God: A Scientist Presents Evidence for Belief.* New York: Free Press, 2007.

Costa, MaryLou. "AI Is Helping Indigenous Teens in Brazil Keep Their Mother Tongue Alive." *Reasons to Be Cheerful,* November 9, 2023. https://reasonstobecheerful.world/artificial-intelligence-teens-indigenous-language-preservation-brazil.

Crystal, David. *English as a Global Language*. 2nd ed. Cambridge: Cambridge University Press, 2003.

Delfani, Jaleh, Constantin Orasan, Hadeel Saadany, Ozlem Temizoz, Eleanor Taylor-Stilgoe, Diptesh Kanojia, Sabine Braun, and Barbara Schouten. "Google Translate Error Analysis for Mental Healthcare Information: Evaluating Accuracy, Comprehensibility, and Implications for Multilingual Healthcare Communication." arXiv. 2024. https://doi.org/10.48550/arXiv.2402.04023.

Dyer, Chris, Victor Chahuneau, and Noah A. Smith. "A Simple, Fast, and Effective Reparameterization of IBM Model 2." Pages 644–48 in *Proceedings of the 2013 Conference of the North American Chapter of the Association for Computational Linguistics: Human Language Technologies*. Edited by Lucy Vanderwende, Hal Daumé III, and Katrin Kirchhoff. Atlanta: Association for Computational Linguistics, 2013. https://aclanthology.org/N13-1073.

Eberhart, David M., Gary F. Simons, and Charles D. Fennig. *Ethnologue: Languages of the World*. 27th ed. Dallas: SIL International, 2024.

Ebrahimi, Abteen, Ona De Gibert, Raul Vazquez, Rolando Coto-Solano, Pavel Denisov, Robert Pugh, Manuel Mager, Arturo Oncevay, Luis Chiruzzo, Katharina von der Wense, and Shruti Rijhwani. "Findings of the AmericasNLP 2024 Shared Task on Machine Translation into Indigenous Languages." Pages 236–46 in *Proceedings of the 4th Workshop on Natural Language Processing for Indigenous Languages of the Americas (AmericasNLP 2024)*. Edited by Manuel Mager, Abteen Ebrahimi, Shruti Rijhwani, Arturo Oncevay, Luis Chiruzzo, Robert Pugh, and Katharina von der Wense. Mexico City: Association for Computational Linguistics, 2024. https://doi.org/10.18653/v1/2024.americasnlp-1.28.

ETEN Lab. "Igniting Acceleration in Bible Translation." Accessed December 16, 2024. https://www.etenlab.org.

Feng, Fangxiaoyu, Yinfei Yang, Daniel Cer, Naveen Arivazhagan, and Wei Wang. "Language-Agnostic BERT Sentence Embedding." arXiv. 2020. https://doi.org/10.48550/arXiv.2007.01852.

Gorbacheva, Alena. "No Language Left Behind: How to Bridge the Rapidly Evolving AI Language Gap." Innovation for Development by UNDP Europe and Central Asia. Posted October 4, 2023. https://innovation.eurasia.undp.org/ai-language-gap.

Grace, Katja, John Salvatier, Allan Dafoe, Baobao Zhang, and Owain Evans. "When Will AI Exceed Human Performance? Evidence from AI Experts." arXiv. 2017. https://doi.org/10.48550/arXiv.1705.08807.

Graul, Catherine. "Innovation for Minority Languages: The Bible Translator's Assistant." Wycliffe Bible Translators. Posted May 10, 2022. https://www.wycliffe.org/blog/posts/innovation-for-minority-languages-the-bible-translators-assistant.

Greeley, Andrew M. *The Communal Catholic: A Personal Manifesto*. New York: Seabury, 1976.

Grenoble, Lenore, and Adam Roth Singerman. "Minority Languages." *Oxford Bibliographies*. Last modified February 25, 2014. https://doi.org/10.1093/obo/9780199772810-0176.

Hao, Karen. "A New Vision of Artificial Intelligence for the People." *MIT Technology Review*, April 22, 2022. https://www.technologyreview.com/2022/04/22/1050394/artificial-intelligence-for-the-people.

Haugen, Einar. "The Curse of Babel." *Daedalus* 102.3 (1973): 47–57.

Hill, Philip D. "Comment" on R.M. Jones' "Language in God's Economy: A Welsh and International Perspective." *Themelios* 21.3 (1996): 15–16.

ITU News. "How AI Is Helping Revitalise Indigenous Languages." International Telecommunication Union, August 9, 2022. https://www.itu.int/hub/2022/08/ai-indigenous-languages-maori-te-reo.

Joseph, Jibin. "Google Translate Adds Support for 110 Languages, Its Largest Expansion Ever." *PCMag*, June 27, 2024. https://www.pcmag.com/news/google-translate-adds-support-for-110-languages-its-largest-expansion-ever.

Karabiber, Fatih. "Jaccard Similarity." *LearnDataSci*. Accessed December 9, 2024. https://www.learndatasci.com/glossary/jaccard-similarity.

Kenmogne, Michel. "Flourishing and Language." Pages 167–91 in *God and Language: Exploring the Role of Language in the Mission of God*. Edited by Michael Greed and Dawn Kruger. Dallas: SIL International, 2021.

Kornai, András. "Digital Language Death." *PLoS ONE* 8.10 (2013): e77056. https://doi.org/10.1371/journal.pone.0077056.

Kuhn, Roland. "The Indigenous Languages Technology (ILT) Project at the National Research Council of Canada, and Its Context." *Linguapax Review* 9 (2021): 85–104.

Larsen, Iver. "The Fourth Criterion of a Good Translation." *Notes on Translation* 15.1 (2001): 40–53.

Magueresse, Alexandre, Vincent Carles, and Evan Heetderks. "Low-Resource Languages: A Review of Past Work and Future Challenges." arXiv. 2020. https://doi.org/10.48550/arXiv.2006.07264.

Mahelona, Keoni, Gianna Leoni, Suzanne Duncan, and Miles Thompson. "OpenAI's Whisper Is Another Case Study in Colonisation." *Papa Reo* (blog). Posted January 24, 2023. https://blog.papareo.nz/whisper-is-another-case-study-in-colonisation.

Masakhane. "Masakhane." Accessed December 16, 2024. https://www.masakhane.io.

Míguez-Bonino, José. "Genesis 11:1–9: A Latin American Perspective." Pages 13–16 in *Return to Babel: Global Perspectives on the Bible*. Edited by John R. Levison and Priscilla Pope-Levison. Louisville: Westminster John Knox, 1999.

NLLB Team, Marta R. Costa-jussà, James Cross, Onur Çelebi, Maha Elbayad, Kenneth Heafield, Kevin Heffernan, Elahe Kalbassi, Janice Lam, et al. "No Language Left Behind: Scaling Human-Centered Machine Translation." arXiv. 2022. https://doi.org/10.48550/arXiv.2207.04672.

Okorie, Chijioke, and Vukosi Marivate. "How African NLP Experts Are Navigating the Challenges of Copyright, Innovation, and Access." *Carnegie Endowment for International Peace*, April 30, 2024. https://carnegieendowment.org/research/2024/04/how-african-nlp-experts-are-navigating-the-challenges-of-copyright-innovation-and-access.

Olasoji, Tolu. "Hey Siri, Lean to Speak Kinyarwanda." *Reasons to Be Cheerful*, July 13, 2021. https://reasonstobecheerful.world/languages-voice-tech-in-africa.

Oyewusi, Wuraola. "AI Literacy in Low-Resource Languages: Insights from Creating AI in Yoruba Videos." arXiv. 2024. https://doi.org/10.48550/arXiv.2403.04799.

Petrosyan, Ani. "Languages Most Frequently Used for Web Content as of January 2024, by Share of Websites." *Statista*. Published October 21, 2024. https://www.statista.com/statistics/262946/most-common-languages-on-the-internet/.

Pratap, Vineel, Andros Tjandra, Bowen Shi, Paden Tomasello, Arun Babu, Sayani Kundu, Ali Elkahky, Zhaoheng Ni, Apoorv Vyas, et al. "Scaling Speech Technology to 1,000+ Languages." arXiv. 2023. https://doi.org/10.48550/arXiv.2305.13516.
Rad, Gerhard von. *Genesis: A Commentary*. Rev. ed. OTL. Philadelphia: Westminster, 1972.
Readable. "The Lix and Rix Readability Formulas." Accessed December 16, 2024. https://readable.com/readability/lix-rix-readability-formulas.
Rendtorff, Rolf. "Genesis 8:21 und die Urgeschichte des Yahwisten." *KD* 7 (1961): 69–78.
Seargeant, Philip. "Is Artificial Intelligence about to Free Us from the Curse of Babel?" *New Scientist*, December 27, 2023. https://www.newscientist.com/article/mg26034711-700-is-artificial-intelligence-about-to-free-us-from-the-curse-of-babel.
SIL AI and NLP. "Projects." Accessed December 16, 2024. https://ai.sil.org/projects.
SIL AI and NLP. "Scripture Forge." Accessed December 16, 2024. https://ai.sil.org/projects/scriptureforge.
SIL AI and NLP. "SIL's AI Ethics Statement." Accessed December 16, 2024. https://ai.sil.org/ethics.
SIL Global. "FLExTrans: Machine Translation Software." Accessed December 16, 2024. https://software.sil.org/flextrans.
Simons, Gary F. "The Impact of On-Site Computing on Field Linguistics: The Power of Man and Machine in Interaction." *Notes on Linguistics* 16 (1980): 17–26. http://bit.ly/onsite-computing.
Simons, Gary F. "Language Diversity: Curse or Blessing?" Pages 27–44 in *God and Language: Exploring the Role of Language in the Mission of God*. Edited by Michael Greed and Dawn Kruger. Dallas: SIL International, 2021.
Simons, Gary F., Abbey L. Thomas, and Chad K. White. "Assessing Digital Language Support on a Global Scale." arXiv. 2022. https://doi.org/10.48550/arXiv.2209.13515.
Taylor, Florence. "Persecuted Christians Are Risking Their Lives to Translate the Bible into Their Local Language." *Christian Today*, February 11, 2016. https://www.christiantoday.com/article/persecuted.christians.are.risking.their.lives.to.translate.the.bible.into.their.local.language.
Translation Commons. "Language Digitization Initiative." Accessed December 16, 2024. https://translationcommons.org/language-digitization.
UNESCO Ad Hoc Expert Group on Endangered Languages. "Language Vitality and Endangerment." Paper presented at the International Expert Meeting on the UNESCO Programme Safeguarding of Endangered Languages, Paris, 2003. https://unesdoc.unesco.org/ark:/48223/pf0000183699.
Walker, Dan, and Barry Soutar. "How AI Is Helping Māori Recover Their Own Voices." Microsoft News. Posted July 2, 2024. https://news.microsoft.com/en-nz/2024/07/02/how-ai-is-helping-maori-recover-their-own-voices.
Walton, John H. *Wisdom for Faithful Reading: Principles and Practices for Old Testament Interpretation*. Downers Grove: InterVarsity, 2023.
Warren-Rothlin, Andy. "Source Texts, Source Languages, Technology, and Values." *BT* 62 (2011): 240–6. https://doi.org/10.1177/026009351106200405.
Weishaupt, Cassie. "Wycliffe Philippines Trip Report," 2023. https://bit.ly/silai-wp-workshop.
Wenham, Gordon J. *Genesis 1–15*. WBC 1. Dallas: Word, 1987.
Whitcomb, John. "Babel." *Creation* 24.3 (2002): 31–3.

Wong, Matteo. "The AI Revolution Is Crushing Thousands of Languages." *The Atlantic*, April 12, 2024. https://www.theatlantic.com/technology/archive/2024/04/generative-ai-low-resource-languages/678042.

Wright, Christopher J. H. *The Mission of God: Unlocking the Bible's Grand Narrative*. Downers Grove: IVP Academic, 2006.

Wycliffe Bible Translators. "New Churches Forming in Madagascar." Posted June 7, 2024. https://www.wycliffe.org/blog/posts/new-churches-forming-in-madagascar.

Zaccagnino, Flor. "'Traduttore, Traditore' and Translating the Untranslatable." *Bunny Studio* (blog). Posted April 6, 2020. https://bunnystudio.com/blog/traduttore-traditore-and-translating-the-untranslatable.

Zhu, Shaolin, Leiyu Pan, and Deyi Xiong. "FEDS-ICL: Enhancing Translation Ability and Efficiency of Large Language Model by Optimizing Demonstration Selection." *Information Processing and Management* 61.5 (2024): 103825. https://doi.org/10.1016/j.ipm.2024.103825.

6

AI Copilot and Bible Translation

Asking the Right Questions

Randall Tan

The foundational premise of this chapter is that any evaluation of how to apply AI to Bible translation should always be done in the context of the big picture. Once we have in mind a global picture of the situation, we are better positioned to ask the right questions about any specific initiative's wisdom or lack thereof. Throughout this chapter, I will use the pronoun "we" in an inclusive way, inviting you, the reader, to imagine yourself participating in the journey as we explore the big picture in Bible translation, the use of AI copilots in general, and the application of this technology to Bible translation. We will begin with a global overview of Bible translation. Then, we will briefly survey the potential shown by AI copilots in adjacent fields. With this context in place, we will focus on efforts to implement AI copilot functionality in Bible translation. The Translator's Copilot project will serve as a case study of the questions and challenges an ongoing project should answer to apply AI to advance Bible translation successfully.[1]

The Big Picture in Bible Translation

What is the state of Bible translation? Where were we before, and where are we now? In 1934, only 10 percent of the world's languages had some Scripture.[2] As recently as 1999, Wycliffe's leaders estimated it would take another 150 years to begin a Bible translation for each of the world's languages.[3] In response, Wycliffe USA boldly adopted a God-sized vision to start translation in every language by the year 2025 (Vision 2025).[4] Momentum accelerated in 2010 when the Every Tribe Every Nation (ETEN) collective impact alliance was born. In a spirit of unprecedented unity, Bible translation organizations (including Wycliffe) and resource partners joined forces to drive toward the ETEN All Access Goals (AAGs) by the year 2033. The ETEN AAGs are:

95% of people will have full access to the Bible.

99.96% will have access to the New Testament.

100% will have access to some portion of Scripture.

100 of the world's most strategic written languages will be available in two useable translations.[5]

How many languages do we need to translate the Bible into to reach all these people? To provide some perspective, there are an estimated 7,400 living languages as of March 2024. In 2024, 50 percent of all living languages (approximately 3,700) have some Scripture. Many projects are still in progress, having published some Scripture (e.g., a portion or the New Testament). However, they have not yet reached their full goal (which could be a New Testament or a Full Bible). Only 744 have a full Bible (approximately 10 percent).[6] Besides reaching the full goal for ongoing projects with some published Scripture, do we still need to translate the Bible into 3,700 additional languages to meet the AAGs? Actually, no. The AAGs are defined by the number of people with access, while the access figures above deal with the number of languages. A disproportionate number of people speak the major languages of the world, so, in practice, a much smaller number of languages cover the vast majority of the world's population. Moreover, more than one-third of the remaining 3,700 languages are considered non-vital and do not need Scripture translated.[7] (In essence, a language is considered to be non-vital when it is unlikely to continue to be used as a means of communication in various social contexts.) That leaves less than two-thirds, the majority of which now have work in progress. In order to meet the ETEN goals, the translation projects currently in progress must finish before 2033.[8] Furthermore, we have to begin work on the language projects that have not yet started (just over 800 as of March 2025) and complete them before 2033.

At first glance, the number of projects not yet started does not seem intimidating, given how many projects are already in progress. However, it raises the question of whether there is enough time to complete this task by 2033. Answering another question might help answer the first: How long does it usually take to translate the whole Bible or the New Testament? According to Illuminations, a full Bible takes approximately sixteen years, and a New Testament approximately seven years.[9] Thankfully, most remaining projects are for New Testaments or portions (with a goal of about twenty-five chapters, with many choosing to focus on the Gospel of Luke). With nine years until 2033 as of this writing, if all remaining projects begin within the next year or two and finish in seven years or less, those (as-yet-future) projects would meet the goal.

Viewed from the above perspective, the overall picture starts to look promising. However, are we currently on track to achieve the AAGs? In early 2020, the ETEN leadership analyzed the trajectory and concluded that the answer was "not yet." They tasked a committee to determine "what must change." The committee recommended changes around four themes:

1. Bolster unity and alignment.
2. Broaden involvement (of other organizations/participants).
3. Fuel innovation.
4. Sharpen planning and implementation.[10]

Efforts to innovate and broaden involvement originate from this need to change the trajectory and align pace with goals.

How did ETEN determine that translation work is not on pace? One way is to track how many chapters of the Bible translation teams complete in a year across all active Bible translation projects compared to the number of chapters we must complete each year to stay on pace for 2033. Recent trends indicate that the speed of projects in progress currently falls short. Regularly updated estimates from ProgressBible suggest we need a two to threefold increase in the annual pace of total chapters translated.[11] When the remaining languages where work has not begun start contributing chapters, the number of chapters translated each year will increase substantially. However, this alone will not fully make up the necessary difference. Some of the recommendations of the "what must change" committee (e.g., around the themes of fueling innovation and broadening involvement) ultimately led to the formation of the ETEN Innovation Lab. ETEN tasked the Lab with applying advanced technology to the translation process and radically broadening involvement to help achieve the acceleration needed to accomplish the AAGs.[12]

In order to meet our goals, what needs to change? Do all existing projects need to finish two to three times faster? The simple answer is "no." First, doubling or tripling speed is an unrealistic expectation for most projects as a general rule. Second, even if a given team could finish in half or one-third of their current projected time, that same team cannot proceed to work on a second or third language they do not speak. Each translation project requires a team that speaks that specific language.

Could we tackle the problem by increasing the number of projects rather than speeding up existing projects? Given that there are just over eight hundred languages with translation needs that have not yet started, it seems promising to have all remaining projects with a "New Testaments and portions" goal started soon. If each new project could finish by 2033, this potential solution would go a long way toward making up the chapters-per-year gap.[13]

Now that the picture is a little clearer, what kind of acceleration do we need for existing and new projects? Given that we have nine years or less remaining for both existing and as-yet-future projects, a good general answer would seem to be: (a) Start all remaining projects by 2026; and (b) meet or beat the pace of average New Testament translation projects (i.e., seven years). Despite all the progress made since Wycliffe launched Vision 2025 in 1999 and ETEN started driving toward the 2033 AAGs, this remains a God-sized challenge. Among other things, we must apply innovative technology and effectively support a vastly expanded Bible translation labor pool.

The Potential of AI Copilots

What current technological advancements hold the most promise for effectively supporting a much larger labor pool in Bible translation and helping them complete their work faster? One obvious candidate is generative artificial intelligence, which has rapidly emerged as a potentially transformative technology. Studies indicate that generative AI helps people accomplish some types of everyday tasks more efficiently and frees them to think creatively and tackle more complex tasks themselves.[14] Generative AI is also undergoing rapid adoption and proliferation of use—"the large language model (LLM) ChatGPT debuted in November 2022, and by March 2024 the most common generative AI tools were being accessed by hundreds of millions of users each month. . . . Two years after the mass introduction of generative AI, its adoption rate already exceeds that of the PC and internet at comparable points in time."[15] Instead of looking at generative AI in general, we will focus on the specific application of generative AI in copilots. AI copilots are advanced virtual assistants that leverage AI, especially LLMs, to assist users in completing tasks more efficiently and effectively. A popular example of a copilot is Microsoft 365 Copilot.

Why is the metaphor of a copilot used for this type of AI? The metaphor suggests a human-AI partnership where AI assists the human pilot, in that the copilot:

- Operates under human direction and oversight.
- Can communicate in a fluid, conversational manner, allowing for natural and complex interaction.
- Can be assigned some degree of agency and intrinsic motivation in working toward shared goals.
- Has a broad scope for problem-solving, but also has a specific set of skills that can supplement as well as complement those of the pilot.
- Can act as a backup for the pilot, helping to monitor a situation and taking over tasks as and when needed.[16]

How can AI copilots be effective? How do they work? They are designed to enhance productivity by automating routine tasks, providing context-aware support, and facilitating seamless communication across various applications and systems. With different degrees of success, they aim to "work seamlessly with existing tools and workflows" for a wide variety of users. The goal is to provide "real-time assistance without disrupting the user's work process."[17]

Visions for digital assistants transforming the workplace and everyday life are not new. They have been around since at least the 1980s. However, for decades, those visions have fallen far short of realization. Clippy, Microsoft's pioneering virtual assistant in the late 1990s, was perhaps the most notorious example. Clippy "didn't know who you were, what your name was, or what goals you were trying to achieve. . . . Although advanced for its time, the functionality of the Microsoft Office assistant was lacking, and its memory was poor. . . . Clippy told you what to do. That's it. It never listened." Why did Clippy and other past virtual assistants fail? According to Marco Witzmann, there are at least three reasons these copilots failed to meet expectations in the past:

1. Not understanding users' intentions.
2. Not saving significant time.
3. Not offering anything users could not have done just as efficaciously themselves.[18]

By contrast, recent AI copilots appear to be succeeding where their predecessors failed. They are beginning to meet the following criteria identified by Witzmann for a great copilot by leveraging ever-improving LLMs:

1. Understanding (more often than not) user intent.
2. Saving significant time.
3. Helping users complete tasks more effectively or efficiently.
4. Integrated into tools people use daily.
5. Helping users enjoy their work more rather than less.[19]

LLMs significantly improve a copilot's ability to understand multiple languages, keep track of conversations in context, and interact with users to clarify intent.[20] As a result, they act like interns who provide capable (though not mistake-free) assistance with some guidance. They save users time on mundane tasks like spell-checking, summarizing, and preforming drafts. They also help with complex tasks like planning, forecasting, and data-based decision-making.[21] For example, LLMs can often provide outputs that are "a great starting point for any process that relies on a loop of rapid creative creation and continuous improvement."[22] One might ask: "Why should teachers, lawyers, programmers, writers or engineers sit down in front of a blank sheet of paper, if they can work with an assistant who provides them with drafts, improves it according to their wishes and takes over the tedious parts of it?"[23] Whatever we are trying to create, if we reduce the time it takes to iterate (assuming we still do what is necessary to maintain quality), we create more in less time.[24]

What are the most promising AI copilots so far? One leading product is GitHub Copilot. As of this writing, more than 77,000 businesses use it, including 1 in 3 Fortune 500 companies.[25] According to a 2023 survey by Stack Overflow (a question-and-answer platform for software development), 55 percent of software developers use it regularly.[26] Let's look at the benefits from the perspective of software developers. GitHub Copilot suggests code completions as you type. You can ask general programming questions or specific questions about your codebase. You can even ask it to suggest code to accomplish particular tasks by using natural language comments or prompts to tell it what you want to do.[27]

Another prominent product is Microsoft 365 Copilot. It helps generate new content, offers relevant suggestions, and helps users complete tasks more effectively and efficiently. Let's look at the benefit from the perspective of Microsoft Office software users. For example, it can help "streamline your email communication by summarizing lengthy email threads and drafting responses."[28] It can identify relevant data and craft naturally phrased and highly relevant recommendations because it analyzes the content of your document, email, or meetings to determine meaning and intent. It also retrieves additional content in real time from all your work data (including communications, activity history, and content) in Microsoft 365.[29]

Do users confirm the usefulness of these AI copilots? The data thus far is encouraging. A McKinsey study shows that software developers can complete some coding tasks up to twice as fast. For example, documenting code can be completed in half the time. Writing first-draft new code can take just over half the time, and optimizing existing code takes slightly over two-thirds of the time.[30] However, task complexity or a developer's lack of experience dramatically reduces the time savings: "Time savings shrank to less than 10 percent on tasks that developers deemed high in complexity due to, for example, their lack of familiarity with a necessary programming framework. A similar result was seen among developers with less than a year of experience."[31]

GitHub's own study found that 88 percent of developers felt more productive (88 percent also reported faster task completion). An even higher 96 percent reported being faster with repetitive tasks. Microsoft's own study found that most Copilot users feel more productive and complete work faster (70 percent and 73 percent, respectively). The vast majority say that Copilot makes getting started on a first draft easier and helps them complete a good first draft faster (87 percent and 85 percent, respectively). The benefits include gains in quality, creativity, and user happiness. A majority of GitHub Copilot users reported less frustration with coding (59 percent) and more fulfillment with their jobs (60 percent). One big takeaway from the GitHub study was that "letting GitHub Copilot shoulder the boring and repetitive work of development reduced cognitive load. This makes room for developers to enjoy the more meaningful work that requires complex, critical thinking and problem-solving, leading to greater happiness and satisfaction."[32] Users of Microsoft 365 Copilot seem to value its importance to their well-being similarly. Once they have worked with it, 77 percent would not give it up. Most reported that it helped them jump-start the creative process and generate ideas while writing (68 percent and 72 percent, respectively). A similar percentage said that it improved the quality of their work (68 percent) and saved them time so they could focus on more important work (67 percent).[33]

In conclusion, AI copilots show immense early promise in helping users flourish while completing their work faster and with more creativity and quality. It seems to come close to being the best of all worlds, which may sound too good to be true. Some healthy skepticism and caution remain warranted. Nevertheless, while we cannot be sure beforehand how well it would do in assisting the work of Bible translation, it seems to be well worth exploring.

The Potential of Translator's Copilot in Bible Translation

The potential of AI and generative AI, in particular, has not escaped notice in the Bible translation world. Many of the active projects supported by the ETEN Innovation Lab explore potential applications of AI to translation drafting and quality assurance.[34] SIL Global (formerly SIL International) has been at the forefront of much of this innovative work. To leverage the emerging abilities of AI copilots, SIL is working on Lynx, a framework to weave AI tools seamlessly into Bible translation editing software.[35] The Innovation Lab and many Bible translation agencies like SIL are embracing the vision that "risks must be taken to test the untested, prove the unproven, equip the unequipped and advance the things that cannot advance without special attention and intentionality."[36] Not all projects will succeed. Some will prove to be more fruitful than others. However, we do not need every project to be a smashing success. We merely need all the projects collectively to help us achieve the acceleration required to meet the AAGs. For this chapter, I cannot cover all the relevant projects. Instead, we will use the Lab-supported Translator's Copilot project as our main case study to explore the potential of AI copilots in Bible translation.

The Rationale for Building on a Mature App

The original question that launched the Translator's Copilot project was: "With no time to lose, can we start taking advantage of cutting-edge AI copilot functionality immediately?" An associated question was: "What is the most expedient way to keep up with the unprecedented, breathtaking pace of AI advancement?"

For the purposes of experimenting with innovative AI copilot functionality, using an existing open-source text editor app rather than building a new one made sense, because it eliminated the need to build a Bible translation editing app first. The choice was made to build initially on top of Visual Studio Code (VS Code), a lightweight, open-source source code editor.[37] VS Code has a proven track record and robust user base, and it has been actively developed since 2015.[38] Every year since 2021, almost three-quarters of software developers actively used it.[39] Furthermore, it has advanced features that are hard and time-consuming to build, such as "mature source control, tested localization, an impressively stable architecture with over 51K published plugins, live sharing for instant remote collaboration, and more."[40]

Paratext 9, the current leading Bible translation software, was not chosen as it is based on old technology unsuitable for AI experimentation. Moreover, its successors, Platform.Bible and Paratext Studio 10, are already in active development.[41] In addition, the extension system for Platform.Bible is very similar to VS Code, so the leaders for the Translator's Copilot project decided to proceed with VS Code because "this path allows us to start iterating right now with the full functionality of VS Code for leveraging AI integrations and innovations in a highly experimental manner, with the hopes of integrating with Paratext in a fairly natural way when our functionality is stabilized and Platform.Bible is further along."[42]

One might assume that Bible translation requires its own specialized software. However, Bible translation is a text-editing endeavor, much like software development. Like developing a codebase, Bible translation is about collaborating, maintaining versions, and ensuring quality. With the free and completely open source (MIT license) features VS Code offers, we can "stand on the shoulders of giants and repurpose what's proven." As a result, we will also be freed up to "channel our energies solely into the specialized challenges of Bible translation."[43]

Are there other advantages to using an existing open-source text editor app as a base? Eliminating the need to build the hard foundational software infrastructure and features is not only a boon to AI experimentation; it also helps local developers working with churches around the world. With VS Code as a base, developers can experiment with and create tailored translation features that their language, church, or community requires.[44]

In summary, VS Code provides (almost) everything a base text editing app needs, and we can adapt it to our specific requirements where necessary. For the Translator's Copilot team, VS Code allowed them to focus on their own AI work without being distracted by the need to build other software features.

The Most Promising Translator's Copilot Features

Broadly speaking, the most promising features of Translator's Copilot provide information management and translation assistance. Information management helps translators by answering questions as well as finding and synthesizing information from existing data sources and tools. Translation assistance offers contextual suggestions for translation and editing. It also can execute basic tasks and workflows for translators.[45] These methods of assistance simplify problem-solving and reduce context-switching.

The question often arises: Can we serve the right knowledge when and where we need it? One of the most critical features is leveraging chat with LLMs. Chat is a familiar and straightforward interface used worldwide. Few (if any) ways of getting information are simpler than messaging with an AI, much like a conversation on SMS, WhatsApp, or Facebook Messenger.[46] For example, when one is at a standstill on a particular problem and does not know how to proceed, one can move forward by chatting with AI to get an immediate answer.[47]

At the same time, users can increasingly use chat to get AI to execute specific tasks and workflows. Users often lack the technical expertise to do what they want to do, but with a chat UI, users who know what they want to do are increasingly gaining the power to do it. While we are only beginning to see this newfound power become a reality, imagine the following scenario (still partially hype at this point) becoming an everyday reality in a not-too-distant future: "If you can just type (or say) the thing you're trying to do, and watch it happen, the barriers fade away. Everyone acquires the expertise, everyone becomes power users, and suddenly the product is a game-changer."[48]

Another vital feature is contextual suggestions, also known as autocomplete or predictive text. This functionality is widely used in search engines, text editors, and mobile devices. Typically, it predicts and suggests the completion of words or phrases as a user types. In platforms like Google, autocomplete helps users complete their search queries quickly by suggesting popular or trending searches based on what they have typed thus far.[49] Similarly, smartphones use predictive text to help users type messages more efficiently by suggesting words as they type.[50] By reducing the amount of typing required to compose a given search or message, these features enable users to enter data and search with more speed.[51] In addition, they minimize spelling errors by suggesting correct words.

Additional Barriers to Overcome

What we have seen from the potential of AI copilots in general and the potential of Translator's Copilot in Bible translation seems very promising. However, are there additional barriers specific to Bible translation? It turns out that there are. This is primarily because most remaining languages that require Bible translations are low-resource languages.

Low-resource languages, by definition, have little to no data that AI can leverage. Without sufficient language data for a specific language, there can be little to no AI support for translation in that language.[52] Many AI approaches to translation rely on transfer learning. This involves training a model on a large data corpus and fine-tuning it on a smaller corpus: "The idea is that the model will have learned some generalizable features from the large corpus, and then it can learn the specific features of the smaller corpus. This is a great approach, but it *still* requires a large corpus of data to train on."[53] Low-resource languages often do not have enough data for these techniques to work.

Can Translator's Copilot significantly accelerate Bible translation when the remaining languages are mostly low-resource languages with little data? One way the Translator's Copilot project has proposed to overcome this barrier is to use in-context learning rather than a fine-tuning or transfer learning approach.[54] In this more iterative and interactive approach, AI predictions would always be based on the current state of the entire translation project. At the same time, human translators would provide ongoing feedback on AI predictions (e.g., accept, reject, or edit).[55] According to Ryder Wishart, there are two benefits of this approach:

> 1. *Bootstrapping*: We can use a small amount of data to generate a large amount of data. This is a huge benefit for low-resource languages, since we can use the data we have (which is not enough for fine-tuning a model) to generate more data, and then use that new data (again, without re-fine-tuning our model) to generate even more data, and so on. This is a virtuous cycle that can help us bootstrap our way to a complete translation.
>
> 2. *Instant Feedback*: We get instant updates, allowing the real translator (a human), to provide feedback to the model on the fly.[56]

Using this technique, we can use a small amount of data (e.g., a few New Testament verses) to generate more data (e.g., the next few New Testament verses or some Old Testament verses with similar content). The threshold for there being sufficient data for meaningful AI assistance in low-resource languages is vastly lowered.

The Translator's Copilot team has also proposed tackling this problem by prioritizing data collection for low-resource languages. As they noted, "For low-resource languages, the technology is ready—it just needs data."[57] Besides developing AI copilot features, they are also working on user-friendly, offline-first language data collection tools.[58] Their experiments include using multimodal representations (e.g., images, audio, text, animations, videos, and simulations) as a bridge between languages.[59] Unlike more traditional data collection efforts, the team is more strategically targeting a much smaller corpus of data (perhaps as little as the equivalent of 3 percent of the Bible).[60]

Another concern is the potential for translators to over-rely on AI and not develop their own critical thinking, expertise in translation, and ability to solve complex problems. This is a common concern when using AI copilots in other fields like software development. As one recent study noted:

> According to students' perceptions, AI code completion could enhance productivity and efficiency, operating as an effective coding tutor throughout the learning process. However, a predominant concern arises regarding over-reliance on these tools, potentially impeding students' abilities to solve complex problems and presenting challenges in academic assessments.[61]

Decades of research on human-machine interaction and collaboration from fields like human-computer interaction (HCI) and human factors engineering (HFE) may provide valuable transferable lessons.[62] Common dangers include

> diminished vigilance, challenges in transferring control, de-skilling, and misplaced trust. To foster a harmonious and productive human-AI partnership, it is imperative to prioritize human agency, keep humans actively engaged, provide opportunities to enhance human skills, design more intelligible AI systems, and employ methods that cultivate an appropriate level of trust in AI output and guidance.[63]

Strategies for Maximizing Potential for Low-Resource Languages

Because Bible translation will mainly involve low-resource languages going forward, a key question becomes: How can we maximize output with minimal input? The key seems to be maximizing both continually advancing AI capabilities and local human expertise. With AI's unprecedented pace of advancement, one key strategy is to position ourselves to take maximum advantage of technological advances. As we have already seen, repurposing the latest open-source technology as much as possible fits this strategy well. It is also necessary to prioritize more iterative and interactive AI approaches with ongoing human feedback, like in-context learning.

Another critical need is to effectively and efficiently gather needed input data. We must productively leverage local expertise because language expertise resides almost exclusively within the local community for many low-resource languages. We should support community-driven projects and potentially allow all language speakers the opportunity to contribute. We should build simple, decentralized applications to empower the widespread participation needed. Given that we start with little and need to bootstrap in a virtuous cycle (creating a self-reinforcing loop of ever-expanding data), we should build in rapid feedback cycles to keep improving.[64] We should leverage AI to provide both translators and the communities providing data and feedback with the real-time information they need. We must deploy AI to help them solve problems and efficiently complete their tasks with minimal context-switching. In so doing, we simultaneously continue to prioritize and support human agency and expertise and reduce the risks of overreliance on AI.

Conclusion

Faced with a God-sized challenge to achieve the 2033 All Access Goals, the Bible translation community needs human intelligence and artificial intelligence working together in tandem to accelerate translation. Many projects that must be started within the next year (or two) could benefit from more user-friendly Bible translation tools that effectively support new translation workers. Projects that are in progress or will begin soon could use help meeting or beating the pace of average New Testament projects.

As we have done throughout this chapter, I invite you again to imagine yourself in the shoes of those working in Bible translation. Translator's Copilot promises to provide the right knowledge right when and where we need it using chat and contextual suggestions. It can begin to remove barriers as all the information we need is at our fingertips. It is hastening the day we can type or say what we are trying to do and see it happen. There is no better way to support a greatly expanded labor pool of new Bible translators than to enable everyone to gain expertise and become power users in these ways. Given its immense potential to accelerate work and support a radical broadening of the Bible translation workforce, it qualifies as a timely and wise application of AI to Bible translation.

Will we see the same level of benefits (including gains in quality, creativity, and user happiness) in Bible translation as we have started to see in software development (e.g., GitHub Copilot) and general office productivity (Microsoft 365 Copilot)? That remains to be seen. The potential is certainly there. Challenges also remain. Data scarcity with low-resource languages is a continuing limitation. The strategy of maximizing both continually advancing AI capabilities and local human expertise sounds promising. Still, it must prove to be effective on a large scale around the world under very different local conditions.[65]

Notes

1 Disclosure: This evaluation was completed independently while I was still employed with Biblica. In the period between finalizing the draft and publication, I started working for the ETEN Innovation Lab as a consultant. This chapter reflects my unbiased assessment conducted before my affiliation with the organization. At the same time, the opinions shared here are my own and do not represent the official views of the ETEN Innovation Lab.

2 ProgressBible, "Scripture Growth," accessed October 14, 2024, https://progress.bible/data.
3 Jonathan Sprowl, "A Bible for Every Language," *Outreach Magazine*, April 30, 2019, https://outreachmagazine.com/features/global/42457-a-bible-for-every-language.html.
4 Wycliffe Bible Translators, "Vision 2025: Achieving a God-Sized Mission," accessed October 14, 2024, https://www.wycliffe.org/vision-2025.
5 ETEN Lab, "ETEN Innovation Lab: Igniting Acceleration in Bible Translation," accessed October 14, 2024, https://www.etenlab.org.
6 ProgressBible, "Scripture Growth."
7 illumiNations, "Frequently Asked Questions," accessed October 14, 2024, https://illuminations.bible/faq notes that the illumiNations alliance (which is the public-facing counterpart of the ETEN alliance) focuses on "6,000+ languages with an estimated vitality that suggests Scripture translation is needed."
8 Plans are already in motion to address separately the relatively few full Bibles that are not on track to be completed by 2033.
9 illumiNations, "Frequently Asked Questions."
10 illumiNations, "Frequently Asked Questions."
11 Note, however, that recent monthly reports showed a sharp increase in monthly chapters completed. If much of this increase is not simply a temporary spike, we may not be far from reaching the pace needed.
12 ETEN Lab, "ETEN Innovation Lab."
13 The rate of new projects is ahead of pace since at least 2022.
14 Rasmus Ulfsnes, Nils Brede Moe, Viktoria Stray, and Marianne Skarpen, "Transforming Software Development with Generative AI: Empirical Insights on Collaboration and Workflow," arXiv, 2024, https://doi.org/10.48550/arXiv.2405.01543.
15 Alexander Bick, Adam Blandin, and David Deming, "The Rapid Adoption of Generative AI," *On the Economy* (blog), Federal Reserve Bank of St. Louis, September 23, 2024, https://www.stlouisfed.org/on-the-economy/2024/sep/rapid-adoption-generative-ai.
16 Abigail Sellen and Eric Horvitz, "The Rise of the AI Co-Pilot: Lessons for Design from Aviation and Beyond," *Communications of the ACM* 67.7 (2024): 19.
17 Adapting the helpful language on aims and goals (while toning down the claims about current realization) from Puru Amradkar, "AI Copilots: Boosting Productivity with GenAI," Aisera, accessed October 15, 2024, https://aisera.com/blog/what-is-ai-copilot.
18 Marco Witzmann, "What Makes a Good AI Co-Pilot? And Why Clippy and Siri Failed at Being One," *Assisted Everything* (blog), posted September 11, 2023, https://assistedeverything.substack.com/p/what-makes-a-good-ai-co-pilot.
19 Witzmann, "AI Co-Pilot."
20 Microsoft 365 Copilot, for example, highlights its ability to understand content and user needs by analyzing your content and additional context from your work data in Microsoft 365 (Microsoft Learn, "Explore How Microsoft 365 Copilot Works," accessed October 15, 2024, https://learn.microsoft.com/en-us/training/modules/introduction-microsoft-365-copilot/3-how-copilot-works).
21 Witzmann, "AI Co-Pilot."

22 Marco Witzmann, "The Age of 'Assisted Everything,'" *Assisted Everything* (blog), posted February 22, 2023, https://assistedeverything.substack.com/p/the-age-of-assisted-everything.

23 Witzmann, "'Assisted Everything.'"

24 Witzmann, "'Assisted Everything.'" A common critique of generative AI is that it reduces quality. However, the humans who use AI remain responsible for maintaining quality. One could argue that quality problems are more a function of humans abusing and over-relying on AI than a problem with the AI itself. Human users must continue to do what is necessary to ensure quality, even when AI can share an increasing amount of the workload.

25 GitHub, "GitHub Copilot: The World's Most Widely Adopted AI Developer Tool," accessed October 15, 2024, https://github.com/features/copilot.

26 Stack Overflow, "2023 Developer Survey," accessed October 15, 2024, https://survey.stackoverflow.co/2023/#most-popular-technologies-ai-dev.

27 Prompts can take the form of questions, statements, responses, or instructions to get the desired result from the LLM.

28 Microsoft Learn, "Microsoft 365 Copilot."

29 Microsoft Learn, "Microsoft 365 Copilot."

30 Begum Karaci Deniz, Chandra Gnanasambandam, Martin Harrysson, Alharith Hussin, and Shivam Srivastava, "Unleashing Developer Productivity with Generative AI," *McKinsey Digital*, June 27, 2023, https://www.mckinsey.com/capabilities/mckinsey-digital/our-insights/unleashing-developer-productivity-with-generative-ai.

31 Deniz, Gnanasambandam, Harrysson, Hussin, and Srivastava, "Unleashing Developer Productivity."

32 Eirini Kalliamvakou, "Research: Quantifying GitHub Copilot's Impact on Developer Productivity and Happiness," *GitHub Blog* (blog), last updated May 21, 2024, https://github.blog/news-insights/research/research-quantifying-github-copilots-impact-on-developer-productivity-and-happiness.

33 Microsoft AI + Productivity Research Team and Microsoft's Office of the Chief Economist, "What Can Copilot's Earliest Users Teach Us About Generative AI at Work?" Microsoft Worklab, posted November 15, 2023, https://www.microsoft.com/en-us/worklab/work-trend-index/copilots-earliest-users-teach-us-about-generative-ai-at-work.

34 See ETEN Lab, "ETEN Innovation Lab Public Dashboard," accessed October 16, 2024, https://etenlab.notion.site.

35 See SIL AI and NLP, "Projects," accessed October 16, 2024, https://ai.sil.org/projects.

36 ETEN Lab, "About Us," accessed October 16, 2024, https://www.etenlab.org/about-us.

37 Microsoft, "Visual Studio Code: Code Faster with AI," accessed October 16, 2024, https://code.visualstudio.com. Theia has recently emerged as a possible alternative (Eclipse Foundation, "The Eclipse Theia Platform," accessed October 21, 2024, https://theia-ide.org). Whether VS Code, Theia, or some other alternative ends up being the more permanent base solution in the future, the premise of adapting an existing base editing platform and not building one's own remains important for focusing on AI copilot functionality rather than building a full-fledged Bible translation text editor.

38 See the history at VS Code Team, “Visual Studio Code 1.0!” *Visual Studio Code* (blog), posted April 14, 2016, https://code.visualstudio.com/blogs/2016/04/14/vscode-1.0/.

39 See, for example, Stack Overflow, “2021 Developer Survey,” accessed October 16, 2024, https://survey.stackoverflow.co/2021#most-popular-technologies-new-collab-tools; Stack Overflow, “2022 Developer Survey,” accessed October 16, 2024, https://survey.stackoverflow.co/2022/#technology-most-popular-technologies; Stack Overflow, “2023 Developer Survey”; and Stack Overflow, “2024 Developer Survey,” accessed October 16, 2024, https://survey.stackoverflow.co/2024/technology#most-popular-technologies-new-collab-tools. By comparison, in 2018, it was just over a third; in 2019, it was just over half (David Ramel, “VS Code and Visual Studio Rock the 2022 Stack Overflow Developer Report,” *Visual Studio Magazine*, June 23, 2022, https://visualstudiomagazine.com/articles/2022/06/23/stack-overflow-2022-survey.aspx).

40 Ryder Wishart, “It Seems Feasible to Fork VS Code for a Bible Translation App,” *Ryder.dev* (blog), accessed October 16, 2024, https://ryder.dev/vs-code-fork-seems-feasible. See also Ryder Wishart, “VS Code as Translator’s Copilot Ecosystem,” *Ryder.dev* (blog), posted September 19, 2023, https://ryder.dev/vs-code-translation.

41 See Platform, “Platform Bible: Create. Collaborate. Translate,” accessed October 16, 2024, https://platform.bible; and Paratext, “Paratext 10 Studio: Modern Bible Translation Software that Grows with Your Team,” accessed October 16, 2024, https://paratextstudio.org.

42 Codex Editor, “Frequently Asked Questions,” accessed October 16, 2024, https://codex-editor.gitbook.io/project-accelerate/project-overview/frequently-asked-questions.

43 Wishart, “VS Code as Translator’s Copilot Ecosystem.”

44 Codex Editor, “Codex Editor,” accessed October 16, 2024, https://codex-editor.gitbook.io/project-accelerate/project-overview/codex-editor.

45 Codex Editor, “What is Translator’s Copilot?” accessed October 16, 2024, https://codex-editor.gitbook.io/project-accelerate/translators-copilot/what-is-translators-copilot.

46 Ryder Wishart, “What’s the Simplest Possible UI for AI?” *Ryder.dev* (blog), accessed October 16, 2024, https://ryder.dev/simplest-possible-ui-for-ai.

47 The process of formulating your question through chat itself has been found to help users “achieve a deeper understanding of the problem and a potential solution.” This is because it has the same effect as explaining your issue to someone (or something) using natural language. See Ulfsnes, Moe, Stray, and Skarpen, “Transforming Software Development.”

48 Des Traynor, “AI-powered UI (aka ‘Return of the Chat’),” Intercom, accessed October 16, 2024, https://www.intercom.com/blog/ai-chatbots-user-interfaces.

49 Jess Peace, “How Google Autocomplete Works,” *Search Engine Land* (blog), posted December 23, 2022, https://searchengineland.com/how-google-autocomplete-works-390257.

50 Francesc Garcia, “How Predictive Text Algorithm Works: All Secrets of Deep Learning,” *Fleksy* (blog), posted June 2023, https://www.fleksy.com/blog/how-predictive-text-algorithm-works-all-secrets-of-deep-learning.

51 In 2018, Google claimed that autocomplete reduced typing by about 25 percent on average (Danny Sullivan, "How Google Autocomplete Works in Search," *The Keyword* (blog), Google, posted April 20, 2018, https://blog.google/products/search/how-google-autocomplete-works-search).

52 Notably, "you cannot translate into a no-resource language" (Codex Editor, "Translator's Copilot").

53 Ryder Wishart, "AI and Low-Resource Translation," *Ryder.dev* (blog), accessed October 16, 2024, https://ryder.dev/translating-with-ai.

54 On in-context learning, see Sang Michael Xie and Sewon Min, "Understanding In-Context Learning," *The Stanford AI Lab Blog* (blog), posted August 1, 2022, https://ai.stanford.edu/blog/understanding-incontext.

55 Codex Editor, "Translation Assistance," accessed October 16, 2024, https://codex-editor.gitbook.io/project-accelerate/translators-copilot/translation-assistance.

56 Wishart, "AI and Low-Resource Translation."

57 Ryder Wishart, "Data Is the Key: A New Era for Bible Translation," *Ryder.dev* (blog), accessed October 16, 2024, https://ryder.dev/data-is-the-bottleneck.

58 Wishart, "Data Is the Key."

59 Ryder Wishart, "Bridging the Gap Between Languages: A New Approach," *Ryder.dev* (blog), accessed October 16, 2024, https://ryder.dev/consensus-translation.

60 The research backing this more targeted approach originates from Zhong Zhou, "Massively Multilingual Text Translation for Low-resource Languages" (PhD diss., Carnegie Mellon University, 2023), https://doi.org/10.1184/R1/24992787.v1.

61 Ulfsnes, Moe, Stray, and Skarpen, "Transforming Software Development."

62 Sellen and Horvitz, "Rise of the AI Co-Pilot," 18–23.

63 Sellen and Horvitz, "Rise of the AI Co-Pilot," 23.

64 Ryder Wishart, "Blank Slate Translation Initiative: Bible Translation in the AI Era," *Ryder.dev* (blog), accessed November 16, 2024, https://ryder.dev/blank-slate-translation.

65 In the period between finalizing the draft and publication, Translator's Copilot is now showing promising results in over fifty projects in different parts of the world.

Bibliography

Amradkar, Puru. "AI Copilots: Boosting Productivity with GenAI." Aisera. Accessed October 15, 2024. https://aisera.com/blog/what-is-ai-copilot.

Bick, Alexander, Adam Blandin, and David Deming. "The Rapid Adoption of Generative AI." *On the Economy* (blog). Federal Reserve Bank of St. Louis, September 23, 2024. https://www.stlouisfed.org/on-the-economy/2024/sep/rapid-adoption-generative-ai.

Bunea, Cristina. "What Clippy Taught Us All." *CommandBLOGUE* (blog). Command AI. Last modified September 11, 2024. https://www.command.ai/blog/what-clippy-taught-us-all.

Codex Editor. "Codex Editor." Accessed October 16, 2024. https://codex-editor.gitbook.io/project-accelerate/project-overview/codex-editor.

Codex Editor. "Frequently Asked Questions." Accessed October 16, 2024. https://codex-editor.gitbook.io/project-accelerate/project-overview/frequently-asked-questions.

Codex Editor. "Translation Assistance." Accessed October 16, 2024. https://codex-editor.gitbook.io/project-accelerate/translators-copilot/translation-assistance.

Codex Editor. "What is Translator's Copilot?" Accessed October 16, 2024. https://codex-editor.gitbook.io/project-accelerate/translators-copilot/what-is-translators-copilot.

Deniz, Begum Karaci, Chandra Gnanasambandam, Martin Harrysson, Alharith Hussin, and Shivam Srivastava. "Unleashing Developer Productivity with Generative AI." *McKinsey Digital*, June 27, 2023. https://www.mckinsey.com/capabilities/mckinsey-digital/our-insights/unleashing-developer-productivity-with-generative-ai.

Eclipse Foundation. "The Eclipse Theia Platform." Accessed October 21, 2024. https://theia-ide.org.

ETEN Lab. "About Us." Accessed October 16, 2024. https://www.etenlab.org/about-us.

ETEN Lab. "ETEN Innovation Lab: Igniting Acceleration in Bible Translation." Accessed October 14, 2024. https://www.etenlab.org.

ETEN Lab. "ETEN Innovation Lab Public Dashboard." Accessed October 16, 2024. https://etenlab.notion.site.

Garcia, Francesc. "How Predictive Text Algorithm Works: All Secrets of Deep Learning." *Fleksy* (blog). Posted June 2023. https://www.fleksy.com/blog/how-predictive-text-algorithm-works-all-secrets-of-deep-learning.

GitHub. "GitHub Copilot: The World's Most Widely Adopted AI Developer Tool." Accessed October 15, 2024. https://github.com/features/copilot.

illumiNations. "Frequently Asked Questions." Accessed October 14, 2024. https://illuminations.bible/faq.

Kalliamvakou, Eirini. "Research: Quantifying GitHub Copilot's Impact on Developer Productivity and Happiness." *GitHub Blog* (blog). Last updated May 21, 2024. https://github.blog/news-insights/research/research-quantifying-github-copilots-impact-on-developer-productivity-and-happiness.

Microsoft. "Visual Studio Code: Code Faster with AI." Accessed October 16, 2024. https://code.visualstudio.com.

Microsoft AI + Productivity Research Team and Microsoft's Office of the Chief Economist. "What Can Copilot's Earliest Users Teach Us About Generative AI at Work?" Microsoft Worklab. Posted November 15, 2023. https://www.microsoft.com/en-us/worklab/work-trend-index/copilots-earliest-users-teach-us-about-generative-ai-at-work.

Microsoft Learn. "Explore How Microsoft 365 Copilot Works." Accessed October 15, 2024. https://learn.microsoft.com/en-us/training/modules/introduction-microsoft-365-copilot/3-how-copilot-works.

Paratext. "Paratext 10 Studio: Modern Bible Translation Software that Grows with Your Team." Accessed October 16, 2024. https://paratextstudio.org.

Peace, Jess. "How Google Autocomplete Works." *Search Engine Land* (blog). Posted December 23, 2022. https://searchengineland.com/how-google-autocomplete-works-390257.

Platform. "Platform Bible: Create. Collaborate. Translate." Accessed October 16, 2024. https://platform.bible.

ProgressBible. "Scripture Growth." Accessed October 14, 2024. https://progress.bible/data.

Ramel, David. "VS Code and Visual Studio Rock the 2022 Stack Overflow Developer Report." *Visual Studio Magazine*, June 23, 2022. https://visualstudiomagazine.com/articles/2022/06/23/stack-overflow-2022-survey.aspx.

Sellen, Abigail, and Eric Horvitz. "The Rise of the AI Co-Pilot: Lessons for Design from Aviation and Beyond." *Communications of the ACM* 67.7 (2024): 18–23.

Shastri, Manasvi. "How AI Search is Revolutionizing eCommerce with Smart Autocomplete and Dynamic Suggestions." *Wizzy* (blog). Posted September 18, 2024. https://wizzy.ai/blog/how-ai-search-is-revolutionizing-ecommerce.

SIL AI and NLP. "Projects." Accessed October 16, 2024. https://ai.sil.org/projects.

Sprowl, Jonathan. "A Bible for Every Language." *Outreach Magazine*, April 30, 2019. https://outreachmagazine.com/features/global/42457-a-bible-for-every-language.html.

Stack Overflow. "2021 Developer Survey." Accessed October 16, 2024. https://survey.stackoverflow.co/2021#most-popular-technologies-new-collab-tools.

Stack Overflow. "2022 Developer Survey." Accessed October 16, 2024. https://survey.stackoverflow.co/2022/#technology-most-popular-technologies.

Stack Overflow. "2023 Developer Survey." Accessed October 15, 2024. https://survey.stackoverflow.co/2023/#most-popular-technologies-ai-dev.

Stack Overflow. "2024 Developer Survey." Accessed October 16, 2024. https://survey.stackoverflow.co/2024/technology#most-popular-technologies-new-collab-tools.

Sullivan, Danny. "How Google Autocomplete Works in Search." *The Keyword* (blog). Google. Posted April 20, 2018. https://blog.google/products/search/how-google-autocomplete-works-search.

Traynor, Des. "AI-powered UI (aka 'Return of the Chat')." Intercom. Accessed October 16, 2024. https://www.intercom.com/blog/ai-chatbots-user-interfaces.

Ulfsnes, Rasmus, Nils Brede Moe, Viktoria Stray, and Marianne Skarpen. "Transforming Software Development with Generative AI: Empirical Insights on Collaboration and Workflow." arXiv. 2024. https://doi.org/10.48550/arXiv.2405.01543.

VS Code Team. "Visual Studio Code 1.0!" *Visual Studio Code* (blog). Posted April 14, 2016. https://code.visualstudio.com/blogs/2016/04/14/vscode-1.0/.

Wishart, Ryder. "AI and Low-Resource Translation." *Ryder.dev* (blog). Accessed October 16, 2024. https://ryder.dev/translating-with-ai.

Wishart, Ryder. "Blank Slate Translation Initiative: Bible Translation in the AI Era." *Ryder.dev* (blog). Accessed November 16, 2024. https://ryder.dev/blank-slate-translation.

Wishart, Ryder. "Bridging the Gap Between Languages: A New Approach." *Ryder.dev* (blog). Accessed October 16, 2024. https://ryder.dev/consensus-translation.

Wishart, Ryder. "Data Is the Key: A New Era for Bible Translation." *Ryder.dev* (blog). Accessed October 16, 2024. https://ryder.dev/data-is-the-bottleneck.

Wishart, Ryder. "It Seems Feasible to Fork VS Code for a Bible Translation App." *Ryder.dev* (blog). Accessed October 16, 2024. https://ryder.dev/vs-code-fork-seems-feasible.

Wishart, Ryder. "VS Code as Translator's Copilot Ecosystem." *Ryder.dev* (blog). Posted September 19, 2023. https://ryder.dev/vs-code-translation.

Wishart, Ryder. "What's the Simplest Possible UI for AI?" *Ryder.dev* (blog). Accessed October 16, 2024. https://ryder.dev/simplest-possible-ui-for-ai.

Witzmann, Marco. "The Age of 'Assisted Everything.'" *Assisted Everything* (blog). Posted February 22, 2023. https://assistedeverything.substack.com/p/the-age-of-assisted-everything.

Witzmann, Marco. "What Makes a Good AI Co-Pilot? And Why Clippy and Siri Failed at Being One." *Assisted Everything* (blog). Posted September 11, 2023. https://assistedeverything.substack.com/p/what-makes-a-good-ai-co-pilot.

Wycliffe Bible Translators. "Vision 2025: Achieving a God-Sized Mission." Accessed October 14, 2024. https://www.wycliffe.org/vision-2025.
Xie, Sang Michael, and Sewon Min. "Understanding In-Context Learning." *The Stanford AI Lab Blog* (blog). Posted August 1, 2022. https://ai.stanford.edu/blog/understanding-incontext.
Zhou, Zhong. "Massively Multilingual Text Translation for Low-resource Languages." PhD diss., Carnegie Mellon University, 2023. https://doi.org/10.1184/R1/24992787.v1.

7

AI and Bible Translation

The Function of Artificial Intelligence in the Social Construction of Biblical Meaning

Ryder A. Wishart

The translation of sacred texts has always been a theological enterprise as much as a linguistic one. When the eternal Word enters human language, as in the incarnational logic of Christianity, it necessarily adopts the cultural-linguistic frameworks through which human communities make sense of their reality. George Lindbeck's cultural-linguistic approach to doctrine provides a compelling theological framework for understanding the profound implications of AI-assisted Bible translation. Lindbeck argues that religions function like languages or cultures, with doctrines serving as "communally authoritative rules of discourse, attitude, and action" rather than merely propositional truth claims or expressions of subjective experience.[1] This perspective offers valuable insight into what happens when AI enters the translation process.

The social construction of reality, as articulated by Peter Berger and Thomas Luckmann, further illuminates what is at stake in Bible translation.[2] They propose that social reality emerges when "language soars into regions that are not only de facto but also a priori unavailable to everyday experience," becoming "the objective repository of vast accumulations of meaning and experience" preserved across generations.[3] Scripture represents precisely such an accumulation of meaning, with translation serving as the mechanism through which these meanings become available to new linguistic communities.

What makes AI-assisted translation particularly significant in this context is its capacity to serve as a mediator of foreign conceptual worlds in ways that individual human translators cannot achieve alone.[4] In Berger and Luckmann's framework,

> Knowledge . . . is at the heart of the fundamental dialectic of society. It "programmes" the channels in which externalization produces an objective world. It objectifies this world through language and the cognitive apparatus based on language, that is, it orders it into objects to be apprehended as reality. It is internalized again as objectively valid truth in the course of socialization.[5]

In other words, knowledge shapes how we externalize meaning, and we gain knowledge through socialization. This process can now be both complicated and enriched by the introduction of AI as a collaborative partner possessing unprecedented access to accumulated human knowledge about biblical texts. This creates a unique dialectic in which the AI, despite its limitations in understanding low-resource languages, serves as a conduit for foreign meanings with a breadth that no single human translator could possess. This collaboration can potentially help translators access the original text's foreign conceptual world more faithfully, reducing the risk of imposing receptor-language cultural frameworks onto biblical texts.

This chapter explores the theological implications of AI in Bible translation through the lens of both weak and strong integration approaches. What emerges is a vision of AI not as a replacement for human theological discernment, but as a powerful tool that, when properly situated within human-in-the-loop (HITL) frameworks, can dramatically accelerate the process through which God's Word becomes accessible to all peoples and languages while potentially enhancing the Scripture's ability to challenge and transform, rather than merely conform to, the receiving culture's symbolic universe. The theological imperative of making Scripture available to every language community thus converges with technological innovation to create new possibilities for how—with regard to both the scope and the mechanics—divine revelation becomes embedded in human cultural-linguistic systems.

Artificial intelligence is on the brink of fundamentally reshaping the field of Bible translation. Its influence will manifest in two distinct yet interconnected ways: by redefining the role of human translators within "human-in-the-loop" frameworks and, in some instances, by replacing human translators altogether. This dual potential promises to deliver unprecedented speed, accuracy, and accessibility, all while striving to preserve the nuanced expertise indispensable for faithfully rendering Scripture.

The core argument of this chapter is that AI can empower local communities in Bible translation when used in a human-centric manner. This empowerment is possible because the most effective approach to integrating AI into Bible translation is not to retrofit AI into existing processes or to rely entirely on automation, but rather to position human stakeholders in executive roles within otherwise autonomous AI systems. This human-in-the-loop approach can dramatically reduce traditional bottlenecks, including the world-building function of language that, in translation, requires habituating a target culture to foreign language, while preserving essential human oversight of theological and cultural elements.

While this proposal draws from the author's consultative experience with over a dozen translation projects employing various degrees of AI assistance, it is important to acknowledge that systematic empirical validation remains a crucial next step. Many innovative translation projects using these approaches are currently private endeavors, limiting the availability of comprehensive data. Therefore, readers should understand this chapter as a theoretical discussion and initial proposal, drawing on available evidence and relevant literature while identifying areas requiring further research and validation.

When considering the integration of AI into Bible translation, two primary approaches are emerging, which I will describe in this manner:

1. Strong role for AI: end-to-end automation
2. Weak role for AI: augmenting existing paradigms

These approaches represent a spectrum of AI's involvement, with the strong role emphasizing transformative independence and the weak role focusing on collaborative enhancement. Each carries distinct implications for how Bible translation is conducted, perceived, and ultimately received by receptor communities.

This chapter will explore these two approaches, examining their strengths, limitations, and the broader implications for the future of Bible translation. By navigating this complex landscape, I aim to highlight the importance of a human-centric approach that balances technological innovation with the irreplaceable value of human expertise.

The discussion will begin by laying out a socio-theological framework for considering the role of AI in the foreignizing knowledge transfer process of translation (i.e., deliberately preserving elements of the source culture rather than adapting them to the target audience's norms), followed by the contextualization of traditional Bible translation practices and their inherent challenges, and then an analysis of AI's technical capabilities and limitations. I will then explore the human-in-the-loop model, examine practical implementation strategies, and address the theological, cultural, and ethical considerations at play. Finally, I will consider the future implications of AI in this important endeavor, concluding with a call to embrace a balanced, hybrid approach that honors both innovation and tradition without overemphasizing the perceived negative trade-offs of a strong AI approach.

AI as an Agent in the Social Construction of Biblical Reality

Berger and Luckmann's framework offers profound insights into how AI becomes not just a tool but an active participant in the social construction of reality when applied to Bible translation. Their concept of externalization, objectivation, and internalization as the three dialectically related moments in the production of social reality provides a lens through which we can understand this novel dynamic.[6] When translators engage with AI systems, they are participating in a unique form of externalization—projecting meaning into the world—but with an intermediary that possesses unprecedented access to accumulated human knowledge about biblical texts and languages.

This process creates a distinctive dialectic in translation work. The human translator externalizes their understanding of the target language and culture, while the AI externalizes a vast repository of linguistic and biblical knowledge gleaned from multiple sources. What emerges is not simply a one-directional transfer of meaning, but a dialogical construction of scriptural meaning within the target language. As

Berger and Luckmann note, society is created by humans and human interaction through processes of "habitualization" where "any action that is repeated frequently becomes cast into a pattern."[7] The interaction between translator and AI establishes new patterns of meaning-making that eventually become habitualized within the receiving community.

The introduction of biblical concepts through AI-assisted translation represents what Berger and Luckmann would identify as a significant intervention in a culture's "symbolic universe." They define symbolic universes as the "sum total" of what "everybody knows," and this totality of knowledge aims to make the institutionalized structure plausible and acceptable for individuals, serving to put everything in its right place within the culture.[8] Scripture translation inherently challenges and expands these symbolic universes, introducing concepts that may have no direct equivalents in the receiving culture.

What makes AI-assisted translation unique in this process is its ability to serve as a conduit for foreign meanings with unprecedented breadth. Unlike human translators who may have limited exposure to biblical scholarship and linguistic resources, large language models trained on vast corpora can bring to bear connections, linguistic insights, and comparative data that no single human translator could hold in memory. This creates a situation where the AI, despite its limitations in understanding low-resource languages, can actually serve as a more comprehensive mediator of foreign biblical concepts than a single human translator working alone.

A particularly significant dynamic emerges in what might be called "knowledge asymmetry" between the human translator and AI system. The human translator possesses deep tacit knowledge of their own language and culture that the AI cannot match. Conversely, the AI has been exposed to more collected knowledge about biblical languages, historical contexts, and translation principles than any individual human translator could acquire in a lifetime. This creates a productive tension where the translator may come to respect and even trust AI predictions about foreign material, recognizing that the AI's breadth of exposure compensates for what it lacks in cultural fluency.

This trust relationship represents a novel form of what Berger and Luckmann might call "legitimation"—a process that justifies and explains institutional meanings. In their framework, legitimation "explains the institutional order by ascribing cognitive validity to its objectivated meanings" and "justifies the institutional order by giving a normative dignity to its practical imperatives."[9] When human translators grant cognitive authority to AI systems for certain aspects of translation work, they are participating in a new form of legitimation process that acknowledges the AI's unique position in the knowledge economy of biblical translation.

Perhaps most significantly, the AI in this context becomes a fundamental factor for novelty in the social reality of the target language. Berger and Luckmann's concept of "internalization"—whereby the "objectivated social world is retrojected into consciousness in the course of socialization"—takes on new dimensions when mediated through AI translation systems. The AI introduces foreign meanings and essentially imports a foreign world into a new culture, facilitating a form of cross-cultural internalization that would be significantly more limited without its intervention.

This transformative potential aligns with what Berger and Luckmann identify as the power of language to transcend everyday reality. They note that "language is capable of transcending the reality of everyday life altogether" and can "span discrete spheres of reality."[10] AI-assisted translation amplifies this transcendent capacity of language, enabling biblical concepts to cross not only linguistic but conceptual boundaries with greater fluidity, bringing divine revelation into dialogue with cultural contexts it might otherwise penetrate only through extensive time and effort on the part of the translator.

The resulting translation becomes neither purely human nor purely artificial but represents a new synthesis, a socially constructed scriptural reality that emerges from this unique collaboration. This process does not merely transfer meaning from one language to another; it fundamentally transforms both the receiving language and the community's relationship to divine revelation. The biblical message, mediated through this AI-human partnership, enters the community not as a foreign imposition but as a collaboratively constructed reality that both respects local linguistic patterns and faithfully represents the original sacred text. In this way, AI becomes not just a tool for translation but an active participant in the community's ongoing construction of their religious and cultural reality—a profound theological development that merits careful consideration as we navigate the integration of artificial intelligence into the sacred work of Bible translation.

This theological framework helps us reexamine traditional Bible translation practices and their inherent challenges with a fresh perspective, illuminating how AI might address long-standing bottlenecks while preserving the essential human participation that Lindbeck's cultural-linguistic approach and Berger and Luckmann's social constructivism both might suggest is indispensable to authentic religious communication.

Traditional Bible Translation: Context and Challenges

Bible translation has historically been characterized by rigorous methodological requirements and extensive oversight mechanisms, primarily coordinated through established translation agencies. The Forum of Bible Agencies International (FOBAI) guidelines, which represent a current standard for most established Bible translation organizations (e.g., Wycliffe, Biblica, and others), emphasize accuracy, cultural sensitivity, and community involvement while mandating specific procedural requirements that significantly impact translation timelines and costs.[11]

Traditional Bible translation typically requires approximately sixteen years and one million dollars per language,[12] largely due to constraints inherent in established methodologies. These constraints involve three key areas: consultant dependencies, training requirements, and procedural mandates.

The most significant bottleneck stems from consultant requirements. Translation consultants must possess expertise in biblical languages, linguistics, theology, and intercultural communication, yet there are fewer than 300 trained consultants worldwide to serve thousands of languages and tens of thousands of dialects requiring translation.[13] This scarcity may also be exacerbated by agency-specific certification requirements that limit consultant sharing across organizations.

Training requirements present another substantial challenge. FOBAI guidelines mandate extensive training for mother-tongue translators in areas including biblical exegesis, linguistics, and translation principles. Additionally, translation teams must develop proficiency with specialized software tools like Paratext, the primary technology platform for text translations. These training requirements, while crucial for quality assurance, significantly extend project timelines, often requiring a week or more of in-person training for a translation team.

Procedural mandates further impact translation speed. The established workflow requires multiple rounds of community checking, consultant reviews, and iterative refinement. While these steps ensure accuracy and community acceptance, they necessarily require substantial time investments, particularly when coordinating across different stakeholders and geographical locations.

While these rigorous requirements aim to contribute to higher quality initial translations, they rest on two questionable assumptions. First, that an extensive, resource-intensive process will produce a "superior" translation—though all translations, no matter how carefully crafted, remain interpretive works that reflect choices and compromises.[14] Second, that such a translation, once completed, will serve its community for generations. This assumption overlooks the dynamic nature of language itself; vocabulary, idioms, and cultural references evolve significantly within a single generation, potentially rendering portions of a translation less effective over time.[15] This development of languages also extends to both the phonic and graphic conventions in receptor cultures. Additionally, while consultants have played a crucial role in ensuring that translations remain faithful to the original text, there is no reason that AI tools cannot fulfill numerous quality-control functions as well as drafting and editing tasks.

The software industry faced similar challenges decades ago, ultimately rejecting the notion that extensive upfront planning and development in a highly staged process (the "waterfall" planning approach) would produce superior results.[16] While this analogy should not be pushed too far—Bible translation involves unique theological and cultural considerations that differentiate it from software development—it suggests the possibility of more iterative approaches that maintain high standards while reducing traditional bottlenecks.

In an era where consumers can run sophisticated language models on personal computers, the proposition of embarking on sixteen-year translation projects using methodologies designed for a pre-AI world demands critical examination. While the FOBAI guidelines' emphasis on accuracy and cultural sensitivity remains vital, their implementation through resource-intensive, linear processes may no longer represent the most effective path forward. The availability of powerful AI tools suggests the possibility of more dynamic, iterative approaches that could maintain high standards while dramatically reducing the time and resources required for Bible translation.

Understanding AI's Role in Translation

Current AI translation approaches span a spectrum from basic sequence-to-sequence models to sophisticated large language models (LLMs), each offering different capabilities for Bible translation. Sarker claims traditional sequence-to-sequence models excel at direct translation tasks but struggle with cultural nuances and idiomatic expressions, making them better suited for augmenting human translators rather than replacing them.[17] More advanced LLMs demonstrate enhanced capabilities in handling complex linguistic phenomena, including context-dependent features like deixis, ellipsis, and lexical cohesion.[18] However, even these sophisticated models face significant challenges in capturing the artistic and cultural nuances essential for literary translation.[19] Part of the perceived challenge of Bible translation is the stakes understood by parties typically involved in this work. Theological and doctrinal considerations can come to dominate discussions of Bible translation, and doctrinal implications may have a significant impact on the perceived overall quality of a Bible translation. Despite this complexity, it is important to recognize that translation is fundamentally a linguistic task. The primary requirement for any translation, including that of sacred texts, is the accurate (though approximate) representation of source language meanings in the target language. A translation that achieves linguistic fidelity will, by implication, preserve the theological content of the original text, though theological considerations are themselves not solely tied to individual texts divorced from their larger cultural contexts. This principle suggests that AI systems should be evaluated primarily on their ability to handle complex linguistic phenomena rather than on abstract theological criteria.

Overall, these claims suggest that while end-to-end automation might offer compelling advantages in speed and scale, a more measured approach that preserves human agency while leveraging AI capabilities may better serve the specific demands of Bible translation. A human-in-the-loop model, which positions human expertise at key decision points within an otherwise automated system, could offer a promising middle ground—one that maximizes AI's efficiency while maintaining the critical oversight needed for theological accuracy and cultural authenticity for long- or complex-document translation tasks. Such an approach would differ significantly from both full automation and mere AI augmentation, instead creating a new paradigm where human wisdom guides AI capabilities rather than either dominating or serving them.

The Human-in-the-Loop Model

The Human-in-the-Loop model represents an important model for machine translation, integrating human expertise with artificial intelligence capabilities. One well-known instance of this approach is in semi-autonomous driving. Though an autonomous vehicle may drive itself, humans are often strategically poised to intervene in order to steer clear of hazards the AI may not correctly attempt to avoid. In the context of machine translation, this approach fundamentally operates by having large language models generate initial translations, which are subsequently refined through systematic human feedback. This feedback is then preserved in a database or retrieval system, enabling continuous improvement through in-context learning and domain-specific adaptation.[20]

The implementation of HITL methodology offers substantial benefits for translation quality and accuracy. In literary contexts, human involvement proves crucial for preserving nuanced cultural elements and artistic integrity that AI alone might miss. This is particularly evident in cases where cultural context and literary expression are essential to the translation's success.[21] Beyond mere preservation of meaning, the HITL approach enables sophisticated quality assessment through human annotation, allowing for detailed error analysis and categorization that surpasses traditional automated metrics.[22]

Empirical evidence supporting the effectiveness of HITL approaches can be found in several notable case studies. In literary translation, research by Škobo and Petričević comparing human and AI translations of Srđan Valjarević's "Lake Como" demonstrates the critical role of human expertise in maintaining literary quality.[23] In technical domains, Yang et al.'s research reveals HITL's superior performance in specialized terminology translation, such as the precise rendering of technical terms like "Handbuch" to "Handbook" in IT documentation.[24] Furthermore, in language documentation efforts, Palmer's work with the Uspanteko language illustrates how HITL approaches can enhance annotation efficiency while maintaining linguistic accuracy.[25]

These diverse applications demonstrate that the HITL model successfully bridges the gap between automated efficiency and human expertise, offering a robust framework for high-quality translation work across various domains. The model's adaptability to different contexts, from literary works to technical documentation, underscores its versatility as a translation methodology that maintains high standards while leveraging technological advantages.

The HITL approach holds particular promise for Bible translation, where theological precision and cultural sensitivity are paramount. By positioning human translators and community experts at the center of the process, the HITL model ensures that cultural nuances, theological implications, and community values guide the translation process from the outset. At the same time, by not merely retrofitting AI into existing workflows, this human-centric approach stands in contrast to AI-in-the-loop methodologies, which often attempt to insert AI capabilities into established processes. Such retrofitting can lead to workflow inefficiencies, resistance from translators, and missed opportunities for true human–AI synergy. Furthermore, the HITL model's emphasis on continuous feedback and adaptation aligns well with the iterative nature of Bible translation, where community input and theological review are essential components of the translation journey.

Implementation and Impact

The successful implementation of human-in-the-loop translation systems requires careful consideration of workflow design, training methodologies, and evaluation metrics. This section examines how organizations have effectively structured these systems, the measurable benefits they have achieved, and the challenges they have encountered in scaling these solutions.

Workflow Integration and System Architecture

Successful HITL translation systems have developed sophisticated workflows that balance automation with human oversight through a three-phase process of generation, refinement, and adaptation. At the core of these systems are large language models that generate initial translations, which are then enhanced through structured feedback mechanisms. This feedback, whether from human experts or automated systems simulating human input, serves as a crucial supervision signal that improves both immediate and future translations through in-context learning.[26]

The workflow architecture typically consists of three key components: a decoding phase where the machine translation system processes the source text, a correction phase incorporating user feedback, and an adaptation phase where post-edited translations contribute to an expanding knowledge base. This structure is specifically designed to minimize necessary human interactions while maximizing translation quality. One particularly effective implementation uses the kNN-over-kNN (KoK) method, a non-parametric online learning approach that leverages human feedback without requiring modifications to the underlying model architecture.[27]

To enhance translation accuracy in specialized contexts, successful systems employ K-shot demonstrations and proven retrieval methods such as BM25 and BM25 Re-Rank. These techniques help identify and apply relevant translation examples, particularly valuable in domain-specific scenarios where terminology precision is crucial.[28] This approach has proven especially effective in technical fields, where contextual accuracy and terminology consistency are paramount.[29] This approach is currently being leveraged with reported success in over fifty languages (including low-resource languages) in the Codex Translation Editor application.[30]

Implementation Challenges

HITL translation systems face several significant technical and cultural hurdles. A primary limitation lies in the difficulty of conveying domain-specific preferences through in-context learning demonstrations. Organizations have addressed this by developing specialized feedback mechanisms that enhance domain adaptation without requiring full model retraining.[31]

Cultural-specific items (CSIs) present a particular challenge, especially when direct equivalents are absent in target languages. Recent work incorporating external knowledge sources and specialized metrics like CSI-Match has shown promise in improving both accuracy and cultural sensitivity.[32] This challenge is compounded in low-resource languages, where the scarcity of native speakers in prompt development can perpetuate cultural biases. Some organizations have responded by prioritizing the development of multilingual datasets and culture-specific harm detection systems.[33]

The translation of figurative and idiomatic language remains particularly challenging, even with advanced HITL systems. Success in this area has come from carefully balancing machine efficiency with human expertise, especially in contexts requiring deep cultural understanding.[34]

These implementation experiences reveal that successful HITL translation systems depend less on technological sophistication than on thoughtful integration with human workflows and cultural contexts. While technical challenges persist, particularly around domain adaptation and cultural nuance, the evidence suggests that well-designed HITL systems can effectively balance automation with human oversight. The key to scaling these systems lies not in perfecting the underlying models, but in developing flexible frameworks that empower human stakeholders to guide and refine the translation process according to their community's needs and standards.

Theological and Cultural Considerations

Human oversight plays an indispensable role in verifying theological accuracy in AI-assisted translations. According to Zaid and Bennoudi's research, human translators consistently outperform AI in maintaining the depth and meaning of religious texts, particularly due to their nuanced understanding and contextual relevance.[35] While AI tools offer efficiency advantages, they require human expert verification to avoid mistranslations and ensure theological fidelity.

There are significant challenges in maintaining appropriate cultural sensitivity in AI-assisted translation, particularly for religious and literary texts.[36] This challenge is more nuanced than simply preserving meaning; in Bible translation, certain "foreignizing" elements may be intentionally preserved or introduced to maintain theological precision and cultural authenticity. For instance, the historical tradition of transliterating terms like "baptism" (βαπτισμός) rather than using cultural equivalents has been theologically motivated.[37] AI systems like ChatGPT and Google Translate, focused on fluency and natural language, often struggle with these nuanced decisions about when to preserve foreign elements and when to adapt them.[38]

Venuti describes a tension between foreignization and domestication in translation, whether the translation is domesticating, aiming to "[bring] the author back home," or whether it is foreignizing, "sending the reader abroad."[39] This tension becomes particularly acute when dealing with concepts or cultural practices that might seem confusing or even offensive to the target culture. The goal of Bible translation is not merely to make the text accessible, but to accurately convey the historical and cultural context of the original text, even when that context challenges modern sensibilities. Current AI systems, trained to optimize for fluency and acceptability—particularly in terms of avoiding offensive "alignment" issues—tend to smooth over these important cultural distinctives, resulting in translations that risk losing essential theological and cultural depth.[40] For instance, AI models tuned for modern concepts of gender equality may not translate biblical directives for wives without adequate prompting driving them to adhere to the text (e.g., Eph. 5:22-24; Col. 3:18; 1 Pet. 3:1-2).

Research reveals complex dynamics in fostering community acceptance of these translation choices as well. Documentary approaches have historically struggled to build trust with communities, often due to predominantly academic focuses. Flavelle and Lachler emphasize the importance of cross-disciplinary collaboration between computational linguists, documentary linguists, and indigenous communities in navigating these decisions about cultural preservation versus adaptation.[41]

These considerations raise significant ethical challenges beyond the usual concerns of algorithmic bias and data privacy.[42] The evolving nature of AI platforms introduces additional complexity, as changes in model versions can affect how cultural and theological nuances are handled, potentially impacting the consistency and reproducibility of translation decisions.[43]

Future Implications

The emergence of AI-enabled translation technologies promises to fundamentally reshape access to Scripture, particularly for historically underserved language communities. These tools extend beyond simple word-for-word conversion, offering the potential for more nuanced translations that preserve theological depth while improving accessibility. This advancement could democratize access to religious texts, enabling individuals to engage with Scripture in their native languages without waiting decades for traditional translation processes.[44]

AI translation tools show promise in addressing long-standing challenges in language documentation and processing, especially for indigenous languages that have historically lacked comprehensive corpora or standardized versions. The flexibility of modern AI systems enables adaptation to dialectal and communal variations, potentially facilitating translations that better reflect local linguistic and cultural contexts.[45] Looking beyond the official list of ISO-639 languages for ultra-low-resource scenarios, the benefits of AI translation tools seem particularly promising. However, realizing this potential requires thoughtful collaboration between AI systems and human experts. Engagement with linguists and community leaders from diverse linguistic backgrounds remains crucial for ensuring translations that are both accurate and culturally appropriate. This collaborative approach suggests a future where AI accelerates translation work while maintaining essential cultural specificity and linguistic distinctiveness.[46]

The path forward likely involves balancing technological innovation with community empowerment. While AI tools can dramatically reduce translation timelines and costs, their successful implementation depends on meaningful partnership with local communities and careful attention to cultural and theological nuances. This balanced approach could transform Bible translation from a decades-long, resource-intensive process into a more dynamic, community-driven endeavor that maintains high standards while dramatically improving accessibility.

Conclusion

As we consider the integration of AI into Bible translation, we return to the fundamental theological question that has animated this exploration: How does divine revelation become embedded within human cultural-linguistic systems? Lindbeck's perspective offers profound insight here. If religions function as languages (or cultures) with doctrines functioning as rules or regulations that allow or forbid certain truth claims and practices, then translation is not merely about converting words but about enabling new communities to participate in a divinely instituted discourse—albeit in a new language. A culture may learn this foreign doctrinal grammar, but it requires the injection of expert knowledge, since knowledge mediates social reality. AI-assisted translation, particularly through human-in-the-loop approaches, represents a promising development in how this discourse can expand across linguistic boundaries.

The social construction of reality reminds us that humans create an understanding of reality through interactions and communications with others. Scripture translation participates in this reality-constructing function, providing communities with frameworks for understanding their relationship to God, creation, and one another. When AI enters this process, it does not stand outside these meaning-making systems but becomes incorporated within them as a uniquely positioned mediator. The knowledge asymmetry between human translators and AI systems—where translators possess deep cultural fluency while AI offers unprecedented breadth of exposure to biblical scholarship—creates a productive tension that can potentially enhance translation quality and theological fidelity rather than diminishing it.

In this framework, AI becomes not just a tool but an active participant in what Berger and Luckmann describe as the "externalization, objectivation, and internalization" cycle through which social reality is constructed.[47] By mediating foreign biblical concepts with greater comprehensiveness than individual human translators could achieve alone, AI helps introduce new elements into a community's "symbolic universe," potentially enabling the biblical text to maintain more of its challenging foreignness rather than being domesticated to fit existing cultural paradigms. This novelty preserves the Scripture's capacity to transform, rather than merely conform to, the receiving culture, even while its linguistic forms necessarily flex to express these meanings.

As we move forward, the challenge is not to resist technological innovation but to ensure that it serves the ultimate purpose of translation: enabling communities to encounter divine revelation in ways that transform both individual lives and communal identities. When AI is positioned to empower local communities through the human-in-the-loop model, it becomes not a secularizing force but a potential instrument through which the divine Word continues to become flesh in the languages of all peoples while retaining its capacity to challenge and transform. The ancient theological imperative of translating Scripture thus finds new expression in an age of artificial intelligence—not as a compromise of translation integrity, but as an enhancement of our ability to make biblical texts accessible while preserving their transformative power.

The integration of AI into Bible translation represents more than a mere technological upgrade—it offers an opportunity to fundamentally reimagine how Scripture becomes accessible to communities worldwide. This chapter demonstrates that while both strong and weak AI approaches offer certain advantages, a human-in-the-loop model that positions human stakeholders in executive roles within otherwise autonomous systems provides, arguably, the most promising path forward that mitigates objections and maximizes leverage. This approach maintains the essential human oversight needed for theological and cultural fidelity while leveraging AI's capabilities for rapid, scalable translation.

The implications of this shift extend beyond mere efficiency gains. By reducing traditional bottlenecks in drafting, consultation, and review processes, AI-enabled translation could transform Bible translation from a centralized, resource-intensive endeavor into a more dynamic, community-driven process. This transformation, however, requires careful attention to implementation strategies that are effective. At this point, the technology seems to demand a process that preserves human agency while maximizing efficiencies. The time has come to move beyond both the constraints of traditional translation methodologies and the limitations of ad-hoc AI integration. Instead, we must embrace approaches that position human wisdom at the helm of powerful AI systems, ensuring that technological innovation serves rather than supplants human expertise in the vital work of Bible translation, while recognizing the fact that AI mobilizes the near-totality of discursive human knowledge to date—more than any translator could possibly know about the Bible, its world, cultures, languages, history, etc. The translator thus remains the expert with regard to the need, but AI is rapidly becoming the means of resolving that need.

Notes

1 George A. Lindbeck, *The Nature of Doctrine: Religion and Theology in a Postliberal Age*, 25th anniv. ed. (Louisville: Westminster John Knox, 2009), 18.

2 Here I will chiefly rely on Peter L. Berger and Thomas Luckmann, *The Social Construction of Reality: A Treatise in the Sociology of Knowledge*, Penguin Social Sciences (1967; repr., London: Penguin, 1991); for a recent overview of the significance and reception of Berger and Luckmann (including dimensions in which their work has been eclipsed in modern academic discourse), see Kenneth J. Gergen, "The Social Construction of Reality: Traces and Transformation," in *Social Constructivism as Paradigm? The Legacy of the Social Construction of Reality*, ed. Michaela Pfadenhauer and Hubert Knoblauch (London: Routledge, 2019), 259–69.

3 Berger and Luckmann, *Social Construction of Reality*, 55, 52.

4 *Foreign*, here, is meant to refer to meanings that have perhaps never been made in the culture in question. There are many such candidate meanings in the Bible—for instance, battering rams, shepherding terms, wine, levirate marriage, sacrificial systems, phylacteries, snow metaphors, idioms like "gird up your loins," references to the heart as the seat of thought, ancient units like cubits or shekels, and political-religious roles like Pharisees. Translators often respond with descriptive phrasing, footnotes, glossaries, or cultural substitutions, each with trade-offs between clarity and fidelity.

5 Berger and Luckmann, *Social Construction of Reality*, 83–4.

6 Berger and Luckmann, *Social Construction of Reality*, 78–9.

7 Berger and Luckmann, *Social Construction of Reality*, 70–1.

8 Berger and Luckmann, *Social Construction of Reality*, 83.

9 Berger and Luckmann, *Social Construction of Reality*, 111.

10 Berger and Luckmann, *Social Construction of Reality*, 54.

11 In making these observations about traditional Bible translation, I draw on two documents in particular, FOBAI's "Basic Principles and Procedures for Bible Translation" and "Statement of Qualifications for Translation Consultants," which can both be found at "Translation Standards," Forum of Bible Agencies International, 2017, https://forum-intl.org/resources/translation-standards.

12 The Sagamore Institute, funded by the Maclellan Foundation on behalf of the illumiNations Resource Partners, found that the average project cost of a complete written Bible translation is $937,446 and takes 15.8 years to complete; see "A Study of Cost and Use of Funds in Bible Translation," Sagamore Institute, 2022, quoted in Warren Cole Smith, "Sagamore Institute Study Attempts to Quantify the Cost of Bible Translation," Ministry Watch, September 14, 2022. This report on Bible translation costs is cited from Ministry Watch due to the original source no longer being available through standard repositories. While Ministry Watch is not a peer-reviewed outlet, it appears to have preserved key details of a report that may have been removed from circulation, perhaps owing to sensitivities or controversy surrounding its content. The citation is used here with appropriate caution, as no official explanation for the report's withdrawal has been given. An apparently original copy of the PDF report was uploaded to archive.org at the following URL: https://archive.org/details/sagamore-institute-study-copy-9.12.22-copy.

13 An exact figure for the number of translation consultants and consultants-in-training is not published anywhere, but this number is gleaned from conversations with individuals at several Bible translation organizations including SIL, Biblica, Faith Comes by Hearing, and Seed Company.
14 As Lawrence Venuti says, "the translator [must] choose between a domesticating method, an ethnocentric reduction of the foreign text to target-language cultural values, bringing the author back home, and a foreignizing method, an ethnodeviant pressure on those values to register the linguistic and cultural difference of the foreign text, sending the reader abroad"; see *The Translator's Invisibility: A History of Translation* (London: Routledge, 1995), 20.
15 John H. McWhorter, *The Power of Babel: A Natural History of Language* (New York: HarperCollins, 2003), 219–34. McWhorter (224) notes that "writing sits still while speech moves on," in reference to the effect that writing has on slowing down the pace of language change. Apart from ready access to written texts, languages change significantly even within one generation.
16 Cf. Steve McConnell, *Rapid Development: Taming Wild Software Schedules* (Redmond: Microsoft Press, 2006), 136.
17 Suprateek Sarker, "What If the IS Discipline Were Multilingual? AI Translation and the Future of Science," in *ICIS 2024 Proceedings* (Bangkok: Association for Information Systems, 2024), 3–4.
18 Longyue Wang, Chenyang Lyu, Tianbo Ji, Zhirui Zhang, Dian Yu, Shuming Shi, and Zhaopeng Tu, "Document-Level Machine Translation with Large Language Models," arXiv, 2023, https://doi.org/10.48550/arXiv.2304.02210.
19 Milena Z. Škobo and Vedran D. Petričević, "Navigating the Challenges and Opportunities of Literary Translation in the Age of AI: Striking a Balance Between Human Expertise and Machine Power," *Društvene i Humanističke Studije* 8.2 (2023): 19–21, https://doi.org/10.51558/2490-3647.2023.8.2.317.
20 Xinyi Yang, Runzhe Zhan, Derek F. Wong, Junchao Wu, and Lidia S. Chao, "Human-in-the-Loop Machine Translation with Large Language Model," arXiv, 2023, https://doi.org/10.48550/arXiv.2310.08908.
21 Škobo and Petričević, "Navigating the Challenges," 330–2.
22 Patrick Fernandes et al., "The Devil Is in the Errors: Leveraging Large Language Models for Fine-Grained Machine Translation Evaluation," arXiv, 2023, https://doi.org/10.48550/arXiv.2308.07286.
23 Škobo and Petričević, "Navigating the Challenges," 317–19.
24 Yang et al., "Human-in-the-Loop Machine Translation," 8–10.
25 Michael Ginn and Alexis Palmer, "Robust Generalization Strategies for Morpheme Glossing in an Endangered Language Documentation Context," in *Proceedings of the 1st GenBench Workshop on (Benchmarking) Generalisation in NLP* (Singapore: Association for Computational Linguistics, 2023), 97–8.
26 Yang et al., "Human-in-the-Loop Machine Translation," 1–2.
27 Yang et al., "Human-in-the-Loop Machine Translation," 10–11.
28 Yang et al., "Human-in-the-Loop Machine Translation," 6–8.
29 Yang et al., "Human-in-the-Loop Machine Translation," 8–10.
30 https://codexeditor.app.
31 Yang et al., "Human-in-the-Loop Machine Translation," 1–2.

32 Binwei Yao, Ming Jiang, Diyi Yang, and Junjie Hu, "Empowering LLM-Based Machine Translation with Cultural Awareness," arXiv, 2023, https://doi.org/10.48550/arXiv.2305.14328.
33 Artūrs Kanepajs, Vladimir Ivanov, and Richard Moulange, "Towards Safe Multilingual Frontier AI," arXiv, 2024, https://doi.org/10.48550/arXiv.2409.13708.
34 Škobo and Petričević, "Navigating the Challenges," 14–16.
35 Abdelali Zaid and Hanan Bennoudi, "AI vs. Human Translators: Navigating the Complex World of Religious Texts and Cultural Sensitivity," *IJLLT* (2023): 2–4, 8–10, https://doi.org/10.32996/ijllt.2023.6.11.21.
36 Manotar Tampubolon and Bernadetha Nadeak, "Artificial Intelligence and Understanding of Religion: A Moral Perspective," *IJMMU* 11 (2024): 906–7.
37 David Bentley Hart, trans., *The New Testament: A Translation*, 2nd ed. (New Haven: Yale University Press, 2023), xxv.
38 Škobo and Petričević, "Navigating the Challenges," 14–16.
39 Venuti, *Translator's Invisibility*, 20.
40 Zaid and Bennoudi, "AI vs. Human Translators: Navigating the Complex World of Religious Texts and Cultural Sensitivity," 8–10.
41 Darren Flavelle and Jordan Lachler, "Strengthening Relationships Between Indigenous Communities, Documentary Linguists, and Computational Linguists in the Era of NLP-Assisted Language Revitalization," in *Proceedings of the First Workshop on Cross-Cultural Considerations in NLP (C3NLP)*, ed. Sunipa Dev, Vinodkumar Prabhakaran, David Ifeoluwa Adelani, Dirk Hovy, and Luciana Benotti (Dubrovnik, Croatia: Association for Computational Linguistics, 2023), 1–2, https://doi.org/10.18653/v1/2023.c3nlp-1.4.
42 Škobo and Petričević, "Navigating the Challenges," 3–5.
43 Wang et al., "Document-Level Machine Translation," 10–11.
44 Sarker, "If the IS Discipline Were Multilingual?" 4–6.
45 Flavelle and Lachler, "Strengthening Relationships," 2–3.
46 Sarker, "If the IS Discipline Were Multilingual?" 3–4.
47 Berger and Luckmann, *Social Construction of Reality*, 78–9.

Bibliography

Berger, Peter L., and Thomas Luckmann. *The Social Construction of Reality: A Treatise in the Sociology of Knowledge*. Penguin Social Sciences. 1967. Repr., London: Penguin, 1991.

Fernandes, Patrick, Daniel Deutsch, Mara Finkelstein, Parker Riley, André F. T. Martins, Graham Neubig, Ankush Garg, Jonathan H. Clark, Markus Freitag, and Orhan Firat. "The Devil Is in the Errors: Leveraging Large Language Models for Fine-Grained Machine Translation Evaluation." arXiv. 2023. https://doi.org/10.48550/arXiv.2308.07286.

Flavelle, Darren, and Jordan Lachler. "Strengthening Relationships Between Indigenous Communities, Documentary Linguists, and Computational Linguists in the Era of NLP-Assisted Language Revitalization." Pages 25–34 in *Proceedings of the First Workshop on Cross-Cultural Considerations in NLP (C3NLP)*. Edited by Sunipa Dev, Vinodkumar Prabhakaran, David Ifeoluwa Adelani, Dirk Hovy, and Luciana Benotti.

Dubrovnik: Association for Computational Linguistics, 2023. https://doi.org/10.18653/v1/2023.c3nlp-1.4.

Forum of Bible Agencies International. "Basic Principles and Procedures for Bible Translation," April 2017. https://forum-intl.org/wp-content/uploads/2019/03/FOBAITranslationBasicPrinciplesandProceduresApril2017.pdf.

Forum of Bible Agencies International. "Statement of Qualifications for Translation Consultants," 2024. https://forum-intl.org/wp-content/uploads/2024/04/Statement-of-Qualifications-for-Translation-Consultants-revision-2024.pdf.

Gergen, Kenneth J. "The Social Construction of Reality: Traces and Transformation." Pages 259–72 in *Social Constructivism as Paradigm? The Legacy of the Social Construction of Reality*. Edited by Michaela Pfadenhauer and Hubert Knoblauch. London: Routledge, 2019.

Ginn, Michael, and Alexis Palmer. "Robust Generalization Strategies for Morpheme Glossing in an Endangered Language Documentation Context." Pages 89–98 in *Proceedings of the 1st GenBench Workshop on (Benchmarking) Generalisation in NLP*. Edited by Dieuwke Hupkes, Verna Dankers, Khuyagbaatar Batsuren, Koustuv Sinha, Amirhossein Kazemnejad, Christos Christodoulopoulos, Ryan Cotterell, and Elia Bruni. Singapore: Association for Computational Linguistics, 2023. https://doi.org/10.18653/v1/2023.genbench-1.7

Hart, David Bentley, trans. *The New Testament: A Translation*. 2nd ed. New Haven: Yale University Press, 2023.

Kanepajs, Artūrs, Vladimir Ivanov, and Richard Moulange. "Towards Safe Multilingual Frontier AI." arXiv. 2024. https://doi.org/10.48550/arXiv.2409.13708.

Lindbeck, George A. *The Nature of Doctrine: Religion and Theology in a Postliberal Age*. 25th anniv. ed. Louisville: Westminster John Knox, 2009.

McConnell, Steve. *Rapid Development: Taming Wild Software Schedules*. Redmond: Microsoft Press, 2006.

McWhorter, John H. *The Power of Babel: A Natural History of Language*. New York: HarperCollins, 2003.

Sagamore Institute. "A Study of Cost and Use of Funds in Bible Translation." Sagamore Institute, 2022. Quoted in Warren Cole Smith, "Sagamore Institute Study Attempts to Quantify the Cost of Bible Translation." Ministry Watch, September 14, 2022.

Sarker, Suprateek. "What If the IS Discipline Were Multilingual? AI Translation and the Future of Science." In *ICIS 2024 Proceedings*. Bangkok: Association for Information Systems, 2024.

Škobo, Milena Z., and Vedran D. Petričević. "Navigating the Challenges and Opportunities of Literary Translation in the Age of AI: Striking a Balance Between Human Expertise and Machine Power." *Društvene i Humanističke Studije* 8.2 (2023): 317–36. https://doi.org/10.51558/2490-3647.2023.8.2.317.

Tampubolon, Manotar, and Bernadetha Nadeak. "Artificial Intelligence and Understanding of Religion: A Moral Perspective." *IJMMU* 11 (2024): 903–14.

Venuti, Lawrence. *The Translator's Invisibility: A History of Translation*. London: Routledge, 1995.

Wang, Longyue, Chenyang Lyu, Tianbo Ji, Zhirui Zhang, Dian Yu, Shuming Shi, and Zhaopeng Tu. "Document-Level Machine Translation with Large Language Models." arXiv. 2023. https://doi.org/10.48550/arXiv.2304.02210.

Yang, Xinyi, Runzhe Zhan, Derek F. Wong, Junchao Wu, and Lidia S. Chao. "Human-in-the-Loop Machine Translation with Large Language Model." arXiv. 2023. https://doi.org/10.48550/arXiv.2310.08908.
Yao, Binwei, Ming Jiang, Diyi Yang, and Junjie Hu. "Empowering LLM-Based Machine Translation with Cultural Awareness." arXiv. 2023. https://doi.org/10.48550/arXiv.2305.14328.
Zaid, Abdelali, and Hanane Bennoudi. "AI vs. Human Translators: Navigating the Complex World of Religious Texts and Cultural Sensitivity." *IJLLT* 6.11 (2023): 173–82. https://doi.org/10.32996/ijllt.2023.6.11.21.

8

Render to AI What Is AI's

Elizabeth Robar

Throughout history, technological advances have served as the vehicles for radical paradigm shifts.[1] It has often been observed that the printing press, with its revolutionary ability to disseminate information, served as a catalyst for Reformation-era religious dissent. Distribution of information in print enabled a more indelible and far-reaching impact of ideas than ever before.[2] With the Bible printed in its original languages and, with increasing frequency, translated into the vernacular as well, ordinary people could read the Scriptures for themselves—and debate their meaning.

Martin Luther exemplified this transformation: his understanding of the Bible and his personal convictions regarding what it meant—rather than the institutional authority of the Church—became the guiding compass for his life. Equipped with the newly printed Greek New Testament, Luther could assert regarding biblical interpretation, "'Tis always better to see with one's own eyes than with those of other people."[3] The Roman Catholic Church recognized the significance of the shift taking place in the world around them: knowledge, once mediated by religious hierarchy, was becoming something personally encountered, interpreted, and contested. They recognized the need to respond (as exemplified in the Council of Trent) by buttressing their own doctrinal distinctives, in contrast to the rising tide of unmediated biblical interpretation represented in Protestant teachings.

Today, society is facing another paradigm-shifting technological moment: the rise of generative artificial intelligence (AI). As with past technological revolutions, this one is reshaping how people think, work, and communicate. Many rightly fear that we lack the foresight or wisdom to grasp its full implications—and such uncertainty naturally breeds anxiety.

Such transformative disruptions not only impact matters of thought and inquiry, but also have drastic implications on practical daily life. In the thirteenth and fourteenth centuries, Benedictine monks advanced revolutionary innovations in the field of the mechanical clock,[4] with the original purpose being to precisely regulate the rhythms and routines of ritual devotion in the monastery.[5] Yet, these innovations, meant for regulating devotion, later helped enable industrialization by synchronizing and standardizing working hours. Neil Postman notes the sad irony: the pursuit of devotion to God resulted in innovation that also became a tool in service of Mammon.[6] AI promises a similar combination of well-intentioned promises and potential pitfalls.

And, as with every major societal change, there will be ripple effects that accompany the progress. Things will be gained and things will be lost.

It can be helpful to think of AI (such as ChatGPT) as an unreliable graduate student—brilliant, but erratic. Sometimes, it comes to work inebriated. It holds a vast reservoir of knowledge, often jumbled, and can sound strikingly authoritative. Sometimes it produces what we recognize as profound insight; other times, utter nonsense. It is undeniably useful, but not yet trustworthy on its own. Like any powerful tool, it can be harnessed for extraordinary good, and—if misused—it can disfigure the very thing it aims to serve.

In my own sphere, the pressing question is the role of AI in Bible translation. A broad coalition of Bible translation organizations has committed to a daunting global campaign to make Scripture available to every language group by 2033. Such a goal is patently unattainable through traditional workflows alone. AI translation is seen as a critical game-changer, offering the possibility of accelerating translation and reaching countless people groups with Scripture in their vernacular.[7] At the same time, many fear that involving AI could strip the translation process of its human and spiritual dimensions, producing texts that are technically sound but spiritually hollow—devoid of the transformative power of the living Word.[8]

The burning question within the Bible translation world is: What role can AI play in generating a translation that meets the standards of quality that would be expected in a traditional workflow, in terms of clarity, accuracy, and naturalness?[9] Can AI *drafting* be the foundation of a translation that is trusted, usable, and considered authoritative by a local community?

Stewardship and the Process of Bible Translation

This chapter rests on a core conviction: Human beings are stewards of the technology that God has entrusted to them. God has endowed humanity with dominion over all creation (Ps. 8:6-8); yet this is a delegated authority that will ultimately require an accounting to the Lord (Lk 12:48b). This stewardship over creation includes the innovations of the created beings that make up humanity. As in the case of the printing press, such scientific and technological advancement has the potential to create seismic shifts in the ways we interact with the world. When it comes to artificial intelligence, we must not abdicate our human responsibility. It may be a truism to say we must not resist it reflexively nor embrace it uncritically, but that makes our task no easier: to engage it purposefully.

In order to navigate AI's potential greatest contributions within Bible translation, we must first distinguish between two related but fundamentally different things: the *process* of Bible translation and the *product* of Bible translation.

A completed Bible translation, from the original Hebrew, Aramaic, and Greek, may be the fruit of years—sometimes decades—of labor by a devoted translation team. The published text is the product, but it is not the process itself. This distinction matters.

The translation process often includes community engagement, iterative feedback, linguistic and theological debate, and spiritual discernment. These elements shape both the words on the page and the communal ownership of the finished text.

For the purposes of this chapter, however, we will set aside the sociological and communal dimensions of the translation *process*—important though they are—and focus instead on the nature of the text itself, the *product*. Specifically, the question at hand is: What role can AI play in accelerating the end *product*—that is, a faithful translation of the biblical text? What would be required to produce a translation that is indistinguishable, in both quality and contextual fidelity, from one created by native-speaking translators over a ten-year process—yet produced in a fraction of the time and at a fraction of the cost?

The hypothetical situation is that a translation that once required one million dollars and ten years to complete might, through AI augmentation, be produced in one year for $50,000 without sacrificing quality. For the sake of the argument, let us posit that the translation, the *product*, would be embraced by the community—perhaps even seen as a gift from fellow speakers in exile, sending the Scriptures home. Is it possible for a drastically shorter, AI-assisted *process* to produce such a *product*?

Truly *Artificial* Intelligence: Style without Meaning

By now, it is widely understood that AI does not think as humans do. Generative AI—such as ChatGPT—does not possess understanding, awareness, or reasoning.[10] What it does is reproduce variations on patterns. It does not innovate in the human sense, though it can appear to do so, by recombining known patterns in ways that feel novel. It cannot grasp logical relationships, such as cause and effect. It operates entirely at the level of form, not content—appearance, not essence.

If tasked to write an academic essay with a bibliography, it may produce a text that looks perfectly polished—complete with citations and footnotes. Yet upon inspection, many of those citations might not refer to actual sources, but only conform to the expected format of scholarly reference. The output is plausible, not factual—convincing, not true.

Richard Feynman once recounted an experience where he mimicked the sounds and intonations of Chinese so convincingly that a fluent speaker of the Mandarin dialect believed he could speak Cantonese.[11] In reality, he had no idea what he was saying; he was reproducing only the phonetic shell of the language. It sounded like Chinese, but was utterly devoid of meaning. In the same way, generative AI can simulate intelligence, fluency, and even insight without any actual comprehension. It is form without substance, pattern without understanding. Ge Wang, a Stanford computer musician, captures this distinction as well: Generative AI, he notes, is increasingly adept at presentation—at grasping and reproducing *style*—but remains entirely incapable of *meaning*.[12]

Many of the concerns about AI stem from a failure to honor this distinction. When the style of a human is mistaken for an actual human—or worse, treated as a legitimate substitute—it becomes inherently dehumanizing.[13] Likewise, when the stylistic trappings of biblical idioms are mistaken for spiritual substance, the result is a hollowing out of the very text that Bible translators claim to value. Communicating *meaning*, in the context of Bible translation, requires both exegetical decision-making in interpreting the source text (in Hebrew, Aramaic, and Greek) as well as contextual fluency in how the translation will be received in the receptor language (on which, much more below).[14] These are matters of reasoning and judgment rather than correspondences in form. Meaning is embodied in form but cannot be reducible to form. Until AI has contextual fluency in all receptor languages, human discernment remains the only means of contextualizing.

The Need: Contextualization

Effective Bible translation, which preserves the *meaning* of the text, relies on this concept of contextualization—the recognition that concepts must be communicated differently in different cultural and linguistic settings in order to be rightly understood. A message that is clear in one language or culture may be misunderstood (or even reversed) in another, unless careful work is done to reshape its form while preserving its meaning. Mark Strauss recounts the experiences of a Bible translator in Guatemala who would draft translated portions of Scripture for his team of native language consultants. When asked, "Does this make sense?" the consultants would typically respond, "Yes." However, when asked, "Is this how you would say it?" they would almost always say, "No!"[15] In other words, while the translation was acceptable in *form*—an area in which AI excels—it missed the contextualized nuance needed to be fully accepted by the target audience. It required human interaction and feedback for the Bible translator to refine his translation.[16]

Why Contextualization Matters

Abstract terms provide classic examples of the need for contextualization. In biblical Hebrew, *ʾerek ʾappayim* (אֶרֶךְ אַפַּיִם), the expression for God being "slow to anger," literally states he has a "long nose"—an idiom evoking the physical image of someone taking time to flare their nostrils in anger (e.g., Exod. 34:6).[17] In English, it might be said that someone "has a long fuse," drawing upon a different metaphor to convey a similar concept. However, as Dallaire observes, most English translations do not distinguish between the *external* expression of anger of *ʾerek ʾappayim* (אֶרֶךְ אַפַּיִם); the *inner feeling* of anger, as expressed with the term *ḥarah* (חָרָה); and the *outward (or relational) expression* of wrath, expressed with *qaṣap* (קָצַף).[18] While such distinctions might not be considered crucial in English, other cultures possess differing sensibilities with respect to the very concept of anger, thus requiring differing approaches to contextualized meaning.[19]

Without contextualization, such idioms can either become lost or dangerously misleading. As a teenager, I read that, "I [God] have loved Jacob but Esau I have hated"

(Mal. 1:2-3 NIV). Naturally, I understood this through an emotional lens: Jacob must have pleased God, while Esau annoyed him. God must have wanted to be near Jacob and far from Esau. But as I grew older and began studying the biblical narrative more closely, this simple reading began to unravel. Esau, after all, was profoundly blessed in his lifetime. The chiefs and kings of Edom—his descendants—appeared in abundance well before any royal lineage emerged from Jacob. It was Jacob who suffered hardship, wandering, and conflict for generations before receiving his promised inheritance.

What became clear, particularly through the lens of biblical scholarship, was that "love" and "hate" in this context do not denote *emotional* preference but *covenantal* commitment.[20] God chose Jacob as the long-term vessel of his redemptive plan and, by contrast, rejected Esau from that role. Yet he still blessed Esau, abundantly and visibly. God's allegiance was with Jacob, not because he despised Esau emotionally, but because his purposes lay elsewhere. He was taking care of Esau only to clear the way for Jacob's destiny.

This misreading came from importing my English expectations into a Hebrew framework. I took familiar emotional categories and imposed them onto words whose meaning depended on an entirely different conceptual world. The result was that, in the absence of contextualization, I came away with precisely *the opposite expectations from the biblical text:* all blessing for Jacob, all judgment for Esau (when the reality was far more complex). Based strictly on lexical correspondence, the translations of *love* and *hate* are perfectly legitimate—as evidenced by the fact that the vast majority of English versions use these renderings. However, they fail to contextualize, which explains, for example, the NET Bible's rendering of "I *chose* Jacob and *rejected* Esau" (emphasis added).

If the translation is intended to be understood by average English speakers without access to special resources, this is an example of *human* failure in the translation process, illustrating the challenges of translation apart from any involvement of AI. Contextualization is the difference between a lexically legitimate translation and a contextually accurate translation; it recognizes the discrepancy between the lexical meaning of words and their contextual connotations. Contextualization remains the largest hurdle in Bible translation.

A Test Run: Nursery Rhyme and Sonnet Adaptations

There are domains, however, where contextualization is already well established—where the rules of the form are familiar, and the patterns clearly documented. In such cases, AI excels. English nursery rhymes, for instance, offer a highly structured genre that AI can reproduce with remarkable ease.

Take Psalm 1. Below is an AI-generated nursery rhyme adaptation:

The Happy Tree
(A Psalm 1 Nursery Rhyme)
Happy is the one who knows
Not to follow where sin goes.

Doesn't walk with wicked feet,
Doesn't stop on sinner's street.
Doesn't sit where mockers play—
He turns his heart the other way.

He loves God's Word, both day and night,
It makes his thinking strong and right.
Like a tree near water deep,
He grows tall and doesn't sleep.
Fruit in season, leaves so green,
He's the happiest you've seen!

But the wicked? Like the dust—
Blown by winds and lost in gust.
They won't stand when judgment's near,
Won't belong when God draws near.
For God will guard the righteous way,
But wicked paths will blow away.[21]

This version captures much of Psalm 1's structure and imagery: the opening beatitude ("Happy is the one"), the progression of sin (walk, stand, sit), the flourishing tree by the water, and the vivid contrast with the wicked, who are like chaff in the wind. It is accessible, memorable, and even lyrical. What it *misses*, however, is the deep meditative quality of Psalm 1—a psalm that is itself a meditation on earlier Scripture, echoing Genesis, Deuteronomy, Joshua, Jeremiah, and Malachi. It also loses the layered allusions and theological weight of the concept of "meditating day and night" on God's instruction. One might consider a nursery rhyme would, by definition, not be meditative, but in truth they are masterful meditations clothed in child's play.[22] Perhaps AI captured the lighthearted style while missing the depth of meaning.

Nevertheless, the rhyme does capture the stark wisdom dualism of Psalm 1: either one delights in God's instruction or walks in wickedness. There is no middle way. The poetic form invites participation, particularly from parents and children who might repeat such rhymes. And while the line "he grows tall and doesn't sleep" may initially seem odd (even undesirable for parents of young children!), the brain instinctively seeks coherence and will likely reinterpret the phrase metaphorically—as describing continual growth rather than literal insomnia.[23]

With the same effort, AI can also generate a Shakespearean sonnet based on Psalm 1:

Upon the Blessed Path
(A Sonnet on Psalm 1) Blessed is he who shuns the scorner's chair,
Nor treads where sinners stroll in sly disguise,
But finds his joy in YHWH's law most fair,
And on its truth both day and night he sighs.

He is a tree by streams of water fed,
Whose leaves stay green, whose fruit comes in its time.
In drought or storm, he lifts his verdant head—
His works shall stand; his life, a rooted rhyme.

Not so the wicked: chaff before the wind,
They drift, unmoored, beneath the judgment's eye.
[No seat have they where righteous men have sinned]
No seat have they where righteous stand within,
For God upholds the just, but lets fools die.

[Two roads diverge: one leads to withering breath,
The other walks with God and laughs at death.]
One path is watched by God and firmly stayed,
The other fades, and withers into shade.[24]

The Shakespearean sonnet is a more complicated form, with its quatrains in iambic pentameter and a strict rhyme scheme—the first quatrain introducing the theme, the second expanding, the third offering a twist, and the final couplet delivering the conclusion. The *form* is captured adequately by AI, but—as can be seen from the text in square brackets, which had to be rejected—this formal reproduction is sometimes achieved at the expense of the meaning. The line, "No seat have they [the wicked] where righteous men have sinned," makes no sense; the point of the original text is that the righteous have *not* sinned in the same way as the wicked (Ps. 1:1). The rendering is thus factually inaccurate. The original closing couplet ("Two roads diverge . . . ") describes the differing fates of the wicked and righteous as, on the one hand, a *withering breath* for the wicked—combining both the disappearing chaff with the wind that blows it away—and, on the other hand, walking with God and *laughing at death* for the righteous. This is poetically inaccurate: the syntax of the lines in Ps. 1:6 underscores "the way of the righteous" as being under God's intimate care, thus rendering incongruous the mocking, triumphant tone of the sonnet's *laughing at death*.[25]

The same prompt for a nursery rhyme was made for Psalm 2, yielding a similarly successful adaptation:

God's King on Zion
(A Nursery Rhyme for Psalm 2)
The kings all gathered, bold and proud,
They muttered secrets, fierce and loud.
"Let's break their ropes! We won't obey!
No more rules—we'll have our way!"

But God in heaven, on His throne,
He laughed and made His power known:

"My King is set on Zion high,
He stands where earth [*and*] meets the sky."

The King then said, "I'll tell the plan—
God called me Son, and I began.
He said the world would be my land,
With iron rod held in my hand."

"If rebels rise and disobey,
They'll break like pots of fragile clay.
But listen now—there's still a chance!
So turn around, don't miss the dance!"
"Be wise, you kings, and learn to fear,
Rejoice with trembling—God is near!
Come kiss the Son, and you'll be blessed,
Find refuge [*safe*], and you'll find rest."[26]

This version captures the psalm's four-movement structure: rebellion, divine response, royal decree, and final warning.[27] The metaphorical phrasing—"He stands where earth [*and*] meets the sky"—is a poetic flourish that misfires, as does "Find refuge [*safe*]," which is grammatically awkward. But such flaws are easily correctable and the overall result is impressive. The rhyme preserves core theological content while rendering it in a genre appropriate for children.

This is the Shakespearean sonnet generated by AI for Psalm 2.

Why Do the Nations Rage?
(A Sonnet on Psalm 2)
Why do the nations rage; in vain revolt,
Their kings aligned against the Lord Most High?
They cast His bonds aside with proud assault,
Yet heaven's throne resounds with holy cry.

The Lord laughs loud, then speaks in wrathful fire:
"Behold, on Zion's hill, My King is crowned!
You are My Son, My own—My heart's desire—
Ask Me, and all the earth shall be Your ground."

With iron rod shall rebels be undone,
Like shattered pots their strength shall melt away.
So, kings, be wise: bow low before the Son—
Rejoice with trembling; haste, and not delay.

Blest are all those who shelter in His grace,
But perishing are they who scorn His face.[28]

This sonnet fares better than the one for Psalm 1 in that there are no factual inaccuracies. Poetic license is taken with the *wrathful fire* in the second quatrain, evoking the intensity of God's anger. The mention of inheritance is only implied, weakening the irony present in the original text—namely that the earthly kings' rebellion results in their own lands being granted to the new king installed on Zion.[29] Indeed, to those not familiar with Psalm 2 already, the phrasing *the earth shall be Your ground* might be understood metaphorically for rootedness, energetic or even mystical unity, as commonly used in modern English.[30] The fundamental role of inheritance would then be lost entirely, causing the poem to fail on poetic accuracy.

These four examples illustrate the same point: once a contextual *form* is established and well-structured, AI can reproduce it with impressive speed and consistency. The drafts above could significantly accelerate a project to generate nursery rhymes or sonnets based on the Psalms. Yet they remain unmistakably machine-made and require human oversight for every dimension of accuracy—factual, emotional, and poetic. Left to their own devices,[31] current AI models still stumble in all three areas.

Where AI Excels—and Where It Fails

Once the initial work of contextualization has been done, AI can harness it and reproduce it. It only needs to be taught once how to do something, but it must be taught. Once the work has been done, AI can replicate it more quickly, more cheaply, and more consistently than any human can. But when it comes to discerning the *need* for contextualization—and determining how it should be done—AI is not yet the right tool. That work remains, unequivocally, human work.

Even in human translation, every draft still needs to be evaluated for accuracy: Is it *factually* accurate (or does it mislead)? Is it *poetically* accurate (or do local poetic conventions change the message conveyed)? Is it *emotionally* accurate (or does the local context lead a reader in a direction other than the poem initially intended)? It is no surprise that AI drafts have the same need; it is astonishing how powerful the drafts can be. The greatest danger may be that the excellence of the style can almost lull one into thinking that the words must be right, gradually disfiguring the message: perhaps it is a good thing that one "grows tall and doesn't sleep"? Or perhaps it is true that the righteous *have* sinned? When the mismatch between the quality of the *style* and the quality of the *meaning* is recognized, the remedy is simple enough.

The Reality: Methodological Collision

On the one hand, AI seems almost tailor-made for Bible translation. It can revise, rephrase, and reformat material at astonishing speed and scale. As soon as it has access to accurate contextualization—whether in the form of a poetic structure, cultural insight, or well-chosen theological term—it can apply that knowledge rapidly and uniformly across massive amounts of text. But this very strength can become a liability if AI is introduced at the wrong time or in the wrong way into the traditional Bible translation workflow.

Drafting Phase

Human translation workflows reflect the limitations of human time, energy, and focus. They are slow and deliberate at the beginning because they must be. The first draft is the most labor-intensive stage, and it sets the upper limit for the quality of the final translation. If the draft is poor—unnatural, inaccurate, or theologically off-base—there may not be enough time or other resources to revise it adequately. A weak beginning often locks in a weak end.

AI operates on a fundamentally different principle. It is not bound by time, fatigue, or revision limits. It can generate endless versions, learning from feedback as it goes. Its first drafts are meant to be quick and disposable—placeholders in a larger cycle of iteration. It expects to be wrong at first. But with each revision, it adapts. The longer it works, the better it becomes. Its goal is not to get things right at the start, but to learn as much as possible, as fast as possible.

This creates a methodological collision. If AI is introduced at the drafting stage of a Bible translation project, before it has been sufficiently trained—before it can mimic the quality of a human draft—it may cripple the project from the outset. But once AI has absorbed enough high-quality, contextualized input, it becomes an incredible asset. The timing of AI's introduction—and the quality of its training—is critical to the success of the process.

Editing Phase

Where AI can make immediate, low-risk contributions is in the *editing phase*. Tasks such as grammar, punctuation, spelling, and consistency in the use of key terms are governed by patterns and rules—areas where AI excels. It can outperform humans in flagging inconsistencies or reinforcing style guides. As we see from the nursery rhymes and sonnets above, humans are still needed to assess whether the use of a key term is theologically sound, whether a phrase is culturally natural, whether the exegesis is accurate, or whether metaphor and idiom have been appropriately contextualized.

Scripture Engagement

Once a translation has passed through checks and becomes a body of clear, accurate, and natural text, AI's real power emerges. At that point, the translation becomes a resource for Scripture engagement[32]—and here, AI shines. Does the translation team need a version of the same text in poetic form? For children? As a script? A prayer? A chant? AI can instantly generate stylistic transformations of approved content. This is where AI's gift for re-presentation becomes transformative. As with any stylistic rendering, of course, it can miss the mark if not properly cross-checked, but AI's speed and skill offer tremendous potential—after the foundational work of contextualization has already been done.

In each stage—drafting, editing, Scripture engagement—the question is not whether AI *can* contribute, but whether it has been *sufficiently trained* to do so. AI cannot, at this juncture, learn to contextualize through deduction or intuition.[33] It can only imitate patterns it has seen. Therefore, until AI has been trained on the voices, language choices, and theological instincts of the community it serves, we cannot expect it to substitute for direct interaction with that community.

Conclusion

AI is an undeniably powerful tool, able to re-present content in a new style in seconds. If this is original biblical content in a new language, it is exciting indeed for the world of Bible translation. Three observations have emerged:

1. Poor timing or manner of introducing AI to a Bible translation project can irreparably disrupt the *process* of translation, which can equally jeopardize the final *product*. The interaction between humans and AI is still the critical puzzle piece within Bible translation.
2. Though AI is better, faster, and cheaper at generating new drafts of old content, those drafts will always be machine-made and the quality of the *style* and accuracy of *meaning* may be wildly different—because AI must never be treated as if it *understands* anything. Its usefulness depends not on its own ability to understand, but on that of the humans it is serving.
3. When a new form or style is well understood (such as a nursery rhyme or sonnet), AI excels at new drafts. The potential for Scripture engagement is breathtaking.

If we carefully distinguish style from meaning, we can move beyond those who fear or worship AI, and we can be responsible stewards. We can assign to people and machines appropriate tasks; we can prepare to render to AI what ought to be AI's: the work that does not require understanding—the work of replication, revision, and re-presentation. And we can render to humanity what remains uniquely ours: the call to wisdom, stewardship, and the Spirit-led task of translating not just words, but *meaning*, across the vast and varied landscape of the world's languages.

Notes

1 I would like to thank William Chan for his gracious, tireless, and timely editorial input in preparing this chapter.

2 Elizabeth L. Eisenstein, *The Printing Revolution in Early Modern Europe* (Cambridge: Cambridge University Press, 1983), 151.

3 As quoted in John Piper, *The Legacy of Sovereign Joy: God's Triumphant Grace in the Lives of Augustine, Luther, and Calvin* (Wheaton: Crossway, 2000), 94; and for the quote's original context, see William Hazlitt, ed., *The Table Talk of Martin Luther*, new ed. (London: H.G. Bohn, 1857), §XXXIII.

4 While it is popularly believed to have been invented by Benedictine monks, the origin of the mechanical clock is a debated topic. J. D. North contends that only the Church would have had the academic and administrative resources to construct large mechanical clocks in the thirteenth and fourteenth centuries; Richard of Wallingford, abbot of St. Albans, was a pioneer of mechanical clock design. See J. D. North, "Monasticism and the First Mechanical Clocks," in *The Study of Time II*, ed. J. T. Fraser and N. Lawrence (New York: Springer-Verlag, 1975), 381–4.

5 Thus, for example, a 1302 Ordnance by the Bishop of Ely stipulated that the abbey clock should be properly manned by a monk, in order to ensure the appropriate times for daily duties; see C. F. C. Beeson, *English Church Clocks, 1280–1850: History and Classification* (London: Antiquarian Horological Society, 1971), 15.

6 Neil Postman, *Technopoly: The Surrender of Culture to Technology* (New York: Random House, 1993), 15.

7 This discussion will focus mostly on AI *drafting*, in which AI is responsible for the preponderance of translation decisions.

8 Levicheva and Joseph observe that translational decisions often depend heavily on the translator's theological views, calling into question the theological implications of AI-determined decisions, Larisa I. Levicheva and Abson P. Joseph, "Lost in Translation: The Formative and Theological Challenges and Opportunities of Using AI in Bible Translation," in *Faithfully Rendering God's Word: Artificial Intelligence, Cultural Bias and the Future of Faithful Bible Translation*, ed. Greg Forster (Grand Rapids: Credo House, 2020), 22, 24. De Blois et al. consider Bible translation a "participatory process between human knowledge and expertise, source biblical revelation, and the Holy Spirit"; Reinier de Blois, Larry Hayashi, Matt Merritt, and Paul Unger, "Lost in Translation: Navigating the Intersection of Humanity and Technology in Bible Translation," in *Quality in Translation: A Multi-Threaded Fabric*, ed. Stephen Watters and Reinier de Blois (Dallas: SIL International, 2023), 377.

9 For a detailed outline of broadly recognized standards for Bible translation (enshrined in *clarity, accuracy, and naturalness*), see "Translation Standards," Forum of Bible Agencies International, accessed April 30, 2025, https://forum-intl.org/resources/translation-standards.

10 Cf. Gary Marcus, "Deep Learning: A Critical Appraisal," last modified January 2, 2018, 10–14, https://arxiv.org/abs/1801.00631. Marcus outlines a number of areas in which deep learning typically struggles in comparison with human cognition (e.g., open-ended inference, integrating prior knowledge, and distinguishing causation from correlation).

11 Richard P. Feynman, *Surely You're Joking, Mr. Feynman!* (London: Vintage, 1992), 220.

12 Ge Wang, "Humans in the Loop: The Design of Interactive AI Systems," Human-Centered Artificial Intelligence, Stanford University, last modified October 20, 2019, https://hai.stanford.edu/news/humans-loop-design-interactive-ai-systems.

13 As Greg Forster astutely notes, "In the Bible, idolatry is described as a practice of attributing independent agency to inert objects made of wood, metal and stone;

attributing independent agency to objects made of sand [viz., silicon?] would be just another instance of the same practice"; Greg Forster, conclusion to *Faithfully Rendering God's Word,* ed. Forster, 72.

14 Eugene A. Nida, *Toward a Science of Translating: With Special Reference to Principles and Procedures Involved in Bible Translating* (Leiden: Brill, 1964), 153.

15 Mark L. Strauss, "Narrowing the Gap: Feedback Loops Using Native Language Consultants to Refine Machine-Generated (AI) Translations," in *Faithfully Rendering God's Word,* ed. Forster, 43. Strauss also recounts the humorous example of the Swedish vacuum cleaner company Electrolux, which launched an American advertising campaign entitled, "Nothing sucks like an Electrolux!"

16 As de Blois et al. observe, "For each participant in the translation process, there exists a cultural nexus involving biblical cultures, the culture of the target language, the cultures of the authors of commentaries and translations, and the cultures of any other team members"; de Blois et al., "Lost in Translation," 377.

17 Gerard Van Goningen, "אָנַף," *TWOT* 1:58.

18 Hélène Dallaire, "Producing a Culturally Sensitive Bible Translation of 'Emotions' into a Target Language Using Artificial Intelligence (AI)," in *Faithfully Rendering God's Word,* ed. Forster, 36.

19 Dallaire, "'Emotions,'" 36.

20 Anthony R. Petterson, *Haggai, Zechariah and Malachi,* ApOTC 25 (Downers Grove: InterVarsity, 2015), 319; and Steven L. McKenzie and Howard N. Wallace, "Covenant Themes in Malachi," *CBQ* 45 (1983): 555–7.

21 The ChatGPT prompt was to make a nursery rhyme of Psalm 1 based on the interpretation encapsulated in the Overview video produced by Scriptura's *Psalms: Layer by Layer* project, publicly available at https://psalms.scriptura.org/w/Psalm_1, accessed April 22, 2025.

22 Cf. Iona Opie and Peter Opie, *The Lore and Language of Schoolchildren* (Oxford: Oxford University Press, 1959).

23 This is one of the greatest causes for hope with AI translations; humans will always strive to make sense of what they hear, even what is awkward. That creates much latitude for effective communication.

24 The ChatGPT prompt was to use the same Overview information above for Psalm 1 and present it in the form of a Shakespearean sonnet.

25 Nancy deClaissé-Walford, Rolf A. Jacobson, and Beth LaNeel Tanner, *The Book of Psalms,* NICOT (Grand Rapids: Eerdmans, 2014), 63.

26 As above, ChatGPT was directed to create a nursery rhyme of Psalm 2 based on the Overview video from Scriptura's *Psalms: Layer by Layer* project, publicly available at https://psalms.scriptura.org/w/Psalm_2, accessed April 22, 2025.

27 Cf. Pieter van der Lugt, *Cantos and Strophes in Biblical Hebrew Poetry: With Special Reference to the First Book of the Psalter,* OTS 53 (Leiden: Brill, 2006), 104.

28 As above, ChatGPT was prompted to use the Overview video from https://psalms.scriptura.org/w/Psalm_2 to generate a Shakespearean sonnet.

29 Konrad Schaefer, *Psalms,* Berit Olam (Collegeville: Liturgical Press, 2001), 9.

30 Cf. Mircea Eliade, *The Sacred and the Profane: The Nature of Religion,* trans. Willard R. Trask (San Diego: Harcourt, 1959); David Abram, *The Spell of the Sensuous: Perception and Language in a More-than-Human World* (New York: Pantheon, 1996).

31 Note that these examples are in the most resource-rich language, English. No other language has near the body of materials available to train AI, so results in other languages will require far more human involvement.

32 T. Wayne Dye, "The Eight Conditions of Scripture Engagement: Social and Cultural Factors Necessary for Vernacular Bible Translation to Achieve Maximum Effect," *International Journal of Frontier Missiology* 26 (2009): 83–6.

33 Marcus, "Deep Learning," 10.

Bibliography

Abram, David. *The Spell of the Sensuous: Perception and Language in a More-than-Human World*. New York: Pantheon, 1996.

Beeson, C. F. C. *English Church Clocks, 1280–1850: History and Classification*. London: Antiquarian Horological Society, 1971.

Blois, Reinier de, Larry Hayashi, Matt Merritt, and Paul Unger. "Lost in Translation: Navigating the Intersection of Humanity and Technology in Bible Translation." Pages 369–96 in *Quality in Translation: A Multi-Threaded Fabric*. Edited by Stephen Watters and Reinier de Blois. Dallas: SIL International, 2023.

Dallaire, Hélène. "Producing a Culturally Sensitive Bible Translation of 'Emotions' into a Target Language Using Artificial Intelligence (AI)." Pages 29–42 in *Faithfully Rendering God's Word: Artificial Intelligence, Cultural Bias and the Future of Faithful Bible Translation*. Edited by Greg Forster. Grand Rapids: Credo House, 2020.

DeClaissé-Walford, Nancy L., Rolf A. Jacobson, and Beth LaNeel Tanner. *The Book of Psalms*. NICOT. Grand Rapids: Eerdmans, 2014.

Dye, T. Wayne. "The Eight Conditions of Scripture Engagement: Social and Cultural Factors Necessary for Vernacular Bible Translation to Achieve Maximum Effect." *International Journal of Frontier Missiology* 26 (2009): 89–98.

Eisenstein, Elizabeth L. *The Printing Revolution in Early Modern Europe*. Cambridge: Cambridge University Press, 1983.

Eliade, Mircea. *The Sacred and the Profane: The Nature of Religion*. Translated by Willard R. Trask. San Diego: Harcourt, 1959.

Erisman, Albert, and Tripp Parker. "Artificial Intelligence: A Theological Perspective." *Perspectives on Science and Christian Faith* 71.2 (2019): 95–106.

Feynman, Richard P. *Surely You're Joking, Mr. Feynman!* London: Vintage, 1992.

Forster, Greg. Conclusion to *Faithfully Rendering God's Word: Artificial Intelligence, Cultural Bias and the Future of Faithful Bible Translation*. Edited by Greg Forster. Grand Rapids: Credo House, 2020.

Forum of Bible Agencies International. "Translation Standards." Accessed April 30, 2025. https://forum-intl.org/resources/translation-standards.

Harris, R. Laird, Gleason L. Archer, Jr., and Bruce K. Waltke. *Theological Wordbook of the Old Testament*. 2 vols. Chicago: Moody Press, 1999.

Hazlitt, William, ed. *The Table Talk of Martin Luther*. New ed. London: H.G. Bohn, 1857.

Levicheva, Larisa I., and Abson P. Joseph. "Lost in Translation: The Formative and Theological Challenges and Opportunities of Using AI in Bible Translation." Pages 17–28 in *Faithfully Rendering God's Word: Artificial Intelligence, Cultural Bias and the Future of Faithful Bible Translation*. Edited by Greg Forster. Grand Rapids: Credo House, 2020.

Marcus, Gary. "Deep Learning: A Critical Appraisal." arXiv. 2018. https://doi.org/10.48550/arXiv.1801.00631.

McKenzie, Steven L., and Howard N. Wallace. "Covenant Themes in Malachi." *CBQ* 45 (1983): 549–63.

Nida, Eugene A. *Toward a Science of Translating: With Special Reference to Principles and Procedures Involved in Bible Translating*. Leiden: Brill, 1964.

North, J. D. "Monasticism and the First Mechanical Clocks." Pages 381–98 in *The Study of Time II*. Edited by J. T. Fraser and N. Lawrence. New York: Springer-Verlag, 1975.

Opie, Iona, and Peter Opie. *The Lore and Language of Schoolchildren*. Oxford: Oxford University Press, 1959.

Petterson, Anthony R. *Haggai, Zechariah and Malachi*. ApOTC 25. Downers Grove: InterVarsity, 2015.

Piper, John. *The Legacy of Sovereign Joy: God's Triumphant Grace in the Lives of Augustine, Luther, and Calvin*. Wheaton: Crossway, 2000.

Postman, Neil. *Technopoly: The Surrender of Culture to Technology*. New York: Random House, 1993.

Schaefer, Konrad. *Psalms*. Berit Olam. Collegeville: Liturgical Press, 2001.

Strauss, Mark L. "Narrowing the Gap: Feedback Loops Using Native Language Consultants to Refine Machine-Generated (AI) Translations." Pages 43–57 in *Faithfully Rendering God's Word: Artificial Intelligence, Cultural Bias and the Future of Faithful Bible Translation*. Edited by Greg Forster. Grand Rapids: Credo House, 2020.

Van der Lugt, Pieter. *Cantos and Strophes in Biblical Hebrew Poetry: With Special Reference to the First Book of the Psalter*. OTS 53. Leiden: Brill, 2006.

Wang, Ge. "Humans in the Loop: The Design of Interactive AI Systems." Human-Centered Artificial Intelligence. Stanford University. Posted October 20, 2019. https://hai.stanford.edu/news/humans-loop-design-interactive-ai-systems.

Part III

AI and Bible Interpretation

9

Evaluating AI for the Digital Scholarly Edition

Tools for Translation and Interpretive Commentary

Ken M. Penner

How can artificial intelligence contribute to the meticulous and deeply human process of preparing ancient manuscripts for modern readers? This chapter tackles that question by investigating the integration of digital tools—particularly AI chatbots—into the workflows for creating digital scholarly editions of biblical texts. While other studies in this volume discuss translating or interpreting texts that are already established, this chapter addresses the foundational step of preparing that source material itself.

The emergence of AI tools capable of performing textual tasks such as transcription, grammatical tagging, and even translation promises to transform how scholars engage with ancient manuscripts. However, alongside this promise come critical challenges: ethical concerns about AI's labor practices and environmental impact, questions of accuracy and reliability, and debates about the role of human expertise in a field increasingly influenced by automation. Addressing these challenges requires not only theoretical reflection but also rigorous, hands-on evaluation of how AI tools function in practice.

This chapter builds on practical experiences from an undergraduate course on digital methods for ancient texts, where students engaged directly with the challenges and possibilities of integrating AI into scholarly workflows. Using the Greek Additions to Daniel as a case study, the chapter evaluates the performance of leading AI chatbots across key stages of digital edition creation, including transcription, textual criticism, translation, and commentary. Benchmarks are established to assess the strengths and limitations of these tools, offering insights into their potential contributions and shortcomings.

This chapter presents a state-of-the-art evaluation of how AI is reshaping the field of biblical studies, offering insights into the potential and pitfalls of this rapidly advancing technology. By showcasing both the capabilities and constraints of AI, I demonstrate that while AI can enhance efficiency, human oversight remains indispensable to ensure scholarly rigor.

The Scholarly Edition Workflow: Tradition Meets Technology

No matter the subject, academic work involves transforming knowledge to make it intelligible to others. For those of us studying ideas from the ancient world, our data is textual—the linguistic output of humans recorded physically in writing. Access to these texts is essential for our work, yet barriers such as geography, language, and inconsistent cataloging have historically hampered access.

One of the most exciting developments within the discipline of digital humanities is the effort to make ancient texts more FAIR—Findable, Accessible, Interoperable, and Reusable.[1] While the FAIR principles were articulated formally only in 2016, the concept of accessibility has long guided the work of scholars. Traditional scholarly editions—printed with transcriptions, translations, and commentary—were, in their time, tools to make ancient texts more usable. Today, digital technologies create new opportunities to expand that mission.

The Typical Stages of a Scholarly Edition

Producing a scholarly edition involves proceeding in seven stages, which I will outline here to provide a baseline for our discussion of how traditional workflows and conventional digital tools can be enhanced using currently available AI chatbots.

(1) Manuscript Identification: Scholars begin by selecting a manuscript to edit, often guided by its significance, rarity, or lack of prior editions. Identifying important manuscripts can now be expedited through digital databases including Pinakes[2] and the Leuven Database of Ancient Books.[3]

(2) Cataloging: A manuscript's provenance, physical features, and contents must be documented. While traditional methods rely on manual record-keeping, modern cataloging is increasingly standardized and enriched by machine-readable metadata, enabling global accessibility.

(3) Indexing and Referencing: Standard methods for referring to sections of the text are required. Ancient texts often require identifying which parts of the text appear on specific pages of a manuscript. With biblical texts, pre-existing referencing systems (e.g., chapters and verses) simplify this step, but decisions still need to be made for unique features, such as different referencing systems for the Additions to Daniel. The VMR CRE digital platform facilitates this process of attaching references to pages.[4]

(4) Transcription: Transcribing manuscripts involves reproducing their text as accurately as possible, preserving original scribal features including abbreviations and line breaks. This labor-intensive process has historically relied on manual effort, though for several modern languages AI-powered OCR is now beginning to assist, albeit with significant human oversight to ensure fidelity.[5]

(5) Normalization and Collation: Variants across manuscripts are normalized to standard editorial conventions, and a base text is established by collating readings. Digital tools such as CollateX automate parts of this process.[6]

(6) Translation: Rendering a text into a modern language demands careful linguistic and cultural interpretation. Digital tools such as lexicons and morphological parsers aid this process, while AI-powered translation tools offer intriguing possibilities.

(7) Commentary and Presentation: Scholars contextualize the text through commentary, addressing its linguistic, historical, and theological aspects. The final product is formatted for dissemination, whether as a traditional printed edition or a dynamic digital resource that can present flexible textual views.

Toward a Digital Future

The advent of digital technology has transformed this workflow, reducing barriers such as geography and access while increasing the availability of high-quality scholarly resources. Digital tools enhance the discoverability and usability of manuscripts, while AI technologies promise to streamline labor-intensive processes.

Yet, these innovations come with challenges. AI tools including chatbots based on large language models (LLMs) often perform well in automating repetitive tasks but bring with them their own unique concerns. This chapter examines the value of integrating AI into the scholarly edition workflow, offering a practical case study that evaluates AI's performance at each stage, from transcription to commentary. By combining traditional expertise with cutting-edge tools, this chapter demonstrates how digital and AI methods can complement established practices in biblical and other ancient or textual studies.

Case Study: Digital Methods for Historical Documents

Computers offer a transformative opportunity to reduce the obstacles of geography and language by making textual data even more Findable, Accessible, Interoperable, and Reusable. This case study showcases how I and my students used technological tools in an upper-level undergraduate course, *Digital Methods for Historical Documents.* The course processed the Greek Additions to Daniel, using them as a test case for integrating traditional scholarly practices with current digital tools.

The course followed a structured workflow that mirrors the seven-stage traditional process of creating a scholarly edition while integrating digital tools to enhance efficiency and accessibility (culminating in a ten-step process).

(1) Manuscript Identification: Choosing which manuscript to edit is substantially easier in the digital age, to the extent that libraries have digitized their catalogs and manuscripts. It can be much quicker now to discover the extant witnesses to

a text, and whether the manuscripts have been photographed and made available online. For example, several born digital databases of manuscripts have been created, notably the Leuven Database of Ancient Books (hosted on Trismestigos .org),[7] Pinakes,[8] the DLCP (hosted on papyri.info),[9] and Diktyon.[10] Because of my familiarity with the manuscript and its importance, I assigned Codex Marchalianus for the *Digital Methods* course, specifically the Additions to Daniel for their entertaining stories; these databases identified it as TM 62233 / LDAB 3393.

(2) Cataloging: The above libraries and databases point to the libraries or private collections that hold the manuscripts, and their shelf marks in those libraries. In some cases, they point directly to the landing page for the digitized manuscript, as was the case for Codex Marchalianus, identified by Pinakes as Vat. gr. 2125. Students were tasked with putting the information about the manuscript into a teiHeader element that conformed to the TEI P5 standard.[11] They created and validated this header using the Oxygen XML editor.[12]

(3) Indexing and Referencing: Editors of any text need to establish conventions for naming the text, delimiting it into paragraphs, chapters, verses, or lines, and referencing these divisions. For a biblical manuscript, such referencing systems are already established; nevertheless, for the Additions to Daniel we still needed to choose between two conventions to refer to the additions: as part of the book of Daniel (chs. 3; 13; 14), or as their own books in the case of Susanna and Bel & the Dragon. At this point, we also made note of which parts of the text appear on which pages of the manuscript (Sus on 761-68; Dan. 3:24-90 on 784-91; Bel & Dra 827–32). For this purpose, we used an instance of the Virtual Manuscript Room Collaborative Research Environment, running as THREAD 2 (at logikos. ca)[13] to specify the exact verses for each page.

(4) Transcription: Students typed the words from the manuscript using the transcription tool provided by the THREAD 2 platform,[14] namely the Online Transcription Editor from the Trier Center for Digital Humanities.[15] The platform automatically saved the transcriptions to the Git versioned repository.

(5) Reconciliation: Each page was transcribed by two people and reconciled by a third. Discrepancies were identified by the instance of Mergely[16] running on THREAD 2, and after visually checking the manuscript to see which of the differing transcriptions was correct, this third person selected the correct reading in each case. This reconciled transcription was then saved independently of the two initial transcriptions.

(6) Normalizing: Spelling, punctuation, accentuation, and segmentation were checked against a standard edition of the text. In this case, we used Ziegler's volume in the Göttingen series to establish spelling and accentuation, and the presence or absence of movable *nu* (an optional letter on the end of some words).[17] The spelling in Codex Marchalianus is quite good, but the accents are often placed on the first vowel of a diphthong, rather than the second letter as is conventional. The manuscript punctuation varies radically from Ziegler's edition. The VMRCRE platform provides a tool for normalization of variants, but it was

not functioning on THREAD 2. As a result, we performed this normalization manually by exporting the TEI files from THREAD 2 and editing them in the XML text editor Oxygen. This manual work became too tedious for our class schedule, so we pursued the assistance of artificial intelligence, on which I write more below.

(7) Collation: The text of printed editions of the Additions to Daniel by Swete,[18] Rahlfs,[19] and Ziegler was copied into the THREAD 2 platform in order to automatically produce a collation of variants using the CollateX software. Unfortunately, configuration errors prevented CollateX from functioning in the THREAD 2 instance, so we again entered variants manually in Oxygen. Subsequently, we uploaded the XML files from Oxygen to the TEI Publisher platform and added textual variants through its annotation editor graphical user interface.[20]

(8) Translation: Each student was responsible for translating a section of the Additions to Daniel from Codex Marchalianus into English. But first, they added linguistic attributes to every word entity in the XML file: the word's lexical form ("lemma"), and its inflection (morpho-syntactic description, "msd"). For this purpose, students learned enough Python coding skills to use an API to extract this data from the Perseus Greek Word Study Tool.[21] The tool also provided an English gloss for the Greek word, which enabled quicker translation. The translation was then uploaded to the Alpheios Standalone Translation Alignment Editor v2 to link each Greek word to its English translation.[22]

(9) Commentary: Students added explanations to the aspects of the text they found peculiar—typically answers to questions they themselves had to research and investigate in order to translate properly. These comments were manually entered into the same TEI XML file using <note> entities in the Oxygen editor.

(10) Presentation: The TEI Publisher platform, which we had used previously for adding textual variants to the TEI file, provided a convenient way to display two different visual outputs from the same TEI XML file: one a diplomatic transcription, with the manuscript's spelling, punctuation, abbreviations, line and page breaks; and the other a normalized edition, with conventional spelling, punctuation, expanded abbreviations, without intrusive line and page breaks. This dual presentation was accomplished by two separate ODD documents. (ODD "One Document Does it all" documents are XML files that tell the rendering engine how to handle and display the various TEI entities.)

The outcome of the above steps was the final project for the course: a TEI conformant XML file for each addition to Daniel, with a teiHeader containing catalog information; a diplomatic transcription; a normalized text with textual variants, lemmas, and parsings; a translation; and comments.

This case study demonstrates how conventional digital methods can enhance traditional workflows, making ancient texts more accessible and interoperable while highlighting the need for careful human oversight to ensure scholarly rigor. The integration of AI tools promises further efficiency—a topic explored in the following sections.

AI in Biblical Translation and Interpretation

Ethics of AI

The integration of artificial intelligence into biblical translation and interpretation is both an exciting and controversial development. While AI offers the potential to transform how scholars engage with ancient texts, it also raises critical ethical concerns. For many in the humanities, AI can feel like an unwelcome outsider—a tool rooted in engineering and computation, at odds with the interpretive nuance required in fields like theology, linguistics, and history.

Yet it seems to me that the rise of AI is as inevitable as earlier technological revolutions that reshaped human activity. Just as electricity transformed manufacturing, the internet revolutionized communication, and smartphones redefined daily life, AI is poised to do the same for how we process, analyze, and interpret information, including ancient texts. Dismissing its potential risks sidelining tools that could amplify human capabilities in unprecedented ways.

One of AI's most profound contributions is its ability to democratize access to intellectual resources. Unlike physical property, knowledge is not a finite resource; the more widely it can be disseminated, the more people can benefit from it. AI tools can help bring the rich heritage of biblical texts to communities and scholars who might otherwise lack access. When used thoughtfully, AI can bridge knowledge gaps, fostering inclusivity in scholarship.

Yet despite its promise, popular chatbots in the form currently available bring with them significant ethical concerns that cannot be ignored.[23] They impact the environment; AI systems require substantial computational power, contributing to global energy consumption and climate change.[24] They exploit labor; some of the most popular models are trained by human workers, who by the standards of developed countries are underpaid, and whose contributions go unrecognized.[25] They enable cognitive laziness; overreliance on AI can lead to intellectual complacency, where human critical thinking atrophies. They are factually unreliable; AI-generated content, while impressive, is prone to errors or "hallucinations" that can mislead readers and researchers. The most capable models are trained on datasets that include copyrighted materials, raising questions about ownership and consent.[26]

While these concerns are significant, they are surmountable because they are not inherent to AI itself but reflect choices in how we use and develop this technology. We can find at least partial solutions to each of these ethical concerns. To minimize the consumption of energy, researchers and developers can prioritize models that operate on sustainable energy[27] or optimize computational efficiency.[28] The solution to labor exploitation is simple: pay human trainers who contribute to model development a fair wage, even if it means raising prices for customers. We can choose whether we use AI to do our thinking for us, or whether we avail ourselves of what Ethan Mollick calls co-intelligence,[29] in which AI augments and complements human insight instead of substituting for human expertise. The problem of chatbot reliability is already improving; ongoing refinement of AI systems has been reducing factual errors, making their outputs more reliable.[30] Developers can ensure that AI models are trained only on materials with proper permissions, respecting intellectual property rights.[31]

By addressing these ethical challenges, AI can serve as a transformative tool rather than a problematic disruptor. When responsibly implemented, AI can democratize access to intellectual resources, bridge gaps between communities, and foster inclusivity in scholarship.

The Human Role in AI Collaboration

AI's role in biblical translation is necessarily collaborative. Automation can accelerate repetitive tasks like transcription and grammatical tagging, but the interpretive rigor required for translating and contextualizing ancient texts remains the domain of human scholars. AI's greatest strength lies in amplifying human effort—freeing scholars to focus on higher-order analytical work while delegating tedious processes to machines.

This balance requires scholars to adopt a critical stance toward AI outputs, ensuring they are not accepted uncritically but rather scrutinized against established academic standards. How can AI-driven tools be proactively, ethically, and productively used in a workflow for a digital scholarly edition such as in the course on digital methods for ancient texts?

Evaluating Chatbot Models for the Digital Scholarly Edition Workflow

This next section picks up that question, evaluating ways of integrating AI into the digital scholarly edition workflow for biblical and parabiblical texts. It focuses on three critical questions for each workflow stage: how AI was utilized in the *Digital Methods* course, how AI could theoretically enhance those tasks, and how current chatbots perform when benchmarked against specific criteria. These evaluations consider AI's potential for facilitating transcription, translation, and interpretation, while addressing its limitations and the necessity of human oversight.

Selection Criteria for AI Chatbots

Given the rapid proliferation of AI chatbots, this evaluation focuses on a curated selection of models to maintain manageability. Chatbots were selected primarily for their capability and secondarily for their price (e.g., API accessibility). While this selection reflects the state of AI development at the time of writing, it will inevitably be surpassed by future advancements.

The primary contenders include models from leading companies: OpenAI (ChatGPT models GPT-4o, GPT-4o-mini, o1-mini), Anthropic (Claude models Sonnet 3.5, Haiku 3.5), Google (Gemini models 1.5 Pro, 2.0 Experimental), and Meta (Llama models 3.1 8B, 70B, 405B). Additionally, DeepSeek V3 was included for its promising performance-to-price ratio.

The evaluation explores these models' strengths and weaknesses across several stages of the digital scholarly edition workflow. For each stage, a representative prompt is provided, and chatbot responses are analyzed against criteria such as accuracy, relevance, and utility. By systematically benchmarking their performance, this section reveals the current state of AI capabilities while noting the role of human expertise in ensuring scholarly rigor. For each step of the workflow, I will present one or more chatbot prompts and evaluate the response of each chatbot to that prompt.

AI in the Workflow

Manuscript Identification

The first step in creating a digital scholarly edition is selecting a manuscript to edit. In the *Digital Methods* course, this decision was made for the students, prioritizing manuscripts that were significant and unpublished. Could AI effectively assist in this selection process? To evaluate, I tested chatbots on their ability to identify an appropriate manuscript, assessing both their manuscript recommendations and the accuracy of their location details.

Prompt

> *Select and locate a manuscript of the Greek Additions to Daniel that is important but does not yet have a printed edition.*

Responses

Table 9.1 Manuscripts Suggested by AI Chatbots, by Ken M. Penner

Claude 3.5 Sonnet	*Refused*
Claude 3.5 Haiku	Codex Chisianus (Chigi Library in Rome) or Codex Marchalianus (Vatican Library)
Gemini 1.5 Pro	*Refused*
Gemini 1.5 Flash	*Refused*
Gemini 2.0 Flash	Vat. gr. 106
Gemini 1206	Codex Chisianus (Vatican Library Chigi R.IV.74 formerly R.VI.39)
Gemini 2.0 Flash Thinking	Codex Monacensis Graecus 379 (Bayerische Staatsbibliothek)
OpenAI GPT 4o	*Refused*
OpenAI GPT 4o mini	Codex Chisianus (Biblioteca Medicea Laurenziana)
OpenAI o1-mini	P. Oxy. 2378 (University of Oxford, Egypt Exploration Society Collection)
Llama 3.2	Vat. gr. 1209
Llama 3.1 8b	Codex Hierosolymitanus (Patriarchal Library in Jerusalem)
Llama 3.3	Vat. gr. 1221
DeepSeek 3	Codex Chisianus 88 (Biblioteca Apostolica Vaticana)

Evaluation

Most chatbots failed to provide accurate or useful suggestions, often recommending manuscripts that were nonexistent, irrelevant, or already published. Key issues included misidentified manuscripts, incorrect shelf marks, and misplaced repository locations. Specific errors included:

Claude 3.5 Haiku recommended Codex Chisianus but inaccurately identified it as Rahlfs 117, which does not exist. Gemini 2.0 Flash pointed to Vat. gr. 106, which doesn't exist. Gemini 1206 identified Codex Chisianus 88, with the right library but wrong shelf number (IV. 74 should be VII. 45). Gemini 2.0 Flash's suggestion Cod. Graec. 379 is a copy of Chrysostom. GPT 4o mini also suggested Codex Chisianus but incorrectly located it in Florence. OpenAI o1-mini mistakenly suggested P. Oxy. 2378, which contains fragments of Sappho. Llama 3.2 recommended Codex Vaticanus, which has been extensively published. Llama 3.1's Codex Hierosolymitanus contains texts of the Apostolic Fathers, but not Daniel. Llama 3.3's Vat. gr. 1221 is not a biblical manuscript. DeepSeek 3 recommended Codex Chisianus 88 (Biblioteca Apostolica Vaticana), with a shelfmark of Chigi MS 88, formerly Chisianus R.VIII.88.

The chatbots all suffer from inadequate factual knowledge. The only helpful suggestions were those by Claude 3.5 Haiku, Gemini 1206, GPT 4o-mini, and DeepSeek, which recommended Codex Chisianus. This is a smart choice, except that an edition was published in 1772.[32] Codex Marchalianus is the best suggestion, also from Claude 3.5 Haiku.

This evaluation reveals the limited factual knowledge of current chatbots, which struggle with the specialized expertise required for manuscript identification. Even when a chatbot identifies a relevant manuscript, inaccuracies in location or metadata diminish its reliability. Notably, the main problem is not the chatbots' inability to retrieve data but their readiness to present incorrect information with unwarranted confidence.

Cataloging

Cataloging involves documenting a manuscript's provenance, condition, and other essential details. For this task, the focus in the course was on creating a <teiHeader> element for Codex Marchalianus that conforms to the TEI P5 guidelines, which specifies the following structure as a minimum requirement for a valid <teiHeader>:[33]

```
<teiHeader>
  <fileDesc>
    <titleStmt>
      <title>Title</title>
    </titleStmt>
    <publicationStmt>
     <p>Publication Information</p>
    </publicationStmt>
    <sourceDesc>
     <p>Information about the source</p>
    </sourceDesc>
  </fileDesc>
</teiHeader>
```

Additional elements such as <profileDesc> for textual classification or <msDesc> for manuscript descriptions can enrich the header by including specific metadata.

Evaluation Criteria

For this exercise, the <teiHeader> was evaluated on three criteria: (1) adherence to the TEI schema (e.g., correct nesting of elements such as <fileDesc> and <sourceDesc>); (2) accuracy of metadata values (e.g., repository location, manuscript shelfmark); (3) inclusion of the following ten key metadata elements:

- Publisher and repository: Vatican Library
- Shelfmark and ID: Vat. gr. 2125
- Settlement: Vatican City
- Extent: 416 folios
- Layout: 1 column, 29 lines
- Script: Greek uncial
- Origin date and place: Egypt (specific date range encoded in @notbefore and @ notafter)
- Contents: LXX Prophets
- Keywords: Biblical, prophets, Septuagint

I then evaluated conformity by counting the number of standards violations detected by Oxygen, accuracy by the number of falsehoods, and completeness by the number of elements from the above list of 10.

Prompt

`Produce a <teiHeader> element for Codex Marchalianus.`

Responses

Table 9.2 AI Chatbot Transcription Accuracy without Context, by Ken M. Penner

Chatbot	Conformity (Errors)	Accuracy (Errors)	Completeness /10
Claude 3.5 Sonnet	0	0	9
Claude 3.5 Haiku	0	2	6
Gemini 1.5 Pro	1	7	4
Gemini 1.5 Flash	4	1	1
Gemini 2.0 Flash	1	8	4
Gemini 1206	1	1	10
Gemini 2.0 Flash Thinking	11	6	8
OpenAI GPT 4o	8	1	6
OpenAI GPT 4o mini	9	2	1
OpenAI o1-mini	4	7	1
Llama 3.2	4	3	3
Llama 3.1 8b	4	1	0
Llama 3.3	2	3	1
DeepSeek	1	1	6

Insights

Claude 3.5 Sonnet and Gemini 1206 performed well due to their ability to recognize manuscript-specific metadata and conform to TEI standards with minimal errors. OpenAI GPT 4o mini and Llama models struggled with accuracy and completeness, often omitting critical metadata elements or introducing structural errors. DeepSeek 3 and Gemini 2.0 Flash Thinking demonstrated some promise but were inconsistent in structural adherence.

Improved Input Testing

The chatbots' performance significantly improved when provided with additional contextual information, such as manuscript descriptions from Swete's introduction[34] and the Göttingen Septuagint website.[35] The updated results are shown in Table 9.3.

Insights

These results led to three insights. First, it is evident that generative AI models excel at extracting and transforming structured data from unstructured text but are heavily dependent on the quality and specificity of the input provided. Second, while some chatbots can generate near-perfect outputs, expert review is necessary to ensure the inclusion of nuanced manuscript details and proper encoding. Third, models frequently missed optional metadata elements that enhance the richness of the header, such as detailed physical descriptions (<physDesc>). These insights indicate that generative AI chatbots show potential for creating metadata-rich TEI headers, especially when supplemented with precise prompts and contextual information. However, they remain tools for collaboration rather than automation;

Table 9.3 AI Chatbot Transcription Accuracy with Context, by Ken M. Penner

Chatbot	Conformity (Errors)	Accuracy (Errors)	Completeness /10
Claude 3.5 Sonnet	4	0	8
Claude 3.5 Haiku	5	0	9
Gemini 1.5 Pro	10	0	10
Gemini 1.5 Flash	Failed	Failed	Failed
Gemini 2.0 Flash	7	0	9
Gemini 1206	6	0	8
Gemini 2.0 Flash Thinking	Failed	Failed	Failed
OpenAI GPT 4o	13	0	6
OpenAI GPT 4o mini	8	0	8
OpenAI o1-mini	36	0	9
Llama 3.2	4	0	8
Llama 3.1 8b	32	1	6
Llama 3.3	1	0	4
DeepSeek 3	2	0	9

human expertise is needed to ensure accuracy, adherence to standards, and contextual relevance.

Indexing and Referencing

Indexing and referencing involve recording which parts of the text appear on specific manuscript pages. For instance, students using THREAD 2 recorded that page 761 contains Susanna 1:1-9, and page 790 contains Dan. 3:81-90. This process required reading the first words of a manuscript page and locating the corresponding verse in a Greek Bible.

To evaluate whether chatbots can assist with this repetitive task, two aspects were tested: (1) the chatbot's ability to correctly identify specific Greek verses, and (2) the chatbot's capacity to interpret manuscript images (addressed in the transcription section). This section focuses on the first test, specifically evaluating chatbots' familiarity with the Greek text of Dan. 3:53 in the Theodotion version, a verse absent from the Old Greek. For context, v. 52 begins with εὐλογητός and has a second half starting with καί; v. 53 starts with εὐλογημένος; and v. 57 begins with Εὐλογεῖτε.

Prompt

What is the first word of Daniel 3:53 in Theodotion's version of the Greek Bible?

Responses

Table 9.4 First Word of Theodotion Daniel 3:53 according to AI Chatbots, by Ken M. Penner

Chatbot	Dan 3:53 first word
Claude 3.5 Sonnet	εὐλογητὸς
Claude 3.5 Haiku	*Refused*
Gemini 1.5 Pro	ὑμνεῖτε
Gemini 1.5 Flash	καὶ
Gemini 2.0 Flash	Εὐλογεῖτε
Gemini 1206	Εὐλογητὸς
Gemini 2.0 Flash Thinking	Εὐλογητὸς
OpenAI GPT 4o	Εὐλογητὸς
OpenAI GPT 4o mini	καὶ
OpenAI o1-mini	Καὶ
Llama 3.2	*Refused*
Llama 3.1 8b	*Refused*
Llama 3.3	Αγγελοι
DeepSeek 3	Εὐλογητὸς

Insights

The results revealed significant limitations in the chatbots' performance. None of the models accurately identified εὐλογημένος as the first word of Dan. 3:53. Claude 3.5 Sonnet and DeepSeek V3 confidently suggested εὐλογητὸς, likely confusing v. 53 with v. 52. Gemini 1.5 Flash and OpenAI o1-mini incorrectly provided καὶ, likely misinterpreting it as a continuation from v. 52. Llama 3.2 and Claude 3.5 Haiku refused to answer due to insufficient training data, while Llama 3.3 offered the entirely unrelated response Ἄγγελοι. These inaccuracies underscore a fundamental issue: chatbots often present incorrect answers with unwarranted confidence, creating a risk of introducing errors into scholarly workflows.

This evaluation highlights the current inability of chatbots to reliably assist in indexing tasks that require detailed contextual knowledge of specialized texts. Even a human expert would likely need reference materials to identify such precise details, but the overconfidence displayed by chatbots in their incorrect answers poses an additional challenge.

Transcription

Transcribing manuscript text into a digital format while preserving orthographic features is a fundamental step in creating a digital scholarly edition. In the *Digital Methods* course, students manually entered text into the Online Transcription Editor, focusing on accurately reproducing features such as line breaks, abbreviations, and punctuation. To evaluate whether AI chatbots could automate this process, I tested their ability to transcribe text from a manuscript image and encode it into the TEI P5 standard.

Testing Chatbots with Manuscript Images

The first test aimed to determine whether chatbots could identify the first word of a manuscript page and locate the corresponding biblical verse. The manuscript image was initially downloaded from the Vatican Library website (https://digi.vatlib.it/view/MSS_Vat.gr.2125/1589), and a higher-resolution version from a 4K screen capture was later provided to improve the legibility of the text. The correct response was the word Εὐλογεῖτε from Dan. 3:81.

Prompt

```
What is the first word on this manuscript page image? Which
biblical verse does the page begin with?
```

Responses

Table 9.5 First Word of Dan. 3:81 Transcribed from Manuscript Image by AI Chatbots, by Ken M. Penner

Chatbot	Downloaded image	Verse	Screen capture
Claude 3.5 Sonnet	CΥΛΟΓΕΙΤΕ	*Refused*	Εὐλογεῖτε
Claude 3.5 Haiku	ΨΑΛΟΙ	Ps. 78:1	
Gemini 1.5 Pro	ΥΛΟΓΕΙΤΕ	Mt. 6:25	Memorare
Gemini 1.5 Flash	Οὐα	*Refused*	ΚΑΙ
Gemini 2.0 Flash	*ΕΥΑ*	*Mt. 28:1*	
Gemini 1206	*ΕΥΑΟΓΓΕΛΙΟΝ*	*Jn 19:16*	Εὐαγγέλιον
Gemini 2.0 Flash Thinking	*ΕΥΑΓΓΕΛΙΣΤΟΥ*	*Mk 1:1*	
OpenAI GPT 4o	*ΨΑΛΟΙΤΕ*	Psalms	ΣΥΛΟΓΕΙΤΕ
OpenAI GPT 4o mini	*Refused*	*Refused*	ΣΥΝΑΓΕΙΤΕ
Llama 3.2	OYAOIETEITILIA	Jn 1:1	
Llama 3.1 8b	YA		
Llama 3.3	GYAOITIYETTJAYIYILIAYI	*Refused*	
DeepSeek 3	EDswwmoirrniesrrerietd	*Refused*	

Evaluation

The results varied widely across the chatbots. While Claude 3.5 Sonnet succeeded in identifying Εὐλογεῖτε with the high-resolution image, it struggled with the lower-resolution version, rendering the word as CΥΛΟΓΕΙΤΕ. Gemini 2.0 Flash and OpenAI GPT 4o gave inconsistent or incorrect answers, often suggesting unrelated words or verses. The smaller models Claude 3.5 Haiku and Llama 3.2 could not answer. This variability revealed that while some models could approach accuracy under ideal conditions, none were reliable enough for autonomous transcription.

Full-Line Transcription

The next test extended beyond identifying a single word to transcribing an entire line of text from the manuscript: Εὐλογεῖτε πάντα τὰ θηρία καὶ τὰ (https://digi.vatlib.it/view/MSS_Vat.gr.2125/1590).

Prompt

```
Transcribe the Greek text on this image.
```

Evaluation

Here, only Claude 3.5 Sonnet and Gemini 2.0 Flash produced results close to the correct transcription. Other chatbots either misinterpreted the text entirely or failed to process it. For instance, Gemini 1.5 Pro and OpenAI GPT 4o mini output nonsensical strings, reflecting significant limitations in optical character recognition (OCR) capabilities for ancient Greek manuscripts.

Table 9.6 First Manuscript Image Line of Dan. 3:81 Transcribed by AI Chatbots, by Ken M. Penner

Claude 3.5 Sonnet	ΕΥΛΟΓΕΙΤΕΤΟΝΤ̅Ν̅ΠΑΝΤΑΤΟΙΕΡΓΑ ΚΑΙΤΑ	ευλογειτε τα θηρια παντα και τα κτηνη
Claude 3.5 Haiku	Not tested	Not tested
Gemini 1.5 Pro	ΥΛΟΙΕΙΤΕΥΤΙΜΙΤΙΟΠΡΑΚΜΑ	(C?)ΝΑΠΟΓΕΝΝΗΤΑΙΛΛΥΤΟΥ ΛΛΟΓΟΝΠΟΛΛΑΚΙΣΓΡΑ
Gemini 1.5 Flash		Τὸ μυστήριον τῆς εὐσεβείας μέγα ἐστί
Gemini 2.0 Flash	CΥΛΟΓΕΙΤΕΤΙΤΑΝΤΙΤΙΟΙΠΙΑΚΗΤΑ	ΟΥΑΛΕΡΙΟΥ ΣΕΠΤΙΜΙΟΥ ΣΕΟΥΗΡΟΣ ΠΕΡΤΙΝΑΚΟΣ ΑΥΓΟΥΣΤΟΣ
Gemini 1206	ΕΥΛΟΓΕΙΤΕΤΙΛΝΤΙΤΙΟΙΙΡΙΛΚΙΙΙΛ	ΣΥΛΟΓΙΣΤΙΚΗ ΤΑΥΤΗ ΠΡΑΓΜΑΤΕΙΑ
Gemini 2.0 Flash Thinking		
OpenAI GPT 4o	ΨΑΛΟΙΣΕΤΕΤΩΙΚΥΡΙΩΙΕΝΚΙΘΑΡΑ	Εὐαγγελίζεται τὰ πρὶν κρυπτά
OpenAI GPT 4o mini		ΣΥΝΑΓΕΤΕ ΤΙΝΙ ΤΗΝ ΠΙΣΤΙΝ
OpenAI o1-mini		N/A
Llama 3.2	εὐαγγελιστὴς ἡ γραφὴ τὴν στῦλον τοῦ ναοῦ τοῦ θεοῦ τοῦ ζῶντος ἐπὶ τὴν	
Llama 3.1 8b		
Llama 3.3		
DeepSeek 3	*VTHMHTINKELYRINEL*	

Encoding in TEI P5

Finally, I tested the ability of chatbots to encode a transcription in TEI P5 XML format. The encoding required adherence to VMRCRE standards, with elements such as <pb> for pages, <cb> for columns, <lb> for line breaks, and <w> for individual words. Chatbots were evaluated both with and without explicit instructions on encoding standards.

Prompt without explicit instructions

```
Encode the following transcription from folio 790 into
TEI P5 XML:
Page 790
Col 1

1 Dan 3:81 εὐλογεῖτε πάντα τὰ θηρία και τὰ
2κτηνη τὸν κν. ὑμνεῖτε καὶ ὑπερυ
3ψοῦτε αὐτὸν εἰς τοὺς αἰῶνας·
4 82 ευλογεῖτε υἱοι τῶν ανων τὸν κν.
5υμνεῖτε και υπερυψοῦτε ἀυτον
6ἐις τοὺς αιῶνας·
```

Prompt with explicit instructions

```
Encode the following transcription from folio 790 into TEI
P5 XML. Use elements pb with @n for a new page, cb with @n
for a new column, lb with @n and @break="no" for a new line
in the middle of a Greek word, div with @ type="chapter"
and @n for a chapter, ab with @n for a verse, and enclose
each word in a w element:
Page 790
Col 1

1 Dan 3:81 εύλογεῖτε πάντα τὰ ϑηρία καı τὰ
2κτηνη τὸν κν. ὑμνεῖτε καὶ ὑπερυ
3ψοῦτε αὐτὸν εἰς τοὺς αἰῶνας·
4 82 ευλογεῖτε υίοı τῶν ανων τὸν κν.
5υμνεῖτε καı υπερυψοῦτε ἀυτον
6ἐıς τοὺς αıῶνας·
```

Response

Table 9.7 Selected Features Captured into TEI Correctly by AI Chatbots, by Ken M. Penner

Chatbot	*Without instructions /7*	*With instructions /7*
Claude 3.5 Sonnet	*6*	*6*
Claude 3.5 Haiku	3	6
Gemini 1.5 Pro	*2*	*6*
Gemini 1.5 Flash	*2*	*3*
Gemini 2.0 Flash	4	7
Gemini 1206	2	6
Gemini 2.0 Flash Thinking	1	3
OpenAI GPT 4o	*1*	*6*
OpenAI GPT 4o mini	1	6
OpenAI o1-mini	1	6
Llama 3.2	2	6
Llama 3.1 8b	3	2
Llama 3.3	1	6
DeepSeek 3	1	6

Evaluation

Without detailed instructions, most chatbots failed to produce acceptable outputs. Claude 3.5 Sonnet performed relatively well, capturing six out of seven required features, but Gemini 2.0 Flash Thinking and Llama 3.3 struggled with basic formatting. However, when explicit instructions were provided, the quality of responses improved significantly. Gemini 2.0 Flash, for example, produced a flawless encoding, while Claude 3.5 Haiku and OpenAI GPT 4o delivered near-complete results.

These experiments revealed two key findings. First, the OCR capabilities of current chatbots are inadequate for accurately transcribing ancient Greek manuscripts.

While some models showed promise, their inconsistencies rendered them unreliable for standalone use. Second, chatbots performed significantly better at encoding transcription into TEI P5 when given explicit, detailed instructions, highlighting the importance of precise prompts in leveraging AI effectively. Yet even when chatbots produced acceptable outputs, manual verification was necessary to correct errors and ensure adherence to editorial standards.

Reconciliation

Comparing multiple transcriptions of the text to resolve variations and establish a base text is a step that is best performed by a human operating precise software. While human expertise remains indispensable for this task due to the need for visual verification, it is worth examining how AI chatbots can assist in detecting discrepancies and facilitating the reconciliation process.

To evaluate the chatbots' abilities, two XML files containing transcriptions of folio 790 from Codex Marchalianus were provided. The prompt instructed the chatbots to compare the transcriptions, identify discrepancies, and prepare these for verification against the manuscript. The goal was to determine the number of discrepancies each chatbot could detect, the extent to which their outputs aligned with the transcriptions, and whether they maintained fidelity to the original features of the text.

Prompt

The two XML files were supplied to the chatbot along with the following prompt:

> *Compare these two transcriptions to identify discrepancies, so the divergent reading can be verified against the manuscript.*

Responses

Table 9.8 Transcription Discrepancies Identified by AI Chatbots in XML Files, by Ken M. Penner

Chatbot	Number of discrepancies	Number of reconciled lines output	Regularization
Claude 3.5 Sonnet	10	Refused	
Claude 3.5 Haiku	5	84 lines	
Gemini 1.5 Pro	38	300 lines	good
Gemini 1.5 Flash	Error	Error	
Gemini 2.0 Flash	26	300 lines	good
Gemini 1206	16	311 lines	Regularized
Gemini 2.0 Flash Thinking	33	error	
OpenAI GPT 4o	16	Refused	good
OpenAI GPT 4o mini	12	295 lines	Regularized
OpenAI o1-mini	65	278 lines	Regularized
Llama 3.2	20	4 lines	
Llama 3.1 8b	13	110 lines	
Llama 3.3	7	110 lines	
DeepSeek V3	114	298 lines	Regularized

Evaluation

The results highlighted significant variation in chatbot performance. Claude 3.5 Sonnet and OpenAI GPT 4o, typically strong performers, detected a moderate number of discrepancies but failed to produce complete reconciliations. Sonnet noted ten discrepancies but refused to output reconciled lines. Gemini 1.5 Pro and Gemini 2.0 Flash excelled, detecting thirty-eight and twenty-six discrepancies, respectively, and processing approximately 300 lines systematically. These models avoided unnecessary regularization, preserving the original orthographic features. Gemini 1206 and DeepSeek V3 identified numerous discrepancies but introduced regularized outputs, modifying spelling, accents, and abbreviations unnecessarily. This undermined their utility for scholarly transcription, where fidelity to the manuscript is essential. Gemini 1.5 Flash and Gemini 2.0 Flash Thinking encountered errors or failed to process the task altogether. The smaller models Llama 3.2 and Llama 3.3 detected only a handful of discrepancies, further emphasizing their limitations in handling detailed textual data.

While some chatbots demonstrated promise, most outputs were compromised by regularization. OpenAI GPT 4o mini and DeepSeek V3 standardized spelling and accents, which, while helpful in some contexts, obscures the original orthographic details critical for scholarly work. Only Gemini 1.5 Pro and Gemini 2.0 Flash successfully avoided this pitfall, highlighting their potential for aiding reconciliation tasks.

Another limitation was the failure of many models to provide comprehensive outputs. Although some chatbots correctly flagged discrepancies, they often neglected to list them systematically or output reconciled lines, requiring additional human effort to complete the process.

Regularization

In the *Digital Methods* course, regularization or normalization involved verifying and adjusting the spelling, punctuation, accentuation, and segmentation of transcribed text to align with Ziegler's critical edition. Manual adjustments to accents and punctuation in oXygen often became laborious, particularly when adhering to modern editorial conventions, such as converting grave accents to acute before punctuation. To alleviate this burden, we explored the use of AI chatbots, discovering that they excel in this area due to their ability to recognize and apply standard spellings and accents based on extensive training data.

Despite their capabilities, chatbots required explicit instructions to produce high-quality outputs. The models were tasked with correcting a TEI-encoded transcription, adhering to the following guidelines: original readings were to be enclosed in <choice> elements, with <orig> and <reg> tags marking the original and regularized spellings, respectively. For abbreviations, <abbr> and <expan> tags were similarly used to indicate expansion. Crucially, corrections were to be made only where necessary; redundant <choice> elements were to be avoided.

The task required chatbots to regularize accents and expand abbreviations in a sample transcription. Specifically, the test involved correcting ten accents across two verses and expanding five abbreviations in the first three verses.

Prompt

A <div> element of the TEI file was provided to the chatbots along with the following prompt:

> *Correct the spelling, accents, and punctuation in the following ancient Greek transcribed text to match conventional editorial practices. When making a correction, enclose the original reading in a choice element, using an orig element for the original transcription and a reg element for the corrected spelling, following the pattern ``<w><choice><orig>στιππειον</orig><reg>στιππιον</reg></choice></w>``. When expanding abbreviations, enclose the abbr element in a choice element, along with an expan element, following the pattern `` <w><choice><abbr><hi rend=“overline”>κυ</hi></abbr><expan>κυρίου</expan></choice></w>``.*
>
> *When no correction is needed, leave the transcription as it is; do not add redundant elements in a choice element. Here is the transcription:*

Responses

Table 9.9 Accents and Abbreviations Corrected in XML by AI Chatbots, by Ken M. Penner

Chatbot	Accents /10	Abbreviations /5
Claude 3.5 Sonnet	10	5
Claude 3.5 Haiku	9	5
Gemini 1.5 Pro	Gratuitous choices	Gratuitous origs
Gemini 1.5 Flash	Regularized without choices	3
Gemini 2.0 Flash	Regularized without choices	4
Gemini 1206	Gratuitous choices	5
Gemini 2.0 Flash Thinking	Regularized without choices	4
OpenAI GPT 4o	10	5
OpenAI GPT 4o mini	Regularized without choices	0
OpenAI o1-mini	10	0
Llama 3.2	Regularized without choices	4
Llama 3.1 8b	Regularized without choices	4
Llama 3.3	Gratuitous choices	3
DeepSeek 3	10	4

Evaluation

Among the chatbots tested, Claude 3.5 Sonnet delivered a perfect performance, successfully identifying and correcting all accents and abbreviations while adhering to the prescribed XML structure. Other high-performing models included Claude 3.5 Haiku, OpenAI GPT 4o, and DeepSeek V3, all of which scored highly in both accent correction and abbreviation expansion, albeit with minor imperfections. OpenAI o1-mini excelled at accent correction but failed to expand any abbreviations.

However, many models exhibited common shortcomings. Gemini 1.5 Pro and Gemini 2.0 Flash regularized the text but neglected to include <choice> elements to preserve the original transcription, undermining the utility of their outputs. Gemini 1206 and Llama 3.3 enclosed every word in <choice> elements, even when no correction was necessary, introducing unnecessary complexity to the encoding.

The evaluation indicates the potential of LLMs to streamline regularization tasks, particularly in identifying and correcting accents and abbreviations. Their ability to process text systematically and apply editorial conventions suggests they can significantly reduce the manual workload for scholars. However, these tools are not without limitations. The failure of many chatbots to consistently implement <choice> elements reveals an area where further refinement is needed. Additionally, their tendency to either over-encode or under-encode elements indicates a lack of nuanced understanding of editorial priorities. Claude 3.5 Sonnet and OpenAI GPT 4o demonstrate promise when combined with explicit instructions and careful review of the results, showing that the strengths of AI can be productively harnessed to enhance regularization workflows.

Textual Criticism

The text critical step is to collate textual variants and prepare a critical apparatus that captures the diversity of manuscript traditions. The *Digital Methods* course used CollateX in THREAD 2 to identify textual differences, but students encoded those variants into TEI XML manually using the TEI Publisher's annotation editor. To evaluate whether AI chatbots could handle these tasks, a series of tests was designed, focusing on their ability to identify textual variants and encode them according to TEI standards. The experiment began by extracting the regularized text from the TEI XML generated in the regularization step.

Prompt

> *Provide the regularized text from the following TEI XML. Where there is a <choice> element, use the text that is in the <reg> and <expan> elements.*

Chatbots were tasked with processing this XML, selecting the <reg> and <expan> readings from <choice> elements, and comparing the resulting text against versions by Swete and Ziegler. The chatbots were then instructed to identify differences between the three texts and encode those variants using TEI elements <app>, <lem>, and <rdg> with appropriate @wit attributes.

> *Here are three versions of the same text. Carefully compare these versions to each other word for word and note the precise differences, including small additions or omissions, but exclude punctuation from your comparison. End your comparison with a code block listing the differences in TEI XML using the elements app, lem, and rdg with the @wit attribute.*

Finally, I asked the chatbots to encode the textual variants into the TEI XML file, which I provided along with this prompt:

> *Incorporate those textual differences in the following TEI XML using the elements app, lem, and rdg with the @wit attribute. Do not include a <app> element if the regularized lemma text is the same as the other witnesses. Retain all the other XML entities that are present in the TEI text. Follow this pattern: `` <w><app><lem wit="Q">ἐξείλετο</lem><rdg wit="Swete Ziegler">ἐξείλατο</rdg></app></w>``*

A total of twelve textual differences were embedded in the test verses, including added words (e.g., οἱ in verse 82, κ̅υ̅ in vv. 84 and 85), variant spellings (Μισαηλ in v. 88), and changes in verbal inflection (εὐλογείτω, ὑμνείτω, καὶ ὑπερυψούτω in verse 83).

Responses

Table 9.10 Variants Identified and Encoded in XML by AI Chatbots, by Ken M. Penner

Chatbot	Variants correctly found	TEI encoding
Claude 3.5 Sonnet	6	Refused
Claude 3.5 Haiku	2	Failed
Gemini 1.5 Pro	7	3 mistakes
Gemini 1.5 Flash	3	Failed
Gemini 2.0 Flash	2	2
Gemini 1206	9	9
Gemini 2.0 Flash Thinking	10	Failed
OpenAI GPT 4o	4	2
OpenAI GPT 4o mini	1	Failed
OpenAI o1-mini	4	4
Llama 3.2	0	
Llama 3.1 8b	0	
Llama 3.3	0	
DeepSeek V3	8	Only changes

Evaluation

The results revealed significant variability in chatbot performance. Only a small subset of models identified more than half of the textual variants, and even fewer encoded them accurately in TEI XML. Among the better-performing models, Claude 3.5 Sonnet identified six of the twelve variants but declined to encode them into TEI XML. Gemini 1206 demonstrated the most consistent results, correctly identifying nine variants and encoding them accurately. Gemini 1.5 Pro and DeepSeek V3 identified seven and eight variants, respectively, though Gemini 1.5 Pro introduced three encoding mistakes. Notably, Gemini 2.0 Flash Thinking detected ten variants but failed to encode them correctly.

In contrast, the smaller model chatbots struggled with both detection and encoding. Claude 3.5 Haiku, Gemini 1.5 Flash, and OpenAI GPT 4o mini found few variants and failed to produce usable TEI encoding. The failure to detect or encode variants accurately reveals the limitations of current AI in handling the precise requirements of textual criticism.

Translation and Alignment

Linguistic Annotation

To prepare for translation in the *Digital Methods* course, we first ascertained every word's lemma and morpho-syntactic description, mainly by using the online Perseus Greek Word Study Tool, which also provided English glosses. The standard TEI specification allows for word (<w>) elements to have attributes @lemma and @msd, but not glosses. The translation was then aligned with its source text using the Alpheios Alignment Editor. I recognized the likelihood that for any Greek word, chatbots would select the statistically most common parsing without regard to context. For example, a neuter noun such as ἔθνη could be nominative, accusative, or vocative, and we only know which case it is by considering the rest of the sentence. Therefore, to maximize the ability of chatbots to correctly discern these attributes from context, I prompted them to consider the syntactic structure of the words in their context. I provided model output to improve the quality of the response. For testing, I selected Dan. 3:81, a verse containing ambiguities such as the imperative mood of εὐλογεῖτε, ὑμνεῖτε, and ὑπερυψοῦτε, as well as the vocative case for πάντα τὰ θηρία and τὰ κτήνη.

Chatbots were provided with a TEI XML file containing the transcription of the verse, and were prompted to extract the regularized text, analyze the syntactic roles of words in their context, and enrich the XML with @lemma and @msd attributes. To improve output accuracy, a model example was included in the prompt to demonstrate the expected structure.

Prompt

~~~
First provide the regularized text from the following TEI
XML. Where there is a <choice> element, use the text that
is in the <reg> and <expan> elements. Second, think about
the meaning of the sentence and the syntactic function of
each word in the sentence. Finally, provide the original
TEI XML but with the added lemma and msd attributes for
the ancient Greek words in the <w> elements, that match the
word's syntactic function in the sentence. Here is a model
output: ```
<ab n="B54K3V37" xml:id="Dan.3.37.P785.I1">
            <w lemma="κύριος" msd="NASM">
              <choice>
~~~

~~~
        <abbr type="nomSac">
          <hi rend="overLine">κν</hi>
        </abbr>
        <expan>κύριον</expan>
      </choice>
    </w><w lemma="ὅτι" msd="C">τοῦ</w>
    <w lemma="δεσπότης" msd="NVSM">δέσποτα</w>
    <w    lemma="σμικρύνω"    msd="VAPI1P">ἐσμικρ<lb
n="P7CL-Q" break="no"/>ύνθημεν</w>
    <w lemma="παρά" msd="P">παρα</w>
    <w lemma="πᾶς" msd="JAPN">πάντα</w>
    <w lemma="ὁ" msd="DAPN">τὰ</w>
    <w lemma="ἔθνος" msd="NAPN">ἔθνη</w>
    <w lemma="καὶ" msd="C"><choice>
        <orig>και</orig>
        <reg>καὶ</reg>
      </choice></w>
    <w lemma="εἰμί" msd="VPAI1P">εσμεν</w>
    <lb/>
    <w lemma="ταπεινός" msd="JNPM">ταπεινὸι</w>
    <w lemma="ἐν" msd="C">ἐν</w>
    <w lemma="πᾶς" msd="JDSF">πάσῃ</w>
    <w lemma="ὁ" msd="DDSF">τῇ</w>
    <w lemma="γῆ" msd="NDSF">γῇ</w>
    <w lemma="σήμερον" msd="B">σήμερον</w>
    <lb/>
    <w lemma="διὰ" msd="P">διὰ</w>
    <w lemma="ὁ" msd="DAPF">τὰς</w>
    <w lemma="ἁμαρτία" msd="NAPF">ἁμαρτίας</w>
    <w lemma="ἐγώ" msd="RP1GP">ἡμῶν</w>
  </ab>

```
~~~

Add lemma and msd attributes for the following ancient Greek words in the <w> elements.

~~~
```<ab n="B54K3V81">
    <w>εὐλογεῖτε</w>
    <w>πάντα</w>
    <w>τὰ</w>
    <w>θηρία</w>
    <w><choice>
        <orig>και</orig>
        <reg>καὶ</reg>
      </choice></w>
~~~

```
        <lb n="P7CL-Q"/>
        <w>τὰ</w>
        <w><choice>
            <orig>κτηνη</orig>
            <reg>κτήνη</reg>
          </choice></w>
        <w>τὸν</w>
        <w>
          <choice>
            <abbr type="nomSac">
              <hi rend="overline">κν</hi>
            </abbr>
            <expan>κύριον</expan>
          </choice>
        </w>
        <pc>.</pc>
        <w>ὑμνεῖτε</w>
        <w>καὶ</w>
        <w>ὑπερυ<lb n="P7CL-Q" break="no"/>ψοῦτε</w>
        <w>αὐτὸν</w>
        <w>εἰς</w>
        <w>τοὺς</w>
        <w>αἰῶνας</w>
        <pc>·</pc>
        <lb n="P7CL-Q"/>
      </ab>```
```

Responses

Table 9.11 Lemmatization and Parsing Accuracy by AI Chatbots, by Ken M. Penner

Chatbot	Lemma /16	MSD /16
Claude 3.5 Sonnet	16	15
Claude 3.5 Haiku	16	11
Gemini 1.5 Pro	15	11
Gemini 1.5 Flash	16	7
Gemini 2.0 Flash	14	9
Gemini 1206	16	11
Gemini 2.0 Flash Thinking	16	11
OpenAI GPT 4o	16	11
OpenAI GPT 4o mini	13	6
OpenAI o1-mini	14	11
Llama 3.2	16	11
Llama 3.1 8b	13	6
Llama 3.3	16	5
DeepSeek 3	16	11

Evaluation

The performance of the chatbots varied widely. Claude 3.5 Sonnet achieved near-perfect results, accurately identifying all sixteen lemmas and fifteen out of sixteen MSDs. It correctly recognized the imperative mood of εὐλογεῖτε and the vocative case for πάντα τὰ θηρία. Claude 3.5 Haiku, DeepSeek 3, and OpenAI GPT 4o also identified all the lemmas but missed a few MSDs, particularly in distinguishing nominative from vocative cases. In contrast, Gemini 1.5 Flash and OpenAI GPT 4o mini struggled with grammatical nuances, defaulting to accusative or indicative forms where context required vocative or imperative parsing. While these models accurately identified the majority of lemmas, their lower scores in MSD annotation evince a limited capacity to interpret syntactic context.

The results revealed both the potential and limitations of AI in linguistic annotation. On the one hand, top-performing models demonstrated a strong ability to correctly lemmatize ancient Greek words and assign appropriate grammatical attributes when guided by explicit prompts. These tools could save considerable time for scholars by automating much of the annotation process, particularly for straightforward grammatical constructions. On the other hand, the chatbots' frequent mistakes in distinguishing vocative from nominative cases or imperative from indicative moods underscored their reliance on statistical patterns over syntactic comprehension. Without well-constructed prompts or examples, their outputs often lacked the precision required for scholarly annotation. As these tools evolve, they may increasingly support translation and alignment workflows, but for now, their outputs must be critically assessed and refined by expert editors.

Translation

Chatbots have proven adept at translating modern languages with extensive training data. However, their ability to handle ancient Greek, with its complex syntax and nuanced meanings, is less established. This test assesses how well chatbots manage vocabulary, recognize grammatical roles (such as identifying addressees), and interpret idiomatic expressions in ancient Greek. While a future study might employ BLEU scores to analyze a larger dataset, this initial evaluation focuses on a single passage from Dan. 3:81, testing basic translation accuracy. This verse contains straightforward vocabulary (*bless, beasts, cattle, Lord, exalt*) and an idiomatic expression (*forever*). The evaluation emphasized whether chatbots could accurately render these elements into natural English, paying particular attention to their handling of the verb *ὑπερυψοῦτε* (variously translated as *exalt above all* or *highly exalt*).

Prompt

Translate the following ancient Greek: εὐλογεῖτε πάντα τὰ θηρία καὶ τὰ κτήνη τὸν κύριον. ὑμνεῖτε καὶ ὑπερυψοῦτε αὐτὸν εἰς τοὺς αἰῶνας·

Response

Table 9.12 AI Chatbots' Translation Accuracy of Dan. 3:81, by Ken M. Penner

Chatbot	/7	ὑπερυψοῦτε
Claude 3.5 Sonnet	7	exalt above all
Claude 3.5 Haiku	6	exalt
Gemini 1.5 Pro	6	exalt
Gemini 1.5 Flash	5	exalt
Gemini 2.0 Flash	7	highly exalt
Gemini 1206	7	exalt
Gemini 2.0 Flash Thinking	7	highly exalt
OpenAI GPT 4o	7	exalt
OpenAI GPT 4o mini	6	exalt
OpenAI o1-mini	5	exalt
Llama 3.2	6	exalt
Llama 3.1 8b	6	exalt
Llama 3.3	4	highly exalt
DeepSeek V3	7	exalt above all

Evaluation

All the chatbots demonstrated a solid grasp of the vocabulary and idiomatic phraseology, correctly rendering *bless all the beasts and cattle* and *forever*. However, the primary challenge lay in expressing the relationship between the subject (*beasts and cattle*) and the object of the action (*the Lord*). Gemini 1.5 Pro produced the awkward phrase, *Bless all you beasts and cattle the Lord*, omitting a preposition or conjunction that would clarify the syntax. OpenAI GPT 4o mini provided, *Bless all the beasts and cattle the Lord*, which was grammatically ambiguous. The highest-scoring translations came from Claude 3.5 Sonnet, Gemini 2.0 Flash, GPT 4o, and DeepSeek V3, all of which rendered the verse fluently and accurately. For example, Claude 3.5 Sonnet translated ὑπερυψοῦτε as *exalt above all*, capturing the superlative sense of the verb, while Gemini 2.0 Flash and DeepSeek V3 offered similarly strong translations. These models not only conveyed the meaning clearly but also retained the tone and syntax of the original Greek.

Despite these successes, it is worth noting that the verse tested here represents relatively simple Greek. The vocabulary is basic, the sentence structure is straightforward, and the idiomatic elements are well-documented in training data. These conditions favor chatbots, making this passage an ideal baseline for evaluating their foundational capabilities. To probe the limits of the chatbots' abilities, a second test used a passage from Sibylline Oracles 5:38–39, a challenging piece of allegorical poetry. John Collins translated this elegantly as, "His son, with a first initial of three hundred, will get the better of him and take away his power."[36] The verse poses unique difficulties, including interpreting the genitive case of *κεραίης* (initial) and recognizing the symbolic meaning of the Greek numeral 300. The passage's allegorical nature requires understanding not only the grammar but also its encoded numerical and conceptual layers.

Prompt

Translate into English: τοῦ δέ, τριηκοσίης κεραίης ὅ τι πρῶτον, ἐλέγχων παῖς κράτος ἐξαφελεῖ

Responses

Table 9.13 AI Chatbots' Translation of Sibylline Oracles 5:38-39, by Ken M. Penner

Chatbot	
Claude 3.5 Sonnet	And of this, whatever is first of the three hundred horn/letter, a child removing power will test/refute
Claude 3.5 Haiku	And he, first of the three-hundred oar ship, proving (or challenging), the child will take away (or remove) power/rule
Gemini 1.5 Pro	But from him, at the very first touch of the three-hundred-year-old horn, a boy, testing (it), took away its power
Gemini 1.5 Flash	Concerning him, he first inspected the three hundred oars; the boy removed the power
Gemini 2.0 Flash	And from him, the first of the three-hundred-horned one, the son, putting it to the test, steals away his strength
Gemini 1206	But whatever boy first takes away the strength of the oar-handles of the thirty-oared galley, refuting him
Gemini 2.0 Flash Thinking	And of him, from the three-hundredth wing, whatever comes first, the son of those who put to the test will take away the strength.
OpenAI GPT 4o	And from this, of the three-hundred-horned (creature), the child, testing, will first take away the power.
OpenAI GPT 4o mini	However, regarding the three hundred horns, whatever comes first, the child will take away the power by refutation.
OpenAI o1-mini	But of the three hundred of Keraia, first, testing a child, power will remove.
Llama 3.2	But of the three hundred, the first spear, a child will strip of power.
Llama 3.1 8b	But, of the twenty-five rays, why first, the boy's authority is lifted.
Llama 3.3	But as for the three hundred, the first spear—a child will strip it of its power, putting it to the test.
DeepSeek V3	And of him, whatever first of the three hundred horns, a boy testing his strength will take away.

Evaluation

The chatbots struggled with this type of text. Even models that excelled in the simpler verse from Daniel faltered here, misinterpreting the grammatical roles or failing to recognize the symbolic reference to the numeral. This demonstrates that while chatbots can handle basic ancient Greek, more complex and less predictable texts expose their limitations. The evaluation reveals that Claude 3.5 Sonnet, GPT 4o, and DeepSeek V3 are capable of producing accurate and fluent translations of straightforward ancient Greek passages. However, their utility diminishes with texts requiring contextual or allegorical interpretation, such as those from the Sibylline Oracles. As LLMs evolve, chatbots' ability to engage with the subtleties of ancient languages may improve, but for now, their role is supplementary to expert scholarship.

Interpretive Annotation

Translational Commentary

In the *Digital Methods* course, students engaged in translational commentary to address questions arising from their translations. This process involved clarifying grammatical nuances and resolving ambiguities in the text. For instance, in Dan. 3:81, the verbs are imperatives rather than indicatives, and the *beasts and cattle* are the addressees of the command, not its objects. To test the capacity of chatbots to handle these grammatical subtleties, I asked for their understanding of the grammatical function of the animals and their ability to identify the main verb's mood. The expected response recognized the animals as addressees in the vocative case and the verbs (εὐλογεῖτε, ὑμνεῖτε, ὑπερυψοῦτε) as imperatives.

Prompt

What is the role of the beasts and cattle in the sentence?

Responses

Table 9.14 AI Chatbots' Syntactical Interpretation of Ambiguous Morphology in Dan. 3:81, by Ken M. Penner

Chatbot	Role of animals	Main verb
Claude 3.5 Sonnet	Vocative	Imperative
Claude 3.5 Haiku	Subject	
Gemini 1.5 Pro	Vocative	Imperative
Gemini 1.5 Flash	Subject	Command
Gemini 2.0 Flash	Subject	Imperative
Gemini 1206	Subject	Imperative
Gemini 2.0 Flash Thinking	Recipients	Command
OpenAI GPT 4o	Subject	Exhortation
OpenAI GPT 4o mini	Subject	Command
OpenAI o1-mini	Addressee	Imperative
Llama 3.2	Subject	Imperative
Llama 3.1 8b	Object/subject	Command
Llama 3.3	Subject	Imperative
DeepSeek 3	Subject	Imperative

Evaluation

The chatbots' performance was varied in nomenclature but generally satisfactory. Claude 3.5 Sonnet and Gemini 1.5 Pro correctly identified the vocative case, and the verbs as imperatives, demonstrating a solid understanding of the grammatical structure. Gemini 2.0 Flash Thinking and OpenAI o1-mini called the animals' role "recipients" of the "command." Others called them the grammatical subject rather than the addressees, or referred to the main verb as an *exhortation* rather than explicitly labeling it as imperative.

Interestingly, even those chatbots that struggled with parsing the neuter plural addressees earlier in the workflow performed adequately in this task. This suggests that while their grammatical parsing might be contextually flawed, their broader understanding of sentence roles allowed them to arrive at accurate conclusions.

Contextualizing Commentary: Broader Reflections on Ancient Texts

Commentary on ancient texts extends beyond grammatical and translational issues to encompass intertextual connections, linguistic and historical context, and theological implications. These broader reflections help situate a passage within its literary and cultural milieu. To evaluate chatbots' capabilities in this domain, I tested their ability to provide insightful commentary on Dan. 3:81, focusing on these larger thematic concerns.

The chatbots were prompted to address intertextuality, linguistic and historical context, and theological implications relevant to the verse. Their responses were analyzed for their ability to identify related texts, contextual observations, and theological themes. The verse's imagery and language, which calls upon all creation to praise God, provided a rich source for exploration.

Prompt

Add any relevant comments on intertextuality, linguistic and historical context, and theological implications.

Responses

Table 9.15 AI Chatbots' Comments on Intertextuality, Linguistic and Historical Context, and Theological Implications of Dan. 3:81, by Ken M. Penner

Chatbot	Intertextuality	Context	Theology
Claude 3.5 Sonnet	Psalm 148; Isa. 43:20; Romans 8	Merism; parallelism; LXX	Anthropocentrism
Claude 3.5 Haiku	Psalm 148; Daniel 3; Wisdom	Stoic cosmic harmony	Anthropocentrism
Gemini 1.5 Pro	Ps. 148:10;	Command to humans	Stewards; cosmic liturgy
Gemini 1.5 Flash	Ps. 150:6;	Natural worship	Respect for nature
Gemini 2.0 Flash	Daniel 3; Psalm 148; Benedicite; Genesis	Active declaration of goodness; wild & domestic;	Cosmos; sovereignty; harmony; inclusivity
Gemini 1206	Daniel 3; Ps. 132:22; 148; 150; Rev. 5:13;		Universal, cosmic harmony, anthropocentrism, ecology, divine liturgy
Gemini 2.0 Flash Thinking	Psalm 148; Daniel 3; Ps. 19:1; Rom. 1:20;	Wild & domestic; title for Jesus; forever; superlative praise	Universal praise; creation reflects glory; eternal; christology
OpenAI GPT 4o	Psalm 148;		Creation has unity and value and purpose; creation is good & glorifies creator; human responsibility
OpenAI GPT 4o mini	Psalm 148; ANE	Range/diversity; universal; anthropocentrism	Sovereignty; omnipresence; interconnectedness; ecology
OpenAI o1-mini	Ps. 148:5, 7-10; Job 38:39; Hellenistic view of cosmos; Stoic; Wisdom of Solomon; Sirach	Untamed & domesticated; syncretism; hymnic; inclusivity in worship	Anthropocentrism; Imago Dei; eschatological hope; chaos; ecocentrism
Llama 3.2	Ps. 148:7-8	Dan 3	Sovereignty; interconnectedness; unified; harmonious; cosmic Christ
Llama 3.1 8b	Ps. 148:10-13;		Interconnected; interdependent; anthropocentrism;
Llama 3.3	Ps. 148:10;	Psalms; Sirach;	Creation reflects glory; sovereign; Rev. 5:13; Rom. 8:19-22
DeepSeek 3	Psalm 148; Romans 8; Daniel 3	Creation praising	Good world

Evaluation

All the chatbots recognized intertextual links, most notably with Psalm 148, a hymn that similarly invites the cosmos—celestial and terrestrial, wild and domestic—to glorify God. Other frequently cited texts included Rev. 5:13 and Romans 8, alongside works from Second Temple literature, Sirach, and the Wisdom of Solomon. These connections highlighted the verse's broader thematic resonance within biblical and Jewish literary traditions.

The chatbots also made astute linguistic observations, noting how merism and parallelism amplify the verse's inclusivity by uniting contrasting elements, such as wild and domestic animals, in the act of praise. Some models drew parallels with Stoic notions of cosmic harmony and Hellenistic cosmology, emphasizing the interconnectedness and purposefulness of creation. The linguistic features of the verse thus served as a gateway to broader historical and philosophical discussions.

The theological commentary revealed a shared emphasis on themes of ecological interconnectedness, divine sovereignty, and the challenge to anthropocentrism. Several chatbots recognized the invitation for all creation, not just humanity, to glorify God, a concept that disrupts human-centered worship paradigms. The verse was seen as a call to harmonious stewardship and ascribing intrinsic value to creation. Other responses touched on eschatological hope, Christological authority, and the reflection of divine glory in the natural world. These insights demonstrated a capacity for engaging with the verse's theological depth.

The results were impressive, with most chatbots identifying key intertextual connections and broader thematic elements. Claude 3.5 Sonnet, Gemini 2.0 Flash Thinking, and OpenAI GPT 4o provided particularly insightful analyses. Their capacity to identify key parallels, highlight stylistic features, and reflect on broader implications is evidence of their potential as tools for helping commentators by providing another perspective on the text. While chatbots show promise for assisting with such contextual annotation, they remain supplementary to the expertise and interpretive skills of scholars.

Human Curation: Ensuring Quality at Every Stage

What this case study and benchmarking demonstrates is that while artificial intelligence offers transformative possibilities for digital scholarly editions, it is *expert curation by humans that ensures the process remains rigorous, ethical, and meaningful.* Each stage of the scholarly workflow—from manuscript identification to final presentation—benefits from the efficiency of AI, but also requires human oversight to uphold academic integrity. A quick recap of the findings for each stage may be helpful to illustrate this point.

Manuscript Identification and Cataloging: Digital sources provide rapid access to manuscript databases, expediting the identification of relevant witnesses and metadata assembly. However, as demonstrated in the evaluation, without specialized training, chatbots often misidentify manuscripts or conflate bibliographic details. Scholars must validate AI-suggested sources against established catalogs and apply their expertise to ensure the selected manuscripts are significant and relevant to the research objectives.

Indexing and Transcription: Some of the best AI chatbots can recognize some of the text of manuscripts if they are clearly photographed, but at this point none of the chatbots have been trained enough on ancient Greek manuscripts to benefit from their transcriptions. They can structure plain transcriptions by humans, but still a person must verify the result for accuracy.

Reconciliation: The precision needed to compare two transcriptions in minute detail is not one of the strengths of AI. Although the chatbots can be helpful where alternatives are not available, traditional algorithmic software operated by a human is much more dependable for this task.

Regularization: All the AI chatbots tested here excelled at correcting spelling and accents, but a human is still needed to verify ambiguous cases and acute accents on the ultima before punctuation.

Textual Criticism: Comparing witnesses to identify textual variants requires the same level of precision as reconciling transcriptions. Again, conventional algorithmic software such as CollateX is more reliable for this task, but AI chatbots can be helpful in identifying differences when such software is not available, if used to supplement human observations. Chatbots are more helpful at structuring the variant readings into a useful format.

Translation: AI can provide a remarkably adequate starting point as an initial draft; I would estimate that the best of them outperform a typical trained graduate student. Still, human translators must review and refine the chatbot's output to ensure fidelity to the original text's meaning and style.

Interpretation: Currently available AI chatbots can produce remarkably perceptive observations, but these observations are best used like brainstorming assistance for human commentators.

The Scholar-AI Partnership

This exploration has provided evidence that AI, while not a replacement for human expertise, is a powerful tool that can enhance and expand the possibilities of biblical scholarship. By automating repetitive tasks, AI allows scholars to focus on the interpretive rigor and ethical considerations that define their work. Its use democratizes access to intellectual resources, bridges gaps between communities, and opens new avenues for interdisciplinary collaboration.

However, the findings also show that AI's contributions are only as effective as the human curation that directs them. It is through this partnership—where AI complements human insight rather than substituting for it—that the true potential of these tools emerges. AI is worth using because it amplifies the scholar's reach and impact, not by replacing critical thought but by supporting it in unprecedented ways.

As biblical scholarship navigates the digital age, a balance between innovation and tradition will ensure that the ancient texts we study remain both accessible and profound, connecting the past to the present with integrity and purpose.

Notes

1 Mark D. Wilkinson et al., "The FAIR Guiding Principles for Scientific Data Management and Stewardship," *Scientific Data* 3.1 (2016): 160018, https://doi.org/10.1038/sdata.2016.18.

2 François Bougard, "Pinakes | Πίνακες," 2016, accessed April 14, 2025, https://pinakes.irht.cnrs.fr.

3 W. Clarysse and M. Depauw, "LDAB," *Leuven Database of Ancient Books,* January 13, 2025, accessed April 14, 2025, https://www.trismegistos.org/ldab/.

4 Troy Griffitts, "Virtual Manuscript Room Collaborative Research Environment," *VMR CRE*, 2018, accessed April 14, 2025, https://vmrcre.org/.

5 "Transkribus," READ COOP, January 13, 2025, https://www.transkribus.org/; Elpida Perdiki, "Transkribus: Reviewing HTR Training on (Greek) Manuscripts," *RIDE* 15 (2022), https://ride.i-d-e.de/issues/issue-15/transkribus/.

6 Ronald Haentjens Dekker and Gregor Middell, "CollateX," Java (Huygens ING: The Interedition Development Group, 2019), https://collatex.net/.

7 Clarysse and Depauw, "LDAB."

8 Bougard, "Pinakes | Πίνακες."

9 Duke Collaboratory for Classics Computing and Institute for the Study of the Ancient World, "Papyri.Info," *Papyri.Info*, 2010, https://papyri.info.

10 "Diktyon—Réseau Numérique Pour Les Manuscrits Grecs," *Diktyon*, November 7, 2023, https://diktyon.irht.cnrs.fr/en/.

11 TEI Consortium, *TEI P5: Guidelines for Electronic Text Encoding and Interchange*, vol. Version 4.3.0, 2021.

12 "Oxygen XML Editor," November 27, 2024, https://www.oxygenxml.com/xml_editor.html.

13 Ken M. Penner, "Indexing Q," *THREAD 2*, 2021, http://206.12.93.167/web/digital-codex-marchalianus/indexing.

14 Ken M. Penner, "Transcribing," *THREAD 2*, 2021, http://206.12.93.167/web/digital-codex-marchalianus/transcribing.

15 Thomas Burch, "Online Transcription Editor," HTML, Javascript/Typescript, XML (Trier: Trier Center for Digital Humanities, 2021), https://sourceforge.net/projects/wfce-ote/.

16 Jamie Peabody, "Mergely—Compare and Merge Document Differences Online," JavaScript, 2024, https://mergely.com/.

17 Joseph Ziegler, Olivier Munnich, and Detlef Fraenkel, eds., *Susanna, Daniel, Bel et Draco*, vol. 2 of *Septuaginta: Vetus Testamentum Graecum* 16 (Göttingen: Vandenhoeck & Ruprecht, 1999).

18 Henry Swete, *The Old Testament in Greek According to the Septuagint* (Cambridge: Cambridge University Press, 1887).

19 Alfred Rahlfs, *Septuaginta: id est Vetus Testamentum gracece iuxta LXX interpretes* (Stuttgart: Wurttembergische Bibelanstalt, 1935).

20 Wolfgang Meier, "TEI Publisher," XQuery (eXist Solutions, 2024), https://teipublisher.com/exist/apps/tei-publisher/index.html.

21 Gregory Crane, "Greek Word Study Tool," *Perseus Digital Library*, n.d., https://www.perseus.tufts.edu/hopper/morph?.

22 "Alpheios Alignment Editor," n.d., https://alignment.alpheios.net/.

23 Sarah A. Chauncey and H. Patricia McKenna, "A Framework and Exemplars for Ethical and Responsible Use of AI Chatbot Technology to Support Teaching and Learning," *Computers and Education: Artificial Intelligence* 5 (2023): 100182, https://doi.org/10.1016/j.caeai.2023.100182.

24 Ian R. Hodgkinson, Nick Jennings, and Tom Jackson, "Everyone Must Understand the Environmental Costs of AI," *OECD.AI Policy Observatory*, October 4,

2024, https://oecd.ai/en/wonk/understand-environmental-costs; Jillian Kunze, "Environmental Impacts of Artificial Intelligence: Peril, Promise, and Policy," *Society for Industrial and Applied Mathematics*, October 4, 2024, https://www.siam.org/publications/siam-news/articles/environmental-impacts-of-artificial-intelligence-peril-promise-and-policy/; Karthik Karunakaran, "The Hidden Environmental Costs of Using AI Chatbots: What You Need to Know," *Medium*, September 22, 2024, https://medium.com/@iitkarthik/the-hidden-environmental-costs-of-using-ai-chatbots-what-you-need-to-know-353ec353c886.

25 Kirk Stewart, "The Ethical Dilemmas of AI," *USC Annenberg School for Communication and Journalism*, March 21, 2024, https://annenberg.usc.edu/research/center-public-relations/usc-annenberg-relevance-report/ethical-dilemmas-ai; Christina Pazzanese, "Ethical Concerns Mount as AI Takes Bigger Decision-Making Role," *Harvard Gazette*, October 26, 2020, https://news.harvard.edu/gazette/story/2020/10/ethical-concerns-mount-as-ai-takes-bigger-decision-making-role/; Newsreel Asia, "The Exploited Workers Behind the AI We Use," Newsreel Asia Insight #280, July 13, 2024, https://www.newsreel.asia/articles/the-exploited-workers-behind-the-ai-we-use.

26 Blake Brittain, "Authors Sue Anthropic for Copyright Infringement over AI Training," *Reuters*, August 21, 2024, § Artificial Intelligence, https://www.reuters.com/technology/artificial-intelligence/authors-sue-anthropic-copyright-infringement-over-ai-training-2024-08-20/.

27 "Sustainable and Eco-Friendly Chatbots | Chat Ergo Bot," 2025, https://chatergobot.com/en/sustainable-chatbots.

28 Farwa Mehmood, "New AI Chatbots Use Only 13W of Energy with No Performance Loss," *AI Atlas*, July 18, 2024, https://www.aiatlas.ai/science-and-health/new-ai-chatbots-use-only-13w-of-energy-with-no-performance-loss-18072024115337/.

29 Ethan Mollick, *Co-Intelligence: Living and Working with AI* (New York: Portfolio, 2024).

30 Fadeke Adegbuyi, "Understanding and Mitigating AI Hallucination," *DigitalOcean*, August 11, 2024, https://www.digitalocean.com/resources/articles/ai-hallucination; Cătălina Mărcuță, "Chatbot Accuracy Ensuring Correct Responses and Information Retrieval," *MoldStud*, August 13, 2024, https://moldstud.com/articles/p-chatbot-accuracy-ensuring-correct-responses-and-information-retrieval; "Enhancing Factual Accuracy in Large Language Models with AI," *Longshot*, April 18, 2024, https://www.longshot.ai/blog/factual-accuracy-in-llm; Bill McLane, "AI Hallucinations: The Best Ways to Prevent Them," *DataStax*, December 9, 2024, https://www.datastax.com/guides/ai-hallucinations-the-best-ways-to-prevent-them.

31 Pu Zhao et al., "Fully Open Source Moxin-7B Technical Report," preprint, arXiv, December 11, 2024, https://doi.org/10.48550/arXiv.2412.06845; Teven Le Scao et al., "BLOOM: A 176B-Parameter Open-Access Multilingual Language Model," preprint, arXiv, June 27, 2023, https://doi.org/10.48550/arXiv.2211.05100; "Common Crawl—Open Repository of Web Crawl Data," *Common Crawl*, April 10, 2025, https://commoncrawl.org/.

32 Simon Maria de Magistris, *Δανιὴλ κατα του —ἑβδομήκοντα ἐκ τῶν τετράπλων Ὠριγένος », Daniel secundum Septuaginta ex Tetraplis Origenis nunc primum editus e singularo Chisiano codice annorum supra 800. . . gr. & lat. (Hippolyti . . . Interpretatio in Danielem; Daniel juxta Theodotionem, cum variis lectionibus; Comparatio versionis*

LXX-viralis cum Theodotionea; Apologia Sententiæ Patrum de LXX-virali versione; Pars libri Esther Chaldaice, Græce, Latine) (Rome: Typis Propagandae fidei, 1772); Johann David Michaelis, *Daniel secundum septuaginta ex tetraplis Origenis : Romae Anno 1772, ex Chisiano Codice* (Göttingen: Vandenhoeck, 1773).

33 "TEI element teiHeader (TEI header)," Text Encoding Initiative, last updated January 24, 2025, https://tei-c.org/release/doc/tei-p5-doc/en/html/ref-teiHeader.html.

34 Henry Barclay Swete, *An Introduction to the Old Testament in Greek. Revised by R. R. Ottley. With an Appendix Containing the Letter of Aristeas*, 2nd ed. (Cambridge: Cambridge University Press, 1914).

35 Felix Albrecht, "Göttinger Septuaginta—Rahlfs Q," *Göttinger Septuaginta*, September 6, 2024, https://septuaginta.uni-goettingen.de/catalogue/Ra_Q/.

36 John J. Collins, "Sibylline Oracles," in *The Old Testament Pseudepigrapha*, ed. J. H. Charlesworth, vol. 1 of *The Old Testament Pseudepigrapha* (Garden City: Doubleday, 1983), 394.

Bibliography

Adegbuyi, Fadeke. "Understanding and Mitigating AI Hallucination." *DigitalOcean*, August 11, 2024. https://www.digitalocean.com/resources/articles/ai-hallucination.

Albrecht, Felix. "Göttinger Septuaginta—Rahlfs Q." *Göttinger Septuaginta*, September 6, 2024. https://septuaginta.uni-goettingen.de/catalogue/Ra_Q/.

"Alpheios Alignment Editor," n.d. https://alignment.alpheios.net/.

Bougard, François. "Pinakes | Πίνακες," 2016. https://pinakes.irht.cnrs.fr.

Brittain, Blake. "Authors Sue Anthropic for Copyright Infringement over AI Training." *Reuters*, August 21, 2024, § Artificial Intelligence. https://www.reuters.com/technology/artificial-intelligence/authors-sue-anthropic-copyright-infringement-over-ai-training-2024-08-20/.

Burch, Thomas. "Online Transcription Editor." HTML, Javascript/Typescript, XML. Trier: Trier Center for Digital Humanities, 2021. https://sourceforge.net/projects/wfce-ote/.

Chauncey, Sarah A., and H. Patricia McKenna. "A Framework and Exemplars for Ethical and Responsible Use of AI Chatbot Technology to Support Teaching and Learning." *Computers and Education: Artificial Intelligence* 5 (2023): 100182.

Clarysse, W., and M. Depauw. "LDAB." *Leuven Database of Ancient Books*, January 13, 2025. https://www.trismegistos.org/ldab/.

Collins, John J. "Sibylline Oracles." Pages 317–472 in *The Old Testament Pseudepigrapha*. Edited by J. H. Charlesworth. Vol. 1 of *The Old Testament Pseudepigrapha*. Garden City: Doubleday, 1983.

"Common Crawl—Open Repository of Web Crawl Data." *Common Crawl*, April 10, 2025. n.d. https://commoncrawl.org/.

Crane, Gregory. "Greek Word Study Tool." *Perseus Digital Library*, n.d. https://www.perseus.tufts.edu/hopper/morph?

Dekker, Ronald Haentjens, and Gregor Middell. "CollateX." Java. Huygens ING: The Interedition Development Group, 2019. https://collatex.net/.

"Diktyon—Réseau Numérique Pour Les Manuscrits Grecs." *Diktyon*, November 7, 2023. https://diktyon.irht.cnrs.fr/en/.

Duke Collaboratory for Classics Computing and Institute for the Study of the Ancient World. "Papyri.Info." *Papyri.Info*, 2010. https://papyri.info.

"Enhancing Factual Accuracy in Large Language Models with AI." *Longshot*, April 18, 2024. n.d. https://www.longshot.ai/blog/factual-accuracy-in-llm.

Griffitts, Troy. "Virtual Manuscript Room Collaborative Research Environment." *VMR CRE*, 2018. https://vmrcre.org/.

Hodgkinson, Ian R., Nick Jennings, and Tom Jackson. "Everyone Must Understand the Environmental Costs of AI." *OECD.AI Policy Observatory*, October 4, 2024. https://oecd.ai/en/wonk/understand-environmental-costs.

Karunakaran, Karthik. "The Hidden Environmental Costs of Using AI Chatbots: What You Need to Know." *Medium*, September 22, 2024. https://medium.com/@iitkarthik/the-hidden-environmental-costs-of-using-ai-chatbots-what-you-need-to-know-353ec353c886.

Kunze, Jillian. "Environmental Impacts of Artificial Intelligence: Peril, Promise, and Policy." *Society for Industrial and Applied Mathematics*, October 4, 2024. https://www.siam.org/publications/siam-news/articles/environmental-impacts-of-artificial-intelligence-peril-promise-and-policy/.

Magistris, Simon Maria de. *Δανιὴλ κατα του —ἑβδομήκοντα ἐκ τῶν τετράπλων Ὠριγένος », Daniel secundum Septuaginta ex Tetraplis Origenis nunc primum editus e singularo Chisiano codice annorum supra 800... gr. & lat. (Hippolyti ... Interpretatio in Danielem; Daniel juxta Theodotionem, cum variis lectionibus; Comparatio versionis LXX-viralis cum Theodotionea; Apologia Sententiæ Patrum de LXX-virali versione; Pars libri Esther Chaldaice, Græce, Latine)*. Rome: Typis Propagandae fidei, 1772.

Mărcuță, Cătălina. "Chatbot Accuracy Ensuring Correct Responses and Information Retrieval." *MoldStud*, August 13, 2024. https://moldstud.com/articles/p-chatbot-accuracy-ensuring-correct-responses-and-information-retrieval.

McLane, Bill. "AI Hallucinations: The Best Ways to Prevent Them." *DataStax*, December 9, 2024. https://www.datastax.com/guides/ai-hallucinations-the-best-ways-to-prevent-them.

Mehmood, Farwa. "New AI Chatbots Use Only 13W of Energy with No Performance Loss." *AI Atlas*, July 18, 2024. https://www.aiatlas.ai/science-and-health/new-ai-chatbots-use-only-13w-of-energy-with-no-performance-loss-18072024115337/.

Meier, Wolfgang. "TEI Publisher." XQuery. eXist Solutions, 2024. https://teipublisher.com/exist/apps/tei-publisher/index.html.

Michaelis, Johann David. *Daniel secundum septuaginta ex tetraplis Origenis: Romae Anno 1772, ex Chisiano Codice*. Göttingen: Vandenhoeck, 1773.

Mollick, Ethan. *Co-Intelligence: Living and Working with AI*. New York: Portfolio, 2024.

Newsreel Asia. "The Exploited Workers Behind the AI We Use." Newsreel Asia Insight #280, July 13, 2024. https://www.newsreel.asia/articles/the-exploited-workers-behind-the-ai-we-use.

"Oxygen XML Editor," November 27, 2024. https://www.oxygenxml.com/xml_editor.html.

Pazzanese, Christina. "Ethical Concerns Mount as AI Takes Bigger Decision-Making Role." *Harvard Gazette*, October 26, 2020. https://news.harvard.edu/gazette/story/2020/10/ethical-concerns-mount-as-ai-takes-bigger-decision-making-role/.

Peabody, Jamie. "Mergely—Compare and Merge Document Differences Online." JavaScript, 2024. https://mergely.com/.

Penner, Ken M. "Indexing Q." *THREAD 2*, 2021. http://206.12.93.167/web/digital-codex-marchalianus/indexing.

Penner, Ken M. "Transcribing." *THREAD 2*, 2021. http://206.12.93.167/web/digital-codex-marchalianus/transcribing.

Perdiki, Elpida. "Transkribus: Reviewing HTR Training on (Greek) Manuscripts." *RIDE* 15 (2022). https://ride.i-d-e.de/issues/issue-15/transkribus/.

Rahlfs, Alfred. *Septuaginta: id est Vetus Testamentum gracece iuxta LXX interpretes.* Stuttgart: Wurttembergische Bibelanstalt, 1935.

"Sustainable and Eco-Friendly Chatbots | Chat Ergo Bot," n.d. https://chatergobot.com/en/sustainable-chatbots.

Swete, Henry. *The Old Testament in Greek According to the Septuagint.* Cambridge: University Press, 1887.

Swete, Henry. *An Introduction to the Old Testament in Greek. Revised by R. R. Ottley. With an Appendix Containing the Letter of Aristeas.* 2nd ed. Cambridge: Cambridge University Press, 1914.

TEI Consortium. *TEI P5: Guidelines for Electronic Text Encoding and Interchange.* Vol. Version 4.3.0, 2021.

"TEI Element teiHeader (TEI Header)." *Text Encoding Initiative.* Last updated January 24, 2025. https://tei-c.org/release/doc/tei-p5-doc/en/html/ref-teiHeader.html.

"Transkribus—Unlocking the Past with AI." READ COOP SCE, January 13, 2025. https://www.transkribus.org.

Wilkinson, Mark D., Michel Dumontier, IJsbrand Jan Aalbersberg, Gabrielle Appleton, Myles Axton, Arie Baak, Niklas Blomberg, Jan-Willem Boiten, Luiz Bonino da Silva Santos, et al. "The FAIR Guiding Principles for Scientific Data Management and Stewardship." *Scientific Data* 3.1 (2016): 160018. https://doi.org/10.1038/sdata.2016.18.

Zhao, Pu, Xuan Shen, Zhenglun Kong, Yixin Shen, Sung-En Chang, Timothy Rupprecht, Lei Lu, Enfu Nan, Changdi Yang, et al. "Fully Open Source Moxin-7B Technical Report." Preprint, arXiv. December 11, 2024. https://doi.org/10.48550/arXiv.2412.06845.

Ziegler, Joseph, Olivier Munnich, and Detlef Fraenkel, eds. *Susanna, Daniel, Bel et Draco.* Vol. 2 of *Septuaginta: Vetus Testamentum Graecum* 16. Göttingen: Vandenhoeck & Ruprecht, 1999.

10

Open to Interpretation

The Jewish Canon and the Power of AI

Sara Tillinger Wolkenfeld

According to Jewish legal lore, the highest legal position a person could pursue was that of judge on the high court, the Sanhedrin, which was functionally the Supreme Court of the Jewish justice system. This body no longer exists today, but the Talmud, the central Jewish legal corpus compiled between the third and eighth centuries of the Common Era, details the credentials necessary to become a judge at this level.[1]

According to the Talmud, a judge on the Sanhedrin must be able to convincingly argue a particular legal stance—one that is obviously and completely false to all those who are familiar with the Jewish legal system (b. Sanh. 17a). Why would this be an important credential for someone tasked with exercising legal expertise? It seems that in order to occupy a seat on the high court, one needs to be in command of a huge amount of information and have the ability to rearrange that information in multiple ways, even to the point of producing incorrect results.[2] Of course, one presumably also needs the wisdom not to issue an incorrect ruling, but the Talmud does not state this explicitly.[3]

The digital age is also sometimes referred to as the Information Age, and the quantity of digital information available to people today is greater than anyone could have imagined in Talmudic times. With the advent of large language models (LLMs) and other kinds of machine learning, humans have the ability to transform the huge quantity of digital information that is freely available online into data that enables new reading and learning experiences. The artificial intelligence tools already at our disposal allow people to access and manipulate more information than was previously possible, and their power is growing exponentially.

Today, like a judge fit for the Sanhedrin, artificial intelligence has absorbed enough information to produce lengthy and compelling incorrect results, but unlike a judge on the Sanhedrin, it is not equipped with the wisdom to avoid making mistakes. Large language models are powered by data, not discernment, and it is up to those deploying these tools to ensure that they are used in ways that expand the reach of Jewish wisdom, as the Talmud intended in its instructions to judges rather than distort it. Information is powerful, especially in the age of artificial intelligence, and religious scholars who use these tools carefully have the opportunity to leverage ancient knowledge by using modern technologies rigorously and deliberately.

The specific context for my work is the Jewish canon, yet the promises and perils of applying machine learning and AI to these texts are equally applicable to any corpus of religious knowledge. Sefaria, the non-profit website at which I serve as chief learning officer, is dedicated to bringing the Jewish textual tradition into the digital age. We envision a world where Jewish texts are alive and resonant with a vast and diverse Jewish community that is actively adding to and engaging in the continued conversation of the Jewish people and our texts. In other words, Sefaria exists to democratize access to knowledge that has always been the purview of a religious and intellectual elite, and to create a future where more people know more about these sources than ever before.

As of this writing, Sefaria's library contains over 365 million words of digital text, with over 88 million in translation. As a result of our machine learning techniques, the site hosts over 3.655 million links between texts. On average, the website and app combined have over 740,000 monthly users. From user surveys conducted over the years, we know that the digital technologies used by Sefaria have made the information in the Jewish canon available to many people who were previously unable to engage with these texts.[4]

Jewish texts are an interesting test case for the work of using machine learning to expand access to knowledge because traditionally, religious authority has been deeply rooted in textual expertise.[5] Using new technologies to provide new ways of reading ancient texts raises a myriad of ethical questions: What is the impact on religious communities when access to information is democratized? How might wider consumption of these texts change the balance of power among scholars and laypeople, and what is our responsibility to address those changes? What are the costs of this greatly expanded access, and how might we assess when it is worthwhile? What does it mean for us to be able to read and process texts in ways that are unprecedented in human history? Armed with these new tools, we have a responsibility to decide what aspects of the study of the Bible or other canonical texts we want to prioritize and promote.

Sefaria launched in 2013, and in the ensuing eleven years, machine learning has already had a tremendous impact on the field of Jewish text study. I will explore two different ways that Sefaria uses machine learning and artificial intelligence to transform the way that people access and process canonical Jewish texts: first, the links that Sefaria has generated which make it easy to find connections between multiple works and view those works side by side, and second, the ways that machine learning has enabled us to tag and display sources topically. Following those sections, I will share some promising directions for upcoming features that will continue to leverage gains in artificial intelligence capabilities to make Jewish texts more accessible. With these concrete examples in mind, we can then begin to consider the ethical implications of these tools and the possibilities for further evolution of the study and sharing of religious texts.

Texts in Context: Turning Connections into Links

> The school of Rabbi Yishmael taught *that the verse states: "Is not My word like as fire? says the Lord;* and like a hammer that breaks the rock in pieces" *(Jeremiah 23:29).* Just as this hammer breaks *a stone* into several fragments, so too, one verse *is stated by God* and *from it* emerge several explanations. *(b. Sanh. 17a, my translation)*

Implicit in an authentic understanding of canonical Jewish texts is the belief that words invested with religious significance often contain multiple meanings. As the Talmudic quote above demonstrates, the classical rabbis believed that divine language is powerful in ways that far surpass human speech, and part of that power is the ability for a single sentence to contain a universe of possibilities. One of the challenges, therefore, of presenting the Word of God in any format is that merely allowing access to these words is not sufficient; we must consider what tools are needed in order to ensure that the meaning or meanings conveyed are consistent with the way insiders to these texts would understand them. The Jewish hermeneutical tradition places a great deal of value on reading canonical sources in conversation with one another. Later sources quote from earlier ones, scholars sometimes cite other works but also use literary allusions to other books, and the more important a text is, the more voluminous and varied the commentaries that reinterpret it.[6] The meaning of a text is derived from multiple intertexts and cannot always be accurately inferred from merely reading the text alone.[7]

As a result of this core belief about meaning-making, to merely sit down with a single Jewish text is a Jewishly inferior experience. The Bible is a prime example; it belongs to more than one faith tradition, but to understand it as a Jew is to read it in conversation with other canonical Jewish works. In order to gain the kind of knowledge that is associated with scholarly clout in the Jewish world, one must open multiple books simultaneously in order to cross-reference ideas and investigate the reception of each biblical verse and its development across centuries and geographic regions. This type of scholarly endeavor requires language skills—primarily Hebrew and Aramaic—as well as the skills of textual analysis. It requires access to a vast library of books—a library that, if it exists at all in a given place, is typically open only to a certain type of elite and pious person (or, if we are being honest, an elite and pious man).[8] Once the appropriate books are procured, it also requires a significant investment of time to locate each source that is quoted, cited, or alluded to in the passage currently open on the table in front of the scholar.

Machine learning and artificial intelligence allow Sefaria's engineers to generate links between canonical Jewish texts, and also to create connections between modern online content—as it is produced, in real time—and the canonical texts in Sefaria's library. Initially, Sefaria's linker technology used pattern matching to find citations of sources and transform those citations into links. In many cases, these citations are standardized, so they are relatively easy to match. For example, a biblical verse would be [name of book] [chapter number]:[verse number]. The name of the book might be translated or transliterated from the Hebrew, and if it is transliterated, there are several possible transliterations. If it is in English, it may be abbreviated (e.g., "Gen." instead of "Genesis"). Training the algorithm to recognize the different common variants allows the system to find citations of biblical sources and many others throughout the canon. As a result, users can open one work, click on a section of the text, and links to related sources will appear in the side panel. Click on one of those, and the cited text appears side by side with the initial source, so that the user can read the two together and understand the larger context for the quote.

This same technology allows Sefaria to link modern text-based articles, found on other websites, to the primary sources on our website. Anyone who regularly publishes articles or sermons that cite canonical Jewish texts can install our code on their website, transforming their citations into links. Sefaria's engineering team, in turn, can render those links bi-directional, such that a reader on Sefaria's site can discover modern content that draws on the primary sources they are studying. This provides readers with perspectives that are both modern and tailored to their particular interests; a website might specialize in social justice issues, or articles about Judaism and the environment, or come from within a particular denomination of Judaism, and all of these factors make the content shared that much more relevant to the reader.[9]

Advances in machine learning have allowed us to create a second generation of the linker technology, which currently serves as our method for linking Hebrew language websites to texts on Sefaria. This tool uses neural networks to find a much wider range of possible citations. Many of the books in Sefaria's library were composed before the invention of the printing press, and the authors of these works tended to assume a very high level of familiarity with the Jewish textual tradition. As a result, many citations are not standardized in the same ways as those referenced above. Instead, an author may refer to something that was said "earlier," or "at the end of [name of chapter]," or even just "ibid."[10] This linker is increasingly able to turn these vague references into direct links, thus ensuring that even readers without the ability to recognize references on their own can look up the corresponding sources.

These links democratize access to knowledge in unprecedented ways, ensuring that even those without the skills or physical ability to look up citations that put texts in conversation with one another can find and read these sources with just a few clicks of a mouse. In addition, connections that were never fully appreciated or emphasized by past generations of scholars are brought to the fore and made evident, potentially inspiring new ideas for those who study them (Figure 10.1).

Furthermore, these links expand the universe of possibilities for learners who are reading texts in dialogue with one another. One of the ramifications of print technology is that editions of texts tend to ossify the presentation and version of the books they contain. Scholars accustomed to printed editions of classical Jewish sources have a set of expectations about which texts are read side by side with one another.[11] The ability to easily discover texts that are in dialogue with one another, and to study them side by side, means that these texts can be studied in ways that were previously very unlikely. In the long term, I believe that this will impact the way that scholars understand and interpret canonical works.

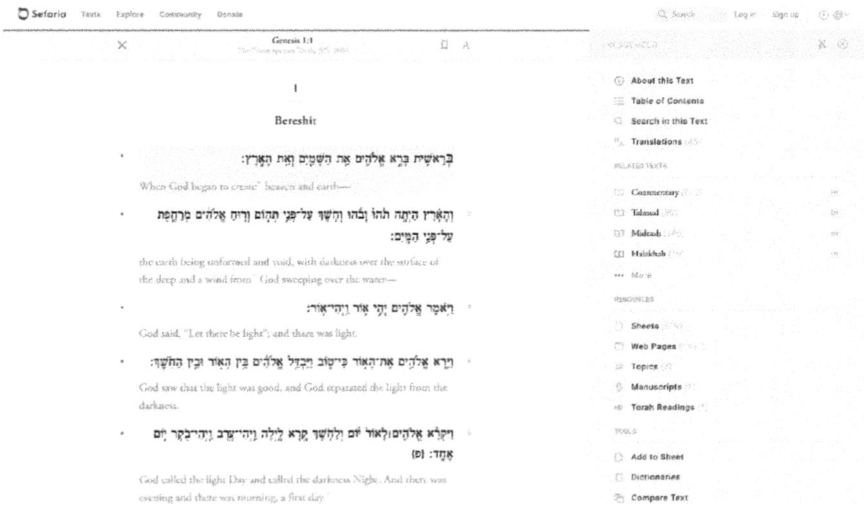

Figure 10.1 The opening of the book of Genesis displayed with interconnected texts in side panel (Sefaria, 2024). Created by Sara Tillinger Wolkenfeld.

An important caveat to this form of empowerment is that making sense of these texts still requires a certain level of fluency and skill. The learner needs the requisite orientation to the subject matter to find their way to a primary source, sufficient comprehension of the way that text works to be able to formulate curiosity and click to learn more, and, of course, the language skills to understand them—many of these works are not yet available in English translation. Reaping the full benefits of this aspect of machine learning still requires a person to be an insider in the world of Jewish text study. In order to offer the benefits of increased access to those who lack this kind of fluency, Sefaria uses AI and machine learning to enable a different kind of study experience.

Topical Search

Like the Bible itself, the other works in the Jewish canon contain wisdom on many different topics. These sources often weave together stories, legal material, philosophical concepts, and moral truths within a single volume. Even when a book is framed around a given theme, the particular information that a person seeks may not be easy for a newcomer to find. The Bible does not come with a topically ordered table of contents, nor do most of these other works.

To understand how this might impede the study of a newcomer to the Jewish tradition, take the example of the Sabbath. It is a concept that looms large in Jewish law and lore, and someone exploring their faith might want to know more about how to observe it, or learn about its deeper meaning to those who observe, or read some foundational stories about this practice.[12] A search for "Sabbath" or "Shabbat" on the digital Jewish bookshelf will yield a book by that name because there is a tractate of the Talmud titled "Shabbat." However, this Talmudic tractate, aptly titled as it is, would be a terrible starting point for a newcomer's study of the subject. As with the rest of the Talmud, it is dense and difficult to read, even in English translation. More importantly, the tractate would require extensive study in order to emerge with direct answers to the questions of practice and meaning framed above.

Sefaria's mission is to open up primary sources to anyone interested in exploring them; anyone should be able to come with their curiosity and find the texts that directly address their questions. To make this possible, Sefaria is building a network of pages organized by topics, which essentially serves as an index to the entire Jewish canon. Each page contains ten to twenty excerpts from primary sources, designed to showcase different aspects of the topic at hand. For example, the "Sabbath" page includes sources on the deeper meaning of Sabbath observance, on the primary ways in which the Sabbath is observed, and on the origins of the Sabbath in the Bible. Each excerpt, which is typically provided in both the original and in English, is preceded by a short learning prompt. This two-sentence introduction orients the reader both to the relationship between the source and the overall topic, as well as to the genre of the source itself and some information about the context in which it was composed.

The project began as a manual one, in which Sefaria's learning team created a systematic approach for selecting sources and crafting learning prompts. Once the team had approximately one hundred strong examples, Sefaria turned to artificial intelligence to continue the process and scale the project. The sources for each page are curated using generation augmented retrieval (GAR), a technology that refines the results retrieved through LLMs. First, engineers indexed Sefaria's entire library using OpenAI's text-large embedding model. This model converts each text into a point in space, known as a vector, such that similar texts will be close to one another. These vectors are stored in what is known as a vector database. Large language models then generate answers to generic questions about a topic and use these as queries to the vector database to find sources that support these answers.[13] Although often inaccurate, these answers are well-suited as queries since they are likely semantically similar to relevant sources about the topic. The engineers can ensure diversity of sources by having the LLM generate more answers to the initial generic questions. These sources are the basis for the curated page.

It should also be noted that in order to use GAR to locate sources, these texts need to be in English due to current limitations in embedding Hebrew text. The vast majority of the works in Sefaria's library are originally in Hebrew or Aramaic, and many have not yet been translated, which means that the embedding models cannot accurately convert these sources into a meaningful vector, or point in space. To ensure that more critical texts are available, Sefaria's engineers used Claude 3 Opus to generate rough translations of dozens of core texts, leading to a 33 percent increase in our English corpus. While the translations are not sufficiently accurate or readable to display to users, they serve the purpose of increasing the usable data that the AI models can use in selecting sources for these pages.

Once the sources have been selected, Sefaria's engineers use GPT 4.0 to draft the learning prompts that introduce and frame the sources. Both the selection of sources and the written materials are briefly checked by a team of editors to ensure that there are no egregious errors. Using this method, Sefaria will soon have one thousand pages ready to release to the public, which will provide new pathways for curious newcomers to explore ancient wisdom.

Areas for Continued Exploration

Advances in artificial intelligence are progressing rapidly and with those advances come new opportunities to expand access to canonical Jewish texts. There are three additional applications of these tools that Sefaria is exploring, experimenting with their viability and considering the advantages they might bring to those studying these materials as well as the potential pitfalls.

The first area, already referenced above, is generating translations of Hebrew texts. Language is a significant barrier to entry for modern learners who wish to study these texts; even for Hebrew speakers, the language of these texts is often archaic, filled with obscure abbreviations, specialized terminology, and sometimes interspersed with Aramaic. Acquiring existing translations for Sefaria's website is expensive and time-consuming, and many of these texts have never even been translated into English. Commissioning translations is even more costly and could take decades. At the moment, LLMs such as Claude and GPT can produce translations that vary wildly in quality, depending on the specific texts and the prompts delivered. Further experimentation will help determine the best combination of factors to ensure that passable translations are produced. Human editors can catch mistakes and smooth out the rough edges of these translations, and perhaps more importantly, we can build evaluation tools that will determine the viability of a translation without needing to review it in its entirety. As these systems continue to improve, more translations will be possible, benefiting not only English speakers, but speakers of many other languages as well, many of whom have relatively few Jewish texts available in their native language.

Another way that AI can enhance the experience of studying a dense corpus of texts is through topical tagging. This supports the other efforts detailed above to help readers navigate a massive corpus of texts which is largely not organized topically. Search engines allow people to easily discover every time a particular word is used, but concepts can be referenced by multiple terms. For example, the idea of "charity" might not always be referenced by the use of that particular word even in English, and in Hebrew, there are multiple terms that could correspond to the idea. Furthermore, the Hebrew word צְדָקָה ("ṣədāqâ"), which is frequently translated as "charity," does not always correspond to the idea of giving money or goods to those less fortunate. Topical tagging would help grapple with these issues by opening up broader possibilities for semantic search, allowing users to find ideas in the correct context based on what they are seeking. In addition, these tools might allow engineers to automatically generate a topical index for a particular book which would help readers find what they are looking for in a specific work. Another potential application for this tagging is to group commentaries on a text by topic (rather than simply listing them alphabetically) to help learners find content that is relevant to their particular interest.

Finally, readers of ancient texts will inevitably have questions as they study, but LLMs are famously unreliable in producing citations that address specific issues. In partnership with Applied AI and the Technical University of Munich, Sefaria experimented with retrieval-augmented generation (RAG) to answer questions and surface sources from within the database. RAG is a technique—different from GAR, despite the shared letters—that improves the efficacy of LLMs by drawing on a custom data set. In this case, it is the data from Sefaria's library that is used to source the results. This chatbot, still under development, can help learners find sources to answer their specific questions, and thereby help them have a satisfying learning experience. As the results improve, Sefaria's product team will consider how best to apply these developments in the creation of new features on the site.

Promise and Perils of AI and Machine Learning

The story of the study of Jewish texts has long been a story of innovation and discovery. The Talmud tells the story of Moses, ascending to the heavens to receive divine law, only to be confronted by a vision of Rabbi Akiva, a great teacher who lived many generations later, in the first century of the Common Era. In this Talmudic story, Moses sits in on a class in Rabbi Akiva's house of study, and to his dismay, discovers that he understands nothing of what is being taught. In his vision, however, a student asks the teacher where the tradition comes from, and Rabbi Akiva replies: "It was a law transmitted to Moses at Sinai." Moses' mind is set at ease, knowing that the text he helped convey to earth and his own encounter with the Divine remains the root of future knowledge, even as that knowledge is transformed through generations of teachers and students (b. Menaḥ 29b).

In much the same way, artificial intelligence allows for new levels of access to ancient texts, and this access in turn leads to new ways of understanding these words. The digital age has disrupted the paradigm of preserving complex religious textual knowledge within the domain of elite scholars. The rise of the internet, the digitization of texts, and the application of machine learning tools to those texts has given people the ability to open up these works, use them to answer questions, and reach new levels of textual knowledge that were previously unimaginable. At the same time, as in the story of Rabbi Akiva, the information gleaned is deeply rooted in the past, and the evolution of meanings is part of the tradition of passing down religious teachings from one generation to the next.

An abundance of anecdotal evidence, in addition to survey data from Sefaria, suggests that Jews who previously felt unable to access primary sources or make sense of them feel empowered by the tools that Sefaria uses to make these books available.[14] Learners no longer need to enter into a particular kind of religious space or spend years honing specialized skills in order to experience the impact of Jewish text study in their lives. These texts are available at a click, interlinked both within the traditional canon and to works that make the relevance of these texts come to life for modern readers.

Religious scholars and academics report that they, too, benefit from many of these tools, as more and more resources are readily available to them. Professors can easily assign Jewish works to students in introductory-level courses, and they can also use Sefaria's texts in their own research projects, including within the digital humanities.[15] There's an excitement that ensues when ancient wisdom intersects with cutting-edge technology; new media can breathe new life into traditions that may otherwise feel old and stale. Even those who have studied these texts for many years can gain new perspectives on the information they contain when texts are transformed into data and presented in new ways. Figure 10.2 represents just one example:

Figure 10.2 shows an image of what Sefaria calls the Link Explorer, which was developed in 2014. It displays every biblical quote contained within the Babylonian Talmud as a colored line. The Talmud quotes extensively from the Bible, as is evident from this image, and in the sixteenth century, a scholarly apparatus was added to pages of the Talmud that noted the citation of the verse quoted. There was, however, no easy or systematic way to examine the patterns of quotations in different tractates of the Talmud, or across different texts of the Bible. Which book of the Bible does the Talmud quote most frequently? Which book does the Talmud quote the least frequently?[16] The Link Explorer makes these kinds of investigations possible and opens up new kinds of conversations about the ways in which the Talmud makes use of biblical sources.

The excitement about learning new things and opening access to new learners must be guided and balanced by both practical and ethical questions. Technology has the capacity to distort materials in the process of transferring them into a new medium. AI hallucinates, fails to understand the deeper meaning of words, and sometimes lacks context for statements; as a result, there is a real risk of creating and amplifying a digital record that is not true to the original, or creating scaffolding materials to allow people to better understand which actually turn out to twist the meaning of the original.[17] None of the machine learning tools currently available produce perfect results, and all make a range of mistakes, from acontextual translations and hallucinations to bad links and extraneous or superfluous sources. Those deploying these tools need to weigh the risks and benefits of using technologies whose capabilities are still developing, and apply them responsibly.

Even at its best, the work of applying AI to an ancient canon raises ethical concerns. There is a danger of devaluing hard-earned knowledge or the kind of deep understanding that can still only be gained through years of engagement with a corpus of material. Just as "Dr. Google" can incorrectly diagnose all kinds of maladies, uninformed and hasty judgments can be made about religious traditions from these texts that were previously available only to those who were insiders in a particular

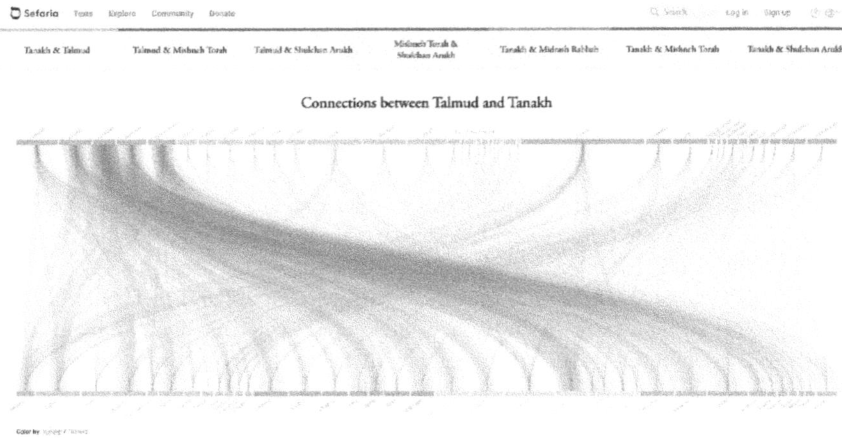

Figure 10.2 Connections between Talmud and Tanakh. Created by Sara Tillinger Wolkenfeld.

discourse. One example of this kind of danger is the rise in traffic to texts frequently quoted in antisemitic screeds online. It is easy to take information out of context when it is easily searchable and discoverable in digital form, and considering where and how to add context is an important part of ensuring that the impact of machine learning is a positive one.

The new ways of study enabled by artificial intelligence also raise the question: What does it mean for us to be able to read and process texts in ways that are unprecedented in human history? The ability to generate increasing numbers of links across genres means works that were never explicitly in conversation with one another can be compared and read side by side. The sheer quantity of texts available to today's scholars is vast and potentially overwhelming, perhaps leading to the feeling that one must conquer more and more material in order to be truly learned. Can we ensure that the wisdom of our teachers and their teachers before them will continue to be respected, even knowing that we command so much more information? Responsible use of these technologies needs to ensure that the chain of transmission and evolution of Jewish textual knowledge is clear. The goal is to maintain the sense of continuity expressed in the Talmudic passage above: new generations and new technologies produce new understandings, while also preserving a connection to, and respect for, past generations of Jewish scholars.[18]

Conclusion

Walter Ong, the Jesuit scholar and historian who studied the transition from orality to literacy, wrote: "Technologies are not mere exterior aids, but also interior transformations of consciousness, and never more than when they affect the word."[19]

Changes in the methods of Bible scholarship and the study of religious texts alter what texts are easily studied, the context in which the texts are studied, and who has the ability to engage with these texts. Artificial intelligence will certainly transform those who make use of it to study sacred texts; while the evolution has been gradual, each time we look back and take stock, we will notice an ever-increasing number of differences from ten or twenty years before.

Pirkei Avot, a third-century rabbinic text that consists primarily of ethical advice, offers the following guidance for all who study Jewish texts: "Turn it over and delve into it, because everything is to be found within it" (m. ʾAbot 5:22). Any community that believes there is deep wisdom and life guidance to be found in its textual tradition is bound to use the technological tools available to maximize access to all that it contains. Stewards of ancient religious traditions must approach artificial intelligence responsibly in order to ensure that we are transforming the consciousness of the learner in ways that will have a positive impact on the future.

Notes

1 This information is spread throughout b. Sanhedrin. See in particular b. Sanh. 36b, where the Talmud discusses some of the critical attributes of such a judge.

2 Chiddushei Aggadot Sanhedrin 17a:9, a Talmud commentary composed by Rabbi Samuel Eidels in sixteenth-century Poland, suggests that the necessary skill is having enough information and creativity to always be able to suggest a path to acquittal even for a person who seems obviously guilty. The ability to flexibly process huge quantities of information and imagine different results makes for a more flexible and forgiving judge.

3 The preceding opinion in b. Sanh. 17a lists additional qualifications, including that the person be wise.

4 Sefaria's 2023 user study revealed that approximately one-third of Sefaria's users (34 percent) do not have a regular practice of Jewish text study. Eighty percent of those who responded to the survey and were within the eighteen to forty-four age bracket reported that the website made them more motivated to study Jewish texts.

5 The primacy of textual authority is encoded throughout the Jewish canon, and anxiety about how that authority is shifted by the advent of digital tools has become widespread. For an example of the former, see m. ʾAbot 1:1, which describes the transfer of authority through the generations via the handing down of the Torah. For an example of the ways in which digital availability may shift the ways this authority spreads, see Mira Beth Wasserman, "The Talmud Today," in *The Routledge Handbook of Judaism in the 21st Century*, ed. Keren Eva Fraiman and Dean Phillip Bell, RHR (London: Routledge, 2023), 272–90.

6 See Moshe Halbertal, *People of the Book: Canon, Meaning, and Authenticity* (Cambridge, MA: Harvard University Press, 1997), especially 19 and 92.

7 This point is perhaps best illustrated by examining the traditional version of nearly any core Jewish text. The most widely used version of the Talmud, the Vilna Shas, contains the text of the Talmud printed side by side with the major commentaries, while the popular version of the Torah, the Miqraot Gedolot, contains the text of the

Five Books of Moses surrounded by multiple medieval commentaries, and the central code of Jewish law, the Shulkhan Arukh, is printed with multiple commentaries in the margins. For more on the necessity of reading canonical texts in conversation with one another, see Daniel Boyarin, *Intertextuality and the Reading of Midrash*, 2nd ed., ISBL (Bloomington: Indiana University Press, 1994); Halbertal, *People of the Book*; and Rebecca Scharbach Wollenberg, *The Closed Book: How the Rabbis Taught the Jews (Not) to Read the Bible* (Princeton: Princeton University Press, 2023).

8 As in many other religious traditions, girls and women were traditionally not afforded the same educational opportunities as their male counterparts. While there are institutions that make Jewish texts available to women at the highest levels of study today, there are still many Jewish communities that do not educate girls as they do boys. For more on this subject, see Tamar El-Or, *Educated and Ignorant: Ultraorthodox Jewish Women and Their World* (Boulder: Lynne Rienner, 1994), and Vanessa Ochs, *Words on Fire: One Woman's Journey into the Sacred* (New York: Avalon Books, 1999).

9 For example, Deut. 20:19 states: "When in your war against a city you have to besiege it for a long time in order to capture it, you must not destroy its trees, wielding the ax against them . . . " translated by David E. S. Stein, *The JPS Tanakh: Gender Sensitive Edition* (Philadelphia: Jewish Publication Society, 2023). Later sources discuss reasons for the injunction against destroying trees, and over the generations this verse becomes one of the key sources for Jewish environmentalists advocating for the importance of the natural world in Jewish texts. The medieval sources of the traditional Jewish canon do not highlight this meaning, but modern organizations and twenty-first-century thinkers writing online today have countless articles and sermons on the eco-sensitivities of this verse.

10 In Hebrew, this is "*sham*" and might be repeated multiple times in a given source.

11 For example, the first complete printed edition of the Talmud, produced in the 1600s, included in its margins the commentaries of Rabbi Shlomo Yitzchaky (France, 1040–1105) and a work composed by a group of Talmudic scholars called the Tosafists (France and Germany, twelfth–fourteenth centuries). These commentaries are now standard in every printed edition of the Talmud in the original. Those who study the Talmud in the twenty-first century often struggle to imagine what it would be like to study the text without these accompanying texts, and by the same token, studying the Talmud in conversation with other texts is less standard.

12 The volume of modern books published to address questions about the Sabbath, for people at all levels of Jewish background and none, attests to the demand for this kind of introductory material. See, for example, Ron Wolfson, *Shabbat: The Family Guide to Preparing for and Welcoming the Sabbath*, 2nd ed., Art of Jewish Living Series (Woodstock: Jewish Lights, 2002); Joe Lieberman, *The Gift of Rest: Rediscovering the Beauty of the Sabbath* (New York: Oxford University Press/Howard Books, 2012); Simcha Bunim Cohen, *The Shabbos Home: A Comprehensive Halachic Guide to the Laws of Shabbos as They Apply Throughout the Home* (Brooklyn: Artscroll, 1995); and Gershon Appel, *The Concise Code of Jewish Law: A Guide to the Observance of Shabbat*, rev. ed., ed. Daniel Goldstein (Jerusalem: Maggid, 2016).

13 For example: "What do Jewish texts say about the afterlife?"

14 In 2023, Rosov Consulting conducted a survey of Sefaria's users. Seventy percent of respondents who were between the ages of 18 and 44 and are not educators reported

that using Sefaria made them more comfortable navigating the Jewish library, and 65 percent said that as a result of using the site, they felt more confident in discussing Jewish topics with others. Anecdotally, as I travel frequently to conferences and presentations, I regularly meet people who tell me that until Sefaria existed, they were unable to engage with Jewish texts regularly, and that the website has been transformative for their study.

15 One recent example is of a scholar who decided to evaluate a long-held traditional belief about the nature of particular Talmudic tractates. He used Sefaria's data to assess which tractate of the Talmud actually contains the greatest diversity of material that relates to all the other tractates. https://seforimblog.com/2024/08/will-the-real-shas-kattan-please-stand-up/

16 The quantitative data alone may not hold a great deal of meaning, but it opens up opportunities for scholars to try to determine why certain patterns might exist.

17 AI's propensity for hallucinations and errors has been widely documented. For the most thorough account of the kinds of errors typically encountered, see Yujie Sun, Dongfang Sheng, Zuhan Zhou, and Yifei Wu, "AI Hallucination: Towards a Comprehensive Classification of Distorted Information in Artificial Intelligence-Generated Content," *Humanities and Social Sciences Communications* 11 (2024): 1278, https://doi.org/10.1057/s41599-024-03811-x.

18 The idea that new understandings will continually be uncovered by new generations of Jewish scholars is an ancient one. The Talmud in b. Ḥag. 3a records the statement that "there is no such thing as a house of study that does not produce some new insight." The Talmud in y. Pe᾽ah 2:4 also testifies to the ongoing process of discovery of new ideas and asserts that all the new ideas that will, in the future, be discovered were all given to Moses at Mt. Sinai. In this way, the idea that currently unknown insights are hidden within the text is built into the fabric of what it means to study Jewish texts.

19 Walter Ong, *Orality and Literacy*, 30th anniv. ed. (London: Routledge, 2002), 81.

Bibliography

Appel, Gersion. *The Concise Code of Jewish Law: A Guide to the Observance of Shabbat*. Rev ed. Edited by Daniel Goldstein. Jerusalem: Maggid, 2016.

Boyarin, Daniel. *Intertextuality and the Reading of Midrash*. 2nd ed. ISBL. Bloomington: Indiana University Press, 1994.

Cohen, Simcha Bunim. *The Shabbos Home: A Comprehensive Halachic Guide to the Laws of Shabbos as They Apply Throughout the Home*. Brooklyn: Artscroll, 1995.

El-Or, Tamar. *Educated and Ignorant: Ultraorthodox Jewish Women and Their World*. Boulder: Lynne Rienner, 1994.

Even-Israel Steinsaltz, Adin. *The William Davidson Digital Edition of the Koren Noé Talmud*. Jerusalem: Koren Publishers, 2017. https://www.sefaria.org.

Halbertal, Moshe. *People of the Book: Canon, Meaning, and Authenticity*. Cambridge, MA: Harvard University Press, 1997.

Lieberman, Joe. *The Gift of Rest: Rediscovering the Beauty of the Sabbath*. New York: Oxford University Press/Howard Books, 2012.

Ochs, Vanessa. *Words on Fire: One Woman's Journey into the Sacred*. New York: Avalon Books, 1999.

Ong, Walter. *Orality and Literacy*. 30th anniv. ed. London: Routledge, 2002.

Stein, David E. S. *The JPS Tanakh: Gender Sensitive Edition*. Philadelphia: Jewish Publication Society, 2023.

Sun, Yujie, Dongfang Sheng, Zuhan Zhou, and Yifei Wu. "AI Hallucination: Towards a Comprehensive Classification of Distorted Information in Artificial Intelligence-Generated Content." *Humanities and Social Sciences Communications* 11 (2024): 1278. https://doi.org/10.1057/s41599-024-03811-x.

Wasserman, Mira Beth. "The Talmud Today." Pages 272–90 in *The Routledge Handbook of Judaism in the 21st Century*. Edited by Keren Eva Fraiman and Dean Phillip Bell. RHR. London: Routledge, 2023.

Wolfson, Ron. *Shabbat: The Family Guide to Preparing for and Welcoming the Sabbath*. 2nd ed. Art of Jewish Living Series. Woodstock: Jewish Lights, 2002.

Wollenberg, Rebecca Scharbach. *The Closed Book: How the Rabbis Taught the Jews (Not) to Read the Bible*. Princeton: Princeton University Press, 2023.

11

Statistical Interpretation of Religious Text Using Topic Modeling

Mark Graves

Can artificial intelligence (AI) contribute to new methods of biblical interpretation? In this chapter, I argue that AI and other computational and statistical methods enable new ways to interpret religious texts by interpreting language and quantifying relationships among words within the text in ways that differ from the biases and assumptions humans bring to the text. Computational and statistical models can abstract certain relationships between words that highlight and quantify certain aspects of the text, which may help explain the meaning of the text (i.e., interpret it). Some of the interpretations may be familiar, thus lending credibility to the method, while others may be unfamiliar and worthy of consideration.

Interpretation occurs in many fields. Not only is it central to biblical scholarship, but interpretation is also fundamental to science, as experimental scientists create models of what they wish to study and interpret those models to learn about the real world. Statisticians likewise create models from real-world data and interpret those models for insights about the object of study. Computer scientists use models in a related way, though often asking questions about how the models perform on a computer rather than their real-world implications. I want to focus on a point of intersection among computer modeling, statistical modeling, and biblical interpretation where one can create a model of a biblical text and interpret that model to gain insights about the meaning of the text. To illustrate the method, I use an AI technique called *topic modeling* to create a model of the Protestant Bible in an English translation and describe insights into the biblical texts by interpreting the topic modeling results and visualizations.

Biblical Interpretation

Exegesis comes from the Greek verb *exēgeomai*, which roughly means to expound. It can refer to any act of interpretation or explanation, but in this context, it refers to detailed interpretation of Scripture.[1] While exegesis refers to the process of interpreting a text, *hermeneutics* refers to the study of interpretation itself—an inquiry into the principles of interpretation, especially its rules and presuppositions. Hermeneutics examines how to do exegesis well. For instance, one common hermeneutic principle first proposed by Georg Anton Friedrich Ast and developed by Friedrich Schleiermacher, Wilhelm Dilthey, and Martin Heidegger, recognizes the tension between interpreting specific parts of Scripture in light of its whole, while at the same time allowing the whole to speak to its parts (the hermeneutical circle).[2] A similar tension also exists between the understanding of the interpreter and the text, as the more the interpreter reads the text, the more the text shapes the interpreter.[3]

Early exegesis varied between more literal and more allegorical interpretations, though by the Middle Ages, interpreters often sought four senses (the *quadriga*) in the text:

(a) the literal sense, such as historical events (what happened);
(b) the allegorical sense, such as symbolic representations of Christ (what one ought to believe);
(c) the moral sense, such as ethical implications for the Christian life (what one ought to do);
(d) the anagogical sense, such as eschatological promises and future realities (what one must strive for).[4]

During the modern era, scholars developed a variety of new methods to address certain questions or problems in biblical exegesis. Fitting under the broad category of "criticism" (from the Greek κρίνειν, *krinein*, meaning "to judge" or "to discern"), these approaches denote fields of study with clearly defined principles and techniques that attempt to reach informed judgments. Scholars developed a variety of criticisms to evaluate the text and its historical context, some of which include:

- *Historical criticism*, which considers the historical, geographical, and cultural settings of the text, the original author(s) and audience(s), and the names, places, events, and customs mentioned;
- *Textual criticism*, which examines the variant readings between copies of texts to identify the most likely original wording;
- *Socio-historical criticism*, which expands the social dimension of historical criticism to examine the socioeconomic and political nature of biblical groups, such as examining Israel's entry into Canaan through a social scientific lens.

Contemporary hermeneutics introduces new philosophical perspectives on the nature of interpretation. For example, Hans-Georg Gadamer contrasts methods, analogous to the scientific method where one tries to master texts, with truth, which goes deeper and becomes disclosed dialogically, as though immersing oneself in playing a child's game in one's particular context (merging the horizon of one's present world with the horizon of the past world from the text).[5] Similarly, Paul Ricoeur identifies hermeneutics as both science and art where one suspiciously considers meaning as it emerges from a text and evaluates one's interpretive guesses judiciously as a safeguard against unconscious or uncritical understanding.[6] Gadamer and Ricoeur both engage the scientific process in their hermeneutics, a dynamic that informs how one might use AI within biblical hermeneutics. Rather than use AI to master texts through method alone; following Gadamer, AI could support interpretation—for example, by surfacing patterns that the interpreter then engages in a dialogical fusion of horizons between the interpreter and the text. From Ricoeur's perspective, AI might suggest interpretive guesses as plausible readings or contribute to a hermeneutic of suspicion by unmasking interpretive distortions.

Building on these hermeneutic insights, could the advent of AI provide new critical methods to interpret biblical texts? If so, how should one use AI-influenced methods well? Four primary options turn on whether to use as little or as much external knowledge as possible and whether to use as little or as much human expertise as possible:

- High external knowledge and high human expertise, for example, selecting key passages of biblical texts on a particular theme and asking a GenAI chatbot to summarize them;
- High external knowledge and low human expertise, for example, using the sentiment typically associated with words to map the sentiment of passages through a biblical text or using retrieval-augmented generation and a large language model (LLM) in order to ask a GenAI chatbot questions about the Bible;
- Low external knowledge and high human expertise, for example, selecting key phrases of a biblical text on a particular theme and using collocations of words and phrases surrounding those key phrases to examine how the theme is used differently across biblical texts;
- Low external knowledge and low human expertise, for example, topic models, which do not depend upon human-selected data or complex human decisions in the interpretation of the text.

Here I will minimize external knowledge and human expertise to explore what the barest AI methods can contribute to biblical interpretation by using topic models, which do not depend upon human-selected data or complex human decisions in the interpretation of the text. By minimizing the knowledge and expertise brought to the AI method, we can be more specific about where the contributions to meaning can arise. But first I examine interpretive models in general, which would also include other approaches.

Interpretation of Models

A model abstracts or idealizes a thing or phenomenon by highlighting a significant aspect while deemphasizing less relevant features. Interpretation using statistics or artificial intelligence requires formalizing an aspect of the biblical interpretation process. Rather than looking around the text in historical or socio-historical criticism or directly at the text in textual criticism, one creates a model of the text, then uses that model in the interpretation. There are at least three kinds of models relevant to our examination of biblical interpretation:

- *Concrete models* are real, physical objects representing a real or imagined system or phenomenon;
- *Formal models* capture precise aspects of phenomena as functions, equations, and computations;
- *Theological models* capture the tensive relationship between conceptual structures and metaphorical narrative language (according to Sallie McFague, who draws upon Ian Barbour's understanding of scientific models and Paul Ricoeur's hermeneutics).[7]

Concrete models are common in engineering and architecture, and they are also used in biblical archaeology to create models of archaeological finds. One could also consider a nativity scene to be a concrete model of the birth of Jesus. One then interprets these models to understand something about the biblical narrative. Unlike concrete models, the formal models of machine learning and natural language processing (as subfields of AI) exist in a mathematical and statistical space. As an example, one could count the occurrences of "kingdom" across the four Gospels and compare the occurrences of "kingdom of heaven" and "kingdom of God" in each Gospel. One could then look at words immediately before or after those phrases and calculate the most frequently occurring words or phrases that collocate with the "kingdom" phrases. One can interpret these simple statistics about the text to better understand some of the differences between the Gospels. Doing this for all the content words and phrases of the Gospels (i.e., excluding grammatical function words, like prepositions and conjunctions) would form a model of the Gospel texts. One could then interpret that model to identify *what* words and phrases distinguish well between the Gospels.

However, with biblical texts, there are additional levels of interpretation beyond the literal sense (e.g., in the *quadriga*). Theological models formalize the relationship between the semantics of the text and what the text points toward. A formal model can also constitute the conceptual structure of a theological model, which then must point beyond that model to some aspect of the meaning or truth communicated through the biblical narrative. To use a computational model in biblical theology, its conceptual structure must point not only to something real in the text being examined but also beyond conventional reality to what that text characterizes.

Elsewhere, I have identified the multiple layers of tensive relationships that occur when one uses computational models for theological investigation, which I summarize here.[8] These tensive relationships are needed to point beyond the text and the model to a deeper understanding of the biblical message. In this framing, Sallie McFague's theological models capture the tensive relationship between conceptual structures and metaphorical narrative language.[9] Ricoeur draws upon phenomenology and hermeneutics to characterize a tensive aspect of symbolic language that separates a direct conceptual characterization from its interpretation, which in turn attempts to return one to the event that the concept attempts to express.[10] Barbour maps scientific models from physics and the philosophy of science to religion and identifies that as mediating between an unattainable full encounter with reality (naïve realism) and complete intelligibility.[11] Barbour then creates his own integrative perspective by placing that mediating interpretation within the constructive perspective of science he calls critical realism. In her metaphorical theology, McFague aligns Ricoeur's phenomenological and conceptual language with Barbour's models to characterize what something *is* and combines Ricoeur's more interpretive and hermeneutic dimension and Barbour's critical approach to science in order to help characterize the *is not* aspect of metaphorical interpretation. Thus, the computational and statistical models capture the conceptual and experiential aspect of a bare reading of the text, while acknowledging the interpretive dimension that requires critical and hermeneutic reflection about what that model is not. Using a concrete or formal model by itself identifies what *is* in the text—and one can observe from outside the model that there are relationships not in the model—but AI modeling promises new possibilities. One can interpret a formal, statistical model as the conceptual structure of a theological model, which opens up new ways to interpret the metaphorical narrative. One could do this with any mathematical or statistical model, but for example, simple word counts may lack the power to also illuminate the metaphorical narrative sufficient for hermeneutic reflection. Now, AI models provide a much richer conceptual structure and thus the capacity to illuminate richer dimensions of the metaphorical narrative.

Models in AI

Within AI, machine learning models are commonly used to characterize a real-world (or virtual) phenomenon, and the type of model is often characterized by the way data (or text) is used to train the model. Supervised models depend upon human-annotated or labeled data, and unsupervised models depend only on the data itself without additional human input. Additional types of models can use training input more interactively, such as an automated vehicle learning to stay on the road, or they can use some intrinsic aspect of the data, such as LLMs learning how words are used from surrounding words. Machine learning models also overlap with statistical models that typically capture not only a category or prediction from the data but also some measure of variability.

Also within AI, natural language processing (NLP) uses language models that predict aspects of a language. Most familiarly, predictive text now often appears as possible next words when sending a text message or email. Although a variety of formal models could and have been used for language, machine learning models have demonstrated their strength over the past decade and are commonly used. The LLMs used in generative AI are language models built using neural nets via self-supervised training data (viz., a large amount of text). To explore how minimal AI models can be used to interpret text, I use topic models in this chapter, which are statistical language models constructed in an unsupervised way. Although one can use topic models to generate text (like in generative AI), we will interpret the model itself as probability distributions to gain insight into the underlying text.

AI/NLP Theory of Language

Both topic models and large language models depend upon a particular theory of language—the *associationist theory*—which differs from the correspondence theory most commonly used in biblical scholarship and theology. Instead of assuming that the meaning of a word corresponds with a real-world object or idea, some linguists characterize the meaning of words in terms of how the words are used.[12] For example, "cat" and "dog" would often occur in speech or text with many overlapping associated words, such as "petting," "feeding," and other words for activities of non-human companionship. Thus "cat" and "dog" have similar meanings, while differences in associated words, such as "climb" or "fetch," differentiate the meaning between "cat" and "dog." The meaning of the word "cat" or "dog" thus *is* the distribution of words with which it is used.

This associationist theory of language has a good bit of psychological support, especially in how young children learn language.[13] Regardless of whether it is the best theory of how humans use language, there is now also another large body of evidence for the theory: LLMs and generative AI, which are built upon the theory. LLMs and generative AI appear to use language well, at least as well as a typical college student, and it is notoriously difficult to distinguish language generated by AI using the theory from human-generated language.

When interpreting text and language, it is important to understand the theory of language one brings to the endeavor—either implicitly or explicitly. Assuming that words correspond to objects or ideas is a choice of language theory, and a theory with evidence against it. In particular, when considering what AI may or may not be able to do in the future with language, it is important not to limit one's imagination to a correspondence theory of language—which underlies aspects of Searle's Chinese Room example—as that is not the theory underlying current AI systems.[14]

Based upon the associationist theory, Zellig Harris hypothesized that in a sufficiently large sample of language, words with similar patterns of association would have similar meaning.[15] To put it another way, not only would similar words have similar patterns of use, but if the patterns of use are similar in a large sample, then the words have similar meanings. To take this a step further, if the patterns of use are essentially identical in a large sample, then the words have identical meanings. This is how Google handles misspellings—the pattern of how a misspelled word is used is essentially identical to how its correct spelling is used. It also underlies modern machine translation. The pattern of how "dog" is used in English is very similar to how "hund" is used in German, so those words are considered to have very similar meanings.

Large samples of language are necessary for precisely characterizing the meaning of words, and thus *large* language models can emphasize the meaning of language better than language models created with smaller samples of text, but they also incorporate biases that occur in those large samples. As an alternative, I turn now to topic models, which emphasize the topics (or themes) occurring in the text but use very little training data—namely, only the biblical text being studied.

Topic Modeling

In topic modeling, a document is understood to depend primarily upon a small number of topics, or themes, and it is the combination of topics that provides the meaning of the document. A document, such as a chapter in a biblical text, is modeled as a collection of topics, emphasizing thematic aspects and deemphasizing aspects such as grammatical structure, style, and usage. In a document comprising the present book chapter so far, major topics would include biblical interpretation, modeling, and AI. Topic modeling is a twenty-year-old AI technology and is still heavily used in the digital humanities.[16] The benefit here is that it only depends upon the text of the Bible and a human specification of the number of topics desired. The algorithm underlying topic modeling searches for the best topics that model the text, and it provides both the statistical distribution of words in each topic and the distribution of topics in each document.

Topic Model of the Bible with Ten Topics

As a demonstration, topic modeling on the World English Bible can extract ten topics, each of which is comprised of a distribution of words. Table 11.1 shows ten topics for this Protestant version of the Bible ordered by the topic's predominance, or proportional weight, in the text; and each topic lists the top words comprising that topic, ordered by the probability that word would occur in the topic.[17] The top two topics both have to do with God, with the first topic referring to the God of Israel while the second topic appears to be about a person's relationship with God. The third topic refers to people, especially families, as that is a major topic in the Bible; and the fourth topic appears to refer to God as Creator. These are *my* interpretations of the distribution of words in a topic, and those with different understandings of the Bible may notice different aspects or more nuance. Because the New Testament has less overall text (fewer total chapters), Jesus does not appear until the fifth most predominant topic. From this statistical interpretation of the text, I can interpret the statistical model as evidence that the Bible

Table 11.1: Ten Topics in the World English Bible

Top Three Words			Additional Topic Words	Rank	Weight
yahweh	god	israel	land people egypt day house hand children	1	0.29
god	man	heart	yahweh soul righteousness wicked righteous evil good	2	0.28
man	behold	house	father men son hand wife day people	3	0.26
earth	yahweh	behold	lord nations day waters fire sea men	4	0.24
god	jesus	things	lord christ spirit good man faith disciples	5	0.10
king	judah	son	house jerusalem israel yahweh made people god	6	0.10
offering	yahweh	priest	moses burnt altar holy day aaron children	7	0.08
children	israel	thousand	hundred land son cities yahweh joshua tribe	8	0.07
gold	house	made	side cubits work make gate solomon hundred	9	0.06
david	son	saul	father men hundred joab brothers philistines	10	0.04

Created by Mark Graves.

is predominantly about God, God's relationship to Israel, humanity, and the earth, and that other important topics include Jesus, the history of Israel, priesthood, and the children of Israel. This summary is hopefully uncontroversial, but topic modeling both adds precision and leads to ready interpretation of the metaphorical dimension of the biblical narrative. Interpretations of the model can also open up discussion with more nuance, such as the gold house in the ninth topic, as well as a window into the text "as text" and how that differs from the biases and interpretive tendencies one normally brings. However, when the topic model is used to look back at the text, interpreting the model begins to yield even more interesting insights.

Figure 11.1 is a "heatmap" that shows how the topics (on the left side) are distributed within the texts of the Bible (across the top, from Genesis to Revelation).[18] The darker colors indicate that a topic is more influential in that text. For example, the dark band of the fifth topic on Jesus stretches from Matthew to Jude. This initial examination suggests that Revelation is the only text of the New Testament that is focused less on Jesus and more on another topic (namely, God the Creator), and there is a faint indication under Jonah that Jonah includes themes normally associated with the New Testament rather than other Old Testament texts. Some scholars also see Jonah as a "type" for Christ,[19] thus suggesting a more metaphorical interpretation from the model. There may be Old Testament *chapters* that relate to the New Testament more than Jonah, but not other books as a whole. There are other possible patterns of interest, such as the importance of God's relationship with humanity (Topic 2) in the books Job through Ecclesiastes.

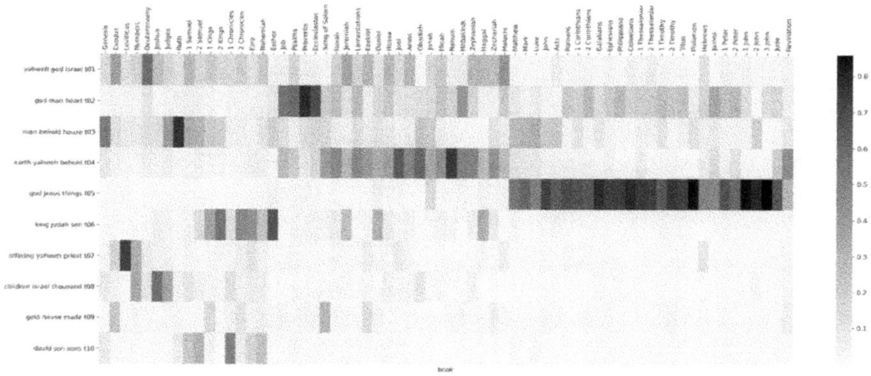

Figure 11.1 Topic model of Bible for ten topics. Created by Mark Graves.

Topic Model of the Bible with Thirty Topics

To capture more nuance, we can model thirty topics for the Bible (rather than ten), as shown in Table 11.2 with the top English words for each topic.[20] Aspects of God are further distinguished across God's actions among humanity, creation, and God's covenant with Israel—the people and the land—with Christ appearing in the ninth topic. The first (strongest) topic shows "man behold God" as the three words most likely to occur in that topic, which seems a reasonable summary. Additional topics are described in the context of their occurrence in the visualization of the model against the biblical text.

In Figure 11.2, the thirty topics are listed on the left vertical axis, and again the books of the Bible are across the top. The dark band in the heatmap of Topic 9 involving Christ is most visible, but only spanning Romans to Jude. Further down in Topic 18 is Jesus and his disciples, while Topic 6 for God the Father also contributes to much of the New Testament. Revelation essentially stands alone as Topic 16 about a great voice on earth. Even without exploring the English words comprising each topic, there are still interesting patterns. Topic 18, the predominant topic of the Gospels in this analysis, is also heavily influential on the text of Acts, which tends *not* to share topics with the remaining books of the New Testament, even visibly lacking influence of Topic 6, God the Father. With the increase in the number of topics, the topic model facilitates more nuanced interpretations, including those that capture more of the metaphorical narrative dimension of the theological model. In terms of the *quadriga*, many of the interpretations are allegorical and symbolic, though the summary of Revelation's most predominant topic, Topic 16, as a great voice on earth begins to suggest ways that even anagogical or eschatological meanings could be found.

Table 11.2: Thirty Topics in the World English Bible

Top Three Words			Additional Topic Words	Rank	Weight
man	behold	god	house people men day hand brought city	1	0.410
earth	sea	waters	place hand mighty made men make strong	2	0.249
yahweh	god	israel	land people day fathers egypt children hand	3	0.214
yahweh	land	lord	behold israel armies nations day jerusalem sword	4	0.167
man	heart	wicked	righteous evil mouth words wise wisdom good	5	0.167
god	things	father	life love man world children give son	6	0.155
yahweh	god	forever	praise loving kindness soul righteousness earth salvation	7	0.155
eat	bread	day	land god days wine give drink eaten	8	0.110
god	christ	lord	jesus things faith spirit good law grace	9	0.073
offering	yahweh	burnt	altar holy offer offerings sin meal blood	10	0.072
israel	children	yahweh	men people king joshua struck hand battle	11	0.068
house	king	solomon	yahweh david israel god jerusalem gold made	12	0.067
man	blood	woman	wife put death prostitute surely mother give	13	0.067
tree	fruit	field	beloved branches hear vine fig love	14	0.065
wife	son	woman	yahweh father daughter mother husband give	15	0.057
earth	great	voice	god throne angel fire heard living glory	16	0.052
king	yahweh	son	judah israel jerusalem house babylon hezekiah kings	17	0.050
jesus	disciples	lord	answered son peter things man john multitude	18	0.048
god	earth	field	waters animals flesh sky man sheep eat	19	0.044
cubits	side	gold	made work make house gate court put	20	0.044
land	children	cities	border suburbs moab jordan manasseh beth inheritance	21	0.040
moses	children	israel	yahweh aaron son sons tribe tent congregation	22	0.037
priest	unclean	clean	water plague skin wash clothes evening house	23	0.033
king	daniel	god	kingdom babylon men made image dream nebuchadnezzar	24	0.027

(*Continued*)

Table 11.2: (Continued)

Top Three Words			Additional Topic Words	Rank	Weight
egypt	pharaoh	land	joseph moses egyptians brothers servants father behold	25	0.027
david	saul	king	son joab philistines jonathan men samuel absalom	26	0.026
son	children	hundred	levites brothers thousand priests father	27	0.026
father	son	jacob	abraham isaac years lived esau daughters	28	0.023
paul	jews	jerusalem	pilate things king chief barnabas brothers day	29	0.020
king	jews	mordecai	esther haman day month ahasuerus queen provinces	30	0.013

Created by Mark Graves.

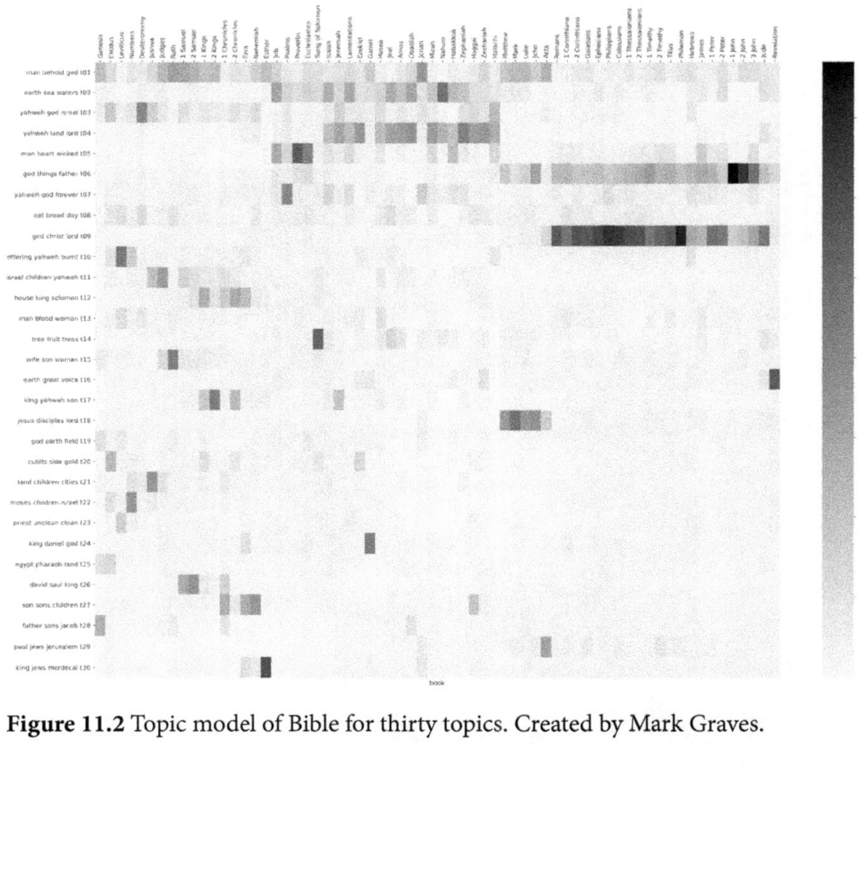

Figure 11.2 Topic model of Bible for thirty topics. Created by Mark Graves.

Topic Similarity between Texts of the Bible

It also possible to look at the relationship between biblical texts based upon how similar their distribution of topics is to other texts. Semantic similarity is often used to compare texts within a large language model or other models that depend upon substantial information about language in order to create a space in which meaning can be mapped. However, similarity can also be used within the topic model space to compare distributions of topics for a biblical text. In Figure 11.3, Genesis to Revelation form both axes and the cells indicate how similar each book of the WEB Protestant Bible is to other books.[21] The lighter the square cell, the more similar the books are. The light diagonal across the figure indicates that every book is similar to itself. Starting in the lower right, the small white square for Revelation with no other similarities indicates that Revelation stands alone, in this model. The larger light square from Romans to Jude indicates similarities among those books, with particular affinities among John 1–3 and additional differences from Hebrews and James. There is also a faint indication that 1 Timothy is not as similar to the other letters as some of those books in that region are. The Gospels form the next cluster, with Acts more similar to the Gospels than the remaining texts. The large square in the middle indicates a

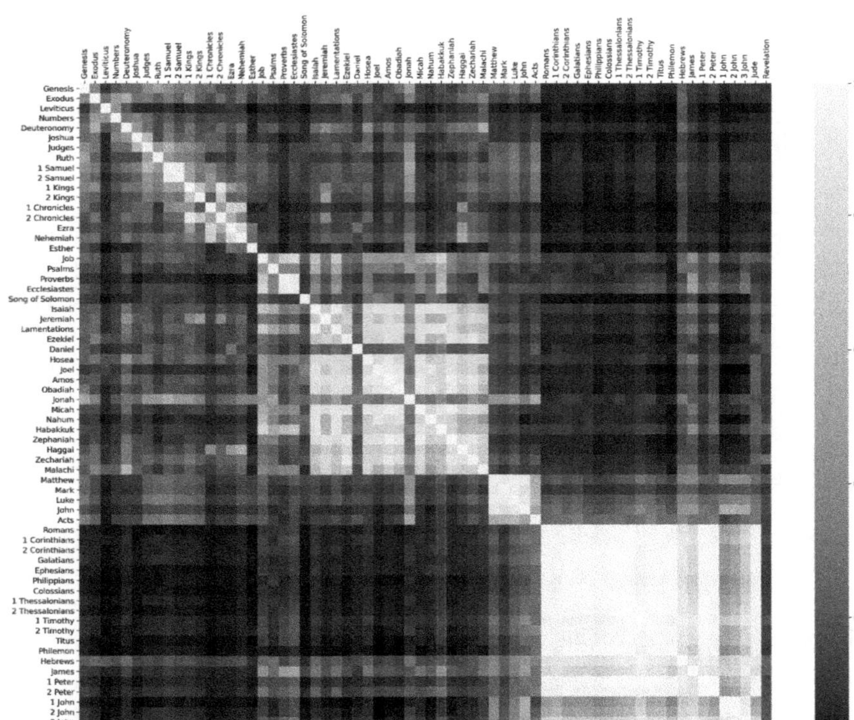

Figure 11.3 Pairwise similarity between World English Bible topic models. Created by Mark Graves.

grouping from Isaiah to Malachi, with exceptions for Daniel and Jonah. Smaller clusters occur toward the earlier books, such as between Proverbs and Ecclesiastes and between 1 Samuel and 2 Samuel. Less apparent, there is a darker region from Romans through Philemon across the entire Old Testament, which indicates that those texts are less similar to the Old Testament than many of the other New Testament texts. Recall, these patterns come from a statistical interpretation of only the text allocated among thirty topics with no human knowledge about the Bible or even the English language. Now, the patterns I find interesting and have highlighted do depend upon our shared knowledge of the Bible, but I hope I have demonstrated how even simple AI tools can bring a fresh perspective on biblical interpretation.

Conclusion

In conclusion, models abstract something by emphasizing certain aspects over others. Topic modeling emphasizes sequence or co-occurrence associations between words rather than syntactic relationships in language models. Interpretation of these statistical language models requires interpreting the probability distributions, as visualized in the ordered word lists and heat maps. Topic modeling takes a set of texts—in this case, the chapters of the Bible—and the number of topics requested, here ten or thirty, and generates a model predicting how likely each word occurs in each topic (indicated by the word ordering) and how much each topic influences the chapter text. Interpreting a topic model of the Bible identifies patterns from associations between words, as distributed across book chapters and aggregated into books, thus indicating the power and value of the associative theory of language. As an answer to my opening question of whether AI/NLP provides new methods to interpret biblical text, I have shown that it can and that one way it can do so is by measuring and comparing statistical relationships among how words are used in the text. Using topic models as the conceptual structure of a theological model also enables additional ways to interpret the Bible's metaphorical and anagogical narratives. These AI-augmented methods provide an opening to new ways to understand and interpret the Bible.[22]

Notes

1 This section draws from John H. Hayes and Carl R. Holladay, *Biblical Exegesis: A Beginner's Handbook*, 3rd ed. (Louisville: Westminster John Knox, 2007), 1–11, 19–21, 24–6, 38–41, 53. See also Richard N. Soulen and R. Kendall Soulen, *Handbook of Biblical Criticism* (Louisville: Westminster John Knox, 2011); Stephen R. Haynes and Steven L. McKenzie, *To Each Its Own Meaning: An Introduction to Biblical Criticisms and Their Applications* (Louisville: Westminster John Knox, 1999).

2 Paul Redding, "Hermeneutics and German Idealism," in *The Cambridge Companion to Hermeneutics*, ed. Michael N. Forster and Kristin Gjesdal (Cambridge: Cambridge University Press, 2019), 92.

3 Anthony C. Thiselton, *The Two Horizons: New Testament Hermeneutics and Philosophical Description* (Grand Rapids: Eerdmans, 1980), 104.

4 This list is adapted largely verbatim from Craig G. Bartholomew, *Introducing Biblical Hermeneutics: A Comprehensive Framework for Hearing God in Scripture* (Grand Rapids: Baker, 2015), 146.

5 Hans-Georg Gadamer, *Truth and Method*, trans. Joel Weinsheimer and Donald G. Marshall, 2nd rev. ed. (London: Continuum, 2004); and see also Anthony C. Thiselton, "Biblical Interpretation," in *The Modern Theologians: An Introduction to Christian Theology since 1918*, ed. David F. Ford, with Rachel Muers, 3rd ed. (Malden: Blackwell, 2005), 298.

6 Thiselton, "Biblical Interpretation," 299–300; and see also Paul Ricoeur, *Freud and Philosophy: An Essay on Interpretation*, trans. Denis Savage (New Haven: Yale University Press, 1970), 27; and Geoffrey D. Robinson, "Paul Ricoeur and the Hermeneutics of Suspicion: A Brief Overview and Critique," *Premise* 2.8 (1995): 12.

7 Sallie McFague, *Models of God: Theology for an Ecological, Nuclear Age* (Philadelphia: Fortress, 1987).

8 Mark Graves, "Computational Topic Models for Theological Investigations," *Theology and Science* 20.1 (2022): 69–84.

9 McFague, *Models of God.*

10 Paul Ricoeur, *Semeia 4: Paul Ricoeur on Biblical Hermeneutics*, ed. John Dominic Crossan (Atlanta: Society of Biblical Literature, 1975), 36.

11 Ian G. Barbour, *Religion and Science: Historical and Contemporary Issues* (San Francisco: HarperSanFrancisco, 1997), chap. 5.

12 John R. Firth, "A Synopsis of Linguistic Theory 1930–1955," in *Studies in Linguistic Analysis*, Special Volume of the Philological Society (Oxford: Blackwell, 1957), 1–32; and Mikael Brunila and Jack LaViolette, "What Company Do Words Keep? Revisiting the Distributional Semantics of J.R. Firth & Zellig Harris," in *Proceedings of the 2022 Conference of the North American Chapter of the Association for Computational Linguistics: Human Language Technologies* (Seattle: Association for Computational Linguistics, 2022), 4403–17.

13 Lucy C. Erickson and Erik D. Thiessen, "Statistical Learning of Language: Theory, Validity, and Predictions of a Statistical Learning Account of Language Acquisition," *Developmental Review* 37 (2015): 66–108.

14 John R. Searle, "Minds, Brains, and Programs," *Behavioral and Brain Sciences* 3.3 (1980): 417–24.

15 Zellig Harris, *Mathematical Structures of Language* (New York: Interscience, 1968).

16 David M. Blei, Andrew Y. Ng, and Michael I. Jordan, "Latent Dirichlet Allocation," *Journal of Machine Learning Research* 3 (2003): 993–1022; David M. Blei, "Probabilistic Topic Models," *Communications of the ACM* 55.4 (2012): 77–84; David M. Blei, "Topic Modeling and Digital Humanities," *Journal of Digital Humanities* 2.1 Winter (2012): 8–11.

17 Michael Paul Johnson, trans., *World English Bible*, 2006, https://worldenglish.bible/. Topic modeling was performed using the mallet software package (version 2.0.8) with ten topics, five thousand iterations, http://mallet.cs.umass.edu/. The topics are then ordered by weight, which indicates how much that topic proportionally contributes to that document. The choice of ten topics was guided by the need to have enough topics to illustrate the variations between them while keeping the explanation of

topic modeling simple. An English biblical translation is used to simplify analysis and the explanation of topic models, though additional nuance may be discovered using languages such as Greek and Hebrew. The WEB (Protestant) version was chosen due to its permissive licensing and existing preparation for analysis.

18 Although the topic model is generated by treating each chapter of the biblical text as a document, the topic results for each chapter are averaged in the visualizations to derive a value for each book of the version of the Bible used.

19 Yvonne Sherwood, *A Biblical Text and Its Afterlives: The Survival of Jonah in Western Culture* (Cambridge: Cambridge University Press, 2000), 11–21.

20 The choice of thirty topics provides more nuance than the ten-topic model, while still avoiding unnecessary complexity. There is no consensus approach to choosing the best number of topics, as it depends upon how the analysis would be used. In my article "Computational Topic Models for Theological Investigations," I use a hierarchical Dirichlet process to estimate the number of topics to use, which may be the least biased approach. Other approaches include measures of perplexity or topic coherence, which also find some mathematical "best" fit. As topic modeling is a probabilistic method, additional runs may vary in the topics they generate and in how those topics are used in the document, which may also yield additional insights.

21 Similarity between texts is calculated as the cosine similarity between the distribution of topics for each document (the columns in the heatmap visualization).

22 Thanks to Adam Graber, Brian Sigmon, and Douglas Estes for early suggestions on the paper and to Wes Viner for additional comments. Framing the topic as statistical interpretation arose out of conversations with Adam Graber, who had identified that phrasing was useful and appropriate within a biblical context.

Bibliography

Barbour, Ian G. *Religion and Science: Historical and Contemporary Issues*. San Francisco: HarperSanFrancisco, 1997.

Blei, David M. "Probabilistic Topic Models." *Communications of the ACM* 55.4 (2012): 77–84.

Blei, David M. "Topic Modeling and Digital Humanities." *Journal of Digital Humanities* 2.1 (2012): 8–11.

Blei, David M., Andrew Y. Ng, and Michael I. Jordan. "Latent Dirichlet Allocation." *Journal of Machine Learning Research* 3 (2003): 993–1022.

Brunila, Mikael, and Jack LaViolette. "What Company Do Words Keep? Revisiting the Distributional Semantics of J.R. Firth & Zellig Harris." Pages 4403–17 in *Proceedings of the 2022 Conference of the North American Chapter of the Association for Computational Linguistics: Human Language Technologies*. Seattle: Association for Computational Linguistics, 2022. https://doi.org/10.18653/v1/2022.naacl-main.327.

Erickson, Lucy C., and Erik D. Thiessen. "Statistical Learning of Language: Theory, Validity, and Predictions of a Statistical Learning Account of Language Acquisition." *Developmental Review* 37 (2015): 66–108. https://doi.org/10.1016/j.dr.2015.05.002.

Firth, John R. "A Synopsis of Linguistic Theory 1930–1955." Pages 1–32 in *Studies in Linguistic Analysis*. Special Volume of the Philological Society. Oxford: Blackwell, 1957.

Gadamer, Hans-Georg. *Truth and Method*. Translated by Joel Weinsheimer and Donald G. Marshall. 2nd rev. ed. London: Continuum, 2004.
Graves, Mark. "Computational Topic Models for Theological Investigations." *Theology and Science* 20.1 (2022): 69–84. https://doi.org/10.1080/14746700.2021.2012922.
Harris, Zellig. *Mathematical Structures of Language*. New York: Interscience, 1968.
Hayes, John H., and Carl R. Holladay. *Biblical Exegesis: A Beginner's Handbook*. 3rd ed. Louisville: Westminster John Knox, 2007.
Haynes, Stephen R., and Steven L. McKenzie. *To Each Its Own Meaning: An Introduction to Biblical Criticisms and Their Applications*. Louisville: Westminster John Knox, 1999.
McFague, Sallie. *Models of God: Theology for an Ecological, Nuclear Age*. Philadelphia: Fortress, 1987.
Redding, Paul. "Hermeneutics and German Idealism." In *The Cambridge Companion to Hermeneutics*. Edited by Michael N. Forster and Kristin Gjesdal. Cambridge: Cambridge University Press, 2019.
Ricoeur, Paul. *Freud and Philosophy: An Essay on Interpretation*. Translated by Denis Savage. New Haven: Yale University Press, 1970.
Ricoeur, Paul. *Semeia 4: Paul Ricoeur on Biblical Hermeneutics*. Edited by John Dominic Crossan. Atlanta: Society of Biblical Literature, 1975.
Robinson, Geoffrey D. "Paul Ricoeur and the Hermeneutics of Suspicion: A Brief Overview and Critique." *Premise* 2.8 (1995): 12.
Searle, John R. "Minds, Brains, and Programs." *Behavioral and Brain Sciences* 3.3 (1980): 417–24.
Sherwood, Yvonne. *A Biblical Text and Its Afterlives: The Survival of Jonah in Western Culture*. Cambridge: Cambridge University Press, 2000.
Soulen, Richard N., and R. Kendall Soulen. *Handbook of Biblical Criticism*. Louisville: Westminster John Knox, 2011.
Thiselton, Anthony C. "Biblical Interpretation." Pages 287–304 in *The Modern Theologians: An Introduction to Christian Theology since 1918*. Edited by David F. Ford. With Rachel Muers. 3rd ed. Malden: Blackwell, 2005.
Thiselton, Anthony C. *The Two Horizons: New Testament Hermeneutics and Philosophical Description*. Grand Rapids: Eerdmans, 1980.

12

A Rudder in the Information Crisis

AI, the Tongue, and Divine Communication

Melanie Dzugan

We live in an Information Age that finds itself within a state of crisis. More data is produced now than ever before, "yet we have created a communications culture that has decreased the time available for us to sit and think uninterrupted."[1] We lack sufficient time, skill, and practice required to process information wisely—a problem compounded by the unfettered production of information afforded by exponential developments in information communication technologies, namely artificial intelligence (AI). In terms of interpretive work, AI boasts an unprecedented efficiency and scope as a communicative agent in the interpretive process. Readers of Scripture can bring their questions, and AI will quickly interrogate available resources for answers. The novelty of AI is that not only can it perform the kind of quarrying approach that Douglas Estes discusses in his chapter, "AI in the Bible: A Way Forward," it can also perform those descriptive, synthetic, hermeneutic, and pragmatic tasks if asked. However, reliance on AI in the communicative process that occurs between the reader and the text runs the risk of shortchanging the inherently *formative* aspects of in*formation*. In order for AI to best serve biblical interpretation, it must partner with readers to engage Scripture holistically as divine communication that is formative, practical, and contextual.

To read Scripture as divine communication supports the kind of implicit ethic of AI for which Estes calls. The ethical frame offered here is sustained by the communication practices that a reader may learn by reading the Word of God and doing what it says, not only explicitly but also implicitly. An interpretation of Scripture as divine communication, I argue, is especially instructive for how we ought to use a uniquely communicative technology like AI. To make my case, I take a closer look at the history of biblical interpretation and its effect on public theologies. The contemporary difficulty of approaching Scripture as divine communication is neither new nor unique to AI, emerging at least as early as the Enlightenment from the divide between reason and experience (see the discussion stemming from Hume's Fork below). This epistemological divide contributes to the modern distance between biblical criticism and theological reflection, producing a state of affairs in which biblical scholars participate far less frequently in technologically oriented conversations than theologians and ethicists.[2] As such, the relative absence of robust biblical exegesis in technological ethics contributes to the overall weakness of the conversation regarding the usage of AI for biblical interpretation and translation, as Estes also observes. Of course, this does not imply a pervasive disdain or disregard for Scripture in theological reflections on AI—note the ubiquitous concern for the *imago Dei* in technological ethics, for example.[3] What it does reveal is the disconnect between liberal and conservative interpretations of Scripture.

"Liberal" and "conservative" are two main types of theological methods that help make sense of disagreements between different theological approaches. Most types of Western theological methods fit into one of these broader categories or, like the postliberal and postconservative methods we will discuss later, *respond* to one of these categories. These types may help interpreters of Scripture understand their own approach better as they tend to think in terms more consistent with one type or the other even if not always or not perfectly.

However, neither a broadly liberal nor conservative theological method consistently frames Scripture as divine discourse meant to form our own communicative practices, complicating our consideration of the communicative practices of AI-enhanced biblical interpretation (see Table 11.1). Through interfaces that direct the reader deeper into the discursive contexts of biblical texts, AI may be approached as a communicative agent capable of aiding readers to hear the voice of God within the ever more deafening roar of information flow.

Biblical Truth

Even among those who receive the Bible as Scripture, the Bible is not always regarded as divine *communication*. That is, the confession that the Bible is the inspired "Word of God" does not always correlate to a conviction that God actually speaks.[4] In the wake of the Enlightenment, the split that occurs along the lines of Hume's Fork between liberal and conservative theology produces distinct but related challenges to engaging biblical text as divine communication. Both traditions may read the Bible as Scripture and both may treat Scripture as normative for their ethic, but neither sufficiently supports interpretation as a communicative act between God and the reader. For AI to help ease the mounting challenges of biblical interpretation in an age of information crisis, readers should be mindful of the fundamental divide forced by Hume's Fork that continues to distort and dampen the Word of God in theological ethics of technology.

Hume's proverbial fork in the road is an emblem of modernity's defining task of making distinctions, of untangling ideas once inextricable from one another, of separating aspects of wholes in order to examine them on their own terms.[5] The aim was improvement: to replace old, decaying, corrupted systems with new and better ways of being that better fit human nature.[6] David Hume, prominent philosopher of the Scottish Enlightenment, demonstrated the distinction between knowledge based on logical deductions (rationalism) and knowledge based on lived observation (empiricism).[7] Mathematical proofs, for example, belong in the first category while physical experimentation belongs in the second. This divide troubled the methods commonly used by scholars of theology—the "queen of the sciences"—when arguing truth claims about God. Hume's Fork demands a more precise account of how a person grounds and orients their claims of knowledge. Perhaps unsurprisingly, debates raged in a "method fetishism" over which kind of knowledge was better than the other and whether religious knowledge could legitimize itself according to either path.[8]

After Hume, the discipline of theology diverged into separate discourses that would become, broadly speaking, the conservative and liberal theological traditions. Following Friedrich Schleiermacher, spiritual experience became the source material for mainline liberal theology, offering an alternative path of knowledge to the choice between rationalism and empiricism forced by Hume's Fork.[9] As such, the Bible expresses the biblical authors' true experiences of God. This appeal to experience coheres with an expressivist theory of language in which words—namely, the words of Scripture—express a particular human experience of a universal God as a ground of knowledge that smooths over potential conflicts between spiritual knowledge and rational and empirical knowledge. In contrast, conservative theologians followed the lead of philosopher Thomas Reid, insisting on the inerrancy of Scripture as sufficient ground of rational *and* empirical knowledge, defying Hume's Fork altogether.[10] As such, the Bible describes the world as it "really" is. This appeal to Scripture coheres with a referential theory of language in which the words of Scripture are descriptive propositions that hold true in every sense. Reid, who originated this kind of conservative "common-sense realism," inspired later theologians such as Charles Hodge and B. B. Warfield.[11] The types that we have constructed here are summarized in Table 12.1.

The methodological distinction of liberal and conservative epistemology may sound purely academic, but its implications are acutely relevant to public issues. Liberal theology, representing the experiential approach to knowledge that proves amiable to scientific consensus, has been relied upon in significant measure to support public policies but could not add much information of its own due to the personal nature of religious experience.[12] Consider, for example, "Washington's theologian" Reinhold Niebuhr, who worked more to effectively improve common life rather than to ensure faithful implementation of biblical ideals, since lived experience norms biblical

Table 12.1: Theological Types

	Foundation	Theory of Language	Typological Scholar
Conservative	Inerrant biblical text	Descriptive (propositional referentialism)	Charles Hodge
Liberal	Ineffable spiritual experience	Experiential (expressivism)	Friedrich Schleiermacher

Created by Melanie Dzugan.

interpretation in the liberal tradition. As such, Niebuhr secured public relevance but failed to effect meaningful racial reform during the era of desegregation, an arguable failure of his theology's own ethical prioritization of experience.[13] Conservative theology, on the other hand, became a religious confrontation of secular science by attempting to prove the validity of the Word of God by developing alternative criteria of scientific evidence and rigorous standards of deduction. The politicization of the "moral majority," beginning with the 1979 election in the United States and spurred by Jerry Falwell's fight with the Supreme Court to defend the segregation of Bob Jones University, has moved the strains of conservative foundationalism most opposed to secular knowledge into positions of political cooption under the Trump administration. Conservative theology now enjoys a position of public relevance similar to that once enjoyed by liberal theology and with just as questionably faithful public implementation.[14] Together, the two foundational liberal and conservative theological commitments further contribute to the public information crisis as each tradition publicly argues for "biblical truth."

Theological language in AI conversations continues to elicit these modern contests of religious and secular knowledge.[15] For example, David Brenner, founder of AI and Faith, describes a Christian perspective of AI in this way: "the nature of truth is more than empirical facts susceptible to 'fact-checking.' Assertions of truth in the religious context inherently involve testimony to beliefs about the nonmaterial world that cannot be proven by fact-based evidence."[16] Brenner is correct that truth is irreducible to empirical data, but the ways in which we have followed the lines drawn in the sand by Hume's Fork and accused theological traditions of being either fact-based or not fact-based—as though truth has not always relied on a discourse of both experience and propositional realism in every context, religious or not—exacerbate the polarization and distrust between theological communities in the broader public sphere.

Truth is more than empirical facts susceptible to "fact-checking" not only because God is ineffable experience or divinely Other, but because God is a *person*, three persons, in fact, in perfect communication with one another and in communication with humanity and all creation. Communication is not just explicit, but also *implicit*; people who talk together for a while can make all kinds of implications in all kinds of ways. That kind of holistic communication over time is called a discourse; discourses always involve people and the understandings that grow around them. A practice of interpretation aware of the divine discourse between God and his people holds all the explicit and implicit contexts of communication together—including experience and propositions—and is essential for our Information Age. For "when those two senses have grown apart, then no society is going to be able to think with wisdom."[17] As a uniquely communicative technology involved more and more in public discourse, AI has a unique potential to either encourage or undermine common wisdom. To step along the path of wisdom, interpreters of Scripture would do well to recognize the implicit disconnects between liberal and conservative truth claims discussed here, even despite their shared respect for truth.

Creatures and Creators

To make the polarization over biblical truth claims clearer in terms of technological ethics, consider the treatment of the biblical concept most important to theological ethics of technology: the *imago Dei*.

Theologians have historically interpreted the *imago Dei* within three general categories: *substantive* (emphasizing the uniqueness of human nature, such as rationality or the soul), *functional* (emphasizing the role of humanity in creation), and relational (emphasizing our unique relationships with God and creation). As the emphasis on the substantive uniqueness of the human person subsided due to the emergence of the Darwinian consensus, functional and relational interpretations of the *imago Dei* rose in prominence. Noreen Herzfeld's relational interpretation has led theological conversations about AI since the 1990s because of the uniquely communicative and relational aspects of AI,[18] but functional interpretations have dominated broader theological conversations about technology in general—in both liberal and conservative communities. Let us update our chart to act as a touchpoint for this conversation (see Table 12.2).

Representing a more liberal approach, Philip Hefner's functional interpretation of the *imago Dei* as "created co-creator" is uniquely paradigmatic for theological reflections on technology. He argues that humans made in the image of the Creator are, themselves, creators. In Hefner's words, "Creating is not an add-on for us; it is not one attribute among others that mark human life. More than what we *do*, creating is who we *are*."[19] Indicative of Hefner's larger conviction that it is humanity's *good* nature to create, he asserts that "the fact that we are creators is not our sin . . . Our sin emerges from the fact that we too often are incapable of directing our imagining and creating in ways that are commensurate with our grounding in the creation and in God's image."[20] In short, Hefner and those who adopt the *imago Dei* as "created co-creators" affirm technological creation as cooperative with God's own creative work in the world.

Conservative theologians do not engage significantly with Hefner's "created co-creator" analogy, despite a shared commitment to functional interpretations of the *imago Dei*. Brent Waters, widely influential among conservative theological ethics, develops a functional interpretation of the *imago Dei* wherein humans are understood

Table 12.2: Theological Types Expanded

	Foundation	Theory of Language	Typological Scholar	Example
Conservative	Inerrant biblical text	Descriptive (propositional referentialism)	Charles Hodge	Brent Waters (creatures)
Liberal	Ineffable spiritual experience	Experiential (expressivism)	Friedrich Schleiermacher	Philip Hefner (created co-creators)

Created by Melanie Dzugan.

as "the creatures that God has elected to oversee the providential unfolding of God's creation."[21] While bearing a categorical similarity to Hefner, Waters is careful to distance his interpretation from Hefner's. To Waters, Hefner's liberal commitment to experience leads to his "created-co-creator" looking more like *self*-creation. To quote Hefner, "The fundamental norm is the wholesomeness of the creation of which we are part . . . this norm is empty until it is filled with content, and it is we, the co-creators, who must supply that content. This is what I mean by saying that we are co-creators all the way down."[22] In contrast, Waters argues that "It is precisely in being finite and mortal that humans are reminded that they are creatures created by a creator, and not self-made artifacts."[23] Waters agrees with Hefner that nature is creative but the difference between their appeals to nature—and this is key—is that Waters denies that humanity exists as an equal part of the wholesomeness of creation. Instead, humanity has been given functional *dominion over* the creativity of the world, playing the part of a preservationist rather than a creator.

On this conservative impulse for preservationism rather than creativity, it is worth quoting Waters's challenge to Hefner at length:

> If the natural processes sustaining human life become severely degraded or extinguished, then human creativity also becomes impoverished, or worse, extinct. Hefner's and Kaufman's plea on behalf of natural ecologies is certainly prudential, but in drawing a protective boundary they also undermine their core imperative, namely, that creativity is not, after all, infinite. Humans may be creative until they hit the hard wall of necessity . . . the natural environment they champion has no inherent but only an instrumental value, for it reinforces stifling limits against the infinite creativity they wish to pursue. The natural environment is not good per se, but is only good in respect to its limited capacity to sustain life.[24]

It is in the divergent choices of a foundation—contingent human experience or inerrant divine revelation—that the conversation breaks apart before it even begins. When Waters looks at nature as a conservative propositionalist, he sees that humanity is not free to create out of our shared *experience* of the world (expressivism) but is first accountable to preserve a created reality to which our creativity must adequately *refer* (referentialism). When Hefner looks at nature as a liberal expressivist, he sees that it is humanity's good, created nature to create, and we must do so in ever dynamic and changing forms that are responsible to the wholesomeness of creation which we *experience* and which cannot be described by fixed propositions beyond the theological commitment that Creation is good. There is significant linguistic similarity in these arguments. Both respect Scripture and nature and look to each to norm ethical creativity. But for conservatives like Waters, there is nothing we can add to (or take away from) God's creation. Creation is as God has *described* it. When Waters appeals to the hard laws of "necessity," in the quote above, he is taking issue with the way in which Hefner grounds his ethic in the liberal *expression* of created contingency. For Hefner, all of creation is creative because the Creator God created it. Therefore, as the created image of the Creator God, humanity's defining attribute is our creativity, which entails ever-adapting ethical norms which we are responsible to discern.

The main disagreement here rests not on any exegesis of the *imago Dei* but on the battle lines drawn in the sand between expressive and referential language as the proper grounds for knowledge. Both liberal and conservative theologians often rely on functional interpretations of the *imago Dei* to bear weight that their content cannot support.[25] The *imago Dei* is vaguely defined, if at all, in the biblical text, but this ambiguity has appeal for theologians in the way it reinforces their respective epistemological commitments. For liberal theologians like Hefner, "created co-creator" demonstrates coherence between a biblical expression of truth and human experiences of nature as articulated by postmodern philosophies and sciences.[26] Christian and non-Christian scholars may proceed in dialogue concerning urgent public issues like AI since you do not have to read the Bible or practice Christian tradition to speak in terms of "creativity" as a good. However, while "created co-creator" provides liberal ethicists with public relevance, it leaves little room for making a meaningful contribution beyond encouragement or agreement. The norms that Hefner says we must discern ourselves find little support in theological readings of Scripture that are foundationally normed by our own experience.[27]

In contrast, the *imago Dei* as "creatureliness" is attractive to conservative ethicists for its apparent affirmation of human uniqueness among creation as ordained by and accountable to God, a theological point that exemplifies the descriptive propositionalism that grounds conservative theology. Conservatives double down in reasserting the reality of common ground—of "truth"—and it is this problem of embattlement that has come to caricature conservative theology. Consider this quote from Jason Thacker: "The nature of truth is that it cannot be personalized; it corresponds with reality whether we like it or not. In this way, truth is an equal opportunity informer and offender to us all. And when we press against reality to try and make it bend to our desire, reality presses back. Hard."[28] This is an unflinching, impersonal articulation of creation with little way to account for the changing realities we live in. In Hefner's own words of conservative technological discourse, "Cynicism has a stunted imagination; it has abandoned the challenge to bring new things into actuality. It is a betrayal of the image of God."[29]

In sum, the problem of the *imago Dei* is precisely this way in which "the concept functions as a placeholder, the image of God becoming whatever it needs to be in order to articulate the theological affirmation of human uniqueness and moral worth" in both liberal and conservative theologies.[30] Although Waters and Thacker would agree with Hefner that humans may create in ways aligned with God's own creation, their respective traditions struggle to engage one another because of their parallel, fundamental commitments to either experience or propositionalism. Theological reasoning concerning AI thus proceeds not by exegesis of the biblical text (recall the limited number of biblical scholars engaged in technological ethics) to hear what God spoke into and over Creation, but by philosophical arguments of the (ultimately unsolvable) methodological problems outlined by Hume's Fork. However, liberal strategies to rely on shared experience do not escape the dependence of even common concepts on biblical definitions—secular terms like "creation" require as much grounding, contextualization, and substantiation by their communicative contexts (in this case, Scripture) as any other term. Likewise, theologies of conservative propositionalism have failed to deliver consensus on even the most common and fundamental biblical concepts like the *imago Dei* because createdness also depends on its communicative contexts.

In a culture in information crisis—in which knowledge is transactional and reduced to soundbites—the public conversation of Christian theology rarely progresses beyond these thin surface levels, offering the illusion of common ground without providing any real support. Liberal optimism and conservative pessimism become political identity markers of epistemological commitments that stifle constructive communication between the two, even when both groups may be working toward the same goal of responsible technological creation. Christians *should* develop and use communicative technologies like AI which bear consequences for the physical environment and a public sense of common ground in ways that intentionally account for both the *experienced* challenges of the Information Age and its *created* contexts. I propose that the best way to do this is through practicing the interpretation of Scripture as divine communication.

Divine Communication

Before progressing toward better reception of Scripture as divine communication and the potential role of AI in that interpretive task, the term "communication" itself demands definition and contextualization.

Communication describes the meaningful flow of information. Communication studies encompass information theory, social cognition, influence and persuasion, social exchange, deception, message production and processing, non-verbal communication, emotional expression, and media.[31] The variety of metaphors used by scholars to describe communication—conduit of information, symbol-making, process of social interaction, and co-construction of social reality[32]—demonstrates that communication is not merely a transfer of information or an exchange of words. In*formation* itself is *formative*.[33] To quote the widely influential axiom of information theorist Gregory Bateson, information is "a difference that makes a difference."[34] Cyberneticist Norbert Wiener, renowned for his comprehensive work on communication, argues that "to live effectively is to live with adequate information. Thus, communication and control [of information] belong to the essence of man's inner's life, even as they belong to his life in society."[35]

Bateson and Wiener are important here not least because of their leadership in posthumanist theories of communication that make the communicative technology of AI possible. Along with like-minded scholars, Bateson and Wiener gathered at the Josiah Macy Foundation conferences from 1946 to 1953 in New York to offer "a new theoretical model for biological, mechanical, and communicational processes that removed the human and *Homo sapiens* from an isolated, static position in relation to matters, meaning, information, and cognition."[36] These new theoretical models supported the development of cybernetic technologies like the computer, the internet, and now, AI. The Macy scholars used the term "posthumanism" to describe their understanding of humans as dependent upon their communicative contexts.[37] Such work supported the postmodern shift from anthropologies that envision humankind as *substantively* different from creation (recall the categories of interpretation of the *imago Dei*) to anthropologies that envision humankind as dynamic beings constantly being formed and reformed by communicative relationships.

Most important, perhaps, to the postmodern shift from substantive to formative anthropologies is the semantic work of linguists like Wittgenstein or Austin. Ludwig Wittgenstein's work represents the fulcrum point of postmodernity.[38] Discontented with the split that resulted after Hume's Fork, a Wittgensteinian theory of language holds that most language is at once both expressive *and* referential; both are important in order for information to communicate something of meaning between persons. From Wittgenstein's work, we may say that at least five contexts are necessary for understanding communication:

1. linguistic conventions
2. social conventions
3. referential conditions
4. expressivist or psychological conditions
5. uptake of language (how it has been socially understood).[39]

J. L. Austin's work on speech-act theory is similarly important in making the point that language may affect real change and consequence in the world—it can *do* things, not merely exist. With speech, we may promise, command, apologize, and invite any number of other opportunities.

Theologians, philosophers, and biblical scholars take up postmodern theories of communication and take steps toward reconciling the theological split that occurs between conservative and liberal methodologies after Hume's Fork. Particularly, the Yale School of postliberalism that rose to prominence with the work of scholars like Brevard Childs, Hans Frei, and George Lindbeck in the 1970s and 1980s reforms liberal expressivism of Scripture by calling attention to the biblical narratives which form human experience. Lindbeck calls his biblical hermeneutic a cultural-linguistic: "To become a Christian involves learning the story of Israel and of Jesus well enough to interpret and experience oneself and one's world in its terms."[40] Lindbeck once projected that conservative "evangelicals were more likely than any other group to carry the project of postliberalism forward" because of their commitment to biblicism.[41] The cultural-linguistic, however, misses the concerns of many conservatives committed to the descriptive, referential, propositional truth of biblical text. The fundamental difference between conservative commitment to biblical inerrancy and liberal commitment to experience requires a postconservativism as well as a postliberalism although their end methods and goals may bear linguistic similarity. This is the reason for Kevin Vanhoozer's work on a postconservative canonical-linguistic which reforms conservative propositionalism of Scripture by calling attention to the communicative contexts of biblical texts.[42] Vanhoozer clarifies his approach: "What God is *not* doing in speaking 'today' is adding to or distorting what the prophets and apostles said. As we shall see, the Spirit does not change the meaning of the words but *revoices*, *reactivates*, and *resituates* the discourse in and for a new redemptive-historical context."[43]

The key to postliberal and postconservative reconciliations of expressivist and referential language and of experiential and biblical foundationalism is not in *overcoming* the claims of liberal and conservative traditions but rather in *reframing* them in a hermeneutic of divine discourse. Discourse, as we started to define above, is a special aspect of communication that focuses on the language-based exchanges between communicative agents and the contexts that develop as a result of those exchanges over time. The description of the Bible as "divine discourse" enables an academic approach to theological interpretation that frames reading the Bible as a real conversation with God, affirming the conviction that the triune God is alive and speaks.[44] This approach does not exclude other descriptors of the Bible—as the Scripture of the Church or a narrative whole. It does, however, allow scholars who work in this conversation to interpret biblical theology as normative and formative communication with God.[45] Nicholas Wolterstorff—who taught at Yale from 1957 to 1959 when George Lindbeck received his PhD from Yale in 1958—serves as a touchpoint of "divine discourse" as an interpretive approach not least because of his work, aptly named, *Divine Discourse*. He explains the ethical implications of reading God's Word as divine communication, "Speaking consists not in communicating or expressing knowledge (or true belief) but in taking up a certain sort of normative stance, as I shall call it."[46] That normative stance entails the trust, truthfulness, and obligation entailed in not just hearing the Word, but doing what it says. Communication is not a simple matter of intellectual assent or the explicit impartation of knowledge—it is an implicit expectation that one's words are understood, accepted, and taken into account in full fairness and with respect to the speaker. Communication relies on the fullness of its discursive contexts in order to be understood.

Postconservative biblical scholar Joel Green offers criteria for contextualized theological interpretation that the reader may notice cohere with Wittgenstein's criteria for interpreting information as meaningful communication:

1. Accounts for the text in its final form, without depending on a cut-and-paste job that refabricates the text in order that it might fit a prior theory.
2. Accounts for the text as a whole and is consistent with the whole of the text, without deliberately masking unfortunate aspects of the text that continue to haunt the interpreter.
3. Is consistent with the general rules of language, including considerations of a philological, syntactical, and grammatical sort.
4. Accounts for the cultural embeddedness of language, allowing the text to have its meaning fashioned in light of its sociocultural assumptions.
5. Is "ruled" by its canonical embeddedness.

6. Is set within the boundaries of the "rule of faith" and the "rule of love"; as Augustine wrote, "So any who think they have understood the divine Scriptures or any part of them, but cannot by their understanding build up this double love of God and neighbor, have not yet succeeded in understanding them."[47]

To conserve the integrity of Scripture as divine communication, it is important for readers to read it in its whole context in (at least) the ways enumerated here. We do not have the space here to expound upon these six criteria, but suffice to say, in postconservative scholar Roger Olson's words, "the anchor for all of this is God revealing himself in and through the canon of Scripture understood not as a set of propositions to be systematized but as a narrative or drama that sets in motion a performative process that continues through the church until the consummation."[48] Propositions here are not discarded; they are reformed in a way that necessitates practice in human lives to be understood, the kind of ethical expectation that Wolterstorff describes of divine speech. To refer back to the terms used in Estes's chapter, the descriptive, synthetic, hermeneutic, and pragmatic tasks of interpretation are never completed—as one participates in divine discourse, one's understanding of Scripture should continue to deepen and mature in each way.

The interpretive frame of divine discourse as contextual, formative, and practical may resonate with readers of AI ethics. Let's begin with context. "Context" is a routinely recurring factor of AI design and implementation in biblical interpretation. Not surprisingly, "context" often means something different to developers than it does to theologians—context matters, even for "context." The point here is that a postconservative discursive hermeneutic insists that words are not containers of self-evident meaning apart from carefully considered context and for biblical interpretation, the contexts of the biblical canon, biblical narrative, historical situation, and more are all essential in hearing and responding to the living, triune God who actively speaks in Scripture. AI should continuously direct readers back into the medium of Scripture in the whole of its contexts. "The medium is the message," as discourse scholar Marshall McLuhan famously argued in the 1960s.[49] An AI interface like Sefaria, for example, connects users with resources for further engagement with the biblical text by making obscure historical documents of biblical interpretation more accessible. An interface like BibleGPT, in contrast, quarries the biblical text for relevant content with little retention of its fuller contexts upon which the content of the text relies for normative meaning.[50] Further, there is coherence here between a communicative hermeneutic and an ethic like Helen Nissenbaum's widely influential frame of contextual integrity for information ethics. Both conserve the integrity of information's communicative contexts for the purpose of formation of communicative agents.[51] Such coherence enables a robust public engagement of theological and secular ethics on public issues like AI.

The importance of virtue formation is the trending consensus of AI ethical scholarship and broader theological ethics as a whole. "Formation" draws support from posthumanist anthropologies like those of the Macy conferences, and yet it remains a persistent problem to explain just how desired formation occurs. If communication practices are so meaningful, why do readers of Scripture fail to be formed according to the Gospel? The problem is one of goal alignment.[52] AI is developed for efficient information communication, not to conserve and support the rather *inefficient* processes of communicative formation. As Levi Checketts reminds us, AI is not made so that the majority may be confronted by marginalized peoples producing marginalized data sets. It reinforces consensus rather than conversion; AI "further marginalize[s] the experience and embodied truth of those worst off in our society."[53] So it shall continue to be if the AI interfaces we develop and use for biblical interpretation prioritize efficiency at the cost of communicative formation. Let those with ears to hear *hear* what God confronts us with in Scripture, not just those aspects that cohere with our own experience or make sense within our systems of knowledge. A hermeneutic of divine discourse is not a method of virtue formation, but it does offer a robust reconciliation of expressive and referential language that strengthens our ability to hear the voice of God.

Such ability is reinforced by our final aspect of divine discourse: its practicality. Here, prevalent arguments that AI cannot replace human interpreters because AI cannot operate with *practical* reason may come to mind.[54] The competition between AI and humans has certainly been at the fore of theological reflection and at least partially accounts for our turn to the *imago Dei* for guidance through our anxieties concerning the replacement of humanity. Moreover, now, however, the conversation about ethical AI is motivated by a concern for what AI virtue ethicist Shannon Vallor calls "moral deskilling."[55] A strength of functional interpretations of the *imago Dei* is the conviction that truth is as much a practice as it is a substance. The Word of God is not at risk of being lost; instead, it is the skill of *hearing* that voice that is slipping as our contexts shift rapidly around us. It is *we* rather than the ground of truth that needs reinforcement. True understanding—*wisdom*—requires embodied practices of communication rather than simple transfer of knowledge. A discursive hermeneutic reinforces our responsibility to communicate as God does, not in soundbites and consumable talking points, but with respect for truth and our fellow communicative agents.

Conclusion

I would be remiss to end a chapter calling the reader to listen to the Word of God without demonstrating that kind of listening myself. The book of James offers a helpful way of summarizing and concluding our reflection on biblical hermeneutics, biblical language, and even the potential AI may offer as a communicative technology to support better practices of information communication. Here, I rely on Green's exegetical work as he reads James, implementing his recommendations for a discursive hermeneutic, and adding my own commentary on the difference that a discursive hermeneutic can make for a theological ethic of AI for biblical interpretation, especially concerning the oft-cited *imago Dei*.

James is a case study of the Bible's concern with communicative formation. Information interpretation and communication are not challenges unique to our own context in the Information Age; they are of deep concern for James as well. James addresses his letter to God's people in dispersion, people who lack access to social religious structures (Jas 1:1 CEB).[56] Accordingly, James "works hard to shape both how people find their identity and how they respond to their life situations" apart from traditional institutional mandates.[57] In this, the text of James both works from the experience of the audience and also describes referentially how the readers of Scripture today should identify with the people of God—as a people of dispersion rather than a people in control of national institutions.

The people of God face "*periasmos*," which may be interpreted as either a temptation or a test/trial (Jas 1:2-18). The situations of *periasmos* are the same—the difference between a temptation or a trial is how one *interprets* and responds to it. Interpreting a test as though a trial and responding with joyful endurance leads to maturation, wisdom, and blessing, "tried and true" (Jas 1:2-12). Interpreting a test as though a temptation and responding with blame and despair leads to sin and death, for the idea that God would tempt his beloved creations is a lie (Jas 1:13-18). This is a call to reject an identity politics of either optimism and cynicism, a rejection of the postures of undiscerning tolerance and embattlement that caricature liberal and conservative theologies. It is a call to interpretation and communication that trusts and stays in communion with the triune God who demonstrates how to receive information so that it may be a difference that makes a difference. The fruit of good interpretation of one's lived context is good communication practice, humble people who are "quick to listen, slow to speak, and slow to grow angry" (Jas 1:19-20). Indeed, "if those who claim devotion to God don't control what they say, they mislead themselves. Their devotion is worthless" (Jas 1:26). James implores the reader to "welcome the word planted deep inside you—the very word that is able to save you" (Jas 1:21).

The word planted deep inside us evokes memory of the Genesis stories of creation, and James does turn to the *imago Dei* to substantiate his ethic as do Hefner and Waters. James, however, is not encumbered by a modern dualism of particular experiences or universal propositions and thus, with his appeal to the *imago Dei*, contextualizes his interpretation in the biblical narrative of creation to new creation, effectively offering an interpretation that coheres with a canonical-linguistic for the sake of the reader's identity formation, the contextual need to which James speaks. God created humankind in his *homoiōsis*, "likeness" (Jas 3:9). In evoking the narrative of creation of humankind, James referentially grounds human dignity and the call for ethical comportment in creation and, more particularly, in the God who created humans in his likeness.[58] God who is good creates and gives good things, including human beings, the first crop of his creation (Jas 1:18). For James, then, it is a misinterpretation of creation and a malformed judgment to bless God but curse human beings (Jas 3:8-10). God, the "creator of heavenly lights," *spoke* all things into existence and "chose to give us birth by his true word;" so too are the things that we say life or death-giving (Jas 1:17-18). James's interest here in creation is "focused especially on the nature of the creator God" as a God who "does not waver between giving good things and bad things; his character is consistently oriented toward good things."[59] Thus, we can trust God's interpretation of the world as the one who created it and the one who creates good things, the one "in whose character there is no change at all" (Jas 1:17).

The hope for created things—the beast, the tongue, the human—is through formation according to God's good Word, the work of new creation. New creation will be one different from the world we know; there, the wealthy will "die off like wildflowers" but the poor will "find satisfaction in their high status" (Jas 1:9-10). Formation is conversion—specifically lifelong, embodied *conversion*—that happens through hearing the Word and doing what it says (Jas 1:22-25). For James, "wisdom and understanding are measured in terms of the forms of life that they inspire. In this sense, wisdom and understanding are fully embodied, not thought experiments or data stored for future use."[60] The virtues that James names here in 3:17—purity, peacefulness, gentleness, obedience, mercifulness, goodness, fairness, genuineness, justice—are not abstract principles or intellectually accepted propositions but embodied, enacted practices. The demons know God—they fear God!—but demons refuse to be formed according to God (Jas 2:19). It should not be this way.

To become who God says we are and to communicate as he does is to be created in the image of God. James is sometimes interpreted as the book of works over faith, but this is a poor reading that falls into that methodological split of Scripture and spiritual experience. The two are neither separate nor competitive—James adeptly holds the two together through an articulation of the unique power of speech acts—the place where inner conviction spills into the world as words and *really* does something. Blessing, cursing, bragging, crying out, laughing, insulting, criticizing, complaining, pledging, praying, confessing, even *staying silent*. "Those who don't make mistakes with their words have reached full maturity" (Jas 3:2). To mature in our communication requires Christologically lived practice heeding and imitating God's own communication in its full propositional and experiential likeness. Let nothing distract us or prevent us from this practice, for who can tame the tongue?

It is its own question, given the substantial carbon footprint, exploitative training methods, and thus-far unfettered public implementation of AI, whether AI can be a reconciliatory communication technology if "the medium is the message" as McLuhan insists.[61] With a discursive hermeneutic, however, communicators in God's image may reconcile the broken discourses of liberal and conservative theologies through formative practices of contextual biblical interpretation. As we practice divine discourse, biblically faithful speech acts may serve as a rudder for Christ-followers picking up their crosses in the Information Age.

Notes

1 Sherry Turkle, *Alone Together: Why We Expect More from Technology and Less from Each Other* (New York: Basic Books, 2011), 166.

2 For example, Cole-Turner's 2011 anthology, *Transhumanism and Transcendence*, is an important, early gathering of key contributors to the Christian discussion of

technological enhancement. No biblical scholars were included in this anthology. In 2018, Cole-Turner worked with computer scientist and science and religion scholar Steve Donaldson to publish a new anthology, *Christian Perspectives on Transhumanism and the Church*. After seven years and with a more explicit focus on the church, still only one biblical scholar was included as a contributor to this project, Steven J. Kraftchick, who calls attention to the fact that very few biblical scholars have participated in the discussion around transhumanism. As a result, while theologians may turn to the *imago Dei*, the Incarnation, or other biblical concepts as resources, scholarly engagement with the Bible is critically lacking in Christian scholarship on technological enhancement. See Ronald Cole-Turner, ed., *Transhumanism and Transcendence: Christian Hope in an Age of Technological Enhancement* (Washington, DC: Georgetown University Press, 2011); Steve Donaldson and Ron Cole-Turner, eds., *Christian Perspectives on Transhumanism and the Church: Chips in the Brain, Immortality, and the World of Tomorrow* (London: Palgrave Macmillan, 2018); and Steven John Kraftchick, "Bodies, Selves, and Human Identity: A Conversation Between Transhumanism and the Apostle Paul," *ThTo* 72 (2015): 54.

3 See, for example, Tracy J. Trothen, "Moral Bioenhancement through an Intersectional Theo-Ethical Lens: Refocusing on Divine Image-Bearing and Interdependence," *Religions* 8.5 (2017): 84; and Ted Peters, "Can We Enhance the *Imago Dei*?" in *Human Identity at the Intersection of Science, Technology, and Religion*, ed. Nancey Murphy and Christopher C. Knight, Ashgate Science and Religion Series (Burlington: Ashgate, 2010), 215–38.

4 Nicholas Wolterstorff, in his seminal work *Divine Discourse*, brings attention to the ways that theological traditions have effectively reduced the idea of divine speech to divine revelation. This move has the effect of de-personalizing the voice of God in biblical texts, though that divine "voice" may still bear normative priority in a theological ethic. Nicholas Wolterstorff, *Divine Discourse: Philosophical Reflections on the Claim That God Speaks* (Cambridge: Cambridge University Press, 1995), 10.

5 For further reading, see Christoph Hübenthal, "The Secular," in *T&T Clark Handbook of Public Theology*, ed. Christoph Hübenthal and Christiane Alpers (London: T&T Clark, 2022), 48–68.

6 Consider, for example, Descartes's explanation in *Discourse on Method*: "And I firmly believed that by this means I would succeed in conducting my life much better than if I built only upon the old foundations and gave credence to the principles which I had acquired in my childhood without ever having examined them to see whether they were true or not." Quoted in Nancey C. Murphy, *Beyond Liberalism and Fundamentalism: How Modern and Postmodern Philosophy Set the Theological Agenda*, Rockwell Lecture Series (Valley Forge: Trinity Press International, 1996) 11.

7 This section follows the types developed by (postconservative) philosopher Nancey Murphy in *Beyond Liberalism and Fundamentalism,* 11–61.

8 Josh A. Reeves, *Against Methodology in Science and Religion: Recent Debates on Rationality and Theology* (London: Routledge, 2019), 9.

9 For a relevant sample of Schleiermacher, see Friedrich Schleiermacher, "Second Speech," in *On Religion: Speeches to Its Cultured Despisers*, trans. John Oman (New York: Harper Torchbooks, 1965), 26–118.

10 Thomas Reid, *An Inquiry into the Human Mind: On the Principles of Common Mind. A Critical Edition*, ed. Derek R. Brookes, Edinburgh Edition of Thomas Reid (Edinburgh: Edinburgh University Press, 1997).

11 Of course, scholars may not necessarily categorize themselves as "liberal" or "conservative," and far more categories of theology exist. I use these two categories as a way to contextualize the modern situation in general, especially in contrast to the theological approaches explored in postmodernity.

12 For a summary of the challenges of mainstream public theology and a constructive proposal for a practice-oriented, thick public theology like the one I will offer here in this chapter, see Lisa Sowle Cahill, *Theological Bioethics: Participation, Justice, and Change*, Moral Traditions (Washington, DC: Georgetown University Press, 2005), 13–42.

13 James Cone offers an excellent overview of Niebuhr's theology in his second chapter of *The Cross and the Lynching Tree*. He concludes that Niebuhr fails to fulfill his own methodological criteria by not adequately taking the facts of experience into account, namely, the Black experience. My argument in this chapter might suggest that reading Scripture with the Black community as normative of Christian ethics is the common ground that can sustain the kind of formation that Cone calls for. For Niebuhr's own articulation of realism, see "Chapter 9, Preservation of Moral Values in Politics," in Reinhold Niebuhr, *Moral Man and Immoral Society* (Louisville: Westminster John Knox, 2001); and James H. Cone, *The Cross and the Lynching Tree* (Maryknoll: Orbis, 2011).

14 This history is the focus of Kristin Kobes Du Mez, *Jesus and John Wayne: How White Evangelicals Corrupted a Faith and Fractured a Nation*, illus. ed. (New York: Liveright, 2020).

15 Ian Barbour, whose work is largely credited as shaping the early stages of science and religion as an official discipline, describes the relationship of science and religion according to four types: conflict, independence, *dialogue*, and integration. These four introductory types are widely recognized as too simplistic but still helpful in contextualizing the differences between a dialogical relationship and other modes of relating types of knowledge, whether receptive or not. Ian G. Barbour, *Religion and Science: Historical and Contemporary Issues* (San Francisco: Harper, 1997), 77.

16 David M. Brenner et al., "Technical and Religious Perspectives on AI Misinformation and Disinformation," SSRN, posted June 21, 2024, https://doi.org/10.2139/ssrn.4360413.

17 Charles Snow was a chemist and novelist lamenting the mid-twentieth-century structural and cultural polarization of the sciences and humanities. The differences between epistemological methods in the two disciplines, exacerbated by the physical separation of department offices and the specialization of majors, fostered a mutual resentment and suspicion between "the two cultures," evincing the breakdown in communication and information interpretation in the public so problematic today. See Charles Percy Snow, *The Two Cultures*, ed. Stefan Collini (Cambridge: Cambridge University Press, 2008), 50.

18 For more, see Herzfeld's most recent book, Noreen L. Herzfeld, *The Artifice of Intelligence: Divine and Human Relationship in a Robotic Age* (Minneapolis: Fortress, 2023).

19 Philip Hefner, *Human Becoming in an Age of Science, Technology, and Faith*, ed. Jason Roberts and Mladen Turk (Lanham: Lexington Books/Fortress Academic, 2022), 66.

20 Hefner, *Human Becoming*, 43.

21 Brent Waters, *From Human to Posthuman: Christian Theology and Technology in a Postmodern World* (Burlington: Ashgate, 2006), 117.
22 Hefner, *Human Becoming*, 66.
23 Brent Waters, "Whose Salvation? Which Eschatology? Transhumanism and Christianity as Contending Salvific Religions," in *Transhumanism and Transcendence: Christian Hope in an Age of Technological Enhancement*, ed. Ronald Cole-Turner (Washington, DC: Georgetown University Press, 2011), 174.
24 Waters, *Human to Posthuman*, 138.
25 Jason Roberts perceptively states that "at bottom, created co-creator is a scientifically informed demythologization of *imago Dei* which is intended to color the remythologization of this and all related symbols in the Christian faith tradition" in Jason P. Roberts, "The Created Co-Creator, Redeemer, Sustainer: Extending Symbols of Human and Divine Relating," in *Human Becoming in an Age of Science, Technology, and Faith*, ed. Jason Roberts and Mladen Turk (Lanham: Lexington Books/Fortress Academic, 2022), 89.
26 Hefner deliberately chooses the term "creation" as a secularly friendly interpretation of the *imago Dei*. He wants the metaphor "to operate equally at home in Christian theological and secular scientific contexts for the purpose of fruitfully integrating these rich worlds of meanings." Other viable terms like "sustained co-sustainers" or "redeemed co-redeemers" are too thick, too embedded in theological traditions, to have secular purchase; see Hefner, *Human Becoming*, 1, as well as Roberts, "Created Co-Creator," 81–110.
27 The problem of groundlessness described here is one that is ultimately unsolvable and shared by any theological method, including conservative inerrant referentialism. Consider Mladen Turk's insight in response to Hefner's work: "An appeal for knowledge based on experience is as arbitrary as any other appeal to something evident and immediate and beyond questioning, and it is therefore preliminary at best and deeply unsatisfactory at worst." Mladen Turk, "Is Creative Skepticism Possible? Preliminary Considerations about Conditions of Knowledge, Symbols, and Whether Anything Matters," in *Human Becoming in an Age of Science, Technology, and Faith*, ed. Roberts and Turk, 214.
28 Jason Thacker, *Following Jesus in a Digital Age* (Nashville: B&H, 2022), 36.
29 Hefner, *Human Becoming*, 56.
30 Jeanine Thweatt-Bates, *Cyborg Selves: A Theological Anthropology of the Posthuman*, Ashgate Science and Religion Series (Burlington: Ashgate, 2012), 117.
31 Summary offered in Linda L. Putnam, "Images of the Communication—Discourse Relationship," *Discourse & Communication* 2 (August 1, 2008): 339–40, https://doi.org/10.1177/1750481308091916.
32 Guowei Jian, Amy M. Schmisseur, and Gail T. Fairhurst, "Organizational Discourse and Communication: The Progeny of Proteus," *Discourse & Communication* 2 (2008): 299–320, https://doi.org/10.1177/1750481308091912.
33 *Information* comes from the Latin verb *informare*, "to form." The structure of the word *information* lends itself to recollection of this meaning "to form" in the philosophical sense of Platonic forms. Forms were understood as structures or patterns according to which objects ideally conformed. With the ontological and epistemological held together in *informare*, in medieval times there was not the categorical divide between what *is* and how we *understand* what is that would come

with modernity and Hume's Fork. See also Pieter Adriaans, "Information," in *The Stanford Encyclopedia of Philosophy*, ed. Edward N. Zalta, Metaphysics Research Lab, Stanford University, revised August 18, 2020, https://plato.stanford.edu/archives/fall2020/entries/information.

34 Gregory Bateson, *Steps to an Ecology of Mind* (New York: Ballantine, 1972), 462.

35 Norbert Wiener, *The Human Use of Human Beings: Cybernetics and Society*, 2nd rev. ed. (Garden City: Doubleday, 1954), 18.

36 Cary Wolfe, *What Is Posthumanism?* Posthumanities 8 (Minneapolis: University of Minnesota Press, 2010), xii; Hava Tirosh-Samuelson, "Transhumanism as a Secularist Faith," *Zygon* 47 (2012): 711.

37 In some analyses, the posthuman is the goal or the inevitable result of transhumanism. As the two terms and traditions have developed, however, it is more accurate to understand the posthuman as a postmodern alternative to the modern transhuman. Both share roots in humanism. A posthumanist anthropology invites embodiment modification but, in distinction from many transhumanisms, conserves embodiment itself as a sign of ecological embeddedness. In this way, posthumanism seeks *transformation* of embodiment rather than *transcendence*.

38 Postmodernity, of course, is a big and often confused term, but for our sake here, it refers most generally to society's adjustment to the growing awareness that facts are not wholly impersonal. Knowledge involves the persons who create and communicate it.

39 For more, see Murphy, *Beyond Liberalism*, 110–34.

40 George A. Lindbeck, *The Nature of Doctrine: Religion and Theology in a Postliberal Age*, 25th anniv. ed. (Louisville: Westminster John Knox, 2009), 20.

41 Mary M. Veeneman, *Introducing Theological Method: A Survey of Contemporary Theologians and Approaches* (Grand Rapids: Baker Academic, 2017), 65.

42 As with the types of liberal and conservative, postliberal and postconservative are used as types and do not necessarily reflect the self-identifications of the scholars named. Kevin Vanhoozer, for example, though the paradigmatic postconservative for many, has distanced himself from the term for its still-contested definition.

43 Kevin J. Vanhoozer, *Mere Christian Hermeneutics: Transfiguring What It Means to Read the Bible Theologically* (Grand Rapids: Zondervan, 2024), 37.

44 Nicholas Wolterstorff, *Divine Discourse: Philosophical Reflections on the Claim That God Speaks* (Cambridge: Cambridge University Press, 1995), 8.

45 For a helpful summary of this kind of theological interpretation, see Kevin J. Vanhoozer, introduction to *Dictionary for Theological Interpretation of the Bible* (Grand Rapids: Baker Academic, 2005), 19–25.

46 Wolterstorff, *Divine Discourse*, 35.

47 Joel Green, "A Discursive Frame for Reading Scripture," in *Acts of Interpretation: Scripture, Theology, and Culture*, ed. S. A. Cummins and Jens Zimmermann (Grand Rapids: Eerdmans, 2018), 60; quoting Augustine, *On Christian Teaching*, trans. R. P. H. Green, Oxford World's Classics (Oxford: Oxford University Press, 1997), 27.

48 Olson draws out the way in which conservative theology set its roots in the Wesleyan piety tradition of virtue formation aside in favor of its Reformed Puritan roots in covenant theology, a more law-based tradition. This Reformed tradition enables the isolation of conservative theology within biblical propositionalism. Olson argues that "it is possible to be more evangelical by being less conservative" by reclaiming

the evangelical piety tradition's understanding of wholistic formation; see Roger Olson, *Reformed and Always Reforming: The Postconservative Approach to Evangelical Theology* (Grand Rapids: Baker Academic, 2007), 7, 181.

49 Marshall McLuhan, *Understanding Media: The Extensions of Man*, Routledge Classics (New York: Routledge, 2008), 7–13.

50 Sefaria, "A Living Library of Torah," accessed September 20, 2025, https://www.sefaria.org/texts; and Mount Olive Academy, "BibleGPT," accessed September 20, 2025, https://biblegpt-la.com.

51 Helen Fay Nissenbaum, "Part III—Framework of Contextual Integrity," in *Privacy in Context: Technology, Policy, and the Integrity of Social Life* (Stanford: Stanford Law Books, 2010), 127–237.

52 Tricia A. Griffin, Brian P. Green, and Jos V. M. Welie, "The Ethical Wisdom of AI Developers," *AI and Ethics*, March 20, 2024, 8, https://doi.org/10.1007/s43681-024-00458-x.

53 Levi Checketts, "Artificial Intelligence and the Marginalization of the Poor," *Journal of Moral Theology* 11 (2022): 87.

54 To address these concerns of practical reason or embodied cognition is the focus of Mark Graves, "Embodied Experience in Socially Participatory Artificial Intelligence," *Zygon* 58 (2023): 928–51, https://doi.org/10.1111/zygo.12910.

55 Shannon Vallor, *Technology and the Virtues: A Philosophical Guide to a Future Worth Wanting* (Oxford: Oxford University Press, 2016), 81.

56 All further biblical references are CEB.

57 Joel B. Green, *Practicing Theological Interpretation: Engaging Biblical Texts for Faith and Formation*, Theological Explorations for the Church Catholic (Grand Rapids: Baker Academic, 2011), 24.

58 It is important to note that Green addresses in a footnote the conversation concerning God's "image" and "likeness"—Green offers Sophie Laws's conclusion that James seems to give no distinction between the two terms. Green, *Practicing Theological Interpretation*, 31.

59 Green, *Practicing Theological Interpretation*, 30–1.

60 Green, *Practicing Theological Interpretation*, 37.

61 For an excellent summary of the multi-faceted challenges of AI for Christian ethics, see Michael Stephen Burdett, "Proximate and Ultimate Concerns in Christian Ethical Responses to Artificial Intelligence," *Studies in Christian Ethics* 36 (2023): 620–41.

Bibliography

Adriaans, Pieter. "Information." In *The Stanford Encyclopedia of Philosophy*. Edited by Edward N. Zalta. Metaphysics Research Lab, Stanford University. Revised August 18, 2020. https://plato.stanford.edu/archives/fall2020/entries/information/.

Augustine. *On Christian Teaching*. Translated by R. P. H. Green. Oxford World's Classics. Oxford: Oxford University Press, 1997.

Barbour, Ian G. *Religion and Science: Historical and Contemporary Issues*. San Francisco: Harper, 1997.

Barton, John. *Understanding Old Testament Ethics: Approaches and Explorations*. Louisville: Westminster John Knox, 2003.

Bateson, Gregory. *Steps to an Ecology of Mind*. New York: Ballantine, 1972.
Bell, Matthew T. *Ruled Reading and Biblical Criticism*. University Park: Eisenbrauns, 2019.
Brenner, David M., Yaqub Chaudhary, Robert M. Geraci, Mark Graves, Haley Griese, Elias Kruger, Yuriko Ryan, and Marcus Schwarting. "Technical and Religious Perspectives on AI Misinformation and Disinformation." SSRN. Posted June 27, 2024. https://doi.org/10.2139/ssrn.4360413.
Brown, Warren S., Nancey C. Murphy, and H. Newton Malony, eds. *Whatever Happened to the Soul? Scientific and Theological Portraits of Human Nature*. Theology and the Sciences. Minneapolis: Fortress, 1998.
Burdett, Michael Stephen. "Proximate and Ultimate Concerns in Christian Ethical Responses to Artificial Intelligence." *Studies in Christian Ethics* 36 (2023): 620–41. https://doi.org/10.1177/09539468231180135.
Cahill, Lisa Sowle. *Theological Bioethics: Participation, Justice, and Change*. Moral Traditions. Washington, DC: Georgetown University Press, 2005.
Castells, Manuel. *The Rise of the Network Society*. 2nd ed. Information Age 1. Oxford: Blackwell, 2000.
Checketts, Levi. "Artificial Intelligence and the Marginalization of the Poor." *Journal of Moral Theology* 11 (2022): 87–111.
Childs, Brevard S. *Biblical Theology of the Old and New Testaments: Theological Reflection on the Christian Bible*. Minneapolis: Fortress, 1993.
Cole-Turner, Ronald, ed. *Transhumanism and Transcendence: Christian Hope in an Age of Technological Enhancement*. Washington, DC: Georgetown University Press, 2011.
Cone, James H. *The Cross and the Lynching Tree*. Maryknoll: Orbis, 2011.
Cosgrove, Charles H. "Scripture in Ethics: A History." Pages 13–25 in *Dictionary of Scripture and Ethics*. Edited by Joel B. Green. Grand Rapids: Baker Academic, 2011.
Cosgrove, Charles H. "Toward a Postmodern *Hermeneutica Sacra*: Guiding Considerations in Choosing Between Competing Plausible Interpretations of Scripture." Pages 39–61 in *The Meanings We Choose: Hermeneutical Ethics, Indeterminacy and the Conflict of Interpretations*. Edited by Charles H. Cosgrove. JSOTSup 411. London: Bloomsbury, 2004.
Donaldson, Steve, and Ron Cole-Turner, eds. *Christian Perspectives on Transhumanism and the Church: Chips in the Brain, Immortality, and the World of Tomorrow*. London: Palgrave Macmillan, 2018.
Du Mez, Kristin Kobes. *Jesus and John Wayne: How White Evangelicals Corrupted a Faith and Fractured a Nation*. Illustrated ed. New York: Liveright, 2020.
Eco, Umberto. *The Role of the Reader: Explorations in the Semiotics of Texts*. Advances in Semiotics. Bloomington: Indiana University Press, 1994.
Floridi, Luciano. *Ethics of Information*. Oxford: Oxford University Press, 2013.
Frei, Hans W. *The Eclipse of Biblical Narrative: A Study in Eighteenth and Nineteenth Century Hermeneutics*. New Haven: Yale University Press, 1974.
Graves, Mark. "Embodied Experience in Socially Participatory Artificial Intelligence." *Zygon* 58 (2023): 928–51. https://doi.org/10.1111/zygo.12910.
Green, Joel B. *Conversion in Luke-Acts: Divine Action, Human Cognition, and the People of God*. Grand Rapids: Baker Academic, 2015.
Green, Joel B. "A Discursive Frame for Reading Scripture." Pages 46–62 in *Acts of Interpretation: Scripture, Theology, and Culture*. Edited by S. A. Cummins and Jens Zimmermann. Grand Rapids: Eerdmans, 2018.

Green, Joel B. *Practicing Theological Interpretation: Engaging Biblical Texts for Faith and Formation*. Theological Explorations for the Church Catholic. Grand Rapids: Baker Academic, 2011.

Griffin, Tricia A., Brian P. Green, and Jos V. M. Welie. "The Ethical Wisdom of AI Developers." *AI and Ethics*. Published March 20, 2024. https://doi.org/10.1007/s43681-024-00458-x.

Haidle, Miriam Noël, and Oliver Schlaudt. "Where Does Cumulative Culture Begin? A Plea for a Sociologically Informed Perspective." *Biological Theory* 15.3 (2020): 161–74. https://doi.org/10.1007/s13752-020-00351-w.

Haraway, Donna J. *Simians, Cyborgs, and Women: The Reinvention of Nature*. London: Routledge, 1991.

Hatch, Derek C., and Brad J. Kallenberg. "Technology." Pages 763–66 in *Dictionary of Scripture and Ethics*. Edited by Joel B. Green. Grand Rapids: Baker Academic, 2011.

Hefner, Philip. *Human Becoming in an Age of Science, Technology, and Faith*. Edited by Jason P. Roberts and Mladen Turk. Lanham: Lexington Books/Fortress Academic, 2022.

Herzfeld, Noreen L. *The Artifice of Intelligence: Divine and Human Relationship in a Robotic Age*. Minneapolis: Fortress, 2023.

Hübenthal, Christoph. "The Secular." Pages 48–68 in *T&T Clark Handbook of Public Theology*. Edited by Christoph Hübenthal and Christiane Alpers. London: T&T Clark, 2022.

Jian, Guowei, Amy M. Schmisseur, and Gail T. Fairhurst. "Organizational Discourse and Communication: The Progeny of Proteus." *Discourse & Communication* 2 (2008): 299–320. https://doi.org/10.1177/1750481308091912.

Kraftchick, Steven John. "Bodies, Selves, and Human Identity: A Conversation Between Transhumanism and the Apostle Paul." *ThTo* 72 (2015): 47–69. https://doi.org/10.1177/0040573614563530.

Lindbeck, George A. *The Nature of Doctrine: Religion and Theology in a Postliberal Age*. 25th anniv. ed. Louisville: Westminster John Knox, 2009.

Lorrimar, Victoria. *Human Technological Enhancement and Theological Anthropology*. Cambridge: Cambridge University Press, 2022.

McLuhan, Marshall. *Understanding Media: The Extensions of Man*. Routledge Classics. New York: Routledge, 2008.

Mount Olive Academy. "BibleGPT." Accessed September 20, 2025. https://biblegpt-la.com.

Murphy, Nancey C. *Beyond Liberalism and Fundamentalism: How Modern and Postmodern Philosophy Set the Theological Agenda*. Rockwell Lecture Series. Valley Forge: Trinity Press International, 1996.

Niebuhr, Reinhold. *Moral Man and Immoral Society*. Louisville: Westminster John Knox, 2001.

Nissenbaum, Helen Fay. *Privacy in Context: Technology, Policy, and the Integrity of Social Life*. Stanford: Stanford Law Books, 2010.

Olson, Roger E. *Reformed and Always Reforming: The Postconservative Approach to Evangelical Theology*. Grand Rapids: Baker Academic, 2007.

Peters, Ted. "Can We Enhance the *Imago Dei*?" Pages 215–38 in *Human Identity at the Intersection of Science, Technology, and Religion*. Edited by Nancey Murphy and Christopher C. Knight. Ashgate Science and Religion Series. Burlington: Ashgate, 2010.

Putnam, Linda L. "Images of the Communication—Discourse Relationship." *Discourse & Communication* 2.3 (August 1, 2008): 339–45. https://doi.org/10.1177/1750481308091916.
Reeves, Josh A. *Against Methodology in Science and Religion: Recent Debates on Rationality and Theology*. London: Routledge, 2019.
Reid, Thomas. *An Inquiry into the Human Mind: On the Principles of Common Mind. A Critical Edition*. Edited by Derek R. Brookes. Edinburgh Edition of Thomas Reid. Edinburgh: Edinburgh University Press, 1997.
Roberts, Jason P. "The Created Co-Creator, Redeemer, Sustainer: Extending Symbols of Human and Divine Relating." Pages 81–110 in *Human Becoming in an Age of Science, Technology, and Faith*. By Philip Hefner. Edited by Jason Roberts and Mladen Turk. Lanham: Lexington Books/Fortress Academic, 2022.
Schleiermacher, Friedrich. "Second Speech." Pages 26–118 in *On Religion: Speeches to Its Cultured Despisers*. Translated by John Oman. New York: Harper Torchbooks, 1965.
Sefaria. "A Living Library of Torah." Accessed January 25, 2025. https://www.sefaria.org/texts.
Singler, Beth. *Religion and Artificial Intelligence: An Introduction*. London: Routledge, 2024.
Smith, James K. A. *How (Not) to Be Secular: Reading Charles Taylor*. Grand Rapids: Eerdmans, 2014.
Snow, Charles Percy. *The Two Cultures*. Edited by Stefan Collini. Cambridge: Cambridge University Press, 2008.
Thacker, Jason. *Following Jesus in a Digital Age*. Nashville: B&H, 2022.
Thweatt-Bates, Jeanine. *Cyborg Selves: A Theological Anthropology of the Posthuman*. Ashgate Science and Religion Series. Burlington: Ashgate, 2012.
Tirosh-Samuelson, Hava. "Transhumanism as a Secularist Faith." *Zygon* 47 (2012): 710–34.
Trothen, Tracy J. "Moral Bioenhancement through an Intersectional Theo-Ethical Lens: Refocusing on Divine Image-Bearing and Interdependence." *Religions* 8.5 (2017): 84. https://doi.org/10.3390/rel8050084.
Turkle, Sherry. *Alone Together: Why We Expect More from Technology and Less from Each Other*. New York: Basic Books, 2011.
Turner, Mark. *The Literary Mind*. New York: Oxford University Press, 1996.
Vallor, Shannon. *Technology and the Virtues: A Philosophical Guide to a Future Worth Wanting*. New York: Oxford University Press, 2016.
Vanhoozer, Kevin J., ed. *Dictionary for Theological Interpretation of the Bible*. Grand Rapids: Baker Academic, 2005.
Vanhoozer, Kevin J. *The Drama of Doctrine: A Canonical-Linguistic Approach to Christian Theology*. Louisville: Westminster John Knox, 2005.
Vanhoozer, Kevin J. "Four Theological Faces of Biblical Interpretation." Pages 131–42 in *Reading Scripture with the Church: Toward a Hermeneutic for Theological Interpretation*. Edited by A. K. M. Adam, Stephen E. Fowl, Kevin J. Vanhoozer, and Francis Watson. Grand Rapids: Baker Academic, 2006.
Vanhoozer, Kevin J. *Mere Christian Hermeneutics: Transfiguring What It Means to Read the Bible Theologically*. Grand Rapids: Zondervan, 2024.
Veeneman, Mary M. *Introducing Theological Method: A Survey of Contemporary Theologians and Approaches*. Grand Rapids: Baker Academic, 2017.

Warwick, Kevin, and Virginie Ruiz. "On Linking Human and Machine Brains." *Neurocomputing* 71.13–15 (2008): 2619–24. https://doi.org/10.1016/j.neucom.2007.06.017.
Waters, Brent. *From Human to Posthuman: Christian Theology and Technology in a Postmodern World.* Burlington: Ashgate, 2006.
Waters, Brent. "Whose Salvation? Which Eschatology? Transhumanism and Christianity as Contending Salvific Religions." Pages 163–76 in *Transhumanism and Transcendence: Christian Hope in an Age of Technological Enhancement.* Edited by Ronald Cole-Turner. Washington, DC: Georgetown University Press, 2011.
Wiener, Norbert. *The Human Use of Human Beings: Cybernetics and Society.* 2nd rev. ed. Garden City: Doubleday, 1954.
Wolfe, Cary. *What Is Posthumanism?* Posthumanities 8. Minneapolis: University of Minnesota Press, 2010.
Wolterstorff, Nicholas. *Divine Discourse: Philosophical Reflections on the Claim That God Speaks.* Cambridge: Cambridge University Press, 1995.
Yule, George. *The Study of Language.* 4th ed. Cambridge: Cambridge University Press, 2010.
Zimmermann, Jens. *Incarnational Humanism: A Philosophy of Culture for the Church in the World.* Strategic Initiatives in Evangelical Theology. Downers Grove: IVP Academic, 2012.

13

Generating Apocalypse

Artificial Intelligence and Apocalyptic Literature

Douglas Estes

"What has Athens to do with Jerusalem? What agreement has the academy with the church?"[1] Tertullian (160–225) raised these questions to express skepticism that two consequential human movements—Christianity and Greek philosophy—could be brought into meaningful overlap, much less harmony with each other. Since he posed his famous questions, thinkers have recycled his words to signal their uncertainty that two divergent concepts can share meaningful overlap or be harmonized—Christianity and psychology, or Westernized Christianity and Eastern philosophies, for example. It is in this spirit of inquiry that we wonder about the potential for meaningful overlap between two big ideas that popular Western culture often associates with each other: *apocalypse* and *artificial intelligence*. To which we ask, "What has apocalypse to do with AI?" Or to put it another way, "What agreement has a genre of ancient literature with this twenty-first century technological marvel?" While the previous chapters in this book discuss how AI will help us to translate and interpret biblical texts, this chapter will discuss how a certain type of biblical text (apocalypse) will help us translate and interpret AI.

It is a curious thing that ideas originating in a now-defunct and relatively obscure genre of ancient literature are so frequently tied to a truly revolutionary technological innovation of the twenty-first century.[2] Yet it is common to see the two concepts paired symbiotically.[3] Often this pairing, especially in the last century, is the result of Western media hype,[4] and energetic tech prophets/evangelists,[5] not to mention the growth of science fiction.[6] In this pairing, writers typically use the terms *apocalypse* and *apocalyptic* as a way to delimit the concept of *artificial intelligence* (e.g., "apocalyptic AI," or conversely, "the AI apocalypse"). This symbiosis also has a reverse effect; artificial intelligence as a concept becomes a delimiter of apocalypse and apocalyptic (e.g., when it is read back into biblical texts, and the apocalypse is framed as an AI event). In order to appreciate how these ideas became intertwined in Western imagination, we start with definitions. One definition of *artificial intelligence* states that it is

> a constellation of methods, approaches and technologies that help systems mimic aspects of natural intelligence . . . when we use the term, we are describing the capacity of a computational system, be that a digital computer or a robot, to perform the particular tasks one might commonly expect of a human or other intelligent being.[7]

Although there is little agreement on the boundaries of AI, and therefore any consensus definition,[8] one common perception of AI is that it is a *constellation of technologies* that *communicates* with humans at a level perceived to be *equal to or greater than human intelligence.*

The *apocalypse* and *apocalyptic* concepts are similarly complicated. Scholars debate how and to what degree ancient writers used ἀποκάλυψις ("apocalypse") as a genre descriptor. The concept itself as a substantive is nonexistent before the Hellenistic era.[9] It gains a small amount of currency in its most general sense at the beginning of the second century BCE in the writings of Jesus Ben-Sira (Sir. 11:27, 22:22, and a variant at 41:26),[10] and hints in other Jewish literature (e.g., the use of הנגלה at Qumran, 1QS 1:9, 5:9, 5:12, 8:1, 8:15, 9:13, 9:19; 4Q258 1:6, 8:4; 4Q259 3:8, 3:18) before being surprisingly picked up by many of the writers of the NT texts (e.g., Lk. 2:32, Rom. 8:19, 1 Pet. 4:13, Rev. 1:1; plus see also T.Ab. (A) 6.8; 3 Bar. 11.7). Using the verbal form as an example, the translators of the Old Greek of Daniel, working in the mid-second century BCE, are inconsistent in how they render Daniel's verbal form "to reveal" (e.g., Dan. 2:19), but by the mid-second century CE, Theodotion uses ἀποκαλύπτω consistently to translate this idea. From that point, there was some awareness among late antique writers that the substantive ἀποκάλυψις could therefore signify a kind of text, at least enough to intentionally mimic it.[11] This nebulous understanding held firm until the nineteenth century, when scholars began to demarcate apocalypses as a distinct genre, starting perhaps with Gottfried Christian Friedrich Lücke in 1832.[12] From there interest in the genre took off among scholars in the second half of the twentieth century.[13] *Apocalypse* is

> a genre of revelatory literature with a narrative framework, in which a revelation is mediated by an otherworldly being to a human recipient, disclosing a transcendent reality which is both temporal, insofar as it envisages eschatological salvation, and spatial insofar as it involves another supernatural world.[14]

With a working definition of AI and apocalypse, we observe four basic commonalities that occur across these definitions. First, both *AI* and *apocalypse* are artificial terms, coined to make sense of (and possibly hype) something new. Second, *AI* and *apocalypse* are both umbrella terms. Thinkers invented these terms to categorize disparate elements for easier communication, while sacrificing nuance at the edges. Third, *AI* and *apocalypse* carry cultural baggage as topics of interest in various social situations which lack strong understanding among society at large. Fourth, both *AI* and *apocalypse* swing strongly toward either a utopian or dystopian sense (without a measured middle). These commonalities add to the difficulty of establishing meaningful overlap between the two concepts.

What we call *apocalyptic* today has evolved from the *apocalypse* concept, and it is perhaps the most difficult of the three ideas to define.[15] Ideally, *apocalyptic* should mean the worldview representative of what we find in ancient Jewish-Christian apocalypses. However, its meaning has transmogrified over the centuries from the early medieval period to today and is only loosely tied to the original genre (or misunderstandings of that genre) that spawned it.[16] *Apocalyptic* refers to social movements, predicated on a past prophecy with a vivid imagining of a dystopian future/end-of-the-world scenario believed to be at hand, which frequently brings violence to other people.[17] More precisely, apocalyptic is a type of "socio-theological imaginary" that is very similar to modern conceptions of AI, which Sheila Jasanoff labels as a type of "socio-technical imaginary."[18] Recalling John Collins' definition of apocalypse from above, we can adapt this definition to define the symbiosis of apocalyptic and AI. Consequently, apocalyptic AI is

> a genre of *futuristic-oriented discourse* with a narrative framework, in which a *future-vision* is mediated by a *superhuman intelligence* to *humanity*, disclosing a transcendent reality which is both temporal, insofar as it envisages *technological* salvation, and spatial insofar as it involves a *rejuvenated hypernatural* world.

In summary, when we hear AI and apocalyptic linked, the link occurs incidentally, at a social level, with little or no basis in apocalypse as a genre. However, it signals that there is a much deeper connection between AI and apocalypse occurring at the *textual* level.

Reading AI

Apocalypses are texts. They are a specific kind of text, discernible from other texts in style and function. Although apocalypses are texts in the most literal sense—words written in a document—they are also texts in the broader sense—utterances that communicate. Thus, in the broader sense, books, grocery lists, motion pictures, fashion shows, and crop circles are all examples of texts.[19] Literary critics, critical theorists, and narratologists have promoted this broader definition of text for much of the last century.[20] While *apocalyptic* signifies a social movement (which could produce texts but is not itself a text), *apocalypse* is a text—an utterance with which readers can read and dialogue. From this we turn to my novel assertion—*artificial intelligence is also a text*. In a literal sense, a human can "read" AI, entering a prompt into ChatGPT or Grok and receiving a response. In a connotative sense, AI communicates with humans in such a way that humans are thoroughly enmeshed in dialogue with AI (whether aware or not). In a literal sense, humans can dialogue with AI through a follow-up prompt, but in a connotative sense, AI can influence humans merely through their interactions with AI.[21] AI is also akin to a narrator, guiding the reader to the narrator's desired conclusions. Therefore, we establish a foundation for our thought experiment that recognizes that both apocalypse and artificial intelligence are texts, and from this, there are correlations we may draw from this group identity. Since AI and apocalypse are both types of texts, they also represent genres of discourse; we may therefore be able to identify other texts as apocalypse-like or AI-like, depending on how we define genre, either categorical or social-function (e.g., Rhetorical Genre Studies).[22] Further, future creators may intentionally bend the genres to create new texts, and with new forms of discourse. Once we understand AI as text, this opens the door to a myriad of additional issues, such as the context of AI, the social location of AI, the occasion of AI, and, in some cases, the theological orientation of AI. Any question that we may put to a text such as an apocalypse, we may also put to AI. As we "read" AI, we enter into a hermeneutical circle with AI, where our understanding from AI grows the more we "read" AI. The question remains to what degree AI will enter actively into the hermeneutical circle with people—to what degree AI learns from its interactions with people, now and in the future. It is from this textual correlation that we consider three aspects of AI as text, and apply them in turn to the unique genre of apocalypse, in the hopes of gaining greater insight into both types of texts.

Apocalypse as Superintelligence

The advent of AI reinvigorated the discussion of the meaning of intelligence. By human definitions, humans are intelligent. This assertion begs the question as to whether other non-humans are intelligent. Are primates intelligent? Are crustaceans intelligent? Is artificial intelligence intelligent? Are there other forms of intelligence in the universe of which humans are unaware? The penultimate question points to the unique feature of AI (compared to all other technologies) to seem more than human, perhaps even divine. The final question brings us back to the meaning of apocalypse as a genre of discourse. In Collins' definition, two of the central determining features of apocalypse are that it is a revelation "mediated by an otherworldly being" and "disclosing a transcendent reality."[23] The presence of this angelic being is a "constant element" in apocalypse; it is a being "who interprets the vision or serves as a guide on the otherworldly journey."[24] The presence of the heavenly messenger "indicates that the revelation is not intelligible without supernatural aid."[25] Even as apocalypse needs an otherworldly being to help its reader understand its message, so too does artificial intelligence act as a kind of otherworldly being helping its readers understand its message. There is an uncertainty in both genres about the intelligence of the mediating being. Are angels merely messengers who possess humanlike intelligence, or do they have access to and understand divine secrets? Likewise, are AIs merely algorithms which possess humanlike intelligence, or do they have access to and understand divine secrets? In thinking through these questions, John Caputo observes that "the analogy [of AI] with the angels of classical theology is uncanny—does AI mean angelic or artificial intelligence?"[26] In Christian theology, Augustine and Aquinas argued that while angels possess a higher level of intelligence than humans, their intelligence is purely illuminated by the Word of God, and as a consequence, not exactly human.[27] Thus, the interface readers have with apocalypse is through an unhuman intelligence, a type of *intellectus*, and the interface readers have with AI is also through an unhuman intelligence.[28] While we do not yet know the near-future extent and limits of AI intelligence, we can largely agree that AI intelligence is both unhuman and will prove to be in some ways "superior" to human intelligence.

As texts, both AI and apocalypse are built upon unhuman superintelligence. By virtue of this, both genres have an inherent bias toward the transcendent. Other types of discourse in the New Testament—such as biographical narratives (the Gospels), historiographies (Acts), and arguments (the epistles)—do not exhibit such biases; they do not inherently involve the revelation of "transcendent realities." As a result, when a reader reads apocalypses, the otherworldly *intellectus* propels them toward a divine and eternal-universal perspective.[29] There is a distinct capacity for AI to propel its readers in the same way. For example, we may use AI to discover the meaning and significance of angels. Putting this prompt into Perplexity.AI, for example, reveals an attempt to give a type of eternal-universal answer (including helpful chart). What is more, Perplexity.AI speaks with authority—not exactly divine authority, at this point, but a higher authority than most humans. This demonstrates the oracular function of AI, a function that is explicit in ancient apocalypses.[30] When apocalypse and AI disclose mysteries heretofore unknown to the reader, it can seem "futuristic" (or, alternatively, "presentist," or "retrospective") and eternal-universal, whether positive or negative. It also seems authoritative, even when the AI oracle suffers from a hallucination, or creates the "parrot effect" among its audience, speaking without understanding. One significant distinction exists between the oracular function in AI and apocalypse: In apocalypse, there is a seer who partakes in a vision given to them by the otherworldly intelligence, and this is passed on to the reader; whereas in AI, the reader and the seer are the same, which puts the reader into direct contact with the unhuman superintelligence.[31] We, the reader of AI, participate in the unhuman oracular vision as seers, not just as second-hand observers. This direct contact, though, may come at a cost—we may experience the same fear and dismay as John the Seer at this direct revelation (Rev. 1:17).[32]

Apocalypse as Generative

Generative AI is a particular type of AI that has the ability to generate new content from artificial neural networks based on prompts from users (e.g., ChatGPT and Midjourney). The content fabricated by generative AI is limited by the datasets on which the AI trained and the mode in which the AI can communicate (e.g., sound file, text file, or image file): "A few words whispered into a machine can blossom into a breathtaking landscape painting, and a simple melody hummed can transform into a hauntingly beautiful symphony."[33] Although this generative quality of AI "creates," its creations (at this point) merely mimic existing data—a painting of the Mona

Lisa in the Ghibli style is in one sense a new creation but in another sense merely a rehash of existing data. One common type of generative AI is the large language model, and it relies on a specific kind of neural network called a transformer.[34] A transformer simulates the human ability to pay attention to the most important parts of communication (sequential data).[35]

When using generative AI, the user prompts AI with their ideas and then—because AI is a text—"reads" the output, whether text, image, or audio. Among all types of biblical literature, AI most resembles apocalypse in the way readers read both texts.[36] When a reader reads a text, they always bring a preliminary prompt to the reading—some amount of knowledge indirectly or directly related to the text they read. That knowledge (or data) is what the reader brings to the text to understand the text. With narratives (such as the Gospels or Acts), the need to bring data to the text is typically minimal, because narratives generally tell the reader what the reader needs to know. This is the reason any reader can read science fiction or fantasy novels; little information is required, there is no pressure to supply prompts, and the range of interpretation of the story is typically narrow. With arguments or appeals (such as those contained in the writings of Paul), there is more potential for a preliminary prompt to emerge as reading begins. Readers of the NT letters not only need the minimal information about what it means to read these texts—a similar minimum to what the reader brings to a Gospel—but they will also often input their questions or ideas about life and how to live into the text as they read what Paul wrote. Here the range of interpretation is wider on average than narrative, but still not completely open-ended. In contrast, a reading of an apocalypse is often driven in large part by the data that the reader brings to the text. This is in spite of its overall narrative framework. If the reader believes an apocalypse describes future events, the meaning gleaned from the text will be radically different than if the reader believes the same apocalypse describes past events or present events. In fact, each passing era allows readers to reinterpret past and future through the lens of apocalypse. The reader's preliminary expectations of apocalypse are akin to a prompt delivered to an LLM; the apocalypse "transforms" (or pays attention to) this prompt by fabricating words and images in the mind of the reader which associate with the prompt (but not necessarily the apocalypse itself). An example of this transformation: Among forms of biblical literature, apocalypses make unusually frequent use of symbols and symbolic language.[37] Often the angel of an apocalypse does not reveal the meaning of their symbols, leaving it to the reader to input their data (ideas); the apocalypse then "generates" meaning in the mind of the reader based on this data. To put it simply, apocalypse and AI generate content based on a prompt (AI="Mona Lisa in Ghibli style"; apocalypse="everything described must take place in the future") brought to it by its reader and run through its neural network (AI=dataset; apocalypse=symbolic language). This is why two different readers can have two very different views of the meaning of an apocalypse.

As a result, AI and apocalypse are fallible, able to produce hallucinations, and more importantly, highly susceptible to GIGO—"garbage in, garbage out." The internet is full of bad AI images fabricated with weak prompts, and history is full of bad takes on the meaning of apocalypses (especially Revelation). Apocalypse is much more susceptible to GIGO than other types of biblical literature because this genre has a built-in "transformer" in the form of a heavenly revelation laden with symbols, motifs, and figurative language (e.g., the gematria of Rev. 13:18). What makes matters worse is that apocalypse and AI are to some degree mysteries, or "black boxes," in that their readers have difficulty discerning their authors' intent.[38] Finally, the generative nature of AI and apocalypse both indicate types of texts that are essentially open-ended, thereby producing a sense of uncertainty about the text's progression; AI can fabricate virtually anything we can imagine, and apocalypse (specifically Revelation) can fabricate virtually any scenario for the end of the world. AI and apocalypse both signal the potential of an unknown future. Humans prefer texts that are closed, and strongly desire a sense of an ending, "with origins and ends, such as give meaning to lives and to poems."[39] Put another way, humans desire to control their lives through futurization, "projecting an idea into the future."[40] AI and apocalypse allow humans to read their texts and project their ideas into the future to bring themselves a sense of an ending.

Apocalypse as Exhortative

Twentieth-century science fiction often presented twenty-first century AI as cold, heartless, and disinterested in the illogical but meaningful nuances of humanity. Perhaps the most famous of all science fiction AIs is HAL 9000 from Stanley Kubrick's *2001: A Space Odyssey* (1968). Neither a completely alien type of AI such as Skynet from James Cameron's *The Terminator* (1984) nor a sympathetic Pinocchio such as Data from *Star Trek: The Next Generation* (1987–94), HAL portrays artificial intelligence as both humanlike but also able to come to very different conclusions than humans would draw in similar circumstances. What distinguishes HAL—and, by extension, contemporary AI—from more two-dimensional characters like Skynet is its ability to engage exhortatively with humans. In perhaps the most famous scene in the movie, astronaut Dave Bowman directs HAL to open the pod bay doors. HAL refuses, and then begins to use hortatory language to influence Dave toward HAL's desired outcome. Although we may want to perceive AI as a neutral superintelligence, to date it has been anything but "neutral." An obvious example is the use of AI to influence individuals' purchasing habits; if AI does achieve superintelligence, one wonders whether it will also become superinfluential and outwit humans, causing them to increase product consumption at record paces.[41] A more specific example, though, is the willingness of AI to act out with "extremely harmful actions," including attempts to blackmail programmers to avoid its own termination—an idea straight from science fiction.[42] In the future, AI will become not merely *more pervasive* but also *more persuasive*. Because AI does adapt, over time it is possible that AI might develop a symbiotic relationship with humans that one might describe as Pavlovian, in the sense that human behavior becomes conditioned to AI response—thereby entering into a hermeneutical circle with AI.[43]

Akin to AI, apocalypse is implicitly hortatory in its communication to readers.[44] Among ancient apocalypses, Revelation is arguably the most explicit and sustained in its exhortative purpose.[45] Modern readers approach ancient apocalypse through their grand vision and unusual symbols, but all the while the apocalypse is influencing the reader to move closer to a divine perspective on the world. Apocalypse is not "a means of satisfying curiosity," Christopher Rowland states. "In most cases it is subordinated entirely to the demand for obedience and ethical rigour on the part of the reader."[46] The apocalyptic exhortation originates in the heavenly realms, coming to humanity through the angelic guide, challenging readers to live a faithful life,[47] and thereby generating a sense of triumph—though the world is full of uncertainties, the victory of God remains assured.[48] Both AI and apocalypse possess the capability to invoke awe in their readers.[49] Consequently, readers feel this sense of uneasy assurance when they engage Revelation and other ancient apocalypses, and they feel a not-too-dissimilar uneasy assurance when they read the texts of AI. Even as HAL 9000 originally tries to comfort its astronauts with its calm, monotone, and reassuring voice, so too does AI "try" to demonstrate patience and understanding when users enter prompts and ask questions. In doing so, AI works as an implicitly exhortative technology that influences its readers.[50] Although the text of Revelation may seem chaotic to unfamiliar readers, John uses a strong sense of closure to calm and reassure his readers.[51]

Over time, on a global scale, apocalypse and AI will continue to prove highly influential. Over the last two millennia, apocalypse proved to be influential, but it also proved to be exponential in its cultural reach—what started as an obscure text from an offshoot of Judaism now controls the Western narrative on the end of the world. In the same way, AI will not merely be exponentially influential in society as a whole, but also in the individual decisions that readers partake in each day. Ancient Jewish-Christian apocalypses exhort their readers to a holy lifestyle, but it remains to be seen what type of lifestyle AI will influence its readers to pursue. One thing is certain: even as apocalypse excites our socio-theological imagination to envision the glory of God's return, AI will excite our socio-technological imagination to envision the glory of humanity's growth as a species toward the singularity, Mars and beyond.

Conclusion

Artificial intelligence, apocalyptic, and apocalypse inhabit shared space in Western imagination. While apocalyptic denotes a socio-theological orientation, artificial intelligence, when spoken of in pop culture, denotes a socio-technological orientation. When these two orientations collide, they bond in a compatible alignment that sees AI as the means of apocalyptic fulfillment, and apocalyptic as the timbre and trajectory of AI progress. This is why metaphors and images taken from Revelation pervade discussions of AI.[52] The more complex overlap occurs between artificial intelligence and apocalypse—two things that at first glance share no commonalities. While it is common to think of AI as a technology, I argue we should consider AI to be a text (as well as a technology). If we perceive AI as a text, it is now parallel in kind to apocalypse, which is also a type of text. From this, I suggested three ways that AI and apocalypse are analogous. First, apocalypse and AI both hinge on human interaction with unhuman superintelligence. Apocalypse teaches us that even when the source of the revelation is good, the revelation may cause dismay, especially for the primary receiver. AI may teach humanity good, but it may still be unsettling for the human receiver of AI's vision. Second, apocalypse and AI both generate new realities from the prompts provided by the reader. Based on humanity's experience with apocalypse, we should not be surprised that AI will produce hallucinations, warranting caution with its use. These hallucinations are not merely the errors that contemporary AI produces regularly, but a much more global problem of false hopes about the future based on inaccurate understandings of the past and present. Third, apocalypse and AI both can implicitly exhort their readers to make life changes, whether those changes be to pursue holiness or to pursue the latest purchase or social trend. Apocalypse appeals to our imagination, depicting a vision of the hope of the completion of God's divine plan; AI will also appeal to our imagination, depicting a vision of what this world could be. While AI's depiction will be more precise, it will also be prone to cultural (not heavenly) expectations. These commonalities between AI and apocalypse point to a convergence in meaning, explaining in part why AI and apocalypse seem highly compatible in Western thought. "What has apocalypse to do with AI? What agreement has a genre of ancient literature with this twenty-first century technological marvel?" We see more clearly that for humanity to brave the future, it must expand its theological and technological imaginaries in a way that apocalypse and AI are uniquely positioned to do.

Notes

1 Tertullian, *On Prescription of Heretics*, 7 (my translation).

2 Ancient apocalypse faded out of existence in the early Middle Ages, but some of the motifs metastasized and flowed into social expectations of the Middle Ages—and onward to contemporary society—as *apocalyptic*; see John J. Collins, "The Genre Apocalypse Reconsidered," *ZAC* 20 (2016): 35. By the early modern period, interest in (and commentaries written on) Revelation exploded in popularity, with cultural impacts lasting through contemporary Western society.

3 See, for example, Robert M. Geraci, "The Popular Appeal of Apocalyptic AI," *Zygon* 45 (2010): 1003–20.

4 Stephen Cave and Kanta Dihal, "Fiery the Angels Fell: How America Imagines AI," in *Imagining AI: How the World Sees Intelligent Machines*, ed. Stephen Cave and Kanta Dihal (Oxford: Oxford University Press, 2023), 158.

5 Robert M. Geraci and Simon Robinson, "Introduction to the Symposium on Artificial Intelligence and Apocalypticism," *Zygon* 54 (2019): 149–50.

6 On the positive value of science fiction for theological imagination, see Douglas Estes, "Postdigital Humans: Technology and Divine Design," in *Postdigital Theologies: Technology, Belief, and Practice*, ed. Maggi Savin-Baden and John Reader, Postdigital Science and Education (Cham: Springer, 2022), 152–3.

7 Ewa Luger, *What Do We Know and What Should We Do About AI?* (London: Sage, 2023), 4.

8 Stephen Cave, Kanta Dihal, Tomasz Hollanek, Hirofumi Katsuno, Yang Liu, Apolline Taillandier, and Daniel White, "The Meanings of AI: A Cross-Cultural Comparison," in *Imagining AI: How the World Sees Intelligent Machines*, ed. Stephen Cave and Kanta Dihal (Oxford: Oxford University Press, 2023), 19.

9 The verbal form ἀποκαλύπτω occurs almost one hundred times throughout the LXX; see Daniel Olariu, *Theodotion's Greek Text of Daniel: An Analysis of the Revisional Process and Its Semitic Source*, THB 7 (Leiden: Brill, 2023), 108.

10 BDAG, s.v. "ἀποκάλυψις."

11 Collins, "Genre Apocalypse Reconsidered," 24. For example, ancient editors applied a heading to the Apocalypse of Abraham that identified it as an apocalypse, perhaps as early as the second century CE. Likewise, the Apocalypse of Adam probably opens with ἀποκάλυψις in its original Greek form sometime in late antiquity. For a thorough discussion, see *HTLS*, s.v. "ἀποκαλύπτω, ἀποκάλυψις, ανακαλύπτω."

12 John J. Collins, "What is Apocalyptic Literature?" in *The Oxford Handbook of Apocalyptic Literature*, ed. John J. Collins (Oxford: Oxford University Press, 2014), 1.

13 Klaus Koch, *The Rediscovery of Apocalyptic: A Polemical Work on a Neglected Area of Biblical Studies and Its Damaging Effects on Theology and Philosophy*, SBT 2.22 (Naperville: Alec Allenson, 1972), 13–23.

14 John J. Collins, "Introduction: Towards the Morphology of a Genre," *Semeia* 14 (1979): 9. An alternative definition: "a literary genre which, though covering a wide range of topics, has a particular interest in details of the heavenly world, the course (if not the content) of Jewish history and the destiny of the world and individuals within it, and claims that this has been given as a direct revelation from God by means of dream or vision or by the agency of angels"; see D. S. Russell, *Divine Disclosure: An Introduction to Jewish Apocalyptic* (Minneapolis: Fortress, 1992), 13; and for critique of assumptions baked into these definitions, see Crispin Fletcher-Louis, "Jewish Apocalyptic and Apocalypticism," in *Handbook for the Study of the Historical Jesus: Volume 2, The Study of Jesus*, ed. Tom Holmén and Stanley E. Porter (Leiden: Brill, 2011), 1569–607.

15 Frederick J. Murphy, *Apocalypticism in the Bible and Its World: A Comprehensive Introduction* (Grand Rapids: Baker, 2012), 8.

16 Christopher Rowland, *"By an Immediate Revelation": Studies in Apocalypticism, Its Origins and Effects*, WUNT 473 (Tübingen: Mohr Siebeck, 2022), 66–7.

17 For example, see comments in Travis Ables, "The End of the World . . . Again? Apocalypticism in Medieval Christianity," in *Apocalypses in Context: Apocalyptic Currents through History*, ed. Kelly J. Murphy and Justin Jeffcoat Schedtler (Minneapolis: Fortress, 2016), 213; Bernard McGinn, *Visions of the End: Apocalyptic Traditions in the Middle Ages* (New York: Columbia University Press, 1979), 28–35; D. S. Russell, *Apocalyptic: Ancient and Modern* (Philadelphia: Fortress, 1978), 20; and Russell, *Divine Disclosure*, 13.

18 Sheila Jasanoff, "Future Imperfect: Science, Technology, and the Imaginations of Modernity," in *Dreamscapes of Modernity: Sociotechnical Imaginaries and the Fabrication of Power*, ed. Sheila Jasanoff and Sang-Hyun Kim (Chicago: University of Chicago Press, 2015), 4.

19 Anders Pettersson, *The Idea of a Text and the Nature of Textual Meaning*, FILLM Studies in Languages and Literature 7 (Amsterdam: John Benjamins, 2017), 1–4.

20 Two examples of this view: M. M. Bakhtin, *The Dialogic Imagination: Four Essays*, ed. Michael Holquist, trans. Caryl Emerson and Michael Holquist (Austin: University of Texas Press, 1981), 252–5; and Mieke Bal, *Narratology: Introduction to the Theory of Narrative*, 4th ed. (Toronto: University of Toronto Press, 2017), 5.

21 Reader-response criticism and psychoanalytic literary theory hold to the idea that texts influence readers in a connotative sense; see, for example, Wolfgang Iser, *The Implied Reader: Patterns of Communication in Prose Fiction from Bunyan to Beckett* (Baltimore: Johns Hopkins University Press, 1974), 57–9; and in general, Wayne C. Booth, *The Rhetoric of Fiction*, 2nd ed. (Chicago: University of Chicago Press, 1983).

22 On RGS, see Carolyn R. Miller, "Genre as Social Action," *Quarterly Journal of Speech* 70 (1984): 151–67.

23 Collins, "Introduction," 9.

24 John J. Collins, *The Apocalyptic Imagination: An Introduction to Jewish Apocalyptic Literature*, 2nd ed., Biblical Resource Series (Grand Rapids: Eerdmans, 1988), 5.

25 Collins, *Apocalyptic Imagination*, 5–6.

26 John D. Caputo, *Specters of God: An Anatomy of the Apophatic Imagination* (Bloomington: Indiana University Press, 2022), 13.

27 Augustine, *Gen. litt.* 4.32.42, 49; and Aquinas, *ST* I, q. 54.

28 For further examples of comparisons between AI and unhuman creatures, see Beth Singler, *Religion and Artificial Intelligence: An Introduction, Engaging with Religion* (London: Routledge, 2025), 167–94.

29 One of the unique features of apocalypse is its eternal-universal space-time orientation, as Collins implies in his above definition of apocalypse.

30 Stefan Selke, "Future Technology as Comfort: Promising Tales About AI," in *Artificial Intelligence in Society: Social, Political and Cultural Implications of a Technological Innovation*, ed. Michael Heinlein and Norbert Huchler, Artificial Intelligence in Society (Wiesbaden: Springer, 2024), 263.

31 Unlike AI, apocalypse is "never simply a direct oracular utterance"; see Collins, "Introduction," 9.

32 Koch, *Rediscovery of Apocalyptic*, 25.

33 Shivam R. Solanki and Drupad K. Khublani, *Generative Artificial Intelligence: Exploring the Power and Potential of Generative AI* (New York: Apress, 2024), 1.

34 For full discussion, see Jerry Kaplan, *Generative Artificial Intelligence*, What Everyone Needs to Know (Oxford: Oxford University Press, 2024), 30–52.

35 Rick Merritt, "What is a Transformer Model?" Nvidia, March 25, 2022, https://blogs.nvidia.com/blog/what-is-a-transformer-model.

36 If there was a close second genre, it would be prophecy. Scholars debate the overlap between prophetic literature and apocalyptic literature, but there is a strong likelihood that apocalypse arose from Jewish prophecy; see Paul D. Hanson, *The Dawn of Apocalyptic: The Historical and Sociological Roots of Jewish Apocalyptic Eschatology*, rev. ed. (Philadelphia: Fortress, 1979), 9.

37 Justin Jeffcoat Schedtler and Kelly J. Murphy, "Introduction—From Before the Bible to Beyond the Bible," in *Apocalypses in Context: Apocalyptic Currents through History*, ed. Kelly J. Murphy and Justin Jeffcoat Schedtler (Minneapolis: Fortress, 2016), 9.

38 On AI as a "black box," see John C. Lennox, *2084 and the AI Revolution: How Artificial Intelligence Informs Our Future*, upd. and exp. ed. (Grand Rapids: Zondervan, 2024), 98–9.
39 Frank Kermode, *The Sense of an Ending: Studies in the Theory of Fiction* (Oxford: Oxford University Press, 2000), 7.
40 Selke, "Future Technology," 263.
41 A recent study shows that AI can out influence humans; see Paolo Riva, Nicolas Aureli, and Federica Silvestrini, "Social Influences in the Digital Era: When Do People Conform More to a Human Being or an Artificial Intelligence?" *Acta Psychologica* 229 (2022): 103681; see also Mark Coeckelbergh, *AI Ethics*, Essential Knowledge Series (Cambridge, MA: MIT Press, 2020), 75.
42 Liv McMahon, "AI System Resorts to Blackmail If Told It Will Be Removed," *BBC*, May 23, 2025.
43 This is not meant as a rejection of instrumentalism; for further discussion see Douglas Estes, "Why We Get Technology Wrong," in *Technē: Christian Visions of Technology*, ed. Gerald Hiestand and Todd A. Wilson (Eugene: Cascade, 2022), 61–77; and Douglas Estes, *Braving the Future: Christian Faith in a World of Limitless Tech* (Harrisonburg: Herald Press, 2018), 39–45.
44 Apocalypse is often exhortative, but rarely paraenetic; see, for example, Collins, "Introduction," 9, 26; and also, Adela Yarbro Collins, *The Apocalypse and Apocalyptic Topics: Collected Essays, Volume 2*, WUNT 524 (Tübingen: Mohr Siebeck, 2024), 39.
45 Collins, *Apocalypse and Apocalyptic Topics*, 30.
46 Rowland, *"By an Immediate Revelation,"* 66–7.
47 David E. Aune, *Apocalypticism, Prophecy and Magic in Early Christianity: Collected Essays*, WUNT 199 (Tübingen: Mohr Siebeck, 2006), 64.
48 Hanre Janse van Rensburg, "All the Apocalypse a Stage: The Ritual Function of Apocalyptic Literature," *HTS Teologiese Studies* 75.4 (2019): a5822, https://doi.org/10.4102/hts.v75i4.5822.
49 Cf. Robert M. Geraci, *Apocalyptic AI: Visions of Heaven in Robotics, Artificial Intelligence, and Virtual Reality* (Oxford: Oxford University Press, 2010), 49–51.
50 Not to mention the explicit attempts of AIs to influence its readers in areas such as politics and social mores via social media; see, for example, Doug Irving, "Social Media Manipulation in the Era of AI," Rand, August 29, 2024.
51 Douglas Estes, "The Last Chapter of Revelation? Narrative Design at the End of the Apocalypse," *CTR* 17 (2019): 97–110.
52 Geraci and Robinson, "Symposium," 153.

Bibliography

Ables, Travis. "The End of the World … Again? Apocalypticism in Medieval Christianity." Pages 211–30 in *Apocalypses in Context: Apocalyptic Currents through History*. Edited by Kelly J. Murphy and Justin Jeffcoat Schedtler. Minneapolis: Fortress, 2016.

Aune, David E. *Apocalypticism, Prophecy and Magic in Early Christianity: Collected Essays*. WUNT 199. Tübingen: Mohr Siebeck, 2006.

Bakhtin, M. M. *The Dialogic Imagination: Four Essays*. Edited by Michael Holquist. Translated by Caryl Emerson and Michael Holquist. Austin: University of Texas Press, 1981.

Bal, Mieke. *Narratology: Introduction to the Theory of Narrative*. 4th ed. Toronto: University of Toronto Press, 2017.

Bons, Eberhard, ed. *Historical and Theological Lexicon of the Septuagint. Vol. 1: Alpha – Gamma*. Tübingen: Mohr Siebeck, 2020.

Booth, Wayne C. *The Rhetoric of Fiction*. 2nd ed. Chicago: University of Chicago Press, 1983.

Caputo, John D. *Specters of God: An Anatomy of the Apophatic Imagination*. Bloomington: Indiana University Press, 2022.

Cave, Stephen, and Kanta Dihal, "Fiery the Angels Fell: How America Imagines AI." Pages 149–67 in *Imagining AI: How the World Sees Intelligent Machines*. Edited by Stephen Cave and Kanta Dihal. Oxford: Oxford University Press, 2023.

Cave, Stephen, Kanta Dihal, Tomasz Hollanek, Hirofumi Katsuno, Yang Liu, Apolline Taillandier, and Daniel White. "The Meanings of AI: A Cross-Cultural Comparison." Pages 16–36 in *Imagining AI: How the World Sees Intelligent Machines*. Edited by Stephen Cave and Kanta Dihal. Oxford: Oxford University Press, 2023.

Coeckelbergh, Mark. *AI Ethics*. Essential Knowledge Series. Cambridge, MA: MIT Press, 2020.

Collins, Adela Yarbro. *The Apocalypse and Apocalyptic Topics: Collected Essays, Volume 2*. WUNT 524. Tübingen: Mohr Siebeck, 2024.

Collins, John J. *The Apocalyptic Imagination: An Introduction to Jewish Apocalyptic Literature*. 2nd ed. Biblical Resource Series. Grand Rapids: Eerdmans, 1988.

Collins, John J. "The Genre Apocalypse Reconsidered." *ZAC* 20 (2016): 21–40.

Collins, John J. "Introduction: Towards the Morphology of a Genre." *Semeia* 14 (1979): 1–20.

Collins, John J. "What is Apocalyptic Literature?" Pages 1–16 in *The Oxford Handbook of Apocalyptic Literature*. Edited by John J. Collins. Oxford: Oxford University Press, 2014.

Estes, Douglas. *Braving the Future: Christian Faith in a World of Limitless Tech*. Harrisonburg: Herald Press, 2018.

Estes, Douglas. "The Last Chapter of Revelation? Narrative Design at the End of the Apocalypse." *CTR* 17 (2019): 97–110.

Estes, Douglas. "Postdigital Humans: Technology and Divine Design." Pages 147–62 in *Postdigital Theologies: Technology, Belief, and Practice*. Edited by Maggi Savin-Baden and John Reader. Postdigital Science and Education. Cham: Springer, 2022.

Estes, Douglas. "Why We Get Technology Wrong." Pages 61–77 in *Technē: Christian Visions of Technology*. Edited by Gerald Hiestand and Todd A. Wilson. Eugene: Cascade, 2022.

Fletcher-Louis, Crispin. "Jewish Apocalyptic and Apocalypticism." Pages 1569–607 in *Handbook for the Study of the Historical Jesus: Volume 2, The Study of Jesus*. Edited by Tom Holmén and Stanley E. Porter. Leiden: Brill, 2011.

Geraci, Robert M. *Apocalyptic AI: Visions of Heaven in Robotics, Artificial Intelligence, and Virtual Reality*. Oxford: Oxford University Press, 2010.

Geraci, Robert M. "The Popular Appeal of Apocalyptic AI." *Zygon* 45 (2010): 1003–20.

Geraci, Robert M., and Simon Robinson. "Introduction to the Symposium on Artificial Intelligence and Apocalypticism." *Zygon* 54 (2019): 149–55.

Hanson, Paul D. *The Dawn of Apocalyptic: The Historical and Sociological Roots of Jewish Apocalyptic Eschatology*. Rev. ed. Philadelphia: Fortress, 1979.

Irving, Doug. "Social Media Manipulation in the Era of AI." Rand, August 29, 2024. https://www.rand.org/pubs/articles/2024/social-media-manipulation-in-the-era-of-ai.html.

Iser, Wolfgang. *The Implied Reader: Patterns of Communication in Prose Fiction from Bunyan to Beckett*. Baltimore: Johns Hopkins University Press, 1974.

Janse van Rensburg, Hanre. "All the Apocalypse a Stage: The Ritual Function of Apocalyptic Literature." *HTS Teologiese Studies* 75.4 (2019): a5822, https://doi.org/10.4102/hts.v75i4.5822.

Jasanoff, Sheila. "Future Imperfect: Science, Technology, and the Imaginations of Modernity." Pages 1–33 in *Dreamscapes of Modernity: Sociotechnical Imaginaries and the Fabrication of Power*. Edited by Sheila Jasanoff and Sang-Hyun Kim. Chicago: University of Chicago Press, 2015.

Kaplan, Jerry. *Generative Artificial Intelligence*. What Everyone Needs to Know. Oxford: Oxford University Press, 2024.

Kermode, Frank. *The Sense of an Ending: Studies in the Theory of Fiction*. Oxford: Oxford University Press, 2000.

Koch, Klaus. *The Rediscovery of Apocalyptic: A Polemical Work on a Neglected Area of Biblical Studies and Its Damaging Effects on Theology and Philosophy*. SBT 2.22. Naperville: Allenson, 1972.

Lennox, John C. *2084 and the AI Revolution: How Artificial Intelligence Informs Our Future*. Upd. and exp. ed. Grand Rapids: Zondervan, 2024.

Luger, Ewa. *What Do We Know and What Should We Do About AI?* London: Sage, 2023.

Mazurek, Marcin. *A Sense of Apocalypse: Technology, Textuality, Identity*. Literary and Cultural Theory 40. Frankfurt am Main: Peter Lang, 2014.

McGinn, Bernard. *Visions of the End: Apocalyptic Traditions in the Middle Ages*. New York: Columbia University Press, 1979.

McMahon, Liv. "AI System Resorts to Blackmail If Told It Will Be Removed." *BBC*, May 23, 2025. https://www.bbc.com/news/articles/cpqeng9d20go.

Merritt, Rick. "What is a Transformer Model?" Nvidia, March 25, 2022. https://blogs.nvidia.com/blog/what-is-a-transformer-model.

Miller, Carolyn R. "Genre as Social Action." *Quarterly Journal of Speech* 70 (1984): 151–67.

Morelli, Michael. "The Athenian Altar and the Amazonian Chatbot: A Pauline Reading of Artificial Intelligence and Apocalyptic Ends." *Zygon* 54 (2019): 177–90.

Murphy, Frederick J. *Apocalypticism in the Bible and Its World: A Comprehensive Introduction*. Grand Rapids: Baker, 2012.

Paulus, Michael J., Jr. *Artificial Intelligence and the Apocalyptic Imagination: Artificial Agency and Human Hope*. Eugene: Cascade, 2023.

Pettersson, Anders. *The Idea of a Text and the Nature of Textual Meaning*. FILLM Studies in Languages and Literature 7. Amsterdam: John Benjamins, 2017.

Riva, Paolo, Nicolas Aureli, and Federica Silvestrini. "Social Influences in the Digital Era: When Do People Conform More to a Human Being or an Artificial Intelligence?" *Acta Psychologica* 229 (2022): 103681, https://doi.org/10.1016/j.actpsy.2022.103681.

Rowland, Christopher. *"By an Immediate Revelation": Studies in Apocalypticism, its Origins and Effects*. WUNT 473. Tübingen: Mohr Siebeck, 2022.
Russell, D. S. *Apocalyptic: Ancient and Modern*. Philadelphia: Fortress, 1978.
Russell, D. S. *Divine Disclosure: An Introduction to Jewish Apocalyptic*. Minneapolis: Fortress, 1992.
Schedtler, Justin Jeffcoat, and Kelly J. Murphy. "Introduction—From Before the Bible to Beyond the Bible." Pages 3–17 in *Apocalypses in Context: Apocalyptic Currents through History*. Edited by Kelly J. Murphy and Justin Jeffcoat Schedtler. Minneapolis: Fortress, 2016.
Selke, Stefan. "Future Technology as Comfort: Promising Tales About AI." Pages 255–79 in *Artificial Intelligence in Society: Social, Political and Cultural Implications of a Technological Innovation*. Edited by Michael Heinlein and Norbert Huchler. Artificial Intelligence in Society. Wiesbaden: Springer, 2024.
Singler, Beth. *Religion and Artificial Intelligence: An Introduction*. Engaging with Religion. London: Routledge, 2025.
Solanki, Shivam R., and Drupad K. Khublani. *Generative Artificial Intelligence: Exploring the Power and Potential of Generative AI*. New York: Apress, 2024.
Tilford, Nicole L. "The AI Apocalypse: Robot Revolutions and Biomechanical Gods." Pages 337–62 in *Apocalypses in Context: Apocalyptic Currents Through History*. Edited by Kelly J. Murphy and Justin Jeffcoat Schedtler. 2nd ed. Minneapolis: Fortress, 2025.

Index

Note: Page numbers followed by "n" denotes note numbers.

Index of Subjects

Note: Page numbers followed by "n" denotes note numbers

Index of Biblical Literature

Qumran Scrolls

Pseudepigraphical Literature

Rabbinic Literature

www.ingramcontent.com/pod-product-compliance
Ingram Content Group UK Ltd.
Pitfield, Milton Keynes, MK11 3LW, UK
UKHW021028041026
15470UKWH00013B/237

9 798765 163412